Richard Berengarten's *Changing*, first published by Shearsman 1 2015, is a single poem consisting of 450 short pieces. This extraordinary mosaic, which took the author thirty years to complete, is both a reflective testament of our times and a homage to the Chinese divination manual known as the *I Ching* (*Yijing, Yi, Book of Changes, Classic of Changes, Book of Transformations*, etc.). Together with its commentaries, this text became the first among the great Confucian classics. Berengarten's *Changing* enters into direct dialogue with the themes, motifs and mathematical structures of this ancient opus, whose influence has been integral to every phase of Chinese history for over 2,000 years.

This present volume, co-edited by Paschalis Nikolaou of the Ionian University, Greece, and Richard J. Smith of Rice University, USA, is a critical and interpretive companion to Berengarten's *Changing*. It contains eighteen essays by contributors from a dozen countries, including a philosopher, a historian, a philologist, an anthropologist, a Jungian analyst, several literary critics, scholarly experts on the *I Ching*, experienced diviners, and practising poets. These essays variously broach the intrinsic qualities of *Changing*, alongside its placement in historical and contemporary contexts, both literary and philosophical: that is, its relationships with the *Book of Changes*, with Daoist and Confucian thought and practice, and with the modern theories of synchronicity and entanglement – as well as with the themes and motifs of Berengarten's other writings.

In this volume, the multivocality of Richard Berengarten's *poeisis* is fully recognised, as is his dedication here both to a field poetics and to an imaginationalist vision. Claiming that Berengarten's *Changing* genuinely belongs among the writings of World Literature, *Under the Sign of the I Ching* transcends the monolithic purities of compartmentalised knowledge in favour of miscellany, diversity and pluralistic inclusiveness.

Under the Sign of the *I Ching*

Essays on Richard Berengarten's
Changing

Edited by
Paschalis Nikolaou
and
Richard J. Smith

Shearsman Books

First published in the United Kingdom in 2023 by
Shearsman Books Ltd
P.O. Box 4239
Swindon
SN3 9FN

Shearsman Books Ltd Registered Office
30-31 St James Place, Mangotsfield, Bristol BS16 9JB
(this address not for correspondence)

www.shearsman.com

ISBN 978-1-84861-849-7

Contents

Editorial Notes

Since the contributors to this book live in many parts of the world, different varieties of English have been adopted. Out of respect for individual preferences and different scholarly conventions, we have refrained from imposing a single house-style and have preserved authorial styles of spelling, punctuation and spacing. Similarly, since some authors have adopted the Pinyin system of transliteration for Chinese words and names, and others, the Wade-Giles system, we maintain these individual preferences too. This variance applies in particular to the titles *I Ching, I-Ching, Book of Changes, Book of Change, Classic of Change*, and so on. All these appellations appear in the essays below. A more detailed discussion of the main differences between the Pinyin and Wade-Giles transliterations that appear in this book can be found in Appendix 3 (346 below). For the transliterated names of Chinese authors, we have respected each individual author's preferences for placing either the family name or the personal name first. As for the Chinese script itself, two different systems are in common use. Some of our authors have chosen traditional-style characters (*fantizi*), and others have employed simplified characters (*jiantizi*). We have encouraged our authors to use whichever form they prefer.

References to *Changing* in this book usually incorporate three elements: (1) the number of the set (cluster), corresponding exactly to that of the hexagrams in the standard *I Ching*; (2) the number of the poem in the set, between 0 and 6; and (3) the page-reference: for example (1/6: 10). Zero (0) always denotes the head-poem for each cluster: for example (21/0: 168). The sixty-four 'head-poems' are always italicised.

While this book has no general bibliography, relevant references appear at the end of each essay. All Internet references have been rechecked shortly before publication in June 2023. And while the book is not intended as a *Festschrift*, we are also happy to note that its publication coincides with Richard Berengarten's 80th year.

Paschalis Nikolaou and Richard J. Smith

Acknowledgements

The editors thank the editors of the following journals for publishing earlier versions of some of these essays, as follows. Eleanor Goodman's review, 'Rich and Varied: Richard Berengarten's *Changing*', first appeared in *Cha*, 39 (April 2018): https://chajournal.blog/2018/02/05/changing/; and the current version of her essay appeared in December 2021 in *Pari Perspectives* 10: 81-87. Gu Ming Dong's 'From the *Book of Changes* to the Book of *Changing*: A Route to World Literature Through Chinese Culture' appeared in the *International Communication of Chinese Culture* 7 (September 2020): 319-335. Lucas Klein's review, 'Lakes and Mountains', appeared in the *Journal of Poetics Research* 8 (April 2018). Hank Lazer's review, 'Welling, Replenishing: Richard Berengarten's *Changing* and the *I Ching*', was first published in the *Notre Dame Review* (Spring 2017) and then online at https://ndreview.nd.edu/assets/267306/lazer_review.pdf. Paul Scott Derrick's essay in this book may also be compared with his earlier review, 'Ringing the changes: *Changing* by Richard Berengarten' in *The Fortnightly Review* (17 Feb 2017), online at: https://fortnightlyreview.co.uk/2017/02/ringing-the-changes/. Roderick Main's essay appeared in March 2022 in *Pari Perspectives* 11: 85-98.

In a special feature on *Changing*, eight essays from this book have also appeared on the website *CHA: An Asian Literature Journal*, edited by Tammy Ho (Hong Kong, 2021–2022). These essays are by Mike Barrett, Paul Scott Derrick, Tze-ki Hon, Sophia Katz, Lucas Klein, Paschalis Nikolaou, Tan Chee Lay, and Alan Trist and Bob DeVine. They appear together with an extract from an otherwise unpublished working journal Richard Berengarten kept while writing *Changing*. We are very grateful to the editor Tammy Lai-Ming Ho for publishing this valuable compilation.

The editors also offer their warmest thanks to Chen Shangzhen, Melanie Rein and Anthony Rudolf, for their valuable advice; to Tony Frazer, the publisher, for his skilful guidance and immense patience in seeing this book through to print; and to Richard Berengarten, for his constant support and encouragement for this project.

Abbreviations

(1) throughout the book

CH	*Changing* (book by Richard Berengarten)
CC	*Cosmic Canticle* (book by Ernesto Cardenal)
CW	*Collected Writings* (of C. G. Jung)
ed./eds.	editor(s); edited by
NIV	*New International Version* (of *The Bible*)
OED	*Oxford English Dictionary* (online)
n.p.	not yet published
RB	Until 2008, Richard Burns; after that, Richard Berengarten
trans.	translator(s); translation(s); translated by

(2) in Index 1

/	and/or
<, <<	see / see further
Hex/hex(s)	Hexagram, hexagram(s)
IC	*I Ching*
n/nn	footnote(s)
Trig/trig(s)	Trigram/trigram(s)

INTRODUCTORY

PASCHALIS NIKOLAOU

The *I Ching* and *Changing*

The *I Ching* is one of the world's most extraordinary texts. In ancient China, by around 136 BCE, it had come to be regarded as the first of the Confucian *classics*: which is to say: of all books, this was the one considered of foremost importance for the practice of both a good life and correct governance. By contrast, in the late twentieth century, this text's very identity as a book – and especially as one that's 'readable' in any conventional sense – has itself been questioned (Jullien 1993: 1).[1]

The *I Ching*'s proto-text is older than Homer. Its earliest known version, the *Zhouyi* (meaning the 'Zhou Dynasty *Changes*') was probably compiled or composed during the last two decades of the ninth century BCE (Shaughnessy 1983: 49). Its complete version, as we know it today, dates from around 300 BCE and includes the addition of its so-called 'Ten Wings' (commentaries).

The *Zhouyi* itself is a manual for oracular divination or foretelling. It's likely, then, that the accreted *I Ching* originates in oral traditions that precede the invention of writing itself and stretch back to the Neolithic age. The core-text embeds an incalculably ancient worldview, rooted in sympathetic magic and in beliefs in *correspondances* between microcosm and macrocosm. For more than 2,000 years, despite blips in the early modern period and acute repression under the rule of Mao Zedong (1949–1976), especially during the so-called Cultural Revolution (1966–1976), the *I Ching* has been regarded throughout Chinese recorded history as a work of profound wisdom and even as one that encapsulates and encrypts the patterns of the cosmos.

---

[1] "On commencera donc par se demander: s'agit-il encore d'*un* livre? Et aussi: à quelle «lecture» celui-ci peut-il se prêter." ("So we need to begin by asking: are we still dealing here with *one* book? And also: to what kind of 'reading' can it lend itself.")

There have been, broadly speaking, two *I Ching* traditions, both at root intimately interconnected, though divergent in directions and expression, and both very much alive today: a popular one that treats the *I Ching* as an infinitely consultable oracular manual within the context of an intuitively-based belief-system; and a scholarly one, which aims to understand and interpret the meanings and structures of all parts of the text in relation to the whole. To this second strand belong mathematical, geometrical and symbological insights. A third, specifically modern strand is the specialised study of the text's origins and history, which incorporates attentive linguistic study and recent archaeological findings.

The entire vision and worldview of the *I Ching* belong intimately to Chinese history and tradition. This ancient text is universally regarded as one of the keys, if not the key-of-keys, to Chinese culture itself, and even to Chinese 'identity'. The ancient text also travelled widely into other nearby languages and cultures, such as Korea, Vietnam and Japan. In all these cultures, the book has been constantly reinterpreted in terms of both Daoist (*aka* Taoist) and Confucianist world-views, as well as, slightly later, Buddhist beliefs. Additionally, since the late seventeenth century, the book has been so widely disseminated into western cultures that by the twenty-first century (despite – or perhaps because of – its age, its mystery, its text's intrinsic obscurities, and the huge challenges presented by translation), the *I Ching* can genuinely be called a 'world text', one that has been assimilated into every literate culture. These historical trends are tracked in the following essay (19-34) by Richard J. Smith, this book's co-editor. This piece, which constitutes the second part of our introduction, is based on many of his previous detailed and scholarly studies of the *I Ching*, especially vis-à-vis its extraordinarily rich and varied travels through space and time (e.g. Smith 1991, 2008, 2012).

வ

More than 2,000 years after the establishment of the *I Ching* as the first Confucian classic, why does an English poet write a complex, composite poem entitled *Changing*, consisting of 450 parts, whose title and structure are both based on the *I Ching*? The poet is Richard Berengarten (*aka* Burns), born in London during the Second World War (1943). He published *Changing* in 2016, at the age of seventy-three.

More specifically, what does Berengarten mean by saying that while his book is consciously intended as a homage to the *I Ching*, he doesn't intend it to be regarded as a commentary, and still less as a translation, but primarily "as a poem, or gathering of poems, in its own right" *(CH,* 'Post-script': 521). Furthermore, precisely how and why does this huge, mosaic-like opus, consisting of many small pieces, relate to an ancient text that wasn't initially conceived as a poem at all? And what, then, are the qualities and characteristics of *Changing*, in terms not only of social, philosophical and/or metaphysical values, but also of literary models, theories, and practices in Chinese, English, and other languages? To summarise: what are the characteristics and qualities of this ambitious and complex work; how is it to be approached and understood; and what is to be learned from it?

While these questions and their implications will inevitably extend far beyond this book's boundaries, they are the ground for the eighteen essays that follow. This volume's *raison d'être* is, modestly, to broach these issues and open lines of further enquiry.

☙

The eighteen essays in this book are grouped thematically into four parts. All overlap with one another. Following the introductions, the first part, entitled 'Precedents, Parallels, and a New Poem', opens with an essay by Jeremy Hooker, aptly entitled 'A Way In'. Here, *Changing* is articulately interpreted as evidence of "a holistic vision" (39). Through this complex, composite poem, "things flow together, and interact, and change, yet remain one continuous generative tissue" (48). Focusing on the melding of unity and diversity in the poem, Hooker shows how Berengarten draws a rich array of changing, confluent experiences [...] "from the 'ever-fresh well' of the *I Ching*" (48). Hooker argues for Berengarten's placement in both a modern international tradition, with particular reference to Pound, Seferis and Paz (37-38), and in a historical line of earlier Anglophone 'metaphysicals', including Donne, Herbert, Vaughan, Blake, Wordsworth and Hopkins. These English and Anglo-Welsh poets, Hooker suggests, viewed heaven and earth as "at once real and grounded upon a mystery that is ultimately inexpressible" (38). "Like the *I Ching*," he clarifies, "Berengarten does not invoke God or gods. He is however a religious poet" with "a strong sense of the sacred" – "a praise poet" (36, 43, 44).

Paul Scott Derrick is an authority on Berengarten. Since he has written several essays and reviews on the poet and also co-edited two previous volumes of essays on different parts of the oeuvre (Jope *et. al.* 2011, 2016; Derrick 2019), he is able to draw insightful comparisons with Berengarten's other books. In accord with Hooker's emphasis on *confluence* as the key to understanding *Changing*, in this essay Derrick explores Berengarten's "nexus of wholeness" (56) through a different yet complementary lens. As his title clarifies, Derrick notes three main strands: 'British Mind. Chinese Soil. American Grain'. Derrick's references include Emerson, Thoreau, Whitman, Stevens and Pound. Arguing that in *Changing*, the presences of three cultures have not only been combined but transcended, Derrick finds qualities in *Changing* corresponding to what Heidegger calls "a patient contemplation". The poet "listens, recalls and responds" (51), by means of a "calm, self-possessed surrender to that which is worthy of questioning" (52, 55). This kind of creative receptivity might well be compared not only with Keatsian "negative capability", as explored by Mike Barrett (243-256) but also with the Chinese concept of *wuwei*, (lit. non-action, i.e. "not striving" or "not overdoing") as also noted by Hank Lazer (74).

Equally attentive to "the vision and content of this grand book" (69), Hank Lazer illuminates the "great range of re-told historical, mythic, ancient, literary *now's*" throughout *Changing*, as he traces how its many short, separate constituent poems "speak in and with and to each other" (75). Like all contributors, Lazer is mindful of the complex relationship between *Changing* and the *I Ching*. He focuses on Berengarten's response to hexagram 48 ('Welling, Replenishing'), which in his 'Postscript' the poet interprets as the 'core' voice or *imagem* for the *I Ching* itself (526-527). Furthermore, Lazer suggests a comparison between *Changing* and George Oppen's *Of Being Numerous* (1968). Lazer draws particular attention to the meditative Daoist current running quietly through Berengarten's book, whether in the radiance of small, familial, domestic details, or in the subtle presence of *wuwei*, which he glosses as "nothing doing, both for the perceiver poet, and for the earth itself" (74).

Clearly, in this part of the book, Hooker's discovery of religious qualities, the contemplative strain tracked by Derrick, and the Daoist elements traced by Lazer – are closely compatible. Significantly, these three contributors are not only interpretative critics but poets in their own right, as are several other presences in the book. Major themes raised by these authors are amplified in what follows; and their qualities of conceptual clarity and perspicacious intuitiveness echo throughout the book.

☙

The contributors to Part 1 are richly aware of the need to view *Changing* in the light of multiple patterns of influence and *in*-formation – across cultures, languages and literatures. In Part 2, entitled 'Within and Among Traditions', this theme is central. It is broached, first, by Ming Dong Gu, who explores Berengarten's own recognition that "associative, analogical and correlative thinking [...] is not only the mental foundation for poetry, ritual and magic in all societies, but specifically underpins the holistic vision of the universe that runs through all traditional Chinese thought [...]". Gu emphasises that this understanding "*first* appeared in the *Book of Changes*. Known as *bixing* 比興, it may be variously translated as 'stimulated analogy', 'inspired comparison', or 'a metatheory of poetry-making'" (90).[2] Finding associative or analogical thinking highly developed in *Changing*, Gu clarifies: "As a successor to Anglo-American modernist poetry, Berengarten's poems have drawn from both techniques and treatments common to ancient Chinese and Western Modernist poets" (104). This theme of *correlative thinking* echoes and re-echoes throughout this book, especially in Main (187ff) and Nikolaou (308ff). And in a keynote passage, whose theme resonates through many other essays, Gu concludes: "Berengarten's *Changing* is a *bona fide* specimen of world literature and blazes a new path for cross-cultural dialogue between Eastern and Western poetry and poetics" (105).

Following these panoramic contextualisations, particular motifs and relationships are gathered and regathered in the essays that immediately follow. Next comes Sophia Katz, who investigates parallels and contrasts between *Changing* and *Cosmic Canticle* by the Nicaraguan poet Ernesto Cardenal (1925–2020), a Christian priest and revolutionist. While noting similar scopes in these two long poems, Katz argues that the two poets differ radically in their ethical and moral worldviews. Whereas Cardenal idealises revolution in Marxist terms, as the way not only to destroy selfishness but also to restore 'broken order', Berengarten finds 'a middle way' rooted in the Kabbalistic idea of *tikkun*, i.e. 'repair, restitution'. And whereas Cardenal sees revolution as *evolutionary*, and thus as an existential necessity, Berengarten warns against the "reckless actions of revolutionaries led by their ideas [...] of truth and justice" (124). Katz continues: "[Berengarten] elevates basic human compassion and sensitivity to the needs of one's neighbor over ideology (*ibid.*)."

---

[2] Gu's acute analysis here is articulated and documented in greater depth and detail in his *Chinese Theories of Reading and Writing* (2005).

Following this, poet Owen Lowery's theme is 'Conflicts, Parallels and Polarities' (130). Lowery is both panoramic and attentive to the detailed manifestations of "the poem's multiple voices" (141).[3] Like Katz, he emphasizes Berengarten's "belief in the importance of *balance* and *wholeness*" (130). He shows how a sense of dynamic balance between *yin* and *yang* – which necessarily includes oscillation and imbalance – pulsates through the entirety of *Changing*, both structurally and thematically, and does so through a huge variety of oppositions, such as "[m]asculinity and femininity, life and death, conflict and peace, speech and silence, and individuality and universality", and also macrocosm and microcosm. Lowery clarifies further: "[T]his set of polarities, in turn, reflects [Berengarten's] interests in Daoism and Jungian philosophy" (131). Lowery's close reading of several poems, especially in the opening cluster, 'Initiating' (1/3-13) clarifies Berengarten's debt to the thinking of quantum physicist David Bohm in *Wholeness and the Implicate Order*. Lowery also explores Berengarten's treatment of extreme imbalance, exemplified in his concern with atrocities, and in particular, the Nazi Holocaust.

Eleanor Goodman, a Sinologist and also a poet, explores Berengarten's vital concern with both "domestic and political spheres" (145). Goodman responds particularly attentively to expressive and textural poetic qualities: for example, "the cautious, considered language" in one poem; "the expert play of consonance and assonance" in another; and the ways in which many poems "pulse with living energy and lived experience" (147, 153, 146, respectively). She also points out that "Berengarten writes evocatively of unity and human connectedness, but just as strongly of dissolution: twin themes that are arguably the basis of the *I Ching* itself" (153). Like Katz, Lowery and Sneller, Goodman reflects that in *Changing* references to the Second World War and the Holocaust abound (150).

Next, Lucas Klein, another Sinologist, and an experienced translator of Chinese poetry, examines image-patterns and tropes in *Changing* "via the transnational and translational *I Ching*", especially "lakes and mountains" (155). Focusing on '*Two lakes, joined*', the first poem Berengarten ever wrote for *Changing* in 1984 (58/0: 464), Klein explores how this piece arose directly out of an *I Ching* divination (155). Emphasising that this small poem expresses joy, Klein suggests that each one of the pieces that makes up the *Changing* is "a microcosm – both of the book in which it

---

[3] *Editors' note*: With great sadness, we record the passing of Owen Lowery in May 2021, during the writing of this introduction and before this book's publication. See also his biographical note (334 below).

takes its part and of its relationship to the *I Ching*" (163). Expanding on two essays by Eliot Weinberger, one on *The Book of Changes* (2016) and the other on Octavio Paz (1992), Klein also highlights the influence of Paz on Berengarten's oeuvre, a fact well-attested by Berengarten himself (e.g. in *RB* 2015).

Drawing this part of the book to a close, philosopher Rico Sneller explores "Spirit and Word" in *Changing* in the context of Jewish prophecy (165-183). Sneller places *Changing* firmly within the Judaic tradition, not least by relating it to Berengarten's keen interest in his own heritage and his study of Kabbalah. This striking thesis draws on the insights and scholarship of a panoply of major Jewish and European thinkers, including Martin Buber, Walter Benjamin, Emmanuel Levinas and Jacques Derrida. Sneller also draws on the Franco-Jewish philosopher André Neher, particularly on the latter's discussion of the polysemic Hebrew words *ruah* ('spirit') and *dāvār* ('word'). Through his examinations of these motifs, Sneller suggests that both the Judaic notion of prophecy and the Chinese practice of divination via the *I Ching* would benefit from being re-imagined and re-contextualised. He suggests that far from being exclusively focused on foretelling the future, exponents of both traditions need to be understood as aiming equally for insight into the "this-here-now" (181). He tallies this idea emphatically with Berengarten's "specific, attentive, and active refocusing" on *presence*.

ಌ

Since the early 1960s, C. G. Jung's influence has been a continuous thread in Richard Berengarten's writings, just as in much *I Ching* commentary. In particular, the theory of synchronicity is frequently encountered in Berengarten's later work, whether as an implicit motivating factor or as an explicit presence. In *Changing*, synchronistic experience and awareness occur often enough to warrant the foregrounding here of a pair of essays exploring the themes of *Changing* from illuminating Jungian perspectives.

In the first of these, Roderick Main clarifies that Berengarten's theory of synchronicity is "[d]eeply informed by Jung's studies and practical experience of the *I Ching*." Iterating key themes also present in Ming Dong Gu's essay above, Main continues: "[Synchronicity] can be seen as a modern Western formulation of *correlative thinking* (189, emphasis added). Main clarifies: "Jung did not use the expression 'correlative thinking', or a German equivalent, but tended to refer more broadly to 'Chinese thinking' or the 'Chinese mind'." Among Main's conclusions, attentively exemplified through discussion of Berengarten's cluster of poems entitled 'Welling, Replenishing' (48: 383-390), is the view that "Berengarten's insight that correlative thinking – and by implication its modern expression as synchronicity" may well be "foundational for poetry". Main adds that this is a "[...] perspective that can generate considerable illumination both in theorising about poetry and in analysing actual poems" (205).

As Main acknowledges, while the association of synchronicity with the *I Ching* has been well established by Jung himself, its connection with the kind of correlative thinking that generates the making of poetry derives from Berengarten's remarks in his 'Postscript' (523-524, 526). These key passages are quoted not only by Main (187), but also by Hooker (38-39), Lazer (75), Gu (90), Goodman (145) and Shen (226).[4] Similarly, the 'Welling, Replenishing' group of poems attracts the attention not only of Main (190-205) but also, significantly, of Hon (257-262), as well as of Derrick, and Sneller (see respectively 54, note 5, and 17,1 note 9).

Heyong Shen, a leading Jungian analyst in China, also writes about synchronicity. He indicates particular stages in Jung's reading of the *I Ching* and, through explorations of Chinese etymology, pinpoints several junctures of analytical psychology and Chinese culture. The etymological core of his discussion lies in the Chinese graph 心 *xin*, itself meaning 'heart' or 'heart-mind'. By amplification, Shen clarifies that this graph is not only a key component of meaning-clusters in many ancient Chinese words and concepts, but also that some of these are particularly relevant both to Jungian analysis and to poetry in our era. This etymological approach enables Shen to throw abundant light onto key motifs and images in both the *I Ching* and *Changing*, especially those involving the heart, and to do so from unusual and revealing angles. Shen's way of putting this perhaps even implies that a specific *kind* of dynamic influence, energetic 'current', or *qi* (气 in simplified script, and 氣 in traditional script) courses through *all* poetry, simply because poetry moves the heart. "Combining Chinese and English resonances together," he suggests, "yields the motif of '*sympathetic or empathetic flow via the living heart*'" (220, emphasis added). These, then, are qualities that Shen amply traces in *Changing*.

---

[4] As explored in my concluding essay to this volume (306-328), this correlation also occurs in Berengarten's memoir on Octavio Paz (RB 2015), published a year before *Changing*. There too, Berengarten quotes a supporting passage about "observation of affinities" from Wordsworth's *Prelude*, which provides one of the epigraphs to *Changing* (see *CH* 1 and 533-534).

Evidently, here Shen also draws on a theme consistent with Ming Dong Gu's and Paul Scott Derrick's arguments above: that *Changing* involves a creative dialogue between traditions; or, to put this the other way round, that out of this kind of inter-cultural dialogue, poetry emerges. This reciprocal, circuitous energetic current is reminiscent, too, of one of Shelley's statements about imagination in *The Defence of Poetry* (1821): "The great instrument of moral good is the imagination; *and poetry administers to the effect by acting upon the cause*" (emphasis added).

Quite aside from their valuable interpretations of key motifs and images in *Changing*, these two essays make unique contributions to Jungian studies.

℘

The final part of this book, entitled '*Changing* and the *I Ching*, *Poeisis* and the *Dao*', contains further reflections on images, themes and philosophical ideas, on internal patterns and structures, and on *Changing*'s specific relationship with *the I Ching*.

Mike Barrett, also a poet, offers a panoramic vision of *Changing*, illuminated by his own explorations of the *I Ching*. The ancient Chinese text, he proposes, "may be regarded as a semiotic system applicable to *all that is, could, and should be*'" (234, emphasis in original). Within this matrix, Barrett identifies eight separable but interconnecting functions: the semiotic, kinesthetic, aesthetic, ethical, civic, mathematical, cosmic, and the hermeneutic. He then proceeds to apply each of these to *Changing*. Combining attentiveness to the text with learned amplifications, Barrett richly illuminates motifs and textural qualities in certain poems. In this way, he connects *Changing* with wider motifs: for example, mathematical theories, writings by other poets, the necessary critique of contemporary capitalism, and Kabbalistic, Daoist and Buddhist beliefs and practices. Barrett's subtle play on John Keats' term *negative capability* (Keats 43) enables him to discover both "positive and negative capability" (233-256) in *Changing*. He suggests that Berengarten, by allowing himself to enter a receptive state, is attentively open to the influences of his sources and readings and, hence, able to proceed to original acts of creation. Overall, Barrett's approach is broadly concordant with those of Derrick, Hooker and Lazer above.

By contrast, the depth study of a single cluster can serve to illuminate the larger scheme of *Changing*. Tze-ki Hon focuses on the motif of 'the well'. Like Main, Lazer and others, he picks up on the hint in Berengarten's 'Postscript' (526) that this motif or symbol might be interpreted as a metonym that "represents" the *I Ching* itself – almost as if it were a kind of microcosm of the entire book. In exploring the cluster 'Welling, Replenishing' (48: 383-390), Hon clarifies that the well is not only polysemic but also expresses antinomies, for it holds both "what is and what will be". And he elaborates: "On the surface, the old well is useless; but it is full of potential, waiting to be tapped." He notes too that the twinned gerundive forms in this title "imply continuous effort, deep-seated commitment, and the will to succeed despite setbacks and disillusionment" (258).[5] From this symbolic reading of "the well as a metaphor of life" (262), Hon spells out a call to responsible moral and social action, broadly in harmony with Confucian ideals.

Next, in a short but far-sighted essay, the main concern of *I Ching* specialist Geoffrey Redmond is with the "literary significance of the book's distinctive structure" (263), since it is so precisely modelled on the *Book of Changes* itself. Drawing on recent studies of the ancient text's origins in the late Zhou Dynasty, Redmond emphasises that Berengarten's book, like the *I Ching* itself, doesn't follow a traditional narrative structure, as does, say, *The Odyssey* (265). Nor, on the other hand, does *Changing* dispense altogether with a structural 'frame', as do modernist long poems such as Pound's *Cantos* (265). Redmond elaborates: "Rather than providing a ready-made narrative, the *I Ching* provides fragments that are made into a narrative *only during divination*" (267; emphasis added).

Here Redmond implicitly draws attention to a structural dimension in contemporary poetics that I, for one, would like to see developed in further studies of Berengarten's ground-breaking poem. While explicit narrative is deployed episodically in many individual poems in *Changing*, and occasionally bonds entire clusters – for example 'Falling (in a pit)' (29: 231-238) and 'Cooking, Sacrificing' (50: 399-406)[6] – the book has no sequentially mapped Aristotelian "beginning, middle and end", but rather,

---

[5] On the use of the '-ing' form in all cluster-titles in *Changing*, see also Katz (126) and Berengarten (*CH* 525). The title of the book itself reflects this pattern.

[6] The former recounts the story, based on fact, of the long imprisonment of Ali Bourequat and his two brothers in twentieth century Morocco. The latter is based on Herodotus' story of the consultation of the Delphic oracle by King Croesus (see *CH* 548 and 556). The collocation of ancient and modern time-zones is a typical feature of *Changing*.

is structured as a 'field'.[7] The overall patterning of *Changing*, then, is not linear but spatial and correlative, as in a mosaic or jigsaw,[8] and perhaps as in a map. Like the *I Ching* itself, it is also configured mathematically.

Next, Tan Chee Lay's stylometric study of *Changing* yields a fascinating and very different interior view of the poem, which, nonetheless, is entirely complementary to Redmond's analysis. Deploying the online digital corpus system *Textalyser*, Tan establishes some of the poem's lexical and semantic frequencies. From this evidence, working within the "Philosophical Sphere of the *I Ching*" (270), he extracts several hypotheses on issues such as word choice and communicability. Although tabulation of his findings offers only a preliminary sketch for a fuller stylometric analysis, Tan shows that while Berengarten's language is usually relatively 'easy' on the surface, beneath these first layers lie many more levels, which embed increasingly complex correlations both of parts with parts and of all parts with the whole. He argues, convincingly, that his method enables "glimpses into [Berengarten's] strategies in composing this poem: simple, direct and highly readable, yet containing a wealth of philosophical profundity" (283). This discussion, incidentally, also throws light on one of the traditionally accepted meanings of the Chinese graph 易 (*I or yi*), in the title 易經 (*I Ching*), as 'easy, simple' (Nielsen 301). Implicit here, too, is the idea of a gradual but progressive discovery of 'layerings' through the various processes of reading and re-reading that constitute interpretation. Tan clarifies that interpreting *means* pattern-finding.

Next, a shift to yet another unusual perspective. An insightful collaborative essay by poet Alan Trist and artist Bob DeVine, entitled 'The Zen of the Tao: Journeys Along the Ridgepole', brings this volume towards closure. Accompanied by photographs, this reflective piece occasionally moves into a form akin to that of a diary. Most significantly, it reflects an experiment, for these authors' readings of several poems in *Changing* are *in*-formed entirely by their authors' own regular practices of *I Ching* divination. Trist and DeVine describe their method as follows: "Our own

---

[7] Apart from Redmond's observations on 'field' patterning in the *I Ching* and *Changing*, see my remarks on 'field' poetics (15 below, inc. note 9), and on Berengarten's "non-linear" modes of composition (313, 315ff below).

[8] The mosaic appears once as a motif in *Changing*, perhaps as a hinted metonym for this entire poem, and, indeed, perhaps for the process of poem-making itself. The former interpretation is implicit in the title: 'A thing like this' (see 17/3: 139). See also *Book With No Back Cover* (RB 2003: 45) where there is a prose-poem about a meeting with a mosaic-maker. See also note 318 below.

active way of reading *Changing* has involved applying it both symbolically and literally to our own lives" (298).

From several viewpoints, the result of this exercise is fascinating and also challenging. For, perhaps surprisingly, Trist and DeVine quickly find answers to personal questions of their own in Berengarten's poetic text, just as they have done or might do in the *I Ching* itself. What is more, the responses they discover turn out to be experientially relevant to their own situations and thinking. Hence, a further question arises: might it be suggested that synchronicity comes into play here too, in the surprising *aptness* (*fittingness*) that Trist and DeVine discern in *Changing*? For here the criterion of *meaning* or *meanings* is construed not merely according to conventional norms of literary interpretation, i.e. as an intrinsic property, such as polysemy, *within* the more-or-less well-defined linguistic field of the text itself, but, rather, as a kind of *non-contiguous connectivity* discoverable in and through uniquely occurring associative resonances *between* the text and the reader's (or readers') personal experiences, which previously were entirely *extrinsic* to the text. For reasons that may seem intuitively obvious, explorations of personal (i.e. private) associations that an individual reader may bring to a text, and discover within it, have not tended to figure prominently in literary theory. But for Trist and DeVine, *meaning* is construed as *meaningfulness*, just as Jung's definition of synchronicity specifies "meaningful coincidence" (Jung *CW* 8, para 840; and see also Lowery 132 and Main 188ff below). Curiously, too, this idea of an experiential approach to *Changing* is mooted by two other contributors, Lazer (72) and Redmond (266). But Trist and DeVine actually put the idea to the test and into practice (286-305).

What is more, Trist and DeVine appear to be alert to the fact that this kind of *non-contiguous connectivity* – which might also be construed as a kind of 'relatedness at a distance' – resonates perfectly both with the Jungian theory of synchronicity (as an "acausal connecting principle") and with the theory of *non-local entanglement* in quantum mechanics (see 287, especially note 2). From Trist's and DeVine's essay, then, it is entirely plausible to envisage the application of entanglement theory to a reading of *Changing* and indeed, of the *I Ching*, or for that matter of any other text – and, more widely, to the theory of synchronicity and to a fuller and richer understanding of how, even more broadly, we interpret meaning and meaningfulness. Barrett also refers to entanglement (254), while Lowery connects entanglement and meaning (134 and 136) via the work of Karen Barad (2007).

Bringing this book to a close, my own recapitulating essay attempts to draw together several of the 'Constants of Change' by tracking the shape and positioning of Berengarten's book within the context of his readings Hence, I focus mainly on intertextualities. This final essay also reiterates the theme that is perhaps the dominant motif of this entire volume: the significance of correlative or analogical thinking in the gradual formation of Berengarten's long poem and, indeed, of all poems, including its consonance with the theory of synchronicity.

⁊

As co-ordinating editor of this volume, I have made half a dozen happy discoveries in reading and sequencing these essays. First, they cross frontiers, including those demarcated by specialisms. Second, assembled together, they foster the realisation that *Changing*, like the *I Ching* itself, deserves the epithet 'easy', at least on one level, as is particularly evident from Tan Chee Lay's piece (270-285). Yet while most of the small poems that populate *Changing* are quickly comprehensible on first reading, their depths and complexities of meaning may become increasingly evident if a reader cares to ponder on symbol-patterns and the mathematically intricate correlative structures of the whole. An initial impression of easiness doesn't preclude a gradual discovery of multiple layerings of complexity.

Third, while I have been struck by the diversity of approaches among contributors, it has been equally fascinating to recognise the degrees and extents of consonances, resonances and coherences among them. I therefore suggest that, together, these reflect the ever-varying holistic worldview of *Changing* itself. The internalised sense of pattern-within-pattern gradually becomes evident among minutiae and broad themes alike. While I have picked out several of these commonalities in the preceding remarks, no doubt an attentive and enquiring reader will discover many more.

A fourth quality in *Changing*, as already suggested above, is that of a 'field' poetics rather than that of a more traditional 'linear' vision. Here, I am thinking particularly of the "geometric" structure noticed by Geoffrey Redmond (264), while also bearing in mind that the term *geometric* necessarily invokes a spatial (and perhaps even a spatio-temporal) model,[9]

---

[9] During the two launches of *Changing* (at the University of Chicago, Chinese Department, October 2016, and at Cambridge University Library, May 2017), Berengarten emphasised his use of a 'field' model of composition rather than one based on sequential narrative (email from RB to editors, 6 March 2021).

and possibly a fractal one too. What is more, since geometric patterning in both the *I Ching* and *Changing* suggests the possibility of an underlying poetics attuned to a relativistic and quantal understanding of space-time, I suggest that Berengarten's 'field' paradigm may well be more relevant to our age than either a 'progressive' or 'developmental' model, traditionally fixed (and fixated) in linear, diachronic time – or, for that matter, any modernistic work, rooted like Pound's *Cantos* or Olson's *Maximus Poems* in the loose, implicit connectivity of parataxis (i.e. proximity, contiguity). And while Olson's notion of a 'field' poetry sets up spatial as well as linear connections (Olson 1950) which may well have influenced Berengarten, it does not necessarily suggest any organisational principle *other than* contiguity. Berengarten's 'field' in *Changing*, however, has a discernible mathematical grammar of its own. This argument also suggests that insofar as the structural patterning of *Changing* bypasses – and even contradicts – the hegemonic models of modernism, Berengarten's poem cannot be classified merely as 'postmodern'. Here, I believe, is an issue that warrants further and fuller discussion; for, as so often occurs in literary history, 'originality' does not arrive out of the blue. *Changing* sets a model for the organisation of long poems that is at once recognizably innovative *and* deeply traditional, in precisely the way that T. S. Eliot describes in 'Tradition and the Individual Talent'.

Even so, fifth, as several contributors clarify by pointing out dominant influences on Berengarten, such as Ezra Pound, George Seferis, Peter Russell, and Octavio Paz, *Changing* does maintain strong links to modernist predecessors. Besides, *Changing*'s connectivity to a particular ancient masterpiece, not to mention its openly stated dependence on it, can hardly fail to recall the reliance of, say, Joyce's *Ulysses* on the *Odyssey*, or Seferis' on the same Homeric text, in his *Mythistorema* and three *Logbooks*. Berengarten's reliance on the *I Ching*, indeed, is even closer to its ancient prototype than are Joyce's or Seferis' works to theirs. The question then arises: can *Changing* be read without the *Book of Changes*? While I believe that Berengarten's poem is resilient enough to enable an 'easy' first reading, it is quite clear that an *in*-formed reading will depend on at least some familiarity with the *I Ching*. This fact alone might be said to generate both a strength and a limiting factor of *Changing*.

Sixth, since this book presents interpretative essays on a poet whose entire oeuvre is attentively attuned to a poetics combining particularity and universality, I think it fitting that this gathering of eighteen contributors includes a philosopher, a historian, a philologist, an anthropologist, a

Jungian analyst, a specialist in the theory of synchronicity, a visual artist, a translation scholar, several literary critics, scholarly experts on the *I Ching*, experienced diviners, and practising poets. Equally tellingly, this book is also marked by its internationalism. Authors come from nine countries: China, England, Greece, Israel, the Netherlands, Singapore, Spain, the USA and Wales. Here, then, is a volume that transcends the monolithic purities of compartmentalised knowledge in favour of miscellany, diversity and pluralistic inclusiveness.

Finally, by investigating some of the multiple ways in which the *I Ching* and *Changing* correlate, the following pages open up a larger field of interpretative possibilities, other areas of which I hope may be taken up by other writers. Overall, in broaching aspects of Berengarten's *poeisis* from multiple viewpoints, it might be said that the eighteen essays that follow this introduction explore three main areas: the intrinsic qualities of *Changing*; the influence of the *I Ching* on the poet; and the enduring qualities of the *Changes*. Above all, such a span of approaches, coming from such a range of professional, linguistic and geographical backgrounds, not only clarifies that this volume of essays is itself enriched by a plethora of perspectives but also suggests that its subject, *Changing*, already belongs among the writings that Ming Dong Gu encounters on the "Route to World Literature" (89-106).

References

Barad, Karen. 2007. *Meeting the Universe Halfway: Quantum Physics and the Entanglement of Matter and Meaning*. Durham, NC: Duke University Press.

Berengarten, Richard. 2015. 'Octavio Paz in Cambridge, 1970'. *The Fortnightly Review*. Online at: https://fortnightlyreview.co.uk/2015/07/octavio-paz/

———. 2016. *Changing*. Bristol: Shearsman Books.

Eliot, T. S. 1919. 'Tradition and the Individual Talent'. Poetry Foundation. https://www.poetryfoundation.org/articles/69400/tradition-and-the-individual-talent

Derrick, Paul Scott and Rys, Sean (eds.). 2019. *Managing* The Manager*: Critical Essays on Richard Berengarten's Book-length Poem*. Newcastle upon Tyne: Cambridge Scholars.

Gu, Ming Dong. 2005. *Chinese Theories of Reading and Writing*. Albany, NY: State University of New York Press.

Jope, Norman, Derrick, Paul Scott, and Byfield, Catherine E. (eds.). 2016 [2011]. *The Companion to Richard Berengarten*. Bristol: Shearsman Books.

Jullien, François. 1993. *Figures de l'immanence: pour une lecture philosophique du Yi king, le classique du changement*. Paris: Grasset et Fasquelle.

Jung, C. G. 1952. 'Synchronicity: An Acausal Connecting Principle'. In *Collected Works*, vol. 8, *The Structure and Dynamics of the Psyche*, 2nd ed. London: Routledge and Kegan Paul, 1969, 417-519.

Keats, John. 1977 [1970]. 'Letter to George and Tom Keats, 21, 27 (?) December, 1817 '. In *Letters of John Keats: A Selection*. Gittings, Robert (ed.). Oxford: Oxford University Press, 43.

Nielsen, Bent. 2003. *A Companion to Yi Jing Numerology and Cosmology*. London: Routledge and Curzon.

Olson, Charles. 1950. 'Projective Verse'. In Allen, Donald M. (ed.). 1960. *The New American Poetry*. New York: Grove Press, 386-397.

———. 1960. *The Maximus Poems*. New York: Jargon/Corinth Books.

Oppen, George. 1968. *Of Being Numerous*. New York: New Directions.

Seferis, George. 1969. *Collected Poems 1924–1955*, bilingual Greek and English edn. Keeley, Edmund and Sherrard, Philip (eds. and trans.). London: Jonathan Cape.

Shaughnessy, Edward L. 2016. 'Preface'. In Berengarten, Richard, *Changing*.

Shelley, Percy Bysshe. 1840 [1821]. 'A Defence of Poetry'. *Poetry Foundation*. Online at: https://www.poetryfoundation.org/articles/69388/a-defence-of-poetry

Smith, Richard J. 1991 *Fortune-Tellers and Philosophers: Divination in Traditional Chinese Society*. Taipei: SMC Publishing.

———. 2008. *Fathoming the Cosmos and Ordering the World: The* Yijing (I-Ching, *or* Classic of Changes*) and Its Evolution in China*. Charlottesville, VA: University of Virginia Press.

RICHARD J. SMITH

Why the *I Ching* Still Matters in the Modern World[1]

THE EARLY FORMS OF THE TEXT AND ITS DEVELOPMENT

The immense authority of the *I Ching* in pre-modern China is seldom fully appreciated. Consider, however, the following quotation from the great Qing dynasty scholar Wang Fuzhi 王夫之 (1619–1692):

> [The *I Ching*] is the manifestation of the Heavenly Way, the unexpressed form of nature, and the showcase for sagely achievement. *Yin* and *yang*, movement and stillness, darkness and brightness, withdrawing and extending – all these are inherent in it. Spirit operates within it; the refined subtlety of ritual and music is stored in it; the transformative capacity of ghosts and spirits emerges from it. The great utility of humaneness and righteousness issues forth from it; and the calculation of order or disorder, good or bad luck, life or death is in accordance with it. (cited in Smith 2008: 3-4)

Throughout the imperial era, from 221 BCE to 1912 CE, the *I Ching* remained a sacred work of nearly unchallenged scriptural authority, serving not only as a moral guide to action but also as a rich source of concepts and symbols.

The basic text of the *I Ching*, dating from around 800 BCE, consists of sixty-four hexagrams (*gua* 卦), each with a name designed to indicate its basic symbolic significance. The first two hexagrams in what became

---

[1] *Editors' note*: In order to focus primarily on material relevant to Berengarten's *Changing*, this text abbreviates a previous essay (Smith 2016a). For the author's writings on the *Book of Changes*, see REFERENCES (33-34). Of particular note, as an introduction to non-specialists, is *The I Ching: A Biography* (Smith 2012).

the conventional (or "received") order are *Qian* (乾) and *Kun* (坤); the remaining sixty-two hexagrams represent permutations of these two symbols.

Most hexagram names (*guaming* 卦名) refer to a thing, an activity, a state, a situation, a quality, an emotion, or a relationship – for example, "Well," "Cauldron," "Marrying Maiden," "Treading," "Following," "Peace," "Obstruction," "Waiting," "Contention," "Great Strength" and "Contentment." Each hexagram is composed of six solid (yang, _____) or broken (yin, __ __) lines in various combinations. Every hexagram also has a "judgment" (*tuan* 彖; *aka* "hexagram statement," "decision," or "tag") and a cryptic "appended statement" (*xici* 繫辭 or *yaoci* 爻辭) for each line.

The judgments are short explanations of the overall symbolic situation represented by a given hexagram. The appended statements (also called "line readings") are usually viewed either developmentally, from the bottom up, or in terms of status relationships indicated by their relative position within the hexagram. From a developmental standpoint, for example, the process leads from a beginning stage (line one, at the bottom of the hexagram), to a developmental stage (lines two through five), and on to an ending or transitional stage (line six). In terms of status relationships within a family, the fifth line might represent the husband and the second line, the wife. The six lines also form a pair of individually named three-line trigrams (also *gua* 卦) juxtaposed within each hexagram, each of which has a set of meanings (originally nature-related).

According to the theory of the *I Ching*, the sixty-four hexagrams represent all of the fundamental situations one might encounter at any given moment in one's life. It followed, then, that by selecting a particular hexagram or hexagrams at a particular moment, and by correctly interpreting the symbolic elements involved (especially, but not exclusively, the judgments, line statements and trigrams), a person could devise a strategy for dealing with issues arising in the present and the future (Smith 2012: 4-5).

To get a sense of how cryptic the basic text of the *Changes* is, let us look briefly at the Qian 謙 hexagram (number 15 in the received order), which I will use at various points in this essay to indicate the problems and possibilities of *I Ching* interpretation. This is how the hexagram may have been understood in China around the eighth century BCE:

Qian 謙

謙：　亨。君子有終。
Judgment: Offering.
For a noble person there will be a conclusion.

初九：　謙謙君子。用涉大川，吉。
First nine [nine indicates a solid line]: "Crunch, crunch."
If the noble person uses this to wade across a big river it will be auspicious.

六二：　鳴謙。貞吉。
Second six [six indicates a divided line]:
A grunting/squealing hamster/rat:
The determination is auspicious.

九三：　勞謙君子。有終吉。
Third nine: A toiling/industrious hamster/rat:
For the noble person there will be a conclusion.
Auspicious.

九四：　無不利。撝謙。
Fourth nine: There is nothing for which this is unfavorable.
A tearing/ripping hamster/rat.

九五：　不富。以其鄰。利用侵伐。無不利。
Fifth nine:
They are not prosperous on account of their neighbors.
Favorable when used for invading or attacking.
There is nothing for which this is unfavorable.

上六：　鳴謙。利用行師，征邑國。
Top six:
A grunting/squealing hamster/rat:
Favorable when used for mobilizing the army, and attacking a town
or state.　　　　　　　　　　　　(trans. based on Kunst: 267-268)

As with most of the other sixty-three hexagrams, very little in the basic text of this hexagram is unambiguously clear. In the first place, the key term, *qian* (謙), is probably a loan word for a similar-looking and similar-sounding character (*qian* 嗛) meaning "to hold in the mouth," which came to be linked, in turn, with the image of a rat (*shu* 鼠) or a hamster (*qian*

21

謙). Second, although *Qian* seems to be an auspicious hexagram (one of very few in which every line has a favorable meaning), we cannot easily determine why from reading the judgment and line statements alone.

Commentaries were thus necessary to make practical, moral and/or metaphysical sense out of cryptic texts of this sort. Over time, thousands of such commentaries were written on the *Changes*, reflecting a wide range of political, social, philosophical and religious outlooks. The most important of these commentaries, at least in the early history of the work, were known collectively as the "Ten Wings" (*Shiyi* 十翼). They became attached to the basic text of the *I Ching* when the work received imperial sanction in 136 BCE as a major "Confucian" classic.

Together, the Ten Wings amplify the basic text of the *I Ching* and invest it with additional symbolism and multiple layers of meaning. Through the use of colorful analogies, metaphors and other forms of imagery, these poetic commentaries elucidate the structure and significance of the hexagrams in terms of their individual lines and constituent trigrams as well as their relationship to other hexagrams. Further, they provide a moral dimension to the *I Ching* and a solid metaphysical foundation based on *yinyang* 陰陽 and five-agents (*wuxing* 五行) principles and an elaborate numerology.

A particularly significant manifestation of the ethical turn in the realm of *I Ching* scholarship was that a number of once value-neutral descriptions of events and objects in the judgments and line statements of the "original" *Changes* came to be seen as heavily value-laden. For instance, the term *fu* (孚), which originally denoted a "capture" or a "captive" in war, came to be seen as a moral quality: "sincerity" or "trustworthiness." Similarly, a term that originally referred to a member of the hereditary nobility (*junzi* 君子) now described a morally upright "exemplary person." Words that previously denoted some sort of "trouble" (like *hui* 悔 and *lin* 吝) came to carry moral connotations of "blame," "remorse," "regret" and even "humiliation." In a striking instance of this phenomenon, the hexagram name *Qian* (謙) (see 21 above), which, as we have seen, was a loan word for two or three more mundane concepts in the earliest stratum of the basic text, came to be understood almost exclusively as the highly valued personal quality of "modesty" or "humility" (see Smith 2013a and Smith 2013b). From the Han period (206 BCE to 220 CE) onward, moral questions were central to *I Ching* hermeneutics – even within interpretive schools that seemed to emphasize "images and numbers" (*xiangshu* 象數) over "meanings and principles" (*yili* 義理).[2]

---

[2] For a discussion of *I Ching* interpretive schools, see Smith 2008 (passim).

THE FUNCTIONS OF THE *CHANGES* IN PREMODERN CHINA

The cultural significance of the *Changes* extended into virtually every area of traditional Chinese life. In the first place, as the "first of the Six [Confucian] Classics" (儒家六經之首), it was a source of intellectual inspiration and moral authority for countless generations of Chinese scholars, from the time of its designation as a classic in 136 BCE until the abolition of the Chinese civil service examination system in 1905. Second, it provided a seemingly inexhaustible repository of symbols with which to represent and explain nearly every realm of human experience, from artistic, musical and literary criticism to science, medicine and technology.[3] Third, from the standpoint of philosophy, it established the conceptual underpinnings for much of traditional Chinese cosmogony and cosmology, as well as the point of departure for most discussions of space and time. It also contributed significantly to an enduring emphasis in traditional Chinese thought on correlations and interconnections, "becoming" over "being," "events" over "things," and "relations over "essences" (on which, see, for example, Raphals; Allen).

The importance of the *I Ching* to Chinese aesthetic life in premodern times is evident everywhere. Artistically speaking, the *Changes* encouraged a preoccupation with nature and natural processes, and provided a symbolic and analytical vocabulary that proved as serviceable in art and literature as it was in philosophy. We can also find many examples of Chinese paintings and line drawings that represent the idea of scholars contemplating the *I Ching*. Furthermore, the classic influenced a wide range of other aesthetically satisfying social activities and occupations, from music and dance to architecture and flower arranging.

Changes symbolism informed a great deal of Chinese literary criticism, and the style of the *I Ching* itself served as a source of direct literary inspiration. The famous fifth century CE critic Liu Xie 劉勰 tells us, for example, that the *Changes* not only provided a model for the linguistic parallelism that was invariably prized in traditional Chinese writing, especially poetry, but that it also was the specific origin of several major types of prose, including *lun* 論 (discussions), *shuo* 說 (argumentation), *ci* 辭 (oracular pronouncements) and *xu* 序 (prefatory statements). Chinese scholars wrote literally thousands of essays on the *I Ching* from the Han period through the Qing, many of which, along with various inscriptions,

---

[3] For an overview, see Zhang, Qicheng (ed.) 1: 401–501 and 2: 3-418; and Smith 2008: 218–240.

memorials, eulogies, and works of rhyme-prose focusing on the classic, found a prominent place in reference works such as the Qing dynasty encyclopedia known as the *Gujin tushu jicheng* 古今圖書集成 (1726).[4]

In Chinese social life, the *I Ching* was particularly influential. As Chinese diaries, memoirs, correspondence and reference books reveal, all of the sixty-four hexagrams had potential application to human affairs, serving as guides to understanding the past, the present and the future. Perhaps the most significant practical use of the *Changes* in Chinese political and social life was in divination – particularly as a means of "resolving [one's] doubts" (*jueyi* 決疑 or 决疑). By definition, all divination had a psychological dimension, but this was especially true of the *Changes*, which emphasized self-awareness, self-understanding, caution and the "alleviation of anxiety (*youhuan* 憂患)." In the words of Tu Yongfeng 屠用豐, a late eighteenth century scholar: "The *Changes* is a book that teaches people to be fearful and to cultivate introspection" (Qian, Jibo: 3: 1-5).

How was the *I Ching* used in divination? I have written extensively on this matter and can only give a very brief summary here.[5] At the most basic level, one needed simply to consult the relevant hexagram(s) of the *I Ching* and then take both the basic text (especially its line relationships) and its commentaries to heart. The hexagram(s) could be chosen deliberately or randomly, with or without preliminary rituals. The actual deliberation could be immediate or it could involve weeks of assiduous study.

The question of the *I Ching*'s place in the history of Chinese science is a complex one. Some scholars, notably Joseph Needham and Peng-Yoke Ho, have argued that the *Changes* inhibited the development of Chinese science (by which they mean a Western model of historical development).[6] It is easy enough to see why. There was, in fact, very little about the natural world for which *I Ching* symbolism did not provide some sort of explanation (as a glance at the index to any one of the many volumes in Needham's monumental *Science and Civilisation in China* under the heading "I Ching" will reveal). The terrain covered by the *Changes* included not only the fields we now know as mathematics, biology, chemistry, physics and medicine but also other areas of scientific knowledge such as geography, topography and cartography. The *Changes* also played a substantial role in the development

---

[4] For translations of several poems from this collection, see Smith 2008: 223 ff.

[5] See, for example, Smith 2008: 24-30, 61-72, 89-100, 226-233; Smith 2012: 4-9, 39-43 and 109-123; and Smith 2013: 146-170. For a wealth of material in Chinese on *I Ching*-related divination, see Zhang, Qicheng (ed.) 419–920.

[6] See, for example, Smith 2008: 235-240.

of theories concerning traditional Chinese medicine. (Zhang, Qicheng (ed.) 2: 108–188).

But to blame the *I Ching* for China's so-called failure to follow a "Western" scientific path is unwarranted. The title of Benjamin Elman's 2005 book, *On Their Own Terms: Science in China, 1550–1900*, explains more fully and more satisfactorily why the history of Chinese science unfolded in the way that it did. In short, scientifically minded Chinese scholars were not trying to imitate European science in the seventeenth and eighteenth centuries; they had their own agenda, and it yielded impressive results in terms of both the recovery of and the expansion upon "lost" Chinese traditions in fields such as astronomy, mathematics and geography (see Elman). It is true, however, that this new information did not produce any major political, social or economic transformation, nor was it likely to. Fundamentally, scholars of late imperial China remained steadfast "moral generalists," who continued to believe that the *Changes* and other classics were the repositories of the most profound and ultimately valuable knowledge (see Smith 2015: 198–206).

The Early Travels of the *Changes* in East Asia and Beyond

By virtue of its pervasive influence in China, and China's great prestige in peripheral areas, the *Changes* gradually spread to other parts of East Asia from the fifth or sixth century onward – notably to Japan, Korea, Annam (Vietnam) and Tibet. During the seventeenth and eighteenth centuries, Jesuit missionaries brought knowledge of the classic to the West; and today there are dozens of different translations of the *I Ching* in various European languages. The work has inspired countless derivative books of various kinds, and is presently used for insight and guidance by millions of people worldwide. How do we account for these developments – particularly the transcultural spread and enduring influence of the *I Ching*?

Clearly the "globalization" of the *I Ching* was in part the product of its alluring "special features (*tezhi*; 特質)"; its exalted position as the "first of the Six [Confucian] Classics"; its cryptic and challenging basic text; its elaborate numerology and other forms of symbolic representation; its utility as a tool of divination; its philosophically sophisticated commentaries; its psychological potential (as a means of attaining self-understanding); and its reputation for a kind of encyclopedic comprehensiveness. The spread of the *I Ching* was also facilitated by the self-conscious strategies employed by those who sought to use it for their own political, social, intellectual or evangelical purposes. In the process the *Changes* invariably became assimilated and transformed in ways that are not only intrinsically interesting but also significant to the broader study of world civilizations.

Although the specific circumstances under which the *Changes* found its way to various countries differed, there were certain common patterns in the way that it traveled. In areas that were closest to China in terms of both geography and culture – Korea, Japan, and Vietnam – the process of transmission was relatively easy because the literati in these places were thoroughly conversant with the classical Chinese language; hence, there was no significant barrier to written communication. Furthermore, since the *I Ching* continued to occupy an exalted position in Chinese culture into the twentieth century, there was never a time when it lacked prestige in peripheral areas. Initially, East Asian elites – and then other sectors of society – embraced the *Changes*, using it for their own often diverse purposes. And in each of these environments the *Yi* became "domesticated," undergoing sometimes radical transformations in the process.[7]

Quite naturally, the early transmission of the *Changes* to the West involved even more substantial transformations. In the first place, unlike the situation in East Asia, in its westward travels the *I Ching* required (and still requires) translation into a variety of European languages that differ substantially from classical Chinese, raising issues of commensurability and incommensurability that are still hotly debated today. Another significant point is that the transmission of the *Changes* to the West paralleled in several ways the process by which Buddhism and Daoism traveled westward. In each case, Western missionaries played a part, and in each case there were varied responses over time, ranging from "blind indifference," to "rational knowledge", "romantic fantasy" and "existential engagement." But in nearly every instance, as in East Asia, there has been some sort of effort, often quite self-conscious, to assimilate and "domesticate" the Chinese classic.

Initially, Jesuit missionaries played the major role in transmitting knowledge of the *Changes* (and other classics) to the West (see, for example, Smith, 2013b, ch. 6). Individuals such as Joachim Bouvet (c. 1660–1732) and his colleague, Jean-François Fouquet (1665–1741) represented a development in Western Christianity known as the Figurist movement, which in China took the form of an effort to find reflections (that is "figures") of the Biblical

---

[7] For an overview of the travels of the *Changes* to Korea, Japan, Vietnam, and Tibet, see Smith, 2012: 129–167. See also Yang, Hongsheng.

patriarchs and examples of Biblical revelation in the Chinese classics – the *I Ching* in particular. Eventually, however, their Figurist enterprise, like the broader Jesuit evangelical movement, fell victim to harsh criticisms and vigorous attacks by Chinese scholars as well as members of the Christian community in China and abroad.

Yet despite the unhappy fate of the Figurists in China, their writings captured the attention of several prominent European intellectuals in the late seventeenth and early eighteenth centuries – most notably, of course, Gottfried Wilhelm Leibniz (1646–1716). And these individuals, in turn, provoked a sustained and substantial Western interest in the *I Ching* that has lasted to this day.[8]

The first complete translation of the *Changes* into a Western language (Latin) did not appear in print until the 1830s, and within decades of its publication, several additional translations of the *Changes* in various European languages appeared. Of these, James Legge's *The Yi King* (1882), remained the standard English-language rendering of the *Changes* until the mid-twentieth century. But in 1924 a German missionary-scholar named Richard Wilhelm (1873–1930) published a translation of the *Changes* titled *I Ging, Das Buch der Wandlungen*, which, when translated into English by Cary Baynes, and published in 1950 as *I Ching, The Book of Changes*, became a global sensation (see Smith 2016b: 385-434).

In certain respects, Wilhelm's translation was like Legge's. It was heavily annotated, produced with assistance from a Chinese scholar, and based on the Qing dynasty's *Balanced [Edition of the] Zhou Changes (Zhouyi zhezhong* 周易折中; 1715), which gave the document a decidedly neo-Confucian cast. But Wilhelm's translation was far smoother, and it reflected a much different worldview. Unlike Legge, Wilhelm made a concerted effort to "domesticate" the *I Ching* in various ways. One was to call upon the authority of classical German philosophers and literary figures, like Kant and Goethe, to illustrate "parallel" ideas expressed in the *Changes*. Another was to cite the Bible for the same purpose. Yet another was to argue that the *I Ching* reflected "some common foundations of humankind … [upon which] all our cultures – unconsciously and unrecognizedly – are based." Wilhelm believed, in other words, that "East and West belong inseparably together and join hands in mutual completion." The West, he argued, had something to learn from China (see Lackner [ed.]: 86-97).

---

[8] Chinese scholars continue to celebrate the connection between Leibniz (and other Western scientists) and the *I Ching*. See, for example, Zhang (ed.): 1: 5.

The Place of the I Ching *in East Asia during the Twentieth and Twenty-First Centuries*

Remarkable transformations in the political, social and cultural environments of China, Japan, Korea and Vietnam during the last century or so have influenced elite and popular attitudes toward the *I Ching*. In China, the fall of the Qing dynasty in 1911 and the rise of warlordism provoked the New Culture Movement (c. 1915–1925), an iconoclastic assault on Chinese tradition by intellectuals seeking new, foreign-inspired solutions to China's pressing problems. Naturally the *I Ching*, as the "first of the Six [Confucian] Classics" came under attack as an outmoded relic of China's "feudal" past (Smith 2008: 195-219). Ironically, however, scholarly study of the *Changes* continued unabated, as intellectuals sought to historicize the document, stripping away the mythology surrounding it and subjecting the work to scientific scrutiny. Much excellent scholarship on the *Changes* grew out of this effort to remove the enormous cultural authority of the document, although the rise of Chinese Marxism after 1920 gave a pronounced political flavor to some evaluations of the *I Ching*. This politicization, in turn, encouraged more "conservative" scholars to celebrate the "humanism" of the *Changes*. Yet another response to the New Culture Movement's emphasis on "Mr. Science" (*Sai xiansheng* 賽先生) was to seek in the *I Ching* scientific principles and possibilities (see Smith 2008: 202-205).

For the next several decades, two successive Mainland Chinese governments – the first under the Nationalist Party, from 1928–1949, and the second under the Communist Party, from 1949 to the present, pursued a "modernizing" strategy aimed, among other things, at building national strength and "destroying superstition" (*po mixin* 破迷信) – including, of course, the use of the *I Ching* for mantic purposes. These campaigns varied in intensity over time, and they diminished dramatically in Taiwan after the Nationalist retreat to the island in 1949. There, the use of the *Changes* for divination, as well as the scholarly study of it, proceeded essentially unfettered. The same was true for Hong Kong, Japan and South Korea. By contrast, North Korea and Vietnam followed the lead of the People's Republic of China.

Things began to change dramatically in the PRC after the declaration of the "Open Policy" in 1978. In fact, during the 1980s and '90s what the

Chinese press described as an "*I Ching* fever 易經熱" swept over China. This enthusiasm for the Classic had both a popular and an academic dimension, and it was manifest in an avalanche of books and journals of every conceivable sort. Two types of scholarship seem particularly significant for our purposes here. One is a continued effort to show that certain features of the *I Ching* are compatible with "modern" science. Thus, we have contemporary individuals such as Yang Li 楊力 arguing in the same basic vein as Fang Yizhi 方以智 (1611–1671) and Jiang Yong 江永 (1681–1762) in the Qing period, that the numbers of the Yellow River Chart and the Luo River Writing are the "deriving coefficient" of everything in the cosmos. Xie Qiucheng 謝求成 maintains that the hexagrams of the *Changes* were originally designed as a high-efficiency information-transfer system analogous to contemporary computer coding based on optimal units of two (the number of basic trigrams in each hexagram) and three (the number of lines in each trigram); and Tang Mingbang 唐明邦, for his part, asserts that the forms of atomic structure in nuclear physics, the genetic code in molecular biology, and the eight-tier matrix in linear algebra all seem to be related to the logic of the *Changes*.[9] Although this sort of thinking remains essentially correlative, it has nonetheless served as a source of satisfaction for Chinese scholars who have long been accustomed to the view that modern science had somehow passed China by.

Another striking development on the Chinese Mainland has been an effort by recent scholars to link the *I Ching* to modern psychology, in particular the ideas of Carl Gustav Jung (1875–1961).[10] The most prominent advocate for this approach is Shen Heyong 申荷永, a Jungian analyst.[11] Professor Shen claims that China is the very "homeland" (*guxiang* 故鄉) of psychology – a country with a long history of scholarly and practical preoccupation with problems of the "heart/mind" (*xin* 心). This preoccupation, Shen argues, is clearly reflected in the *Changes*, where, he claims, one can find a great many psychological insights that are expressed not only in the Ten Wings but also in a number of psychologically potent hexagrams, including *Bi* (#8), *Kan* (#29), *Xian* (#31), *Mingyi* (#36), *Jiaren* (#37), *Yi* (#42), *Jing* (#48), *Gen* (#52) and *Lü* (#56) (see Smith 2008: 216-217).[12]

---

[9] See Smith, 2008: 141, 184-186, 193, 208-11, 240 and 266; also Homola: 733-752.

[10] *Editors' note*: For Jungian interpretations of *Changing*, see PART 3, 167-228.

[11] *Editors' note*: For Shen Heyong's essay on *Changing*, see 208-228 below.

[12] For a general overview of psychology in China, see Yan Guocai.

Professor Shen has written widely on topics such as "Jung's psychology and Chinese Culture" ("Rongge xinli xue yu Zhongguo wenhua 榮格心理學與中國文化") and "The *Classic of Changes* and Chinese Cultural Psychology" ("Yijing yu Zhongguo wenhua xinli" 易經與中國文化心). As one of several examples of the psychological orientation of the *Changes* and the primal power of its "archetypal" images, Shen cites a line in the "Explaining the Trigrams" commentary 説卦傳 that refers to the duplicated trigrams of *Kan* (#29) as the symbols for anxiety (*you* 憂), and "heartsickness" (*xinbing* 心病) in the realm of human affairs (see Shen, Gao and Cope). Shen goes on to say that a number of traditional Chinese commentators, including both Cheng Yi 程頤 (1033–1107) and Zhu Xi, have identified *Kan* as a hexagram reflecting not only the problems but also the potential powers of the mind. Thus, for example, in his famous commentary on the Judgment of Kan, which refers explicitly to the "success" or "prevalence" (*heng* 亨) of the heart/mind of a person who possesses true sincerity, Cheng avers that "With the most highly developed sincerity, [the heart/mind of a human being] can penetrate metal and stone, and overcome water and fire – so what dangers and difficulties can possibly keep it from prevailing?" (至誠可以通金石蹈水火何險難之不可亨也) (see Yan 26-31).

The Place of the Changes in the West during the Twentieth and Twenty-First Centuries

As is well known, Richard Wilhelm was a strong advocate of Jungian psychology. Indeed, Wilhelm asked C. G. Jung to write a foreword to the English translation of his *The I Ching or Book of Changes*. In it, Jung downplayed certain metaphysical assumptions of the work – namely that (1) it duplicates relationships and processes at work in the realm of Heaven-and-Earth; (2) these relationships and processes are knowable, since the mind of Heaven and the mind of Man are considered one (天人合一); and (3) as a reflection of the cosmic Way (*Dao*), the *I Ching* provides guidance for proper conduct in the present and for the future. Jung did, however, view the *Changes* as a document that not only encouraged "careful scrutiny of one's own character, attitude, and motives," but also had "uncommon significance as a method of exploring the unconscious" – that is, providing a vehicle for projecting one's previously unrealized thoughts into the ancient Classic's "abstruse symbolism" (Jung xxxiii-xxxiv).

Many of the most distinctive epistemological features of the *I Ching* are those that encourage creative thinking – especially an emphasis on interconnections, indirection, and the discovery of hidden implications in manifest phenomena" (see Smith 2015: 198–206). The idea of indirection is expressed in the Great Commentary by a reference to language that "twists and turns but hits the mark" (*yan qu er zhong* 言曲而中), while the idea of finding hidden implications in manifest phenomena can be found in the same passage by the provocative notion that "things and events are obviously set forth but they carry hidden [meanings]" (*qi shi si er yin* 其事肆而隱). And, of course, the *I Ching* places great emphasis on the idea of seeking "meanings that lie beyond words" (*yan wai zhi yi* 言外之意). All of these qualities encourage intuition (*zhijue* 直覺) and what has been described by Chinese scholars as "image-thinking" (*xiang siwei* 象思維) (Smith 1997: 5-7).[13]

To be sure, many mainstream Western philosophers have tended to disparage intuition as a way of knowing. Yet there is abundant evidence that in the Western tradition itself this sort of epistemological approach yields all sorts of interesting benefits. Isaac Newton once wrote that "[no] great discovery is ever made without a bold guess"; and Max Planck, a pioneer in quantum theory, summed up the importance of creativity this way in his autobiography: "pioneer scientists must have a vivid intuitive imagination for new ideas, ideas not generated by deduction, but [by] artistically creative imagination." Along the same lines, Max Born, one of the great mathematical physicists of the twentieth century, wrote: "Faith, imagination and intuition are decisive factors in the progress of science … [just as they are] in any other human activity." The celebrated inventor Michael Faraday advised: "Let the imagination go, guarding it by judgment and principle … [and] holding it in and directing it by experiment" (see Smith 1977: 5-7).

As I have discussed at length elsewhere, a wide variety of modern-minded individuals in Europe and the Americas have looked to the *I Ching* for intellectual, spiritual or creative sustenance. The choreographers Merce Cunningham and Carolyn Carlson, for example, found inspiration in the *Changes*, as did such noted composers as John Cage, Udo Kasemets and Joseph Hauer. It has been a significant element in the art of individuals such as Arnaldo Coen, Felipe Erenberg, Eric Morris, Augusto Ramírez and Arturo Rivera, in the architecture of I. M. Pei, and in the writings of a wide

---

[13] The literature on intuition (*zhijue* 直覺) and "image-thinking" (*xiang siwei* 象思維) in Chinese culture is vast. See, for example, Wang.

range of Western authors, including Jorge Luis Borges, Will Buckingham, Philip K. Dick, Allen Ginsberg, Herman Hesse, Octavio Paz, Raymond Queneau, and most recently, Richard Berengarten. It also appears in the lyrics of Bob Dylan (a newly minted Nobel Laureate in Literature), among other songwriters (see Smith 2012: 194-210; and Redmond and Hon: 192-236).

Concluding Thoughts

For those of us who teach and write about texts and traditions, it is virtually impossible to avoid cross-comparisons of one sort or another – not least because we seek answers to questions inspired by what we already know. But how should we go about it? Opinions naturally differ (see Smith 2003a: 783-801). This much seems clear in any case: we all can benefit from being introduced to different ways of "world-making" as a means of expanding our mental horizons. As Clifford Geertz reminds us, the greater the reach of our minds – that is, the broader the "range of signs we can manage somehow to interpret" in our effort to understand the cultural ways of "other" people – the more expansive and rich our own "intellectual, emotional and moral space" will become (Smith 2003b: 5). At the same time, sympathetic engagement with the "other" defamiliarizes what may appear to be normative. That is, an honest effort to appreciate the way "alien" cultures see the world provides us with fresh perspectives on our own society. The more we can understand what it is like to be the "other," the more likely we are to understand ourselves. And if we can do this with the *I Ching*, then we can do it with any document.

References

Allen, Barry. 2015. *Vanishing into Things: Knowledge in Chinese Tradition* Cambridge, MA: Harvard University Press.

Elman, Benjamin A. 2005. A. *On Their Own Terms: Science in China, 1550–1900.* Cambridge, MA and London: Harvard University Press.

Homola, Stéphanie. 2014 (August). 'The Fortunes of a Scholar: When the *Yijing* Challenged Modern Astronomy,' *Journal of Asian Studies* 73.3: 733–752.

Jung, C. G. 1967. "Foreword" to Wilhelm, Richard. *The I Ching or Book of Changes.* Princeton, NJ: Princeton University Press.

Kunst, Richard A. 1985. 'The Original "I Ching": A Text, Phonetic Transcription, Translation, and Indexes, with Sample Glosses.' Berkeley, CA: PhD dissertation, University of California at Berkeley.

Lackner, Michael. 1999. 'Richard Wilhelm: A "Sinicized' German Translator".' In Viviane Alleton and Michael Lackner (eds.). *De l'un au multiple. La traduction du chinois dans les langues européennes.* Paris: Maison des Sciences de l'Homme.

Qian, Jibo 錢基博. 1990. 'Zhouyi wei you huan zhi xue 周易為憂患之學' (The study of the *Zhou Changes* as a means of alleviating anxiety). In Wang, Shouqi 王壽祺 and Zhang, Shanwen 張善文, eds., *Zhouyi yanjiu lunwen ji* 周易研究論文集 (Collected essays on research into the *Zhou Changes*). Beijing: Beijing daxue chubanshe.

Raphals, Lisa. 2013. *Divination and Prediction in Early China and Ancient Greece.* Cambridge: Cambridge University Press.

Redmond, Geoffrey and Hon, Tze-ki. 2014. *Teaching the I Ching (Book of Changes).* New York: Oxford University Press.

Shaughnessy, Edward L. 2022. *The Origin and Early Development of the* Zhou Changes. Leiden and Boston: Brill.

Shen, Heyong *et al.* 2006 (January-June). '*I Ching*, Psychology of Heart, and Jungian Analysis.' *Psychological Perspectives.* 49.1: 61-78.

Smith, Richard J. 1977. "The Tao of Physics." Address to the Freshman Class, Rice University. Online at: https://www.academia.edu/29138380/The_Tao_of_Physics.

———. 2003a. 'The *Yijing* (Classic of Changes) in Comparative Perspective: The Value of Cross-Cultural Investigations.' *International Journal of the Humanities* 1, 783–801.

———. 2003b. 'The *Yijing* (Classic of Changes) in Global Perspective: Some Pedagogical Reflections.' *Education about Asia* 8.2.

———. 2008. *Fathoming the Cosmos and Ordering the World: The* Yijing (I-Ching, *or* Classic of Changes) *and Its Evolution in China*. Charlottesville, VA: University of Virginia Press.

———. 2012. *The I Ching: A Biography*. Princeton, NJ: Princeton University Press.

———. 2013a. 'Fathoming the *Changes*: The Evolution of Some Technical Terms and Interpretive Strategies in *Yijing* Exegesis.' *Journal of Chinese Philosophy* 40: 146–170.

———. 2013b. *Mapping China and Managing the World: Culture, Cartography and Cosmology in Late Imperial Times*. Abingdon: Routledge.

———. 2015. *The Qing Dynasty and Traditional Chinese Culture*. Lanham, MD: Rowman and Littlefield.

———. 2016a. 'Why the *Yijing* 易經 (Classic of Changes) Matters in an Age of Globalization'. In Ming Dong Gu, (ed.) *Why Traditional Chinese Philosophy Still Matters: The Relevance of Ancient Wisdom for the Global Age*. London and New York: Routledge.

———. 2016b. 'Collaborators and Competitors: Western Translators of the *Yijing* (*Classic of Changes*) in the Eighteenth and Nineteenth Centuries.' In Lawrence Wang-chi Wang and Bernhard Fuehrer (eds.). *Sinologists as Translators in the Seventeenth to Nineteenth Centuries* Hong Kong: Chinese University Press.

Wang, Shuren. 2005. *Huigui yuanchuang zhi si – xiang siwei shiye xia di Zhongguo zhihui* 回歸原創之思 – 象思維視野下的中國智慧 (A return to original creative thought – Chinese wisdom viewed from the standpoint of image thinking). Nanjing: Jiangsu renmin chubanshe

Wilhelm, Richard (ed. and trans. into German) 1967. *The I Ching or Book of Changes*. Baynes, Cary F. (trans. from German). Princeton, NJ: Princeton University Press.

Yan, Guocai 燕國才. 2005. *Zhongguo xinli xue shi* 中國心理學 (History of Chinese psychology). Hangzhou: Zhejiang jiaoyu chubanshe.

Yang, Hongsheng 楊宏聲. 1995. *Bentu yu yuwai: Yixue di xiandaihua yu shijiehua* 本土與域外: 易學的現代化與世界化 (The native land and beyond: the modernization and globalization of *Changes* studies). Shanghai: Shanghai shehui kexue yuan.

Zhang, Qicheng 張其成 (ed.). 1996. *Yijing yingyong da baike* 易經應用大百科 (A practical encyclopedia of the *Classic of Changes*). Taibei: Dijing qiye gufen youxian gongsi.

Zhang, Shanwen 張善文 (ed.). 1990. *Zhouyi yanjiu lunwen ji* 周易研究論文集 (Collected essays on research into the *Zhou Changes*). Beijing: Beijing daxue chubanshe.

PART 1

Precedents, Parallels,
and a New Poem

JEREMY HOOKER

Changing: A Way In

This heaven-and-earth Cosmos is also the Cosmos of our immediate experience, and if we don't think of heaven and earth as mere abstractions, we can see that heaven and earth are indeed an accurate description of the physical reality in which we live. The generative life-supporting reality of earth requires the infusion of energies from heaven: sunlight, rain, snow, air. We dwell in our everyday lives at the origin place where this vital intermingling of heaven and earth takes place, at the center of a dynamic cocoon of cosmic energy, an all-encompassing generative present.
David Hinton, *I Ching* (x-xi)

There is order in being.
Richard Berengarten, *The Manager* (146)

My title is an accurate description of what I intend this essay to be: an initial entrance to Richard Berengarten's *Changing*. 'Way in' is also a pun on The Way, Tao (*aka* Dao), "the most common term for nature in premodern China" (Smith 3). First, it is a way in to Berengarten's book that I have found for myself. I have been a reader of Berengarten over the years, and have written about his earlier work. I am also a poet and critic of his generation who, as a student in the 1960s, shared his counter-cultural influences, including Zen and Taoism. Yet, before reading *Changing*, I literally knew nothing about the *I Ching*. What I know of it now I owe to *Changing* and the reading to which it points. *Changing* draws upon the *I Ching* as an "ever-fresh well" (48/4: 388). Berengarten finds it "solid yet flowing / firm yet yielding / radiating images". *Changing* is rooted in the wisdom of ancient China. It is also a major contribution to modern English poetry. Berengarten is Anglo-Jewish by birth and upbringing. He is also fully justified in thinking of himself rather as "a European poet who writes in English than an English poet" (RB 1999: back inside cover). Furthermore, with his acknowledged poetic masters, George Seferis and

Octavio Paz, his particular vision expresses a universal humanism. Keeping in mind the relation between the particular and the universal, I shall focus here on *Changing* as poetry in the English language, which draws on and contributes to the English poetic tradition.

Among epigraphs to *Changing* in several languages, including Chinese, Greek, and Latin, we find several in English. Each is at once specific and contributes to the universalism of the book. Shakespeare is represented by Hamlet's words: "There are more things in heaven and earth, Horatio, / Than are dreamt of in your philosophy." Heaven and earth are key terms in the cosmology of the *I Ching*. In the words of David Hinton quoted above, the terms describe "the physical reality in which we live, [...] at the centre of a dynamic cocoon of cosmic energy, an all-encompassing generative present" (Hinton xi). This is the language of Tao, not of Shakespeare's Christian universe. Like the *I Ching*, Berengarten does not invoke God or gods. He is however a religious poet – as I shall discuss later. Like Shakespeare and the poets who follow him – Donne, Herbert, Vaughan – he writes in the tradition of metaphysical poetry, in which heaven and earth are at once real and grounded upon a mystery that is ultimately inexpressible.

A note to the sixth epigraph (534) refers us to the following lines from *The Prelude* (1805), in which Wordsworth speaks of 'a toil' resembling 'creative agency':

> I mean to speak
> Of that interminable building rear'd
> By observation of affinities
> In objects where no brotherhood exists
> To common minds.   (Book 2, ll. 401-405)

"Building" accurately describes the architectonics of *Changing*: a work whose sixty-four clusters of six poems based on the hexagrams of the *I Ching* give it a solidity of numerical structure that contains a wide range of fluid expression. Here, however, I want principally to observe the link between Berengarten's work and the Romantic idea of imagination, in which 'creative agency' unites the human mind with nature. "affinities / In objects where no brotherhood exists" is also an idea consonant with C. G. Jung's concept of synchronicity, which reading the *I Ching* helped Jung to define. 'Creative agency', thus understood, is at the heart of Berengarten's thinking:

> As for associative, analogical or correlative thinking, sometimes also known as 'correlative cosmos-building', this is not only the

mental foundation for poetry, ritual and magic in all societies, but specifically underpins the holistic vision of the universe that runs through all traditional Chinese thought – most evidently so in Daoism. (*CH*, 'Postscript' 526)

In the 'ever-fresh well' of the *I Ching*, Berengarten has found his "holistic vision", his understanding of "all phenomena, including the forces of nature, the interaction of things, and the circumstances of change" (Smith 64).

Like Wordsworth's words from *The Prelude*, a quotation from Gerard Manley Hopkins used as another epigraph may be seen as prefiguring synchronicity: "All the world is full of inscape and chance left free to act falls into an order as well as purpose" (Hopkins 230; *CH* 533). Chance falling into order could be a brief description of both the *I Ching* and *Changing*. With equal succinctness, words from *The Manager* encapsulate the belief on which all Berengarten's work is founded: "There is order in being" (RB 2011: 146).

This is a belief Ezra Pound shared. Berengarten is among the modern poets indebted to Pound, described by T. S. Eliot, in his introduction to Pound's *Selected Poems* (1928), as "the inventor of Chinese poetry for our time" (Eliot 1928: 14). Pound, in turn, was indebted to Ernest Fenollosa, and together they introduced the force of Chinese poetry to the West. By force, I mean 'the forces of nature', the generative energy of Tao, and the affinity this shares with the 'active universe' of Wordsworth and other Romantic poets. Pound, inspired by Confucian ideas, tried to force an idea of order onto *The Cantos,* with tragic political consequences. With humility, he finally admitted his "errors and wrecks", and affirmed: "it coheres all right" (Pound 1970: 26-27). With this affirmation of coherence, of order in being, as its final epigraph, *Changing* begins.

Berengarten is closest to William Blake among Romantic poets. For Berengarten too, "Energy is eternal delight" (Blake 182), and the dynamic universe is a unity of binary forces. Blake's "without contraries is no progression" (*ibid.* 181) has affinities with *yin* and *yang*, the complementary opposites in process of constant interaction and transformation, which compose the ancient Chinese cosmos. As Richard J. Smith explains:

> From the late Zhou period onward, yin and yang came to be [...] viewed as modes of cosmic creativity (female and male, respectively), which not only produced but also animated all natural phenomena. (Smith 50)

Berengarten shares with Blake a vision consonant with this view of things, in which the dynamic Cosmos vibrates with sexual energies, and the female is liberated from subjection to the male. In the twentieth century the new physics revealed a universe in which ideas such as complementarity supported the holistic vision of Blake and the Taoists. Significantly, in *Changing* Berengarten cites the physicist David Bohm and his book *Wholeness and the Implicate Order* (*CH* 535).

Blake's spirit is invoked in a number of poems in Berengarten's book. In 'Oh my (our) country'. for example, which begins with lines that include a resonant Blakean word:

> Oh my (our) country, replete
> with privileges and snobberies
> accumulated over centuries,
>
> laid out in every enclosed
> and cultivated land-parcelling,
> built into wall and roof
>
> plotted, mapped, chartered
> into every street [...]   (27/3: 219)

"Chartered", echoing a keyword in Blake's 'London', belongs to a comprehensive critique of present-day England:

> Since your
> walls, fences, hedges, ditches block
> him, her, us, each other in/out,
>
> your mad sales and purchasings
> on beauty behind bodymind barriers
> demoralise age, destroy youth.   (*ibid.*)

As in Blake, inner and outer, flesh and psyche ("bodymind") are united here, and a whole repressive system is condemned as life-denying on aesthetic, economic and moral grounds. Geoffrey Hill is the contemporary English poet closest to Berengarten in this particular poem of enraged and frustrated love for his native country. Hill's social radicalism is closer to John Ruskin, but his anger at the condition of the English working class has more than a tinge of Blake, and is present throughout his work. What both poets are responding to is a failure of vision that has produced a strictly limited sense of human possibility, and a deathly ethos in all aspects of life in modern England.

Death preoccupies Berengarten in *Changing*. This is not surprising, as it is the work of an aging poet. Death is of course the most personal matter, and Berengarten confronts it as a poet who passionately affirms life. In his poetry, as in the *I Ching*, death is not simply the negation of life. Early on, in his introduction to *Ceri Richards: Drawings to Poems by Dylan Thomas*, he describes:

> the eternal round of birth, growth, fertilisation and death, the unitary quality of all these taken together, and the inevitability of struggle within this process – since, as Blake said, "Without contraries is no progression". For only by confrontation of death can "death have no dominion."   (RB 1980: xiii)

Confrontation of death in *Changing* proceeds with the wisdom of the *I Ching*. In the fifth poem in 'Darkening', Berengarten replies to Theodor Adorno's assertion, "To write a poem after Auschwitz is barbaric," Adorno "misconstrues what / poems are, do, are for":

> To call out love and justice,
> born of the heart's oldest and
> simplest imperatives – hope,
>
> compassion, courage, truth,
> *and* defiance of death-makers.   (36/5: 293)

Defiantly, Berengarten reverses the trend in modern literature based on the belief that modern atrocities have invalidated the 'big' words – love, justice, hope, compassion, courage, truth – as if these values were vapid abstractions. In accordance with his universal humanism, he links poets across the ages. Both ancient and modern poets express "the heart's oldest and / simplest imperatives." This faith in poetry as the voice of humanity recalls the thought of Octavio Paz, a major influence on Berengarten, who was deeply impressed by Paz's affirmation in *The Labyrinth of Solitude* that: "For the first time in our history we are contemporaries of all mankind" (Paz 1967: 194).[1] The continuity of poetry is a defining feature of humanity. In the words of Paz:

---

[1] *Editors' note*: Berengarten often repeats this *bon mot* of Paz's, almost as if it were a mantra: for example, as an epigraph to *Avebury* (1972, 2018), and *Imagems 1* (2013).

The first hunters and gatherers looked at themselves in astonishment one day, for an interminable instant, in the still waters of a poem. Since that moment, people have not stopped looking at themselves in this mirror. And they have seen themselves, at one and the same time, as creators of images and as images of their creations. (Paz 1992: 159)

Since the Stone Age, poetry has been integral to the life of all human societies, and an art by which we know ourselves.

One of the finest poems about death in *Changing* brings together an evening walk in Cambridge, when the poet sees "a zinc-and-nickel // half-moon in cloudless sky", and his reading that night of Cesar Vallejo's line "C'est la vie, mort de la Mort!" He concludes the poem: "Poetry is a criticism of death" (41/5: 333). In simple language, characteristic of the clarity of *Changing* as a whole, Berengarten intimates a complex experience. The radiant image of the half-moon brings a particular fineness to the poet's home city; it also suggests the life-and-death wisdom of the *I Ching*. The "even finer" conviction of the Peruvian poet enables Berengarten to correct Matthew Arnold's prosaic half-truth that poetry is "a criticism of life". The traditionally feminine image of the moon and Vallejo's line come together as a vision of wholeness. The poem also contains an implicit answer to Arnold's despairing belief that Wordsworth was the last poet with "healing power". To Arnold's mind, in the condition of England in his time "of doubts, disputes, distractions, fears", there could be no more sacred poetry (Arnold 1949: 118).

There is nothing cavalier about Berengarten's defiance of death. In 'Meditation at Majdanek', site of a Nazi concentration camp in Poland, the poet writes: "*Memory, mother / of poems, shrinks away / to scream not mourn*" (36/0: 288). These too are expressions that define our humanity, and part of what makes *Changing* a profoundly human document. 'Warsaw Ghetto, April-May 1943' begins: "Remember / and honour them // all who perished" (39/5: 317). To remember and honour the dead are primary functions of poetry; and sometimes, as in this instance, "The only possible/ words are modest. And very quiet."

True to the spirit of change and transformation, *Changing* contains a wealth of human experience and a wide range of emotions, and addresses, or refers to, a large number of people – family and friends, fellow poets, contemporary and historical figures, and figures of myth, such as Arthur. It is hospitable poetry: "for what // use is a voice, / of being human, / to restrain gifts // on a tight leash" ("Hospitality," 37/3: 299). Berengarten can often be celebratory, a praise poet. Contending with death, he is most Wordsworthian in his frequent recourse to the pleasures which there are in life itself. An excellent example of this is 'Lara's garden in August', which records an afternoon enjoyed in the company of his daughter and other family members:

> [...] we sat and drank
> elderflower cordial and
>
> chilled white wine in the long
> garden and looked at old photos
> and chattered about
>
> family things, nothing
> in particular.   (37/1: 297)

Together, they enjoy "Pleasures so / simple they're almost // incommunic-able, // fabric of most / people's everything". Such "fabric" can hardly be "nothing / in particular". The words are quietly deceptive. Berengarten's poems are built of particulars – here, named individuals, drinking elderflower cordial, looking at old photos, and other specific details. As noted above, an epigraph to *Changing* quotes Hopkins describing the world as "full of inscape". Hopkins is among the poets Berengarten values highly for his love of what Blake called "minute particulars" (see Foster Damon 280-282). Walt Whitman is another. It is a democratic vision that Berengarten shares with Whitman, and with Paz, of whom he has said:

> I believe that Octavio's poetics of universalism has an urgency that is rooted in the moral and humane issues born (and borne) out of the ashes of Auschwitz and Hiroshima. Formulated in the immediate wake of the United Nations' *Declaration of Human Rights* in 1948, his idea that "we are contemporaries of all humanity" encapsulates the integral poetics and morality of that Declaration. (RB 2015 online)

The "poetics of universalism" requires particularism. Thus, in 'In the spirit of Walt Whitman', Berengarten writes:

> It's villages and small
> towns across the world
> I'm interested in and
>
> care for, not countries.   (7/2: 58)

The poem concludes by identifying its many particulars as "each unique *this*, familiar / to a person, to persons".

A phrase in *Changing* that describes Earth as "*mother of particularities*" (2/0: 14) is, surely, an echo of David Jones's 'Tutelar of the Place', in which he invokes the "mother of particular perfections" and passionately defends the local and particular against the imperial and megalopolitan (Jones 62). Jones admired Hopkins and was influenced by him, and, as a Roman Catholic, shared his sacramental vision. Berengarten is not, like Hopkins and Jones, a poet of the Christian universe. He is, however, a poet who perceives the "radiance of the ordinary" or "radiance of the commonplace" (RB 2017: 124), and a religious poet with a strong sense of the sacred. In this context, it is instructive to bring Jung's definition of religion together with Berengarten's.

In his 'Foreword' to Richard Wilhelm's translation of the *I Ching*, Jung describes "the original meaning of the word *religio*" as "a careful observation and taking account of (from *religare*) the numinous". In a footnote, he observes: "This is the classical etymology. The derivation of *religio* from *religare*, 'bind to', originated with the Church Fathers" (Jung xxviii). In *A Portrait in Inter-Views*, Berengarten discusses the meaning of *religio*:

> The Indo-European root of the word 'religion' is the same as for words like 'yoke', 'join' and 'conjugal'. The poet is always trying to 'yoke', to 'join', to find connectivity [...] is connected and the poet realises these connections. (RB 2017: 86)

In this context, 'conjugal' strikes me as being an especially significant word. It relates to marriage, and brings to mind the contraries of Blake's 'The Marriage of Heaven and Hell'. It also suggests *yin* and *yang*, and interactions of male and female forces, that have had a profound influence on both Berengarten and Paz. Berengarten's description of connectivities, to which Paz introduced him in conversation, encapsulates the spirit of what might be termed their shared cosmic erotics:

> themes and patternings broached by him constantly recur. Recursion and iteration; cyclicity and spirality. Motion in stillness, stillness in motion. Chaos and order in a similar binary correlation. 'Notness' and 'isness' intertwined like lovers; eros and psyche interpenetrating and wound around each other like a caduceus – the universal dance that meshes being with not-being.
>
> (RB 2015 online)

The interpenetration of eros and psyche has been both an early and continuing preoccupation of Berengarten. It is present for instance in the male and female symbolism of *Avebury*, and in *the* Jewish mysticism of Adam Kadmon and the Shekhinah in *The Manager*. Sex as a sacred, creative phenomenon, active as complementary forces in the universe, is fundamental to Berengarten's vision in *Changing*. We can see, therefore, that taken together, Jung's and Berengarten's definitions of religion stress the duality of a single process, in which conjugal connectivity is manifested in luminous particulars.

We may well ask why a sophisticated poet growing up in the 1940s and 1950s, a poet keenly aware of modernity in all its forms, should have been drawn to a Chinese text originating in the Bronze Age. The same question might be asked of the poet's decision to base an early work on the prehistoric stones of Avebury (RB 1972 and 2018). In both cases the answer would be the same. In a time under the shadow of the atom bomb, a time at once universally life-threatening and subject to widespread cultural superficiality and a sense of existential meaninglessness in the West, he was seeking some fundamental ground of meaning on which to base his life and work. Not an abstract ground, but a bodymind spirituality, with a vibrant creativity activated by the complementary powers of male and female. Mainstream English poetry at that time had, with few exceptions, lost touch with the larger Self and the world beyond the social realm.

Egotism blights poetry. Blake describes Selfhood as the Spectre in *Jerusalem*, and prays: "Annihilate the Selfhood in me: be thou all my life!" (Blake 436). This may be compared with Berengarten's account of the twentieth century sage Xiao Yao, who "changed himself and

> [...] went down
> into darkness and silence,
> where he shedded *things,*
>
> spacetime, life-and-death,
> even his own breath. Then
> from that core that is
>
> nothing and everything,
> a fire inexhaustible flowed
> in streams through and
>
> along his fingers, to and
> into whatever he touched.   ('Shedding', 49/5: 397)

45

Shedding everything, Xiao Yao comes to "that core that is" which releases an inexhaustible fire. This primal energy may be compared to the life Blake prays to *be*. We may think also of Charles Olson's prescription for the poet's mental efficacy: to get "rid of the lyrical interference of the individual as ego", and write as "a creature of nature" (Olson 25). In each instance what is at issue is the relationship between mind and world – an idea of human creativity as part of the generative energy of the active universe. Berengarten finds in the *I Ching* what he finds in great Romantic poets such as Wordsworth and Blake. The *I Ching*, with commentaries and interpretations added to it over the centuries, is an immensely complex book. But at its heart is something simple: observation of nature. And the nature the sages observed is dynamic, rhythmic, patterned, and transformative. In nature, "everything is process / *in* process, changing to something else" ("Ways and whys," 8/5: 69).

This *way* of nature, this dynamic vision, is what *Changing* restores to English poetry. Berengarten writes from within a reality both physical and metaphysical, and his sense of the sacred has affinities with that of the Catholic poets, Hopkins and Jones. It also calls to mind the Eliot of *Four Quartets*, and Dylan Thomas's 'The force that through the green fuse drives the flower'. In fact, Berengarten is closer to Thomas than to the Christian poets, since his is a secular sacred; it has no need of an external divinity to engender life in the seed. Energy at once physical and spiritual informs the nature he apprehends, as in '*Seed, seeding, seedling*':

> *A seed hardly visible to*
> *human eyes swells, splits,*
>
> *opens, pushes up and down,*
> *down and up, powered in each*
> *and every one of its expansive*
>
> *nano-changes by latent pre-*
> *patterned responses to chemical –*
> *physical signals and triggers [...]*   (3/0: 24)

Here, as elsewhere in *Changing*, observation of a primary natural process unites with a modern understanding of physics and chemistry, and science becomes poetry:

> *Pausing to*
> *register this, how can one not*
> *be stunned by the ordinary*

extraordinary miraculousness
of this epiphany, this thisness,
this entire matter of living?   (*ibid.*)

Changing is a highly personal book that draws on the poet's life-experience and the immediacy of his daily living. In the latter respect it contains vivid vignettes of life in Cambridge. But it is not bounded by a narrow egotism. It is poetry of the larger Self, and in freeing itself from a linear sense of time, it finds images for the eternal now. Observing effects of wind in grass, Berengarten sees:

how here, across grass, time

may flow backwards too, as
floods of *was* and *will-be* inter-
penetrate, the unpredictable

unlikely casual tomorrow
and the firm and sure causal
arrow being mere surface

of this immense, patterned
dense-packed, multilayered
field you float in [...]   ('Wind across grass', 19/1: 153)

Again, this phenomenal process is closely observed; and observation reveals synchronicity: the "casual tomorrow" and the "causal arrow" of time are "mere surfaces" of the "whole field".

As Jung wrote, in order to understand the *I Ching*, "it is necessary to cast off certain prejudices of the Western mind" (Jung xxxv). Jung also notes: "The ancient Chinese mind contemplates the cosmos in a way comparable to that of the modern physicist" (*ibid.* xxiv). This view corresponds to Jung's idea of synchronicity, which "takes the coincidence of events in space and time as meaning something more than mere chance, namely, a peculiar interdependence of objective events among themselves as well as with the subjective (psychic) states of the observer or observers" (*ibid.* xxiv). The way of the *I Ching* also, like that of Jung and the modern physicists, is participation: the observer is not a spectator of what he or she observes, but part of the living whole. In the words of David Hinton, the *I Ching* "divination practice operates on the very primal assumption that we are an integral part of the Cosmos" (Hinton xiv). What the ancient Chinese sages observed, and made available for divination purposes, modern countercultural artists, musicians, and poets, including Richard Berengarten, have used to renew an idea of human 'creative agency' as integral to the active universe.

"There is order in being." The way of nature is form-making, patterning, and humans, implicated in natural processes, learned from nature to create the kind of patterns that we know as art. Ancient sages observed changing movements, positions, forms in heaven and earth: day and night, stars, clouds, 'mountain-shapes in mist', textures, animal tracks, all the phenomena of the world they lived in, and:

> observing these high
> and low with eyes peeled
> we learned to copy
>
> and with fingers mark
> patterns of our own in shell,
> wood, clay, hide, stone.　　　　　　　　('Patterns of our own', 20/1: 161)

'Man-the-maker' is our evolutionary boast. We may see it perhaps as a peculiarly Western assumption, that asserts human mastery over nature perceived as conquered and turned into passive matter. This is not the view of the *I Ching*, or of the Romantic poets with their essentially participatory metaphysics. Paz reminds us that Jung "maintained that the principle that rules the hexagrams is not causality but confluence" (Paz 1992: 48). Confluence, I think, is the best word to sum up the way into *Changing* that I have offered here. It intimates how things flow together, and interact, and change, yet remain one continuous generative tissue. Berengarten's book is a highly patterned, solidly structured work. Within it, from the "ever-fresh well" of the *I Ching*, he draws a wonderful array of changing, confluent experiences. *Changing* is a book of constant surprises, with recurring themes undergoing change and appearing in ever-new manifestations. It is a monumental "building" and my attempt to enter it is only one way. There will be other, different ways.

In addition to Octavio Paz, George Seferis is another key influence, and his presence in *Changing* is manifested in recurring images of "black light".[2] As these and other influences demonstrate, Berengarten is certainly "a European poet who writes in English". But he is also a major poet

---

[2] *Editors' note:* See *CH* 2/5: 19; 10/2: 82; 30/2: 242; 33/0: 264, 36/2: 290; 53/0: 424, and 63/5: 509. *Black Light* is the title of a sequence which RB dedicated to Seferis. See RB 2011a: 147-176.

who extends the tradition of English poetry that is open to mystery, and alive to human creativity as a natural energy. With his luminous "minute particulars", he writes in the spirit of Blake and Gerard Manley Hopkins; and he develops the art of Imagism, which Ezra Pound helped to bring into poetry in English from the Chinese. *Changing* is both a powerful work of the intellect, and one in which, as in the medieval *Pearl*, "simplicity / and complexity keep // opening out into each / other, interpenetrating, / blurring, irradiating" (*CH* 64/5: 517). "Solid yet flowing / firm yet yielding", *Changing* is a radiant book.

References

Arnold, Matthew. 1949. *The Portable Matthew Arnold*, Trilling, Lionel (ed.). New York: The Viking Press.

Blake, William. 1956 [1927]. *Poetry and Prose of William Blake*. Keynes, Geoffrey (ed.). London: The Nonesuch Library.

Berengarten, Richard. 2011a. *For the Living: Selected Longer Poems 1965–2000*. Exeter: Shearsman Books.

————. 2011b. *The Manager*. Bristol: Shearsman Books.

————. 2015. 'Octavio Paz in Cambridge, 1970'. *The Fortnightly Review*. Online at: http://fortnightlyreview.co.uk/2015/07/octavio-paz/.

————. 2016. *Changing*, Bristol: Shearsman Books.

————. 2017. *A Portrait in Inter-Views*, Nikolaou, Paschalis and Dillon, John Z. (eds.). Bristol: Shearsman Books.

————. 2018. *Avebury*. Bristol: Shearsman Books (Shearsman Library 5).

Burns, Richard. 1972. *Avebury*. London: Anvil Press Poetry with Routledge and Kegan Paul.

————. 1983. *Black Light*. Cambridge: Los Poetry Press.

————. 1999. *Against Perfection*. Norwich: King of Hearts.

Burns, Richard (ed.). 1980. 'Introduction' to Richards, Ceri: *Drawings to Poems by Dylan Thomas*. London: Enitharmon Press.

Eliot, T. S. 1928. 'Introduction' to Pound, Ezra, *Selected Poems*. London: Faber and Faber.

Foster Damon, S. (1979). *A Blake Dictionary*. London: Thames and Hudson.

Hinton, David (trans.). 2015. *I Ching: The Book of Change*. New York: Farrar, Straus and Giroux.

Hopkins, Gerard Manley. 1966. *The Journals and Papers of Gerard Manley Hopkins*. House, Humphrey (ed.). Oxford: Oxford University Press.

Jones, David. 1974. *The Sleeping Lord and Other Fragments*. London: Faber and Faber.

Jung, C. G. 1983. 'Foreword' to *The I Ching or Book of Changes*. Wilhelm, Richard and Baynes, Cary F. (trans.). London: Penguin Books.

Olson, Charles. 1966. 'Projective Verse'. In *Selected Writings,* Creeley, Robert (ed.). New York: New Directions.

Paz, Octavio. 1967. *The Labyrinth of Solitude*. Kemp, Alexander (trans.). London: Allen Lane: The Penguin Press.

_____. 1992. *The Other Voice*. Lane, Helen (trans.). Manchester: Carcanet Press.

Pound, Ezra. 1970. *Drafts and Fragments of CANTOS CX-CXVII*. London: Faber and Faber.

Smith, Richard J. 2012. The *I Ching: A Biography,* Princeton, NJ and Oxford: Princeton University Press.

Wordsworth, William. 1969 [1933]. *The Prelude, or Growth of a Poet's Mind* (1805 text). De Selincourt, Ernest (ed.). London, New York, Toronto, ON: Oxford University Press.

PAUL SCOTT DERRICK

British Mind. Chinese Soil.
American Grain.

Richard Berengarten's accomplishment in *Changing* is too broad, too complex and too intricately detailed to explore satisfactorily in a single essay. There's just too much to account for. So I intend to narrow my focus here to what I suspect to be the book's central and possibly deepest concerns, encompassed in Berengarten's vision of wholeness.

A sequence of 448 eighteen-line poems and two villanelles that compose a contemporary epic in verse, *Changing* grew slowly out of the poet's extended interaction with the Chinese *Book of Changes*. More than thirty years of asking questions, casting hexagrams, reflecting on their contents as answers and elaborating those answers into his own responses in poems – not to mention poring over a host of other commentaries and critical studies on the origins, the history, the organization, the structure, the philosophy and the reader's possible uses of that intriguing, compelling text.

But this kind of careful and unhurried, deliberate and thoughtful approach to writing is not unusual for Berengarten. For example, he gradually accumulated his book-length poem *The Manager* over a period of about twenty-two years, from 1978 to 2000 (RB 2001). And the initial inspiration for another complex sequence, *The Blue Butterfly*, came in 1985 and led to the composition of two poems, "The Blue Butterfly" and "Nada: hope or nothing" (RB 2006: 123-124). The other forty-seven poems in that collection were written over a span of twenty years. As I have argued elsewhere, this kind of composition is akin to what Martin Heidegger called *ein andenkendes Denken* (Derrick, online), a patient contemplation that listens, recalls and responds. For Heidegger, this way of thinking, this way of using the potent tool of the mind, offers a needed antidote to the aggressive kinds of thought that have characterized Western society in modern times, and is best represented by the mindset of modern science and, especially, technology.

By the middle of the twentieth century, Heidegger saw quite clearly the threats to the survival of the world posed by thinking that imposes human will and intervenes, too often rashly, in natural processes. The initial intentions of science are to a large extent benign and philanthropic: to expand knowledge, to improve living conditions for human beings, to combat disease, to ease the struggle for life. But we know from our Romantic forebears that it doesn't take long for those noble intentions to be contaminated by the push of the ego and for the scientist, or the culture that science nurtures, to be intoxicated by the temptations presented by the power over nature that science grants us. No one would deny that we live in perilous times. And it seems to me that one of the deepest causes of the many dangers that face us now is the essentially destructive path our culture's tampering with the world has led us to.

We need to take a different path, and for Heidegger the key to that path lies in learning to use the potential of the mind differently, less aggressively and more receptively. His term for that is *reflection*. In the essay "Science and Reflection"[1] he says that "Reflection is of a different essence from the making conscious and the knowing that belong to science […]" (1977: 180). After elucidating how that making conscious and knowing impose the human will on nature, he sums up what he means by reflection: "To venture after sense or meaning [*Sinn*] is the essence of reflection [*Besinnen*]. This means more than a mere making conscious of something. We do not yet have reflection when we have only consciousness. Reflection is more. It is calm, self-possessed surrender to that which is worthy of questioning" (*ibid.*). And I would argue that this passage gives a good description of the process by which Berengarten produced *Changing*.

It has long been my contention that there is a deeply embedded strain of nihilism in Occidental culture, and that the Romantic movement stemmed from a recognition of that strain and marked the first glimmering of a need to resist it. On the heels of the Enlightenment, numerous writers, painters and thinkers perceived the dangers inherent in an over-dependence on rational thought, and so initiated what I like to think of as the "recessive" line of thinking in Western culture, which has been, over the intervening centuries, examining and criticizing our drive toward fragmentation and destruction. This subversive countermovement necessarily advocates a return to unity and wholeness. That is, to a holistic paradigm. And I believe that one of its finest representatives in contemporary poetry is Richard Berengarten.

---

[1] *Wissenschaft und Besinnung*, originally published in 1954.

The gods speak to us through the poets, diviners and holy prophets, but the poets, diviners and holy prophets also speak to the gods for us. [...] Our poems and our prophecies are also our prayers.
Edward L. Shaughnessy, Preface to *Changing* (x)

When Ruth Halkon asked Berengarten if he considered himself a religious poet, he gave a typically holistic reply:

I do, in a way. [...] 'Religio', the Latin antecedent of 'religion', means 're-binding'. [...] The poet is always trying to 'yoke', to 'join', to find connectivity, and that is engrained in the structure – and stuff – of metaphor [and] of language itself, and of experience itself. Everything *is* connected and the poet realizes these connections. Pound reminded himself of that, quasi-tragically, at the end of his *Cantos*: "It coheres all right – even if my notes do not cohere." As Wordsworth says in *The Prelude*, "I mean to speak / Of that interminable building reared / By observation of affinities / In objects where no brotherhood exists / To passive minds." "Observation of affinities" will inevitably result in perception of connectivity, yoking: *religio*. As is assumed in the entire endeavors of science and mathematics, there is a pattern, and there are inherent, intrinsic laws governing pattern. This sense of pattern, connectedness, connectivity, is inherent in all poetry. The physicist David Bohm calls this "implicate order".[2]
(Nikolaou and Dillon, 85-86)

The question of religion is significant in a book that has its origins in the *I Ching*. In that ancient book Berengarten found the perfect interlocutor to ruminate on and cultivate his conviction that "Everything *is* connected." Edward L. Shaughnessy is right to focus in his Preface to *Changing* on the "relationship between prayer, prophecy and poetry"(ix). I take it that he is implying that the kind of serious questioning of the *Book of Changes* that

---

[2] A reference to Bohm's innovative book *Wholeness and the Implicate Order* (1985). In it, based on a novel interpretation of the postulates of quantum physics, he proposes a new model of reality. As the book's blurb describes it: "Bohm argues that if we are guided by a self-willed view we will perceive and experience the world as fragmented. Such a view is false, because it is based on our mistaking the content of our thought for a description of the world as it is. Bohm introduces the notion of the implicate order in which any element contains enfolded within itself the totality of the universe – his concept of totality includes both matter and consciousness" (front page). As I develop my argument here, the many underlying similarities with Bohm's proposed new model of reality should become evident.

was the source of Berengarten's book is a form of prayer – not in the selfish sense of pleading for some kind of personal favor or privilege, but as a way of seeking a deeper understanding of what we are and how to be, that is, a clarification of life. And I would postulate that prayer in this sense also corresponds with what Heidegger called *Besinnung*, or reflection.

Gaze into a mirror, or a well or a pond. You see yourself (and you see yourself looking back at yourself). For many, this can be a cause of wonder: the visual image of consciousness. Henry David Thoreau is looking into his own mind when, using both scientific knowledge and imagination, he plumbs the depths of Walden Pond. Walt Whitman sees the reflection of his own divinity when he stares over the rail of the Brooklyn ferry and

> Saw the reflection of the summer sky in the water,
> Had my eyes dazzled by the shimmering track of beams,
> Look'd at the fine centrifugal spokes of light round the shape of my
> head in the sunlit water [...]   (Whitman 1989a: 2033)

Emily Dickinson peers into a well ("Like looking every time you please / In an abyss's face!") and realizes that there are things in the world (and in herself) that empirical science can never completely account for:

> But nature is a stranger yet;
> The ones that cite her most
> Have never passed her haunted house,
> Nor simplified her ghost.   (Franklin 1254)

And in 'For Once, Then, Something,' following on Dickinson, Robert Frost peers into another New England well,

> [...] never seeing
>
> Deeper down in the well than where the water
> Gives me back in a shining surface picture
> Me myself in the summer heaven godlike
> Looking out of a wreath of fern and cloud puffs   (Frost 145)

and almost sees something in his own reflection that he realizes is finally ungraspable. They all discover some aspect of themselves in the image the water gives back to them.[3]

---

[3] For Berengarten's version of this theme see Section 48 of *Changing*, "Welling, Replenishing," especially 48.6, where the *Book of Changes* is described as a "Well, inexhaustible" (390).

Similarly, when we stare into the deep waters of the *I Ching* and elaborate meaningful answers from the ambiguous images of its hexagrams, we are also plumbing the depths of our own minds. To "speak," as Berengarten has done, with the *I Ching* is "a calm, self-possessed surrender to that which is worthy of questioning."

This isn't the first time I've alluded to Martin Heidegger's thinking in relation with Berengarten's work, nor is it the first time I have talked about the subversive and poetical thinking of Ralph Waldo Emerson in this respect. But I need to repeat the point that Heidegger's philosophy of the twentieth century "rhymes" with Emerson's deep thinking in the nineteenth century. That is, they both form a part of that line in Western intellectual development deriving from our Romantic forebears.

In his foundational Transcendental text, *Nature*, first published in 1836, Emerson foresaw the threat of fragmentation inherent in the dominant rational line of Western thought. He comprehended how easily things could fall apart. I never tire of returning to this passage, because we forget so easily and we constantly need to be reminded – especially today, when things do seem to be spectacularly falling to bits.

> The problem of restoring to the world original and eternal beauty, is solved by the redemption of the soul. The ruin or the blank, that we see when we look at nature, is in our own eye. [...] The reason why the world lacks unity, and lies broken and in heaps, is, because man is disunited with himself. He cannot be a naturalist until he satisfies all the demands of the spirit. (Emerson 1989a: 930)

Emerson had been trained as a Unitarian minister in the Harvard Divinity School, not as a formal philosopher, so he had no qualms about using an undefined term like "soul." But I hope most of us know what he means. As both ex-minister and Romantic thinker, he believed in a spiritual component of human being – whatever it is that gives us our ability to think, and feel, and intuit, and imagine – which must be acknowledged and potentiated for our continuing survival. Both rational thought and intuitive feeling are, he argued, necessary elements of what we are. We only see a part of the world, and therefore fragment it, if we only observe through the lens of rationality. This is why he continues,

> Love is as much its demand as perception. Indeed, neither can be perfect without the other. In the uttermost meaning of the words, thought is devout, and devotion is thought. [...] There are innocent men who worship God after the tradition of their fathers, but their

sense of duty has not yet extended to the use of all their faculties. And there are patient naturalists, but they freeze their subject under the wintry light of the understanding. (*ibid.*)

That is, we need to learn to use all of our capacities, rational thought (which Emerson called Understanding) and intuition and feeling, in order to perceive the world properly and in this way keep it and ourselves whole. "Is not prayer also a study of truth, – a sally of the soul into the unfound infinite? No man ever prayed heartily without learning something" (*ibid.*).

The purpose of this digression is to suggest how Richard Berengarten's collaboration with the *I Ching*, his protracted conversation through question and answer, is also a form of prayer – that deepest form that Emerson is describing. And what is learned through this kind of prayer, or reflection, goes far beyond mere factual knowledge or empirical data.

What I'm talking about, of course, is wisdom – an alternative way of knowing ourselves and our world that contemporary societies are very much in need of. In his sensitive review of *Changing*, Hank Lazer is exactly right when he says what Berengarten gives us here are "*wisdom poems*" (76 below). The poems in this book are the result of a union – or perhaps even better, communion – of a reflective mind with the deep reservoir of accumulated thought on timeless human experience that is the *Book of Changes*. In this sense, *Changing* becomes a kind of nexus of wholeness, connecting its readers' minds, through Berengarten's, to that same source. And this is why the idea of coherence constitutes one of the most important of the many themes that thread their way through *Changing*.

❧

The invariable mark of wisdom is to see the miraculous in the common.

Ralph Waldo Emerson, *Nature* (930)

If *Changing*, as many commentators have suggested, is the culmination of Berengarten's impressively rich and varied poetic accomplishment, then it stands to reason that one of its central concerns would be the issue of connectedness. I propose that this book forms a highly significant part of what I am describing as the (very) late Romantic countermovement, a rearguard action to resist our culture's headlong drive toward fragment-ation and recover a holistic worldview. Berengarten's focus on wholeness – and its related quality, coherence – is announced in the ten epigraphs to *Changing*, written in six languages and coming from texts that span centuries. Two of them are particularly pertinent for my point. The first of these comes from *The Journal and Papers of Gerard Manley Hopkins*: "All the world is full of inscape and chance left free to act falls into an order as well as purpose" (1). This is a brilliantly chosen passage. The idea that chance falls of its own accord into order is a perfect representation of how the oracular facet of the *I Ching* functions. And the other one comes from Ezra Pound. We've already seen it in Berengarten's comments on religion and wholeness in the interview with Ruth Halkon: "it coheres all right" (*ibid.*).

This passage from the late *Cantos* obviously occupies an important place in Berengarten's creative consciousness. Shouldn't we think of it as an aged poet's hard-won insight into human experience? One that Berengarten clearly assumes for himself and advocates? The quote has appeared before in Berengarten's work. When Charles Bruno, the protagonist of *The Manager*, is pulling himself together after a personal breakdown into existential confusion and despair, he (or a supra-personal voice that represents the consciousness of the author) identifies with Pound's complaint and resolution:

> I cannot make it cohere is what the old man said. Try though he did through his art. Willing that bridges be built where none had ever existed.
>
> And looked through his eyes' windows. And saw the blue flash of kingfishers. And the moment *benedetto*. And before he went back into silence
>
> Answered himself thus: The light sings eternal … i.e. it coheres all right. Even if my notes do not cohere … Aye, old man, through thick and thin, the world
>
> Sticks together right loyally.   (RB 2011: 146)

Taken together, these two epigraphs indicate that beneath or behind or within what may seem to be a mélange of random phenomena, there lies a scaffolding of order. And if there is order, then there is, presumably, also meaning.

Or, to hone my phrasing more precisely, could they perhaps indicate that the world – the amalgamation of the physical environment and our experience of it – *can be* invested with order and meaning? Can be. There is undoubtedly a universe of physical phenomena and processes, but what it is *for us* depends in subtle ways on how we think it. Unity, wholeness, connectedness, coherence are not necessarily pre-existing conditions. They are contingent on our readings of experience and arise – or not – from the way we interact with the material world we are immersed in. The complete process of interacting with the *I Ching* – eliciting chance through casting coins or yarrow stalks, consulting the hexagram thus attained, pondering its ambiguous images and statements, and then constructing a meaningful answer to the question posed – all of this is a model, or pattern, for the act of creating sense or meaning through the interaction of mind and world.

The "it" that Pound was talking about *can* cohere, as long as we conceive our thoughts about it properly, and learn to see "the moment *benedetto.*" This theme runs through *Changing* from beginning to end and binds it together as a keel holds true the hull of a ship.[4] It begins almost immediately in the fourth poem of the book, "Cohering, Inhering," which is, significantly, dedicated to David Bohm:

> All day long and
> all night long it starts
> now now. To
>
> keep everything
> (every *thing*) in mind
> in its entirety, and
>
> still focus entire on
> *this*? As the universe
> keeps all measures
>
> and all in measure,
> and each thing main-
> tains its own seams,
>
> stains, marks, patterns
> edges, pleats, horizons
> may the same quiet

---

[4] Those poems that contain the word *cohere* or any of its variants are *CH* 1/3, 2/5, 14/0, 23/6, 27/0, 32/5, 43/5, 45/4 and 64/6. I shall be dealing with several of them in the following discussion. But other, less direct allusions to coherence could also be included in this cluster.

                patient appetite for
                order cohere, inhere
                in this, in here.   (1/3: 7)

This quiet, patient appetite for order is a later variation of Wallace Stevens'
"Blessed rage for order." Berengarten talks about Stevens' poem, "The Idea
of Order at Key West" (Stevens 128-130), in the Ruth Halkon interview.
There he seems to suggest that Stevens refers to a pre-existing order "that
emerges out of the matrix [in this case, the sea] it has been embedded in"
(Nikolaou and Dillon 96). My reading offers a slightly different nuance,
in that I stress that the mind is the conduit through which order emerges,
and that the perception or appreciation of that order is contingent on
how the mind is used. It is, after all, the *idea* of order Stevens is talking
about. The nameless singer in the poem absorbs her experience of "the
grinding water and the gasping waves" through her senses and expresses all
of those roiling non-human phenomena in her song. The speaker and his
friend, "pale Ramon," observe that process of transformation of the natural
world into art, and as a result they perceive order in their surroundings:
"[…] when the singing ended and we turned / Toward the town […] /
The lights in the fishing boats at anchor there, […] Mastered the night
and portioned out the sea […]" (ll. 45-9). The nature of their perception
has been changed. That is, order results from a "correct" fusion of mind
and world. For Stevens, that fusion is best achieved through the creative
imagination, i.e. art.

Stevens was arguably the most Romantic of the great American
Modernist poets, and this poem in particular links him directly to Emerson.
For to sing "beyond the genius of the sea" is a distinctly Transcendental
concept. The singer's voice *elevates* an unconscious world into consciousness.
The whole poem illustrates Emerson's belief that the way the mind interacts
with the rest of the world – how we observe and think about what we
observe – creates significant meaning, or not. And this, I believe, is the
lineage to which Richard Berengarten belongs.

∾

Do you think there is anything not attached by its unbreakable cord
to everything else?
                                Mary Oliver, "Upstream" (5)

Both the *I Ching* and *Changing* are rooted in, emerge from and encourage
a holistic worldview, according to which all things are connected with

everything else, including the mind. This synthetic reading of the world facilitates those forces or processes that favor life, as opposed to the analytic or mechanistic reading of the world that underlies the dominant line of Western thinking. As we all know by now, analysis, by definition, breaks things down into separate parts. And these separate parts, eventually, become isolated fragments. The subversive role of art in a time when the world is undergoing this kind of de-construction is to restore a comprehension of the need for wholeness.

Mary Oliver's sentence above, though, contains a flaw. Those cords that attach all things are by no means unbreakable. They are fragile and can only endure if we recognize and protect them. Isn't this what Berengarten wants us to glean from "*Summer, svemir*"?[5]

> On our big round table
> a vase of campanula. On
> our small table a potted
>
> Flowering hibiscus. On
> windowsills, four orchids
> two speckled, one white
>
> one pink. Outside,
> two doves sit side-by-side
> in our rowan tree.
>
> Our bowl has been
> replenished, our cup
> overflows with juices
>
> and still this singular
> flood pours in and
> through us. Today
>
> our lives are
> a garden. Nothing
> doesn't cohere.   (27/0: 216)

---

[5] *Editors' note*: For a quite separate yet interestingly coincidental comparison between Berengarten and Oliver, see also Eleanor Goodman's essay below (147).

60

So, on this peaceful summer day, the speaker's cup runneth over; his life – and ours if we can also see this moment *benedetto* – "is a garden."[6] Everything coheres when the mind opens up and, rather than imposing our will, receives and nourishes.

If there's any doubt that the poet is thinking in terms of wholeness here, we need only take a look at the explanatory note he appends to this poem's title:

> In Serbian and Croatian, *svemir* means 'universe, space'. Derived from Old Slavonic, the word is constructed from two parts, *sve* ('all') and *mir* (мир 'world', 'universe', 'community'). The conflation of the homophone *mir*, meaning 'peace, calm, tranquillity', creates an interesting ambiguity. Hence the modern word *svemir* simultaneously suggests not only 'entire world' but also 'all-encompassing peace, complete tranquillity'. (*CH* 547)

World, universe and community. The suggestion seems to be that when everything is connected, peace and tranquility result. But of course the opposite condition also obtains: without connectedness, peace and tranquility fail.

Poem 30/0, "*Over whole skies*" (240), offers clear evidence that Berengarten fully understands the fragility of such wholeness. The base-line for this poem, announcing its source hexagram in the *I Ching*, is "*fire* [...] *brightness doubled.*" And this idea is presented in the first two stanzas: "*No fire flames once. / That which is bright / happens twice. Sunset // and dawn repeat their / blaze over entire skies / in glory.*"

But what is this "brightness doubled"? Is it simply the fact that natural processes like sunrise and sunset repeat themselves? Perhaps. Yet when the poet says, "that which is bright happens twice," it seems to me that he is talking about the kind of peaceful and receptive perception that "*Summer, svemir*" exemplifies. The first brightness is the natural phenomenon and the second one is the illumination in the receptive mind. What Berengarten celebrates here is, once again, very close to Heidegger's understanding of reflection, a non-aggressive acceptance of the world which devolves into a different way of participating in it. "*When flame,*" the poem continues

---

[6] The same Biblical echo (Psalm 23:5) appears in *The Manager* when Bruno is putting himself back together again. An important part of growth into wholeness is learning to accept and assimilate the inevitability of death. And Bruno does: "Cradling death upturned in my arms, I stand on the doorstep, shivering. And know this vessel my Grail, my singing head. Now blessèd I backwalk up Hope Street. My cup runneth over" (RB 2011: 149).

clings to the palpable
it connects the world
with invisible power

shattering mountains
to memory, graveyards
into present gardens

and flaring where
boundaries of May trees
bloom white snows.   (*ibid.*)

The point is that human perception – *"brightness doubled"* – is a component of the whole. Human perception is indeed a key component, for it contributes consciousness, will. We can choose the will to power or we can choose to renounce power and strive to participate (*connect the world with invisible power*) rather than to dominate. "*When brightness clings* / *to brightness, nothing* / *happens alone.*"

The secret then, or the key, is to learn again how to permit the world to go on being what it already is. If this is an echo of Heidegger's term "letting be," it is also what Emerson means when he talks about "the problem of *restoring* to the world original and eternal beauty" (1989a: 930, emphasis mine). And too, this is almost certainly what Berengarten has in mind when he says at the end of 45/4 ("Beautiful September Morning" 364), "Things of their // own accord fit and / cohere, including our / breaths in this air." That modest internal half-rhyme, cohere / air, nicely serves to reinforce the idea. Things fit and cohere of their own accord (though the implicit *if we let them* is left unsaid). Our breaths, that is our being in the world, and the words our breaths produce, can and should form a harmonious part of all that is. This is poetry whose aim is to bring us back home to the world. We too need to learn, of our own accord, how to fit in and cohere.

And if anyone needs more proof that Berengarten is consciously engaged in the task of recovery and renewal – what I prefer to think of as a late Romantic subversion of the primary line of Western thought – well, we have "Mist dispersing":

Meanings gather, adhere,
cohere. Those cunning eroders –
who ran and ruined our city

and confused its ministries
and academies by trouncing
sense out of words and

wheedling purpose from
thought – have gone suddenly quiet
They'll be back soon

enough [...]

    They
aren't to be believed now
any more or less than

before. Time to move
on past them, as if they
were mist dispersing.   (43/5: 349)

℘

In China, the *Classic of Changes* is thought to encompass every
aspect of human experience, from the beginning and end of heaven
and earth back to the beginning again.
           Edward L. Shaughnessy, Preface to *Changing* (xii)

After a long poetic sequence that does indeed encompass every aspect of
human experience, the final poem of *Changing* echoes the book's opening
epigraphs and in this way completes an intentional circle of coherence. It
wouldn't be an exaggeration to read the light that bestows a renewed sheen
on the world in "Brightness diffusing" as entering in the train of the "mist
dispersing" (43/5: 349). The first four stanzas convey a sense of the beauty
of existence – or the potential beauty of existence – in the kind of direct,
simplified and delicate language that Berengarten has perfected over the
course of his career and which reaches its culmination in this book.

Sunlight bronzes sea.
Everything sighs. Mid-
October, still warm.

Olive leaves' undersides,
Dull metallic sheens, flicker
Across sandy hill groves.

Our sunflower heads
are harvested. Light flames
Oleanders and cypresses.

Prickly pears swell,
lobes topping green oval
Faces, golden grenades.   ("Brightness diffusing", 64/6: 518)

When we perceive it – reflect it – reflect on it in this way, the world coheres
in all of its transient beauty and glory. Transient, yes. And yet, it coheres
through these words that save it for us from oblivion.

"Attention is the beginning of devotion," writes Mary Oliver (8). And
from this kind of attention, both to the *Book of Changes* and to the world
it helps us to see in a deeper light, a personal knowledge arises. Recall those
words of Emerson: "No man ever prayed heartily without learning something." Through the poems in *Changing*, Berengarten shows us how to
cleanse our vision and see the world anew, by changing what Emerson
called our "axis of vision" (1989a: 930).

The last two stanzas circle back to the epigraph from Pound:

Instress, pattern, glory.
It all coheres, no question,
as do these notes of mine.

Come sit at the table
out here on the balcony.
Drink a glass of wine.   (*ibid.*)

Once again, the rhyme, "mine/wine," reinforces the sense of order attained,
as the poet invites us to share this vision of a thriving world in an act of
deep communion. Perhaps the final message is that, in order to preserve
and protect a living world, we need to learn to think of our participation in
it as this: a form of communion.

The first definition of *communion* in my much-loved *American Heritage
Dictionary of the English Language* is "a possessing or sharing in common,
participation" and the second is "a sharing of thoughts and feelings; intimate
talk." The specifically Christian sense of the word is secondary to the idea of
an intimate sharing of thoughts and feelings and mutual participation. But
it, too, has to do with connectedness.

That larger sense of the word is what Walt Whitman has in mind when
he announces at the beginning of *Song of Myself* that his poem will be
celebrating a new, secular kind of Eucharist, or communion:

I celebrate myself, and sing myself,
And what I assume you shall assume,
For every atom belonging to me as good belongs to you [...]
(Whitman 1989b: 1974)

What more thorough sharing of essences and intimate talk can there be? Whitman leans and loafs at his ease observing a spear of summer grass, and in the remaining one thousand three hundred and forty-odd lines of the poem he allows nature to well up through his calm, receptive mind and speak through his voice "without check and with original energy" (*ibid.*).

Communion, communication, commingling, community. Whitman took his cue directly from Emerson, who wrote for example in "The Poet," "I know not how it is that we need an interpreter, but the great majority of men seem to be minors, who have not yet come into possession of their own, who cannot report the conversation they have had with nature" (1989b: 985). And just as Whitman loquaciously reports his conversation with nature, so Berengarten reports his own conversation, and communion, with the ancient Chinese compendium of wisdom that is the *I Ching*.

ᘓᘒ

I learned from Whitman that the poem is a temple – or a green field – a place to enter and in which to feel. Only in a secondary way is it an intellectual thing – an artifact, a moment of seemly and robust wordiness – wonderful as that part of it is. I learned that the poem was not made just to exist, but to speak – to be company.
Mary Oliver, "My Friend Walt Whitman" (12)

Changing is, without a doubt, an intellectual thing. And one of the myriad qualities that make it so impressive is its "robust wordiness". Its intricate interlacings with the intricacies of the *I Ching*, the multiple layers of meaning, suggestion and rich ambiguity conveyed by Berengarten's appendix of explanatory notes, the disciplined stanzaic form of the poems, based on the structure of the Chinese hexagrams: all of this, and much more, attest to the deep intelligence that created it. But this is also poetry that speaks directly to its readers in a very human, very understandable voice.

Berengarten has often stated that he doesn't think of himself as a specifically English or British poet. Rather, he prefers to be thought of on a broader scale as a pan-European voice. But the more I read and reflect on his work, the more convinced I am that he can also be placed quite comfortably within what William Carlos Williams called "the American grain." Even in a work inspired in ancient Chinese thought and culture, I can't help finding lines of continuity with Emerson, Thoreau, Whitman, Stevens and, of course, Ezra Pound.[7]

But then, simply to make that claim without any further qualification would be too facile. The real point is that the American grain is essentially a European grain, once removed. The profound and striking similarities between Emerson's transcendental thinking and Heidegger's existential philosophy make the point well.[8] What is in play is the larger, underlying counterforce (to employ a term from *Gravity's Rainbow*) initiated by the Romantics to subvert the tendency in our culture toward fragmentation and to reunite thought and world in a holistic synthesis. I suspect that this synthetic comprehension of experience, in which language is conceived as the adhesive that fuses all things into an interconnected whole, is what originally called out to Berengarten from the Chinese thinking that produced the *Book of Changes*.

He is aware that he's taking this alternative but necessary path; though it would be more in keeping with the temper of *Changing* to invoke the concept of *Tao* and say that he is *following* this way through thought. Berengarten also knows full well that he is taking a step beyond Pound, for these carefully crafted notes of his do cohere. In the poem "A yellow lower garment" (2/5: 19), describing the light that bathes everything in the world in the same rich glow, he writes: "yes, you flow and cohere / all right, very right, // as do these notes, in / white light, black light, / alternating, oscillating" – an affirmation repeated, as we've seen above, in the final poem of the book.

And so, to finish – and possibly to begin – I want to take just one last look at the title. Doesn't it also apply to us? Isn't this book's ultimate aim to contribute to a change in how, both individually and as a culture, we think ourselves and our world? Emerson understood how important it is for us to perceive everything-that-is as constant process, constant becoming. "Beauty," he wrote, "is the moment of transition, as if the form were ready to flow into other forms" (1957: 178).

---

[7] "In the spirit of Walt Whitman" (*CH* 7/2: 58) clearly acknowledges Berengarten's awareness of this American dimension in his work.

[8] These particular lines of continuity have been brilliantly explored by the contemporary American philosopher Stanley Cavell. See, for example, "Thinking of Emerson", esp. 194-195; *In Quest of the Ordinary*; and "Aversive Thinking: Emersonian Representations in Heidegger and Nietzsche" in *Emerson's Transcendental Etudes*: 141-170.

Many of the poems in *Changing* capture those fleeting moments of transition and reveal the beauty of a world that still has not been frozen and dissected by the meddling intellect. Will they change our axis of vision? We can only hope (or maybe pray) it's not too late for the world we have been given to flow and cohere.

References

Baym, Nina *et al.* (eds). 1989. *The Norton Anthology of American Literature,* Vol. I. New York: W. W. Norton.

Berengarten, Richard. 2016. *Changing*. Bristol: Shearsman Books.

_____. 2011. *The Manager: a poem*. (3rd edn.). Bristol: Shearsman Books.

Bohm, David. 1985 [1980]. *Wholeness and the Implicate Order*. London: Routledge and Kegan Paul.

Burns, Richard. 2001. *The Manager: a poem*. (1st edn.). London and Bath: Elliott and Thompson

_____. 2006. *The Blue Butterfly*. (1st edn.). Cambridge: Salt Publications.

Cavell, Stanley. 1993 [1972]. 'Thinking of Emerson' in Buell, Lawrence (ed.). *Ralph Waldo Emerson: A Collection of Critical Essays*. Upper Saddle River NJ: Prentice Hall, 191-200.

_____.1988. *In Quest of the Ordinary*. Chicago, IL: University of Chicago Press.

_____. 2003. *Emerson's Transcendental Etudes*. Stanford, CA: Stanford University Press.

Derrick, Paul Scott. 2017. 'Ringing the Changes: A Fortnightly Review of Changing by Richard Berengarten' in *The Fortnightly Review*. Online at: http://fortnightlyreview.co.uk/2017/02/ringing-the-changes/

Emerson, Ralph Waldo. 1989a [1836]. *Nature*. In *The Norton Anthology of American Literature*, Vol. I, Baym, Nina *et al.* (eds.). New York: W. W. Norton, 903-931.

_____. 1989b [1844]. 'The Poet'. In *The Norton Anthology of American Literature*, Vol. I, Baym, Nina *et al.* (eds.). New York: W. W. Norton, 984-999.

_____. 1957 [1860]. 'Beauty' in Miller, Perry (ed.) *The American Transcendentalists*. Garden City, NY: Doubleday Anchor Books, 171-186.

Franklin, R. W. (ed.) 1998. *The Poems of Emily Dickinson*. Variorum edition (3 vols.). Cambridge, MA: The Belknap Press of Harvard University Press.

Frost, Robert. 1965 [1955]. *Selected Poems*. Harmondsworth: Penguin Books.

Heidegger, Martin. 1977. *The Question Concerning Technology and Other Essays* (trans. Lovitt, William). New York: Harper Colophon Books.

Lazer, Hank. 2017. "Welling, Replenishing: Richard Berengarten's *Changing* and the *I Ching*" in *Notre Dame Review* 45 (winter/spring 2018), 189-204.

Nikolaou, Paschalis and Dillon, John Z. (eds). 2017. *Richard Berengarten: A Portrait in Inter-Views*. Bristol: Shearsman Books.

Oliver, Mary. 2016. *Upstream: Selected Essays*. New York: Penguin Press.

Stevens, Wallace. 1987 [1954]. *Collected Poems*. London: Faber and Faber.

Whitman, Walt. 1989a [1856]. "Crossing Brooklyn Ferry". In *The Norton Anthology of American Literature*, Vol. I, Baym, Nina *et al.* (eds.). New York: W. W. Norton, 2032-2036.

_____. 1989b [1855]. "Song of Myself". In *The Norton Anthology of American Literature*, Vol. I, Baym, Nina *et al.* (eds.). New York: W. W. Norton, 1974–2016.

HANK LAZER

Welling, Replenishing: Richard Berengarten's *Changing* and the *I Ching*

While it is a responsible and even pleasurable thing to pay considerable attention to the structure and history of composition of Richard Berengarten's *Changing*, such an approach to the book, at least for me, misses a more essential aspect.[1] I want to pay close attention to the vision and content of this grand book. Berengarten's work may not be widely known or recognized (particularly in the USA) in part because of his independent, skeptical, shape-shifting nature. His poetry is not part of any particular movement or group, though it is helpful to note that one of his most profound influences was his friendship with Octavio Paz, inheriting his friend's sense of the poet's participation in a global or universal poetry. In the current age of poetry in the West, with the reigning fear being that of "appropriation," it is absolutely refreshing to find a poet – after 50 years of studying and reading the *I Ching* – who proceeds and writes a beautifully

---

[1] In brief: *Changing* consists of 450 poems, 7 for each of the 64 hexagrams of the *I Ching*, plus two additional poems. 448 poems are 18 lines long: 3 lines per stanza, 6 stanzas; and 2 poems are villanelles. The review by Paul Scott Derrick in *The Fortnightly Review* is especially excellent on form and structure (Derrick 2016 online). Derrick considers *Changing* in relation to Berengarten's many other books of poetry, noting that "Structural and formal control have always been essential for Berengarten. This is one of the many qualities that make him such a fascinating contemporary poet." Silvia Pio's informative review, "Prayer, Prophecy, and Poetry: Richard Berengarten's *Changing*," is also excellent. (Pio online). Owen Lowery's review (2017) places *Changing* within the context of Berengarten's overall literary career. See also Berengarten's own remarks on form and structure in his "Postscript" (*CH* 525).

Editors' note, added: See the essays by Paul Scott Derrick (51-68 above) and Owen Lowery (130-144 below).

multifaceted homage to this great Chinese source-text.[2] Berengarten's Postscript to *Changing* makes clear what his book of poems is and is not:

> *Changing* is conceived as a single work, a composite poem made up of many small poems. It is based closely on the Chinese *Book of Changes* or the *I Ching*, and it is intended in part as an act of homage to this ancient text. But while many of its parts are rooted in the *I Ching*, and most take their inspiration from it and make repeated reference to it, and while its overall concept, plan, structure and themes have been configured through the *I Ching*, *Changing* is not a translation or a commentary. My hope is that this book will be read first and foremost as a poem, or gathering of poems, in its own right and for its own sake. (521)

For my money, the best (current) translator of ancient Chinese poetry is David Hinton.[3] In *Hunger Mountain: A Field Guide to Mind and Landscape*, he begins by telling us that "Ancient China had a long and diverse philosophical tradition centered on the nature of consciousness, the empirical world, and the relationship between them" (Hinton 2015: xi). But it is the fully extended version of Hinton's introductory remarks that

---

[2] As one poet (John Matthias) who has known 'Berengarten' for many years puts it: "He's always been at odds with Cambridge poetry orthodoxy, esp. Prynnians (though he does admire Prynne himself, and was in fact the first to introduce me to him). It's hard to take Richard's measure as he has been so many things – English, Jewish, Greek, Serbian, and now Chinese. But I do think *Changing* is his masterpiece." (email to author: December 1, 2016). Until somewhat recently, Berengarten published under the name Richard Burns. He now publishes under his ancestral family name, affirming his Jewish identity. *Wikipedia* offers this helpful summary of the range of his affinities: "Richard Berengarten (born 1943) is a European poet, translator and editor. Having lived in Italy, Greece, the USA and the former Yugoslavia, his perspectives as a poet combine English, French, Mediterranean, Jewish, Slavic, American and Oriental influences. His subjects deal with historical and political material, with inner worlds, relationships and everyday life. His work is marked by its multicultural frames of reference, depth of themes, and variety of form. In the 1970s, he founded and ran the international Cambridge Poetry Festival. He has been an important presence in contemporary poetry for the past 40 years, and his work has been translated into more than 90 languages."

[3] Hinton's own translation of the *I Ching* (2015), which was too recent a translation to figure into Berengarten's writing, is also a poetic interpretation of the source-text. In fact, Hinton, in contrast to so many before him, understands the *I Ching* itself as a poetic text. See Hinton 2015.

point us toward the informing affinity and vision of Berengarten's book:

> Ancient China had a long and diverse philosophical tradition
> centered on the nature of consciousness, the empirical world, and
> the relationship between them; but virtually all of that tradition's
> diversity begins with the same, relatively simply conceptual frame-
> work. This framework, apparently originating at the earliest levels of
> Chinese culture, in Neolithic and Paleolithic times, appears in the
> Taoist and Ch'an (Zen) Buddhist philosophical traditions and, even
> more fundamentally, in the structures of classical Chinese language
> itself. (*ibid.* xi)

As will become more evident as I discuss specific poems from *Changing*,
Berengarten's affinities are principally with the ancient Taoist textual
perspectives (as opposed to later, institutional Taoist practices). As Hinton
explains, "*Tao* originally meant 'way,' as in 'pathway' or 'roadway,' a
meaning it has kept. But Lao Tzu redefined it as a spiritual concept, using
it to describe the process (hence, a 'way') through which all things arise and
pass away" (*ibid.* 16). Berengarten's book lives within (but not exclusively
within) such a Taoist mode of thinking and being. Berengarten's book
affirms *poetry itself* as a way, a pathway, and roadway – a process itself that
expresses, affirms, and embodies the way that things arise and pass away.

Changing is also a book that affirms friendships and kinships, sometimes with family members, but more often with poets, philosophers, and
historians who share the poet's vision of the intertwining of language,
cosmos, and consciousness. And as Jacques Derrida made a crucial distinction between *religious* and *religion*, so also Berengarten's own spirituality (a
fusion of Jewish, Buddhist, and Taoist thinking about poetry and wisdom)
is profoundly religious without developing a rigid set of institutional
insistences or dogmatic tenets. To Berengarten's credit, he has written a
book that does not shy away from being wise, even as that wisdom may
entail limitation and humility, but nonetheless moments and poems of
beautifully moving insight do emerge. After all, this book is a life's work,
and it benefits greatly from 50 years of thinking and reading (and 30+
years of writing the book), and it benefits as well from Berengarten's own
aging and the insights that perhaps can only come about through aging,
vulnerability, and the death of close friends.

໑

I have read *Changing* several different ways. As I usually do when I am dipping into a new book of poetry, I flipped around randomly throughout the book, finding out if there would be enough poems that engaged me to invite a more sustained reading. Over the period of a few weeks, I also explored *Changing* as one typically consults the *I Ching*: each morning, I would pose a question; I would throw the coins; and I would read the hexagram/section that turned up (first in the *I Ching*, in the classic Wilhelm translation, and then in David Hinton's more recent translation, and then the series of poems in *Changing* associated with the specific hexagram).[4] I found this method to be quite enjoyable (and deeply affirming of the kinship of *Changing* and the *I Ching*). For this essay, I engaged in the academically respectable practice of reading the book in order, from cover to cover, including the copious and extremely helpful notes at the back of the book, as well as Berengarten's insightful and informative Postscript. As the book is not based on a discernible narrative trajectory, any of these methods of reading will work just fine, and may eventually lead to a fuller appreciation of this remarkable book.

Berengarten sees the *I Ching* as "a generative and transformative structure which remains entirely passive and latent until it is 'activated.'" What he has to say about a reader's relationship to the *I Ching* applies equally well to his own book. Once this activation happens, the book

> presents itself as immediately available for *practical application in the field of now*, in and through which it creates a flow of information for and through its user. As I have suggested, this information flow is based on a set of pre-formulated binary conversion rules which at their basic level are extremely simple. In this respect the *I Ching* functions like (as) a kind of proto-computer. What 'switches on' the *I Ching* is the personal user's asking a question in the first phase of the divination procedure. Use of the word *user* here reiterates the prime intended function of the *I Ching*, in contradistinction to any other books of comparable intellectual and imaginative scope, reach or magnitude in world history. It is a manual. (*CH* 524)

Reading either book, or both books, provides (sporadic) access to *the field of now*.

☯

---

[4] *Editors' note*: See the essay by Alan Trist and Bob DeVine (286-304 below), which adopts this approach.

Changing is a life-path book. From the very beginning, often told through characters researched and absorbed from Chinese history and philosophy, as well as European history, Berengarten asks about how best to live this life. In "What Zhang Zai thought" – Zhang Zai being an 11th century philosopher and astronomer – Berengarten identifies totally with Zhang Zai's perspective:

> Zhang Zai sat on a tree stump
> and quietly forgot about time and
> mortality and himself awhile
>
> as he soaked himself into
> and through things. Not much of
> a life, he thought, if you can't
>
> or don't get a chance to see
> patterns and images of heaven
> and earth as merely sediment
>
> of marvellous transformations.
> And not much of a view if you've
> forgotten it. Better be poor and
>
> remember this than have power
> and wealth and forget heaven is
> text and context for all wisdom.   (1/2: 6)

When I describe Berengarten's thinking as Taoist, this poem and the one that follows are good examples of what I mean. The Zhang Zai poem, particularly the final three stanzas, could just as easily have appeared in Lao Tzu's *Tao Te Ching*. (Perhaps all of us who write poetry are, whether we know it or not, heading toward that mountain pass, and our writing, or the guard at the mountain pass, asks of us to write down what we know?). As the *I Ching* participates in divination, in ordering and directing our lives and choices in an effort to make cohere the extensiveness of our perceptions, so too does *Changing*, as in the poem "Cohering, Inhering," a poem that appears early in the book, and acts as one of several early overviews:

> All day long and
> all night long it starts
> now now. To

keep everything
(every *thing*) in mind
in its entirety, and

still focus entire on
this? As the universe
keeps all measures

and all in measure,
and each thing main-
taining its own seams,

stains, marks, patterns,
edges, pleats, horizons –
may the same quiet

patient appetite for
order cohere, inhere
in this, in here.   (1/3: 7)

Bearing some similarity as well to the task in George Oppen's *Of Being Numerous*, Berengarten's hope and petition is to attend to the one and the many, to attune to the order (and disorder) of the universe. In a wonderfully rich homophonic pun, Berengarten's plea for coherence (co-hearing?) rests with what is in here, and with what we can hear here. It is a writing fully informed by the Taoist concept of *wuwei* (no overdoing; doing what comes naturally), both for the perceiver poet, and for the earth itself:

you crusted ball of lava balanced on
one invisible axis, indiscernible strings
keeping your modest place, your

rolling pace, as doing nothing, you
revolve and spin   ("Earth," 2/0: 14)

ↄ

The overall collection of poems offers many different pathways for reading, linking, and interconnection. Berengarten's notes help us to locate these interconnections, for example, "The force that fills and empties (2/6: 20), which relates directly to "Light fills and fails" (1/6: 10) as well as with "Brightness diffusing," the last poem of the book (64/6: 518). His poems do speak in and with and to each other. Sometimes, the connectivity stems from a key set of Chinese characters (which, at times, appear at the bottom of a page), as with *zhongdao*, the central path or middle way. All of these pathways lead me to think carefully about what are the many units of sense available in *Changing*. First, there is the particular poem, and there is also the layout of the page itself as another unit of composition, particularly with the subscript material at the bottom of the page (which links rather directly to the particular line of the hexagram that has "generated" the specific poem). Perhaps a more complete unit of thinking occurs at the level of the seven-poem series (or what I think of as a "chapter") associated with each of the 64 hexagrams. Again, I would emphasize the very fresh, independent thing that Berengarten is (and is not) doing in *Changing*. He is *interpreting* each hexagram, but that does not become an all-exclusive focus or a confining elucidation of the prior text. Berengarten is, more accurately, taking off from the particular hexagram – riffing, improvising, updating (not in the sense of improving, but in the sense of offering new historical information that re-enforces and deepens the particular hexagram), extending, and replying to it.

Berengarten's description of the principles that order and do not order the *I Ching* are equally applicable to his own book:

> The *I Ching* operates transversally to sequential linearity. It cuts across both logical and narrative modes, intersecting them by applying a mode of thinking and perception – and hence also, by invoking a way of being – that is irreducibly synthetic, correlative, resonant, and poetic. To amplify these remarks: the *I Ching* does not function primarily in the way that any myth, tale, story or novel must proceed and operate, even though it may admit all such narrative elements. Nor is it 'rooted' in one or more particular places, as all fictions necessarily are. Nor does it proceed in the manner of developing argument. (*CH* 523-524)

This peculiar structuring of the *I Ching* is replicated in *Changing*, with important implications for Berengarten's ongoing sense of how his own book *coheres*. Both books create a sense of a governing set of rules and structures, while eluding any sense of a strictly unified text. Or, as Berengarten observes about the *I Ching*, "Its symmetrical structure itself suggests not only an over-arching 'pattern' or 'frame' but one that has no need to be dependent on the Aristotelian unities of time and place or, for that matter, on any other kind of insistent narrative or dramatic form" (*CH* 525).

Structure (form) in *Changing* (and elsewhere) acts as a provocation; structure is heuristic. It provokes the poet – is one aspect of a poet's being called – to write. It is a lens through which something new (and old) might be seen and known. As with the Buddhist story about the finger that points to the moon, I am not so interested in writing about the nature of the finger; I am interested in thinking about what we learn about the moon.

∽

In response to hexagram 48, which he calls "Welling, Replenishing", Berengarten, in his Postscript (526-527), indicates that this particular hexagram is what he finds to be the central voice or "imagem" for the *I Ching* itself. A poem in this set that he dedicates to the memory of Richard Wilhelm, the classic translator of the *I Ching*, is itself titled "*I Ching*":

Fifty years my
friend, companion
and spirit-guide

always trustworthy,
never diffident
never irrelevant

solid yet flowing
firm yet yielding
radiating images

self-replenishing
inexhaustible
fathomless

ever-fresh well –
in plumbing you
I soar

feet still
grounded rooted
in *this here now*.   (48/4: 388)

The multiplicity of senses for the final line enrich the variegated nature of *Changing*. While I tend to be drawn to more immediate present-tense *now* instances in *Changing*, there is also a great range of re-told historical, mythic, ancient, literary *now*'s throughout Berengarten's grand book.

Changing, as the ultimate (though not final!) book of Berengarten's writing life, while it is a book that the poet insists does cohere, is also a book that opens outward and onward: "The book is constantly/ being written" ("You," 17/5: 141). And in our particular age and time, when poetry itself is a marginalized activity rarely read with care, depth, and patience, it becomes increasingly necessary for poets to be their own best readers, or at least to articulate their own reading experience as a corollary of the writing experience. Berengarten's *Changing* thus, at times, reads itself, or offers perspectives on how reading the book might be approached:

What the book said about itself

In opening this book
you open a locked chamber
in which, before words,

you have to read lines
to unlock the meanings
hidden in the words.

Meanings lie neither
in words nor in lines but
cluster behind both. Nor

will these leap to greet you
like puppies wagging tails
to welcome Master home.

You have to sit and wait
in a patience within patience
without praise or hope

for meanings to grow
like ferns unscrolling from
cracks between lines   (20/1: 160)

As the writer of such a book, Berengarten's task – one among several – involves simplification: *"You have told me, / Throw away your / craft, your tricks, // your techniques, all / you have learned"* (*"Lean and Strong,"* 21/0: 168). He writes: "Our job is to foster and grow // (a) coherent language" that enables us "to reaffirm the dignity // of the dead" so that this newly found language ultimately allows us to "mend and change the real / regrow and rebuild hope" (23/6: 190). Or, as he puts it in the companion poem "*Tikkun*, Majdanek," "Our task, to restore/ the fallen. Nothing else or / less" (36/6: 294). Part of that act of repair, of *tikkun*, of healing, involves detailed and heart-felt acts of remembering.[5] Thus, many of the hexagrams (see 23, for example) are built upon archaeological reporting and the re-telling of historical atrocities and massacres – tales of the suffering and injustice that must not be forgotten if *tikkun* is to take place. Berengarten's book of divination – *Changing* as the multifaceted homage to and extension of the *I Ching* – moves forward and backward in time, offering pointers and visions for the future, but also an equally strong movement into an understanding of or bearing witness to the past, particularly the human past of cruelty, often enacted on a large scale.

The mandate for simplicity leads to some beautifully paced, patient poems – what I am tempted to call *wisdom poems*. There are a number of these scattered throughout *Changing*, and I will only offer remarks on a couple of them.[6] In "Winter Solstice" Berengarten writes,

> Sky a frosted pearly
> porcelain blue as I walk
> down Mill Road this
>
> morning to post a last
> Christmas card. A mass
> of people out, traffic
>
> honking, blocked solid.
> Yesterday, I heard another
> friend has died – that's
>
> two gone this week.
> Today consciousness, life
> itself, seems improbable;

---

[5] I think that an interesting essay about the intersection – kinships and differences – between Jewish and Buddhist thinking could be written based on *Changing*.

[6] For another poem of similar simplicity and beauty, see "Somewhere to go" (16/0/128), this particular poem being a superb answer to that question often posed to the elderly: based on your life experiences, what advice would you give to someone much younger?); and also "Now I confess" (56/4: 452), and "Beautiful September morning" (45/4: 364).

miraculous. Presences
of small glories mean more
than all or any of

heaven's promises.
At home I boil a sky
blue egg for lunch.   (35/6: 286)

This understated, beautifully compressed moment – of grace, glory, the intrusion of a sense of the miraculous in the commonplace, even as it is juxtaposed with the death of friends – becomes a sporadically reoccurring element woven throughout the complex, non-unitary texture of *Changing*. That very pressure of mortality drives the poet toward such moments of intensified love of being itself.

And in "Adhering, inhering":

The way the light
adheres and inheres
to or in things

as if glued or
as part of their
fabric, stuff,

very grain
and yet constant
in its changing

is surest gift
of world and time.
Whatever else

may go or come
this light changing
on surfaces

is delight, is
glory, the unique
common miracle.   (55/1: 441)

Such poems exhibit a compelling gratitude – for being, for being incarnate, for the perfection of simple moments and simple deeds, for the miraculous seen (and felt) in the commonplace. And gratitude for change itself. As *zazen*

(Zen meditation) often produces intensified gratitude for and awareness of one's breathing, Berengarten's poems are stripped of intellectual display and reduced to their essential words with rarely a wasted or redundant word. What emerges is that profound kinship between *thinking* and *thanking*. While that kinship is crucial to Heidegger's "What Is Called Thinking?," it is also a perspective and linkage central to Zen thinking as well. As David Hinton notes: "we can trace *think* far enough back to see that it converges at its vanishing point with *thank* in the Indo-European *tong-*, which means *love*. So it seems likely that thinking was early on experienced as gratitude or love for the world" (2012: 57).

One might argue, perhaps somewhat reductively, that these simplified, stripped-bare wisdom-poems are what happens as one gets up in years. But Berengarten's poems of old age (as with virtually every other topic in this book) do not occupy one perspective, especially not merely the nostalgic, melancholic backwards glance. One is equally likely to find Berengarten taking up a rather different perspective:

> Getting old brings
> not sadness and regret
> but more hunger for
>
> more life, more
> energy, more desire
> for doing, making
>
> more – more of *now*,
> more worlds.   ("All I could ever," 42/4: 340)

Berengarten grapples with his own eventual non-being – "my mind // completely fails to conceive / of its own non-being / before birth returning" (62/6: 502) – acknowledging the difficulty of even imagining that eventuality. While that process of disappearance is painful to admit, it is also a pathway toward a more insistently Taoist view of the importance (or non-importance) of self and toward intensified gratitude:

> Now how can there be
> no now-any-more? I go
>
> into the dustless zone
> into gone deathcall, calling
> *Glad to have lived.*   ("In negative," 63/5: 509)

While Berengarten's ultimate end might be a complete self-erasure – "Seek me nowhere. / Whoever or whatever I / was dissolves." (53/6: 430) – it is the encounter with the cosmos (with the stars) that takes us along with Berengarten through a chastening and pedagogical shift in perspective, as in the poem "Consoling, abundant, terrifying stars":

> Consoling, abundant,
> terrifying stars, you humble
> the identity of me to
>
> a point less than zero,
> to zero's irreducible core,
> whatever such might be.
>
> What an irrelevance
> any such entity as 'I'
> compared with your
>
> high hushes and rushes
> mastering unimaginable
> time-space, vast zones
>
> of your habitations.
> Here, away from city glare,
> and faced with you and
>
> my death, you squeeze
> all identity out of me. And
> that's fine, majesties.   (55/3: 443)

In part, there is in Berengarten's thinking a movement toward self-erasure, though that diminution of the centrality of the self, of 'I,' comes from and out of personal experience and moments of insight fully within the context of a fairly traditional poetry of self and by means of a distinctly personal voice. The insights that come out of these moments of meditative observation feel to me to be profoundly Taoist in their nature, as when Berengarten writes of "us who, being / on earth, thereby / reside in heaven, // among heavens, / made of the same / heaven-stuff as they" ("Heaven-stuff," 55/5: 445). In such moments, as Hinton describes it, "in the moment of perception, there is no 'I' perceiving, there is simply perception" (2012: 113). Or, even more in keeping with Berengarten's "Heaven-stuff"), in writing of the poets of Chuang Tzu's time, Hinton calls "the deepest level of their wisdom: their experience of consciousness itself, not just the body, as woven wholly into the *ch'i*-tissue that is our physical universe" (*ibid.*). Or, as Alan Watts describes such moments, "Ultimately, of course, it is not really a matter of oneself, on the one hand, trusting nature, on the other. It is a matter of realizing that oneself and nature are one and the same process, which is the Tao" (Watts 32).

In hexagram 24 ("Returning"), in Berengarten's head-poem "*Everyone knows the ways,*" it is the ancient Chinese voice, the foundational voices and poets of Taoist and Zen thinking, who help take him to the edge of a profoundly different perspective on human incarnation:

> *But who except voices like these*
> *will take you and me on*
>
> *into zones the other silent*
> *and unwritten side before*
> *birth and after death, where*
>
> *light itself gleams brilliant*
> *black and angelic against*
> *interiors of mountains?*   (24/0: 192)

What I've been calling self-erasure may more accurately be thought of as a displacing of the centrality and drama of the self through a broader and more-encompassing cosmic perspective, the kind of meditation that we find in "Tracks to stars and back":

> Complex thoughts,
> many-dimensioned, fling
> tracks to stars and back.
>
> 'I' dissolves. 'I' keeps
> on dissolving. That's hard at
> first. But better that way.
>
> When all's said and done,
> 'I' matters little to anyone.   (25/4: 204)

But if we compare Berengarten's realizations about the self, and his commitment to a process of self-dissolving, to those of another great partisan of the *I Ching*, a considerable difference opens up. Whereas John Cage's displacement of the self becomes central to his own methods of composition – chance determined (through consulting the *I Ching*) and an embracing of randomness – in poetry, in painting, in musical compositions, and in filmmaking (particularly in editing), Berengarten's changing perspective on the self comes about through a poetry that remains intensely self-centered within a compositional tradition of a recognizable self with a particularly distinctive voice. In other words, Berengarten's poems tend to enact (or summarize) conclusions about the proper place of the self in this universe, but the method of writing the poem (while intensely and carefully structured by the poet's relationship to the *I Ching* as the exemplary source-text), does not undergo a correspondingly radical compositional change.

☙

There are so many possible pathways in and through *Changing*, many of which have evaded my attention in this essay, sometimes due to my preferences for some strands over others, sometimes for my own lack of preparedness to fully appreciate particular strands. But one pathway that continues to resonate with me is Berengarten's interrogation of and gratitude for our – human being's – nuanced relationship to language. In fact, the first poem that Berengarten composed for *Changing* propels us down that very pathway, for example "The complete art of drowning":

Being 2½ years old
this child falls, every
day she wakes, into

the lake of language.
Sometimes I watch her
from under this water

I swim my life through
having drowned here long ago.
Each day she gets better

at diving. Already she frog-
paddles on the surface. Her
gills are growing, lungs

disappearing. Soon
she'll learn the complete
art of drowning.

When engulfed in words
what worlds will she lose
and what world gain?   (41/6: 334)

It could be argued that this fall into language is what this book – what
poetry? – is about, though *Changing* would make us wary of any singular
assertion. Berengarten, in "Roots, roofs, routes" summarizes the complex
dance that human consciousness and language have been doing ever since
we became capable of entering the dance:

The central nervous
system – most evolved of
teleonomic structures.

Whose purpose prompts
this? Is it we who pattern
language? Or does it us?   (46/1: 369)

While Berengarten has confidence (and perhaps faith) in a natural process
of coherence – "Things of their // own accord fit and / cohere, including
our / breaths and this air" (45/4: 364) – perhaps it is the penultimate poem
of *Changing*. "Alchymical Perle," that provides the best summary of his
perspective on the nature of things. It is, as I have been suggesting all along,
a classically Taoist (and Zen Buddhist) act of equivocation, expressing and
choosing both/and over any singular assertion:

Axiomatic, our *precious*
perle wythouten spotte is to be
found at home, in our own

hearth, heart, guts. And in
the core of commonplace, among
ordinary (ornery) things

is where we're to look
again and again, before our
noses, behind our backs,

in and through darkest
deepest blind spots. What
at first seemed simple

may turn out quite
complex – yet simplicity
and complexity keep

opening out into each
other, interpenetrating,
blurring, irradiating.   (64/5: 517)

References

Berengarten, Richard. 2016. *Changing*. Bristol: Shearsman Books.

Derrick, Paul Scott. 2017. "Ringing the Changes: A Fortnightly Review of *Changing* by Richard Berengarten." *The Fortnightly Review*. Online at: http://fortnightlyreview.co.uk/2017/02/ringing-the-changes/

Heidegger, Martin. 1968. *What is called thinking?* Wieck, F.D. and Gray, J.G.. (trans.), New York: Harper & Row. [1968]

Hinton, David. 2012. *Hunger Mountain: A Field Guide to Mind and Landscape*, Boston, MA and London: Shambhala.

———. (trans. and ed.). 2015. *I Ching: The Book of Change*. New York: Farrar, Straus and Giroux.

Lao Tzu. 2015. *Tao Te Ching*. Hinton, David (trans.). Berkeley, CA: Counterpoint Press.

Lowery, Owen. 2017. "I Ching-influenced poet who confronts borders." *The Jewish Chronicle* 46. Online at: https://www.pressreader.com/uk/the-jewish-chronicle/20170303/282291025018949

Oppen, George. 1968. *Of Being Numerous*. New York: New Directions.

Pio, Silvia. 2017. "Prayer, Prophecy, and Poetry: Richard Berengarten's *Changing*." *Margutte*. Online at: [http://www.margutte.com/?p=21380&lang=en

"Richard Berengarten." *Wikipedia*. Online at: https://en.wikipedia.org/wiki/Richard_Berengarten

Watts, Alan and Huang, Al Chung-Liang. 1975. *TAO: The Watercourse Way*. New York: Pantheon Books.

Wilhelm, Richard (ed. and trans. into German). 1967. *The I Ching or Book of Changes*. Baynes, Cary F. (trans. from German). Princeton, NJ: Princeton University Press.

PART 2
Within and Among Traditions

Ming Dong Gu

From the *Book of Changes* to the Book of *Changing*: A Route to World Literature

The *I Ching*, also known as the *Zhouyi* (the *Book of Changes*), is the first Chinese classic and has served as both inspiration and source material for writings of history, philosophy, literature and art. While numerous Chinese poets have made major use of it in their poetic writings, it has never given rise to a complete poetic work in a Western language. The English poet Richard Berengarten has changed this situation. His recent poetic work, *Changing*, is not only the most ambitious poetic work ever to have been inspired by the Chinese classic, but it also constitutes an admirable artistic achievement that contributes to cross-cultural dialogues in poetics and poetic practice.

In terms of poetic themes and techniques, Berengarten's opus charts a direct route from the *Book of Changes*, through ancient Chinese poetry and Anglo-American modernist poetry, to a remarkable work of world literature. And although it draws its creative inspiration and thematic sources directly from the first Chinese classic, the book is "not a translation or a commentary" on it, as it is "to be read first and foremost as a poem, or gathering of poems, in its own right and for its own sake" (*CH* 521). Since the *Book of Changes* is a philosophical text or divination handbook, a reader might well ask: In what way is it related to Berengarten's poetic collection, other than being the main source of inspiration for it?

In the author's postscript, he gives us a brief account of how the overall conception, planning, structure, and themes have been configured through the *Book of Changes*. He also tells us how closely he has modelled his poetic work on the Chinese classic, from both macrocosmic and microcosmic perspectives, by "replicating and adapting its architectonic patterns" and by following the *I Ching*'s sixty-four hexagrams with their image statements and line statements, with the result of producing 450 poems (each of the hexagrams yields a group of seven poems with two additional poems for the first two hexagrams: 64 x 7 + 2 = 450). Moreover, he informs us: "Consisting primarily of visual symbols patterned on binary mathematical option, which are combined with verbal 'images', 'statements and judgements', it is, rather a generative and transformative structure which remains entirely passive and latent until it is 'activated'" (524).

In terms of poetic composition, I would call the structural organization of Berengarten's poetic work one of 'external form' because its formal organization is readily apparent in just the same way that we can see the external structure of a building or a piece of sculpture. As a literary critic, however, I am more interested in its internal form and the creative principle in the poetic composition.

Berengarten and the preface-writer Professor Edward Shaughnessy have both supplied hints towards finding answers. According to the poet, by following the patterning principle of the *I Ching* itself, his poetic composition employs "the kinds of modes, models and devices that have developed out of the great Symbolists, Modernists and Surrealists as 'connecting' principles – such as associative linkage, parataxis, focus on the 'arbitrariness' of language, or attentive highlighting of the apparent gulf between the *signifiant* and *signifié*" (526). In this statement, Berengarten touches upon a deep source of poetic inspiration and creative principle in the *I Ching*:

> As for associative, analogical or correlative thinking, sometimes also known as 'correlative cosmos-building', this is not only the mental foundation for poetry, ritual and magic in all societies, but specifically underpins the holistic vision of the universe that runs through all traditional Chinese thought – most evidently so in Daoism. It also gives rise to C. G. Jung's theory of synchronicity, which is itself rooted in the *I Ching*. (*ibid.*)

Understandably, Berengarten does not engage in exploring his deeper poetic source or techniques any further than this and prefers to leave any such task to literary critics. In my view, his main 'poetic' source, which itself either originates in or is identical to associative, analogical and correlative thinking, is also the fundamental poetry-making principle in Chinese literature – which, moreover, *first* appeared in the *Book of Changes*. Known as *bixing* 比興, it may be variously translated as 'stimulated analogy', 'inspired comparison', or 'a metatheory of poetry-making' (Gu 1997: 1-22). This creative principle has of course been widely recognized to have grown out of the first anthology of Chinese poetry, 詩經 the *Shijing* – or the *Book of Songs* in Arthur Waley's majestic version, or the

Shih-ching: The Classic Anthology Defined by Confucius, according to Ezra Pound's poetic translation. Even so, this principle initially arose from the hexagrams and line statements of the *Book of Changes*.

The images created on the principle of *bixing* abound in both the *Zhouyi* 周易, the earliest model of the *I Ching*, and the *Shijing*. Both use analogy as a fundamental way of thinking. According to simple common sense, there are two basic modes of analogical thinking: analogy by images and analogy by logical reasoning. In the *Zhouyi*, however, the hexagram images and line statements reveal a mode which, while employing both kinds of analogy, allows these to penetrate each other, superimpose themselves on each other, and supersede each other, giving rise to a mode of thinking that transcends three dimensional limitations and creates multiple dimensions, multivalence, and polysemy. In a word, this resulting complex model differs radically from the common modes of analogy. The 'common sense analogy,' as posited by Aristotle, is called 'scientific' or 'logical,' because it is based on qualities which two different things may have in common from an 'objective' point of view. The hexagram statements and the *Shijing* poems also employ this kind of analogy. But there is another kind of analogy which is widely used both in the *Zhouyi* hexagrams and line statements and in the *bixing* poems of the *Shijing*. Tentatively, I call this kind of analogy 'correlative analogy' or 'literary analogy.' The characteristics of this mode are well exemplified by a comparative discussion of several hexagram images and Berengarten's poems.

Since the *I Ching*'s statements are verbalizations attached to each hexagram and line, how can they be related to poetry in general and to Berengarten's poems in particular? To inaugurate this exploration, I cite Hexagram 28 (大過 *Da Guo*) to illustrate the intimate connection between line statements and the *Shijing* (*Book of Songs*), the first anthology of Chinese poetry:

2. 枯楊生稊，　　　A withered poplar grows new shoots.
   老夫得其女妻。　An old man gets a young wife
   無不利。　　　　Nothing is unfavorable.

5. 枯楊生華，　　　A withered poplar grows flowers.
   老婦得其士夫。　An old woman gets a young husband.
   無咎，無譽。[7]　No misfortune and no honor.

---

[7] Unless otherwise indicated, all translations of Chinese texts and poems are my own.

The two line statements share a prominent feature in many poems in the *Book of Songs*: the use of *bi* 比 (analogy) and *xing* 興 (inspired comparison) in the composition of a poem. Li Jingchi, a well-known scholar of the *Book of Changes* is perhaps the first modern scholar to notice the similarity between hexagram statements and the *Shijing* poems. In his essay '*Zhouyi* shici kao' 周易筮辭考 ('Investigating the Hexagram and Line Statements of the *Zhouyi*'), he compares some *I Ching* statements with some *Shijing* poems:

> There are many *bi* and *xing* style poems in the *Shijing*. It is natural that commentators have explained them in the light of *bi* 比 and *xing* 興 styles It has never been known that in the *Zhouyi*, there are poems of similar styles; nor has there been any attempt to comment on the *Zhouyi* in terms of poetic styles of the *Shijing* (Li Jingchi 38).

Long before Li Jingchi, however, the Song Dynasty scholar Chen Kui 陳騤 (1128–1203) had already noticed the similarity between some hexagram statements and poems in the *Shijing*. For example, he cited the statement of Hexagram 61, *Zhong Fu* 中孚: "If one includes it in the 'Ya' section of the section of the *Shijing* poems, who would be able to tell that it is merely a line statement of a hexagram" (Chen Kui 5). In his preface to *Changing*, Edward Shaughnessy observes a similar pattern of composition in the poetic lines of both the *I Ching* and the *Shijing*. In identifying the organizational pattern of prayer and prediction in the *Shijing* poem 'Taoyao,' he notices a similar pattern to some *I Ching* statements, and he goes on to suggest how this pattern has inspired Berengarten's poems (*CH* x-xiv). While Shaughnessy views this way of thinking as an act of divination consisting of "prayer, prediction, and fulfillment," Berengarten regards it as associative and analogical thinking. However, bearing in mind that identical or at least very closely similar patterns or modes of poetic creation occur in both the *I Ching* and the *Shijing*, I offer a different view and consider the common approach as *bixing* ('inspired comparison').

Even a casual reading of the hexagram statements in Hexagram 28 shows their poetic qualities. Moreover, it displays a clear analogical correspondence. In the first three lines, "a withered poplar grows new shoots" is in a parallel correlation to "an old man gets a young wife." In a patriarchal society, it was relatively common for an old man to take a younger wife. The analogy offers a prediction: "nothing is unfavorable." In the second three lines, "a withered poplar sprouts blossoms" offers an analogy for "an old woman gets a young husband." In a patriarchal society, this kind of marriage is not favored but not prohibited, and the prophecy is therefore understandable: "no misfortune and no honor."

The line statements in Hexagram 28 have inspired Berengarten to compose a poem with a similar theme: 'Old willow.' By deploying similar images, the poem adopts a similar mode of associational thinking and a similar approach to composition:

> By the stream an old
> willow is sprouting we
> thought had dried up.
>
> The widower who lived
> on the hill at the far end
> of the track leading
>
> up to the high plains
> has come down to our
> village and taken a
>
> neighbour's eldest
> brightest daughter
> as wife. Both now
>
> wear fat smiles.
> Her belly is already
> rounding nicely.
>
> She is tall, strong,
> and firm-breasted. She
> will inherit his land. (28/2: 226)

In this poem, the "old willow" is a duplicate image of "withered poplar" in the hexagram statement. People thought it had dried up, and thus displays an analogical relationship between the "old willow" and the "widower." The old willow stands in the same condition as the widower. Just as the withered tree grows new shoots, so the widower acquires renewed energy by marrying a younger wife. Berengarten also poetically presents the positive result of the marriage in the same way that the hexagram statement predicts the beneficial situation. The widower marries the neighbor's brightest daughter and the resultant situation is auspicious: the woman gets pregnant and the land will have its inheritor.

Thus, hexagram 61, *Zhong Fu* 中孚 (rendered by Berengarten as 'Inner Trusting') has inspired him to compose a poem with a similar theme. The hexagram statement itself reads:

鳴鶴在陰,	A crane sings in the shade;
其子和之;	Its offspring harmonizes with it.
我有好爵,	We have a fine beaker of wine;
吾于爾靡之。	I will empty it with you.

The analogy in this statement is also quite clear. In Chinese culture, to drink alone is often a sign of sorrow or sadness, whereas to sing in harmony with someone suggests enjoyment and conviviality. One feels most happy when one's singing is accompanied by other singers. In a like manner, a wine drinker feels happier when drinking with a companion. Just as the song of a crane in the shade is echoed by its responding offspring, so a person who is drinking is kept company by a fellow drinker. In this line statement, the associative relation lies in the condition of enjoying something together with a companion. What is more, two further analogies are embedded here: first, between the wild natural world and the civilised human world; and second, between the familial intimacy of parent and offspring on the one hand and the cordiality of two friends on the other.

This poem has also inspired Berengarten's 'Seagull's wings,' which has a different theme but the same associational logic:

For an instant
beating
seagull's wings

take up the whole
sky. This heaven-
filling happens

both at zenith and nadir
of their pulsing and
drumming on wind.

Time, unstitched
from history, goes
into reverse. At the

ferry's stern we stand,
so wholly held by this
watching, that distances

slip into haze. Everything
broken is mended. Where we
are is the horizon.   (61/2: 490)

While the statement for hexagram 61 has the image of a singing crane,
Berengarten's poem features a crying seagull. Although this poem contains
the similar image of a crying bird, its theme is radically different from
the Chinese hexagram statement. But the associational link between the
image of the bird and the feelings of the humans who observe the seagull
is similarly imparted. The seagull flying up to the zenith and down to
the nadir, its cry filling up the whole sky, offers a spatial conception of
time, which connects the past with the present, and objects near and afar.
Through the associational presentation of the seagull, Berengarten adroitly
breaks the demarcation line between time and space, far and near.

Each hexagram has inspired Berengarten to composed a group of seven
poems. In hexagram 53, *Jian* 漸, which he translates as 'Shifting,' the statements focus on the image of a wild goose and its movements, together with
the corresponding situations and predictions drawn from the analogical
comparison:

5. 鴻漸于陸， A wild goose gradually flies to the land;
    夫征不復， A husband on a campaign never returns;
    婦孕不育， His pregnant wife has not given birth.
    兇利禦寇。 Inauspicious but favorable for warding off enemies.

There are implicit connections between the image and the situation here.
First, in Chinese, there is notable sound association: *lu, fu,* have the same
vowel sound. But the association goes beyond mere rhyme to meaning. As
Zhu Xi points out, "The wild goose is a kind of water bird; the land is not
a place where it feels comfortable" ("鴻，水鳥，陸非所安也," Zhu Xi
245). On land, the bird might fall prey to a land predator or huntsman.
Going out on a campaign is a similarly uneasy venture; the campaigner
might lose his life and never return home. A water bird usually lays eggs in a
hidden place in a habitat where there are favorable conditions for hatching;
and when the eggs are hatched, the bird is in its own territory and knows
how to protects its offspring. But now the bird is on land, in a strange
place where all sorts of dangers lurk. If it lays eggs in this inhospitable
place, it is more than likely that the eggs won't have a chance to hatch, with
still fewer chances for its fledglings to survive. If a similarly unfavorable
situation befalls a woman in the human world, she may become pregnant,
but the pregnancy may well end in a miscarriage. That is why the result of

this particular divination is "inauspicious." Why, then, is it beneficial for defence against enemies? Since the bird or person is on dangerous ground, it/he must be on the alert all the time, hence it will be easier to fend off attacks. The line statement's meaning may thus be rendered as follows: it is as uncomfortable for a wild goose to be on land as it is dangerous for a man to be on a campaign; and as unfavorable for a woman to be pregnant when her husband is away. What is more, the subsequent statements for individual lines may be interpreted in the same vein. Here are several examples of line statements:

1. 鴻漸于幹，　The wild goose advances to the shore.
   小子厲，　　A dangerous place for a youngster.
   有言，無咎。There will be talk, but no misfortune.

The wild goose leaves water and swims to the bank, almost out of its home territory. This is dangerous because predators may be lurking on the bank. In the human situation, a youngster ventures out of his/her known area and is likely to meet with danger. Fortunately, s/he is cautioned at the right time by some mature person. So s/he escapes unharmed.

2. 鴻漸于磐，　The wild goose advances to a boulder.
   飲食衎衎，　It is joyful to drink and eat.
   吉。　　　　Auspicious.

Here, the wild goose flies to a big rock in the middle of the swamp. This is a safe place, where it can find plenty of food and eat it with joy, without any need to worry about predators. In a human situation, to have plenty to eat and drink is of course a happy situation. Hence it is auspicious.

4. 鴻漸于木，　The wild goose flies into the wood.
   或得其桷，　It may reach a 'rafter.'
   無咎。　　　There will be no misfortune.

In this line, the wild goose flies into the woods. One commentator notes, "When the goose flies to the wood and finds a branch which can serve as a 'rafter', it takes it because it is straight and easy to perch on" (*Ciyuan* 856). Here the rafter obviously symbolizes a secure place. Just as the bird may find a safe branch to perch on, so in the human situation, a person might find a comfortable place to stay. Hence no harm.

5. 鴻漸于陵，　The wild goose flies onto a mountain ridge.
   婦三歲不孕；A wife won't get pregnant for three years.

| 終莫之勝, | Finally, nothing can overpower her. |
| 吉。 | Auspicious. |

Next, the wild goose flies to a high mountain, far from its home. In the human situation, a husband goes to a distant land, leaving his wife at home alone. It is natural that she does not get pregnant. Nevertheless, her husband returns home after a long separation. Husband and wife are reunited. Nothing can overcome the wife's steadfastness and faith in her husband. Hence, auspicious.

6.	鴻漸于陸,	The wild goose advances to high ground.
	其羽可用為儀	Its plumes can be used for ceremonies.
	吉。	Auspicious.

In this line, the wild goose gradually flies to land. It is caught by a huntsman. It is a misfortune for the goose, but good fortune for the human world. The goose's feathers can be used for ceremonial purposes at rituals. Hence, auspicious.

To sum up, the above line statements contain a clearly analogical correlation between the natural world and the human world.

Berengarten's poem 'Wild geese' simply sketches the bird's movements and its destinations:

Slow the wild
geese in V formation
approach the shore

Slow the wild
geese land on the crag
settle high up

Slow the wild
geese wing ways
to highlands

Slow the wild
geese settle on
tree branches

Slow the wild
geese arrive among
blue-grey hills

> Slow the wild
> geese pace cloud-avenues
> over mountains   (53/1: 425)

This is the first poem in this cluster based on individual lines. Unlike the *I Ching*'s statement, this poem expresses neither personal feelings inspired by the birds nor any correlation in the human world. Instead, these become explicit in other poems, for example in the fifth poem, 'What the tinker said' (2):

> The road ahead
> swirls in and out
> of rainbow
>
> no path could
> be more clear
> way of sky
>
> and way of stone
> way of oak and way
> of leaf, way
>
> of river
> and cloud, way
> of swan and
>
> snake, way of
> tortoise and tiger
> way of dragon
>
> way of word
> and not-word way
> of air and fire.   (53/5: 429)

This poem is directly related to the previous one quoted. In the former, the wild geese settle in various places, but the routes to their destinations are not mentioned. In the latter, the poet contemplates possible ways towards them, whether for the birds or for a person. These 'ways' are of two kinds: on the one hand, positive, bright, and colorful, as symbolized by the images of rainbow, clear sky, and green foliage; and on the other, negative, tortuous and dangerous, as suggested by images such as snake, tigers, and fire. What is more, the image of the wild goose leads the poet to further contemplations of the possible ways of meeting the challenges of aging, sickness, and eventual death, as expressed in the third poem in the group:

> To die of sickness isn't
> inevitable. Why not instead
> prepare for living well
>
> until life's last moment
> comes? And though sickness
> in old age be expected
>
> norm, why not step out
> of such mind-habits, such
> conditioned addictions?
>
> Time to simplify and
> purify things, eat less, even
> cut out grains (hard),
>
> drink water and teas,
> walk, meditate, practise
> *taiji, daoyin, qigong,*
>
> become more supple
> in body and spirit, write
> clear, finer poems.   (53/3: 427)

This poem reveals the strong influence of traditional Chinese thought and life-style on the poet. Sickness is a major cause of death and constitutes one of the four main categories of human suffering. How to meet the challenges of sickness is a problem that modern human beings must address. Stanzas 1 and 2 present a Daoist view of the issue, which accepts sickness and death as a natural course for human beings. By declaring "To die of sickness isn't inevitable," the poet adopts a Daoist attitude towards life and death. In the following stanzas, the poet methodically lays out an alternative to the old way of life, which includes the rejection of over-indulging physical appetites and the adoption of a more moderate way of life, characterized by fasting, meditation, *taiji, qigong,* and breath control. Moreover, the last stanza advocates strengthening one's body and mind by engaging in poetic creation.

The next poem, 'All the best books,' continues this theme of self-cultivation:

All the best books say
you can't do it through books
You have to find a teacher.

Then you have to follow,
cultivate, practise daily. Years
he went looking. Several

proclaimed or self-proclaimed
Masters took him on. Their paths
turned away. Or he wasn't ready.

Others disappointed or
saw through him. Then looked
across him, far, way off.

He worked his own passage,
learned truths from friends and
companions, from other

creatures, nature, and dead
masters, whose words/deeds re-
corded in books outlive Death.   (53/4: 428)

This poem may well be interpreted as an abbreviated story of the poet's own self-cultivation. At first, he learned to cultivate himself by reading books, which directed him to learn from so called "masters." He has learned a little from a few who were self-proclaimed masters, as well as from authentic masters, but he was not ready. The real problem lies in the fact that self-cultivation must be accomplished for and by oneself, even though books and teachers may offer guidance and assistance. The poet only comes to this realization once he has decided to work "his own passage." The gently-hinted seafaring image here clarifies that he 'works' his own way as an active crew-member, not as a merely passive passenger. It is through his own practice that he realizes that "teachers" may appear in many different forms: books, friends, companions, dead masters, creatures, and, above all, Nature. Clearly, this poem may also be read as a poetic footnote to the famous parable of 'Wheelwright Bian' in the Daoist master Zhuangzi:

Duke Huan was reading in his hall. Wheelwright Pien, who was cutting a wheel just outside the hall, put aside his hammer and chisel and went in. There he asked Duke Huan, "What do those books you are reading say?" The duke answered, "These are the words of the

Sages." The wheelwright said, "Are the Sages still around?" And the duke answered, "They're dead." Then the wheelwright said, "Well, what you're reading then is no more than the dregs of the ancients."

The duke became very angry with the wheelwright and threatened to put him to death if the latter failed to offer a reasonable explanation for his claim. The wheelwright explained his claim in terms of his own profession and told the duke why it was impossible to pass on something to another person through transmission. His conclusion was: "The ancients have died and, along with them, that which cannot be transmitted. Therefore what you are reading is nothing more than the dregs of the ancients." (Owen 35-36)

Berengarten translates the title of Hexagram 62 (小過 *Xiao Guo*) as 'Overstepping.' The last poem in this cluster, 'Bird falling out of sky,' is a reflection on the mutual transformation of life and death:

So too when I fly
or fall into my own
death all thoughts

ideas words music
will flutter or drop
to the ground plop

plummeting into
completion smashing
into perfection. Just like

that bird, into the blasting
ring of the sun. Stench
of frazzled feathers

and shit and blood will get
cleaned. Though that burning
is not hard to see, my mind

completely fails to conceive
of its own non-being
before birth returning.   (62/6: 502)

The poet's focus on the sudden, brutal physicality of this creature's death, which leads to thoughts of his own mortality, suggests that this bird symbolizes life itself. There are hints, too, that this this is no ordinary bird, for in several respects it is remarkably phoenix-like. First, the bird flies "into the blasting ring of the sun." A phoenix is known as a sun-bird. The death of the bird in the poem has evidently been caused by the sun's heat, so that the creature drops suddenly to the ground. This detail might well be a representation of the phoenix, which in Western mythology consumes itself in fire. Second, the mess of its death, including the "stench of frazzled feathers" and "shit and blood," is cleansed by burning. Third, the bird does not tumble to *mere* destruction, but plummets into a kind of purified "completion" by dint of smashing itself into perfection. Last but not least, even though the bird has met physical destruction, it does not die. It is implied that it reincarnates in the spirit of non-being and resurrects in a rebirth. In this way, the implicit image of the phoenix fuses bird and poet into an entity that embodies continuity *across* mortalities.[8]

‿

Berengarten readily admits that *Changing* was influenced by "the kinds of modes, models and devices that have developed out of the great Symbolists, Modernists and Surrealists" (*CH* 526). There is little doubt that his poetry is influenced by Anglo-American modernist poets like Ezra Pound and T.S. Eliot, who in their turn received influence from classical Chinese poetry. In particular, Pound's fascination with ancient Chinese poetry is well-known. In his Imagist Manifesto, Pound called on poets to make direct treatment of 'things' in their poetry and to consider this injunction as the first Imagist tenet (Pound 11). Eliot, who was influenced by the Metaphysical poets, advanced the idea of the "objective correlative" (Eliot 1919: 89) and advocated the necessity in poetic composition to digest various experiences and to perceive analogical correspondence among disparate things. In assessing the achievement of the 'Metaphysical' poets, Eliot sums up a few points that modern poets might put to good use. These points parallel similar poetic techniques to those of classical Chinese poetry. For instance, Eliot appreciates the "elaboration of a figure of speech to the farthest stage to which ingenuity can carry it." He cites several examples: Cowley's comparison of the world to a chess-board in 'To Destiny,' Donne's comparison of two lovers to a pair of compasses

---

[8] The discussion here evidently concerns the phoenix of Western tradition, rather than the Chinese mythical bird known as the *fenghuang* (鳳凰)—often translated "phoenix." In East Asian cultures, *fenghuang* mythology does not involve the motif of rebirth. As a further aside, we can't help wondering if, in writing this poem, Berengarten might also have had in mind the Icarus myth.

in 'A Valediction: Forbidding Mourning,' and the latter poet's relating tears to a globe and a deluge in 'A Valediction: Weeping' (Eliot 2010: 962). Although this fact may not be widely known among Anglophone literati, Classical Chinese poets share with the Metaphysical poets the love of using strange and obscure metaphors. Qian Zhongshu, the foremost expert on traditional Chinese poetry and poetics in the twentieth century, extensively discusses features that are common to ancient Chinese poets and the English Metaphysical poets. He translates 'conceits' as *quyu* 曲喻 (i.e. 'twisted metaphors') (Qian 22).

Berengarten has clearly absorbed many of these insights from Pound, Eliot, and other modernist poets. This can be seen in his penchant for using striking metaphors and direct treatment of things in his poems. Wind and rain are two topics which frequently appear in Berengarten's poems. I would like to discuss these poems in relation to some traditional Chinese poems with similar themes. The first Chinese example of a poem focusing on rain and wind is by the Northern Sung poet Liu Ban 劉攽:

新晴　　　　　Clear Day after Rain

青苔满地初晴后，The ground is full of moss shortly after rain.
绿树无人昼梦余。No one is in the green wood after my day dream.
惟有南风旧相识，There is only an old acquaintance – the south wind
偷开门户又翻书。Who sneaks through my door and leafs
　　　　　　　　　　　　　　　　　　through my books.

In this poem, the southern wind after rain is depicted as an old friend who stealthily opens the door to the poet's studio and reads his books. For further comparison, here is another poem on wind by the Tang poet He Zhizhang 贺知章:

咏柳　　　　　Ode to a Willow

碧玉妆成一树高，A tall tree is decorated with blue jade;
万条垂下绿丝绦。Dangling with thousands of green silk braids.
不知细叶谁裁出？I wonder who tailors fine leaves with scissors?
二月春风似剪刀。February's spring wind cuts them into shape.

While the tree is compared to a beautiful girl wearing a silky pigtail and decorations of jade, the wind is compared to a pair of scissors used by a skilful tailor, who makes a gorgeous robe for the girl.

Critics have written extensively about Pound's Imagist tenets, William Carlos Williams' espousal of the "thing" and his idea of "total metaphor," and T.S. Eliot's theory of the "objective correlative." All these Modernist ideas can be compared with the methods of poetry-making demonstrated in the two poems above from the *Book of Songs*, as well as many statements in the *Book of Changes*. At the beginning of the Anglo-American Modernist movement, Hulme, Pound, Hilda Doolittle, Amy Lowell, Williams and other poets were busily engaged in searching for a new poetic sensibility and techniques for modern poetry. All of them were fascinated by the Cathay poems translated by Pound and showed a great interest in Chinese images and imagery, which had also arisen from the direct treatment of observed things. T. E. Hulme, who insisted that a poet should develop the "particular faculty of mind to see things as they really are" (Hulme 134), was the first to advocate the direct treatment of observed objects, which was later developed by Pound into a central tenet of Imagism. As a successor to Anglo-American modernist poetry, Berengarten's poems have drawn from both techniques and treatments common to ancient Chinese and Western Modernist poets.

Following these two Chinese poems, whose topics are rain and wind, here are two by Berengarten with the same theme. The first is entitled 'Under rain':

All summer rain
has been falling on
this thin flat roof –

brushing of cymbals
hammers drumming
gongs chiming –

as if wolves were
howling rocks clashing
forests tumbling –

and no blocking of
ears will keep out this
baying thrumming –

is this the onset of
the world's end
eve of judgement –

```
and in this heavy
sultriness will this
head crack open?                    (9/6: 78)
```

The poem is concerned with a storm and the poet's responses to it and reflections on it. To present the magnitude of the storm, the poet does not resort to abstract descriptions. Instead, he depicts it as a chorus of drums, gongs, and cymbals – which might well be Chinese, since these are all traditional Chinese instruments – all reinforced by the howling of a wolf and the suggestion of a solid 'cracking,' perhaps like a stone, or perhaps even like an egg. This cacophony of concrete noises suggests an apocalyptical evocation of the Day of Judgment, i.e. a metaphysical reflection on the end of the world. In other words, the poet does not stop simply at the direct presentation of wind and rain by means of vivid images; he goes on to turn the images into what Pound calls "an intellectual and emotional complex" (Pound 1969: 4).

ᘒ

My brief comparative study of Berengarten's poems with some hexagram statements and ancient Chinese poems has offered evidence to suggest that *Changing* is indebted to the Chinese tradition in more ways than simply as a source of creative inspiration. It not only draws inspiration and poetic resources from the *Book of Changes*, but also makes innovative use of techniques that are characteristic of traditional Chinese poetry. Berengarten's deployment of images, metaphors, and direct treatments of objects, which carries forward the pioneering experiments by such Modernist poets as Pound, Eliot, and Williams, not only enriches the Anglo-American modern poetic tradition but also makes a significant contribution to the meshing and blending of Chinese and English poetry in the context of the now-flourishing world literature. Within the category of writing that may legitimately be regarded as world literature, most works are produced, circulated and consumed around the globe through the medium of translation. But it is rare to come across literary works that are not only inspired by the subject matter of several literary traditions but also deploy poetic techniques derived from them. In this respect, Berengarten's *Changing* is a *bona fide* specimen of world literature and blazes a new path for cross-cultural dialogue between Eastern and Western poetry and poetics.

References

Berengarten, Richard. 2016. *Changing*. Bristol: Shearsman Books.

Chen Kui 陳騤. 1962. *Wenze* 文則 [*Models of Writing*]. Guo Shaoyu and Luo Genze (eds.). Beijing: Renmin wenxue chubanshe.

Ciyuan 辭源. [*Origins of Words*]. 1995 [revised edn.]. Beijing: Shanwu yinshuguan, 856.

Eliot, T. S. 1919. 'Hamlet and His Problems.' In *The Sacred Wood: Essays on Poetry and Criticism*. London: Methuen, 87-94.

———. 2010. 'The Metaphysical Poets.' In Leitch, Vincent *et al.* (eds.). *The Norton Anthology of Theory and Criticism*. New York: Norton, 961-968.

Gu, Ming Dong. 1997. '*Fu-Bi-Xing*: A Metatheory of Poetry-Making.' *Chinese Literature: Essays, Articles, Reviews* 19, 1-22.

Hulme, T. E. 1965. *Speculations: Essays on Humanism and the Philosophy of Art*. London: Routledge and Kegan Paul.

Li Jingchi 李鏡池. 1978. 'Zhouyi xici kao 周易筮辭考' ['Investigation of Divination Statements in the *Book of Change*']. In *Zhouyi tanyuan* 周易探源 [*Exploring the Origins of the Book of Changes*]. Beijing: Zhonghua shuju.

Owen, Stephen. 1996. *Readings in Traditional Chinese Literary Thought*. Cambridge, MA: Harvard University Asia Center.

Pound, Ezra. 1954. *Shih-ching: The Classic Anthology Defined by Confucius*. Cambridge, MA: Harvard University Press.

———. 1969. *Literary Essays of Ezra Pound*. Eliot, T. S. (ed.). London: Faber and Faber.

———. 1974. 'A Retrospect.' In Schulman, Grace (ed.). *Ezra Pound: A Collection of Criticism*, New York: McGraw-Hill, 11-22.

Qian Zhongshu. 1993. *Tanyi lu* 談藝錄 [*Records of Discourses on Art*] [photocopy edn.]. Beijing: Zhonghua shuju.

Waley, Arthur (trans.). 1960. *The Book of Songs*. New York: Grove Press.

Zhu Xi, *Zhouyi benyi* 周易本義 [*The Original Meanings of the Zhouyi*]. 1986. Tianjin: Tianjin guji shudian.

SOPHIA KATZ

An Ongoing Revolution:
Cosmic Canticle, Changing,
and the Problem of Broken Harmony

In the *Book of Changes*, the Chinese classic that was believed to encode all possible contingencies of human existence, the dynamic of 'revolution' is addressed by hexagram 49 革 (*Ge*). The literal meaning of this character is "the hide of an animal" (Huang 389). "In its verbal sense *ge* (hide) means 'skin,' 'get rid of' – certainly a radical change" (Lynn 449). *Ge* is also part of the expression 革命 *geming*, 'shedding the mandate'. In modern Chinese *geming* means 'revolution.'

In his *Changing*, Richard Berengarten translates *Ge* as 'Shedding' (391-398). Richard Wilhelm translates it elsewhere as 'Revolution (Molting)' (Wilhelm 1977: 189), Richard Lynn as 'Radical Change' (Lynn 444), and Alfred Huang as 'Abolishing the Old' (Huang 389). In the first poem in the cluster associated with this hexagram, Berengarten summarizes the psychological makeup of persons involved in a 'typical' revolutionary movement:

> *Our self-appointed task*
> *questioning, challenging myths,*
> *based on our own longing*
>
> *to see them tumble,*
> *collapse, crumble, wither away –*
> *towers of bricks brought*
>
> *down by us – and what*
> *pleasure to see this happen*
> *before our very own eyes.*   (49/0: 392)

In this poem, entitled 'Revolutionary Cadre,' the individual voice is replaced by the voice of 'collective consciousness': 'we' is used in place of 'I,' while 'us' is perceived in sharp opposition to 'them.' Yet both the internal, self-searching questions and the external ones arising in the hearts and minds of individuals remain unanswered:

> *Our dreams? We invested them*
> *in debunking, interrupting,*
>
> *clashing. Why? Not to*
> *put up with the blur and glaze*
> *of half-truth?*   (*ibid.*)

The act of "*abolishing the old*" (as implied in the poem's 'base-line'), involves the wish to find the whole truth, believed to exist in an ideal world, as opposed to the half-truth of the current reality. The entire revolutionary procedure opens real dangers, all the more so because "catastrophe beckons us repeatedly." Yet it also holds great potential, as "we remain a reservoir untapped" (*ibid*). In the hexagram *Ge* the lower trigram is 離 (*Li*) 'fire' and the upper, 兌 (*Dui*) 'lake.' As this structure suggests, the uncertainty of this time is symbolized by the motif of fire burning under water, which itself epitomizes a dynamic state of accumulated energy that has not yet been expressed. The outcome is still unknown: it may turn out to be either "increasing light" and the reconstruction of "the entire state edifice" (49/2: 394), or "making mistakes and enemies" and total destruction (49/3: 395).

This tension between the search for truth, justice, and harmony on the one hand and fierce violence and intense pain on the other is at the center of my discussion in this essay. I explore these questions by specifically referencing two indicative poetic works: Ernesto Cardenal's *Cosmic Canticle* (1993)[9] and Richard Berengarten's *Changing* (2016).

Written from very different philosophical/theological perspectives and distinct in style, *Cosmic Canticle* and *Changing* nonetheless share many common characteristics. Both are ambitious book-length poems, composed of shorter pieces. Both are universal in the range of questions they address, and encyclopedic in their use of references. And both employ Eastern and Western perspectives, tightly interwoven. While Berengarten's *Changing* intentionally follows the structure of the Chinese *Book of Changes*, it is nonetheless very personal and, as such, discloses the

---

[9] Ernesto Cardenal (1925–2020) was a Nicaraguan Catholic priest, liberation theologian and poet. On his life and work, see Cohen 2009.

thoughts and yearnings of the author. Cardenal's *Cosmic Canticle* employs the form of a Christian hymn of praise; yet, the textual themes of this work are inspired by science and various traditions, including South American, Chinese, and Indian sources.

Seen as wholes, *Changing* and *Cosmic Canticle* are both progressive and cyclical. As Berengarten's comments in his 'Postscript' reveal (525), the structure of his work can be explained by that of the *Book of Changes*, in which the progression from one situation to another occurs due to the interaction of two opposing yet complementary powers, *yin* and *yang*. The double structure of Cardenal's *Cosmic Canticle*, which describes progression from the 'Big Bang' (Cantiga 1) to 'Omega' (Cantiga 43), appears to stem from the author's sense of poetic harmony and his integrative philosophical vision. This cyclicity is embedded in the book's very structure. The first lines of Cantiga 1 and the very last lines of Cantiga 43 are connected: hence the conclusion of *Cosmic Canticle* is a 'back-reading' of its beginning (*CC* 1, 481).

Intriguingly, these two works exhibit very different approaches to the violence associated with revolution. Sharing the ideas of liberation theology, Cardenal perceives violence as *an integral part of creation*, necessary for breakthrough and the liberation of the oppressed (see Jimmerson 2009). Following the Chinese holistic worldview, Berengarten sees violence as a manifestation of excessive energy, often destructive, which needs to be harmonized through the balancing of *yin* and *yang*.

"In the Beginning":
Cardenal on the Poetic Word and Harmony

Elements inspired by the Chinese tradition appear as early as Cantiga 1 of *Cosmic Canticle* (*CC*), where Cardenal connects the mythological story of Pangu (P'an Ku) with primordial oneness (*CC* 3). This oneness, as Cardenal suggests, was the Dao (Tao) itself, before it received its name:

> [...] Then the Tao had no name.
> A name came and it was creation [...]   (*CC* 4)

The idea of ineffable 'namelessness' here clearly refers to the opening lines of the Chinese classic, the *Daodejing* (Ivanhoe 2002). Basing his narrative equally on the Gospel of John, in Cantiga 2, 'The Word,' Cardenal describes the appearance of the 'Word' as the primary act of creation, which is both poetic and dynamic in nature.

> In the beginning
> > – before spacetime –
> was the Word
> All that is then is true.
> > Poem. (*CC* 13)

Creation, bringing "the light out of the darkness" (*ibid.* 15), is a deeply poetic act. Yet Cardenal perceives the moment of creation not as a single centralized movement, but rather as "a simultaneous explosion on all sides, filling / the whole space from the beginning, every particle / of matter drawing away from every other particle" (*CC* 7). The continuous mutual interaction between these particles constitutes the cosmic song, "united by rhythm." [...] "In harmony"

> The cosmos sings.
> > The two choruses.
> "The yang calls;
> The yin responds."
> > Dialectically. (*CC* 17-18)

The dialectical movement of *yin* and *yang* or, as Cardenal calls it, "the celestial dialectical dance" (*CC* 16), is directed toward union of these forces. This union, in Cardenal's view, is the essence of love, both as a physical act between lovers, and as metaphysical love between creator and creatures:

> He is in that which each thing is.
> > And in that which each thing enjoys.
> Each thing coitus.
> > The entire cosmos copulation.
> All things love, and he is the love with which they love.
> "The yang calls;
> > the yin responds." (*CC* 16)

The movement and copulation of opposing forces, *yin* and *yang*, as the movement of female and male lovers, creates harmony. This kind of harmony is rhythmic, poetic and musical:

The whole universe musical harmony.
Everything is number and harmony
in music and in heavenly bodies. (*CC* 46)

Cardenal's description of a harmonious universe reaches its crescendo in Cantiga 20, 'The Music of the Spheres' (*CC* 187-196). Here, this harmony is described as cyclical and constantly changing:

A harmonious universe like a harp.
Rhythm is equal beats repeated.
The beating of the heart.
Day/night.
The coming and going of birds of passage.
Cycle of stars and maize.
Mimosa which unfolds during the day
and at night folds back. (*CC* 187)

In describing the universe as "harmonious," Cardenal makes it clear that in his understanding harmony does not imply uniformity. Rather, harmony for him is polyphony, "a music closer to jazz than to classical music," "disorderly dance of things" (*CC* 188), guided by change:

The cosmos as change.
Its structure is change.
Ever-changing spider web of light.
Meditation as contact with the rhythms of the universe.
Returning is the motion of the Tao. (*CC* 190)

It is noteworthy that in order to express the idea of change as a foundation of harmony, Cardenal employs explicitly Chinese philosophical concepts, such as the alternation of *yin* and *yang* as the principle of the Dao (Tao). Unusually for a Christian thinker, Cardenal perceives harmony not as an ideal 'state' of things, existing in "in the beginning," that is, in the form, whether symbolic or literal, of a Biblical Paradise, but rather as a dynamic process associated with continuous creation, most notably exemplified by the *Book of Changes*.[10]

---

[10] On the concept of 'dynamic harmony,' see Li 2014.

"Meeting Christ and Reading Marx":[11]
Cardenal on Broken Harmony

Following this 'Chinese' line of thought, Cardenal extends the concept of cosmic harmony to the realm of politics, which in his view links cosmic and earthly orders. He claims that a close connection exists between political, social, and cosmic harmony:

> Political, moral and cosmic harmony:
> *Yin* and *Yang* for the Prime Minister too.
> The four seasons pass in order
> when the right thing is done in everything.   (*CC* 196)

According to the Chinese understanding of dynastic circles, rulers have the legitimacy to rule as long as the right order is preserved. This means that order is based on the moral behavior of those in power. Yet when rulers' corruption increases and the people's hardships intensify, order is broken. The dichotomy between the harmonious life of the privileged minority and sufferings of majority of the people who remain oppressed constitutes one of the major themes in the *Cosmic Canticle*. The brokenness is expressed most strongly in Cantiga 25, 'Visit to Weimar' (*CC* 240-244). Opening this cantiga with the usual reference to the Biblical "In the beginning" and noting that the multiplicity of forms and creatures in the world is made of 92 atoms, Cardenal recollects his visit to this locus, which epitomizes German civilization and civility. The detailed and painstaking description of the interior of Goethe's house, the milestones in the poet's life, his intellectual search and contacts with remarkable men of his epoch, his belief in the healing power of poetry, and his vision of "a free people living on this earth" all add up to create a feeling of peaceful routine in the city that was "the intellectual capital of Germany" (*CC* 240-241). But this languid description then crashes headlong into a shocking later reality, half-hidden from the eyes of Weimar residents – that of Buchenwald:

> And 15 minutes from there
>   set in the woods
> we enter the "Highway of Blood."
>   The prisoners themselves paved it.
> [...]
> Barbed wire within barbed wire within more electrified barbed wire.

---

[11] Cohen 2019.

> The horrendous watch-towers.
> And we saw the cremation ovens in red brick.   (*CC* 241-242)

"With as many inhabitants as Weimar," this is "another city" (*CC* 242), and the site of horrendous atrocities, which did not result from disorder and chaos but from meticulously planned organization:

> Everything well-ordered.
> The name of each one who was going to arrive
> sent beforehand to the concentration camp
> with a copy to the Central Management of Concentration Camps
> cc. to the Gestapo, etc.   (*CC* 242)

Describing the horrors of Buchenwald, the unbearable human suffering and dehumanized, cold-blooded actions of the Nazis, Cardenal makes it clear that this entire 'machine' was operated by people who continued to read books, write love poems, appreciate Goethe, and take pride in Germany's cultural heritage:

> Human skin was good for parchment.
>   For writing poems on, love poems.
> For binding books.
>   For lamp shades.   (*CC* 242-243)

The reason for this dehumanization, at least to some degree, is the failure of those in power to understand that all things in the world are interconnected, through "[t]he unity of humanity and the union / with all that surrounds it." (*CC* 244). This is an ever-present theme. As Cardenal writes more explicitly in Cantiga 8, 'Condensations and Vision of San José de Costa Rica' (Cantiga 8, *CC* 60-65), human life can be meaningful and valuable only in community. Therefore, communism, with its emphasis on communal wellbeing, is perceived by Cardenal as the political system best able to bring about unity and harmony.

Nazi atrocities are not the only sources of suffering perpetrated by other humans. In Cantiga 16, 'The Darkest Before Dawn' (*CC* 132-140), Cardenal describes the terrors in Nicaragua:

> I'm going to tell you now about the screams from the Cuá
>   screams of women as though in labor.   (*CC* 132)
> [...]
> Two girls told what happened:
> They discovered a pistol on a boy from the neighborhood,

And they didn't search anymore.
They pushed the women, children and elderly to one side.
Made the boys lie on the ground.
Three of their brothers were on the ground;
a guardia ordered them to look away.
After the shots they saw the bodies writhing on the ground.
They drove a tractor over the bodies.
The tractor then piled them up, a single red mass.   (*CC* 136-137)

Through detailed descriptions of victims' suffering, the cruelty of op-
pressors, and the indifference of the rest of the world, in this part of his
poem Cardenal portrays a situation of despair with no visible exit. Even so,
he insists that neither individual nor collective pain is meaningless. Just as
the suffering of a woman crying in labor will bring forth new life, so the
collective suffering of humanity is a stage in bringing forth a new reality.
As the title of this cantiga promises, darkness is not eternal. The oppressed
will wake from their dreams and realize the power of community with the
light of morning:

We'll see the water deep blue: right now we can't see it.
[...]
The shades fly off like a vampire before the light.
        Get up you, and you, and you.   (*CC* 139-140)

BROKENNESS AND *TIKKUN* ('REPAIR')
IN BERENGARTEN'S *CHANGING*

One of the strongest examples of the theme of brokenness in *Changing*
occurs in the poem-cluster associated with hexagram 23 剝 (*Bo*), 'Peeling'
(*CH* 183-190). The title of this hexagram is a reference to peeling the "skin
from fruit or vegetables."[12] 'Peeling' is intimately connected to the title
of hexagram 49 革 (*Ge*), 'Shedding,' which is based on an animal image,
and expresses the motif of 'revolution', as noted above. For Berengarten,
bo 'peeling,' is concerned above all with archaeology: peeling off layers
of earth and, by implication, whatever masks the darknesses buried deep
within the human soul. Like the archaeologist who peels off layers of soil

---

[12] Richard Lynn notes: "Kong Yingda glosses *bo* as *boluo*: 'to peel off,' as skin
from fruit or vegetables, bark from a tree, etc. As such things so peel (and split),
this indicates their 'deterioration' or 'decay,' which is what *boluo* means by extension." (Lynn 1994: 284).

in order to discover fragments and so to reconstruct the past, Berengarten gathers evidence into a terrifying picture of a human reality that has been repeatedly dehumanized. Referring to Vienna after Nazi Germany annexed Austria in 1938, in a poem entitled 'We thank our Führer,' Berengarten describes the life of Austrian Jews, who overnight were turned from being respected citizens into ridiculed victims and outcasts:

> March 1938: the most popular sport that
> weekend was to round up all ranks of Jews
> particularly middle class specimens
>
> and make them clean streets
> and scrub pavements decorated with pro-
> Schuschnigg posters and slogans
>
> and kick and beat them especially
> older and feebler ones if they stumbled
> or collapsed. The Jews were forced
>
> to work with bare hands onto which
> acid was poured. Meanwhile Viennese
> citizens stood by jeering and laughing
>
> and occasionally breaking into roars
> of delight as they chanted: "Work for the
> Jews at last! At last work for the Jews!"   (CH 23/1: 185)

Resembling the twofold reality of Weimar described by Cardenal, where "no one knew anything" (CC 244), here the citizens of Vienna were ready to condone the barbaric treatment of Jews. Moreover, they took pleasure in humiliating their neighbors, many of whom were later transferred to concentration camps and perished.

The Holocaust is not the only zone of human suffering Berengarten confronts. In the next poem in this cluster, he directly quotes the testimony of Margaret Cox, a British forensic anthropologist whose job was "to locate, excavate and exhume mass graves believed to hold the victims of genocide" (Warner 2004; CH 545). In 1994, during the genocide in Rwanda, within a period of 100 days, hundreds of thousands of people were tortured and murdered at the hands of their former neighbors (see Gwin 2014 and Epstein 2017). Berengarten dedicates his poem, 'After the Massacre,' to the memory of Annonciata Mukandoli, a young Tutsi woman who was gang-raped and then horrendously murdered:

In the area of Nyamata Church
atrocity was so widespread and
gang-rape so systematically

organised that men with
HIV waited their turn till last.
In a vault below that church

a particularly large coffin
was found, at least three
metres long. The body

inside was a woman's
of merely average height. She
needed this long coffin

because she had been raped
with a sapling. The tree had been
forced right through her.

The local people
buried her with the
tree inside her.   ('The forensic archaeologist,' 23/2: 186)

The lines of the poem, written as a simple historical record, reveal the almost inconceivable reality of premeditated torture and murder inflicted by people of one ethnic group upon members of another, who only days before had been their fellow-villagers. The description of extreme violence within the grounds of the church, where people, old and young, desperately sought refuge in the vain hope of protection and mercy, leaves the reader with a sense of helplessness and despair: skulls crushed, clothes torn, human bodies burning alive – the graphic epitome of broken humanity.

The agony of meaningless suffering, which is all the more intensified by the calm discursive narration, is not, however, the final word. As the cluster of poems proceeds, it becomes apparent that, following the inner dynamic of the hexagram, tendrils of hope slowly manifest as a web of connections between past and present. In the third poem of the cluster, the "bespectacled young forensic / archaeologist" reports finding "a silver chain / [which] surrounded several / joined vertebrae," while she herself is "wearing / a blue *hamsah* medallion / around her slender throat" ('After the Massacre,' 23/3: 187). The *hamsah*, possibly signifying the archaeologist's belief that the amulet "will ward off [...] Evil" (545) connects the living and the dead, the latter being directly embodied in the unearthed vertebrae of a person who was also wearing a necklace. The identical image is taken up elsewhere in 'Words for a *hamsah*' (31/5: 253). So, life continues. In the fourth poem, entitled 'Language Palazzo,' continuity is epitomized by children "playing hopscotch" in the Campo de la Bragola in Venice, even after general destruction and the breakdown of language, when "[m]eanings / collapsed to rubble" (23/4: 188). Then, the need for meaningfulness, implied here, is taken up in the last poem in this cluster:

> Enough of battering, blasting,
> storming, excavating, carving.
> Our job is to foster and grow
>
> (a) coherent language, little
> by little, in patience, in respect.
> And how can this be but
>
> by following the heart's
> paths and injunctions – to
> reaffirm the dignity
>
> of the dead, and reclaim,
> recall, rediscover – or find for
> the first time (a) language
>
> fit for, capable of examining,
> expressing, understanding, *in*
> and *through* words, what had
>
> been unsaid, unsayable, and
> so mend and change the real,
> regrow and rebuild hope.   ('[A] coherent language,' 23/6: 190)

Finding appropriate words to address the painful past and doing so "by following the heart's paths and injunctions" is necessary in order to rebuild hope. For this reason, the initial act is to find "(a) coherent language", which for Berengarten is, first and foremost, the language of poetry. Like Cardenal, who views the poetic word as the impulse of creation itself, Berengarten imbues poetry with the power of mending the broken world, the power "from depth of dark to confront and conquer evil" (36/5: 293; base-line), and so to prepare the way to repair the broken reality. Challenging Theodor Adorno (1903-1969), who claimed that "to write a poem after Auschwitz is barbaric" (551), Berengarten insists that the poetic word has the power to transform pain into hope:

I shall find words, my
own, after, despite *and* because
of this. *And* speak of it.

Your call, in words, to
silence, misconstrues what
poems are, do, are for.

To call out love and justice,
born of the heart's oldest and
simplest imperatives – hope,

compassion, courage, truth,
and defiance of death-makers.   (36/5: 293)

These lines imply the motif of *tikkun* תיקון, meaning 'repair, restoration, restitution'. Berengarten relies considerably on this Hebrew word, "a fertile and resonant term in Kabbalistic thought" (*CH* 545-546). He quotes Gershom Scholem's explanation: "The task of man is seen to consist in the direction of his whole inner purpose towards the restoration of the original harmony which was disturbed by the original defect – the Breaking of the Vessels – and those powers of evil and sin which date from that time." (Scholem 275). The same redemptive theme appears explicitly in the following poem, '*Tikkun*, Majdanek' (*CH* 36/6: 294).

Therefore, not silence, but rather the poetic word, according to Berengarten, is able to serve as the means for *tikkun*: restoring the broken reality, slowly and carefully, to the original oneness, to the wholeness of the Biblical "in the beginning":

In the beginning was
Word – and Word was
wholly *way why one.*

Word was number
and unison. Word was
one and all. And

Word was not spoken
but heard. In silence.   ('Way Why One', 20/5: 165)

Heard first by humans in the solitude of their hearts, this is the very Biblical "Word," ultimately poetic, that can restore broken harmony.

Berengarten, like Cardenal, depicts primordial harmony by means of the image of copulation between lovers. Aspects of this motif appear throughout the poem-cluster associated with hexagram 44 姤 (*Gou*), 'Coupling.' Significantly, *Gou* is structurally related to hexagram 23 (*Bo*), 'Peeling,' mentioned earlier, by a double change: each hexagram is both the inversion and the *yin* and *yang* opposite of the other.[13] This means that in Berengarten's *Changing*, the poems describing brokenness (in the cluster associated with hexagram 23) and harmony (in the cluster for hexagram 44) are connected on deeper levels. Referring to the harmony of sexual union between lovers, Berengarten suggests that the "*[e]ntire fabric / of the human orgasm / meshed of timeless / space and light*" (44/0: 352), embodied in the unity of "I" and "you," leads to the dissolving of private identity and the appearance of a "*fourth / person singular.*" This entity seems mysterious. Is the key to this idea, perhaps, the simple fact that procreation results from sexual union and that out of the state of the oneness experienced by two emerges a third, an entirely new being? So might the embryo in the mother's womb then, perhaps, be this "*fourth person singular*" (*ibid.*), as both outcome and embodiment of physical love?

Another kind of intuitive and intimate connectivity also passes between mother and daughter, when it becomes possible to hear what otherwise would remain hidden: the 'sound' of 'a silent smile' – a manifestation, perhaps, of what is described in the Bible as "the voice of finest silence" (Hebrew קול דממה דקה *kol dmama daka*; Kings 19: 12):

> I'm pregnant,
> she told her mother on
> her (mother's) birthday.
>
> [...]

---

[13] The relationships between the hexagrams in the *I Ching* are dynamic: hexagrams can turn into one another. There are two major patterns that describe such changes: 錯卦 *cuogua* ('counter-changed hexagrams') and 綜卦 *zonggua* ('inverted hexagrams'). Counter-change means that all *yin* and *yang* lines of a particular hexagram become their opposite, while inversion means that a hexagram is turned upside down. Double change means that a particular hexagram is both counter-changed and inverted. Such is the relation between hexagrams 44 and 23. This is also the relation between hexagrams 49 and 3. For more details about the relationship between these hexagrams, see Ooi 2014: 111-118.

> In and through
> the silence at each
>
> end of the line
> both women heard
> the other smiling.   ('Hearing the other smiling,' 3/2: 26)

The image of a woman hearing a smile in silence, the interplay between birth and motherhood, giving and receiving life, not only enhances the sense of harmony, but also emphasizes the unbreakable power of life represented by hexagram 3 屯 (*Zhun*), 'Beginning.'[14] Intriguingly, hexagram 3 is the opposite of hexagram 49 革 (*Ge*), 'Shedding,' by a double change in just the same way as hexagrams 23 剝 (*Bo*) 'Peeling' and 44 姤 (*Gou*) 'Coupling' oppose and balance each other. The connection between the two hexagrams emphasizes the importance of harmony as a healing power that can balance the crisis brought forward by revolution. As Berengarten emphasizes, the feeling of being embraced, "breathing gently," being cared for and carried "away to dreamland" ('For a very small child,' 3/5: 29), where one can dwell safely and in harmony, is the experience of an infant.

A perhaps comparable 'quiescence' can be consciously adopted by an adult too, to cope with uncertainty and instability, even in the most turbulent times:

> The entire national economy has
> cracked up. He has a job and works
> hard but doesn't get paid. [...]
>
> [...]
>
> This isn't his time or anyone else's.
> In the capital students and workers
> demonstrate outside parliament.
>
> With bare hands they tear down
> walls. Pull up flagstones. Hoist parked
>
> cars on top. Then torch the piles.
> [...] He, meanwhile, stays
>
> at home in his provincial town.
> Borrows money. Tightens his belt.
> Goes on working. Bides his time.   ('Biding [his] time,' 3/6: 30)

---

[14] See also the reference to this poem in Shaughnessy 2016.

Berengarten dedicates this poem to his friend Paschalis Nikolaou (537). It refers to the 2011 anti-austerity protests in Greece, when thousands of young citizens of Athens and many other Greek cities occupied public squares and clashed with police, protesting for a better future. The fervor of the moment, generated in solidarity with others, may have been what propelled the young protesters to the barricades. However, for Berengarten, the *Book of Changes* espouses the wisdom of waiting, tending the fire rather than burning within it. This motif is evident in another poem, associated with hexagram 33 遯 (*Dun*), 'Retreating.' During the Cultural Revolution, the Buddhist monk, Xiao Yao, "retreated" from his previous retreat, a monastery high in the mountains, to the city of Xiangtan, where he worked in a boiler room:

> Calling himself Mr. Tan, he slept
> on a mattress in the boiler room. So,
> incognito, Xiao Yao retreated
>
> from his mountain retreat to find
> safer retreat in the city, by the river,
> servant to the blazing heart of fire.   ('Retreating,' 33/5: 269)[15]

Retreating and tending the fire of life rather than running headlong into it is for Berengarten the appropriate way to act in such a situation of uncertainty and danger. Berengarten believes that genuine revolution occurs first and foremost within one's own being. Before a person can revolutionize the world, 'shedding' the old and bringing forward the new, s/he must 'shed' her/his old self by transforming her/his own inner being:

> Before Xiao Yao
> effected changes in the world,
> in others, he changed
>
> himself. He went down
> into darkness and silence,
> where he shedded *things*,
>
> spacetime, life-and-death,
> even his own breath. Then
> from that core that is

---

[15] For brief information about Xiao Yao and sources for further reading, see *CH*: 550.

nothing and everything,
a fire inexhaustible flowed
in streams through and

along his fingers, to and
into whatever he touched.
Were you, who were

lucky enough to meet
him, charged through
his charge? Changed?   ('Shedding,' 49/5: 397)

While "[i]ncreasing light" (49/2: 394) is often perceived by revolutionaries as their mission, according to the *Book of Changes* this process cannot be forced. Rather, changing the future for the better is possible only after inner transformation of one's own self.

Breaking Through or Breaking Down? Cardenal and Berengarten on Revolution

The philosophical vision of the *Book of Changes*, which perceives harmony as dynamic process, is clearly manifested in both Ernesto Cardenal's *Cosmic Canticle* and in Berengarten's *Changing*. This process is portrayed as the movement of lovers, the mutual changes of *yin* and *yang*, and the dynamic oneness of musical sounds. Harmony reflects: *"order, not only already / within, but discoverable and / not imposed"* (*'Order in grand design,'* 14/0: 112). It also demands unity, equality, and the well-being of all members of society. Therefore, as long as injustice prevails, as long as human beings are exploited or suffer, both the order of the world and harmony are broken, and still need to be restored. For Cardenal, restoration of the broken order is the function of revolution:

> the whole of creation down to the hoardings groaned with pain
> Because of man's exploitation of man. The whole of creation
>   was clamoring, clamoring in full cry for
> the Revolution.   (*CC* 65)

Revolution is not merely an act of violence imposed by one group of people on another; rather, it is an existential necessity. Revolution is evolutionary, and therefore opposing it is perceived not merely as an act of counterrevolution, but as counter-*evolution* – an opposition to the entire existential order based on love:

> The enemies of evolution (Somoza etc.)
>   Counter-evolutionaries.
> How can there be unemployment on this planet?
> But there is a tower we wish to build, Chuang-tse said,
>   that might reach to infinity.   (*CC* 72)

Referring to both Christian and Daoist sources, and perhaps being influenced by interpretations of Daoism by his friend Thomas Merton (1915–1968),[16] Cardenal claims that the eventual extinction of selfishness and of capitalism is certain as the change of seasons. Building "the tower of the spirit," based on the "entire sincerity of Tao" (Merton 134), is possible only by means of destroying selfishness:

> Capitalism will pass away. You'll no longer see the Stock Exchange.
> – Just as sure as spring follows winter...
>
> [...]
>
> And if "the last enemy destroyed will be death"
> selfishness will be destroyed before.   (*CC* 62)

Revolution is necessary for destroying selfishness and restoring unity. Yet Cardenal makes it clear that a single revolution may not suffice: "the battle's already twenty thousand million years old" and will continue; "the revolution doesn't end in this world." As light and darkness alternate, new disturbances will appear, leading to new revolutions until death, the eternal "status quo," will be defeated (*CC* 63-64).

Although Cardenal employs Chinese concepts, among them 'dynamic harmony,' his philosophical vision is directed by his Christian faith: the final goal of human struggles and revolutions is the defeat of death. On the way to this ultimately Christian goal (1 Corinthians 15: 54-55), humanity will proceed in a spiral, through alternation of light and darkness, yet always progressing towards a better future:

> Lying in my bed in Managua
> I'm dropping off to sleep
>   and suddenly I ask myself:

---

[16] On the friendship between Merton and Cardenal, see Sandoval 2017.

> Where are we going? We are
> on the dark side of the earth,
> > the other side, lit up.
> Tomorrow we will be in the light
> and the others in darkness.
>
> [...]
>
> take it easy boys, we're doing fine.
> > Spinning around in black space
> wherever we're going, we're doing fine.
> And also,
> > the Revolution's doing fine.   (*CC* 88)

Cardenal perceives revolution as ultimately positive, as the way in which harmony will be restored and community revived. Although he condemns violence associated with the broken order of things, he does not criticize violence associated with revolution. For Cardenal, revolution which sets as its goal the restoration of equality and the end of suffering is the manifestation of love, for "[o]nly love is revolutionary" (*CC* 60).

Berengarten, perhaps disenchanted by the history of world revolutions, warns against the reckless actions of revolutionaries led by their ideas, no matter how noble, of truth and justice. He claims, again and again, that the goal cannot justify the means. This theme is particularly prominent in the cluster of poems associated with hexagram 49 革 (*Ge*), 'Shedding.' In the third poem in this cluster, Berengarten elevates basic human compassion and sensitivity to the needs of one's neighbor over ideology. When self-reflection is distorted by an individual's sense of his/her group's 'unique mission' combined with his/her own 'personal purity,' then "making mistakes" and creating innocent victims are unavoidable:

> In making mistakes
> and enemies, we did not
> do so languidly, but
>
> deliberately and un-
> hesitatingly cut competitors
> and opponents down.
>
> So we destroyed many
> we still loved or once had
> loved and many more we

didn't give a damn about
who happened to occupy
any position blocking

our road to our goal – *the*
Road and *the* Goal. Those
we wiped out included

unwary, innocent and
ignorant passengers. We got
good at creating victims.   ('Making mistakes and enemies,' 49/3: 395)

The poem associated with the fourth line of this hexagram continues:

While we suffered
losses keenly, believing
ourselves sole

light spreaders, […]

[…]
we built on destruction.   ('While we suffered losses,' 49/4: 396)

Building "on destruction" by means of intentional action, rather than
slowly 'mending' the cracked world through the power of the poetic
word and enabling *tikkun* and reconciliation, cannot and will not lead to
creation of a better reality. Even though such an action may be victorious,
the price of this victory, paid by all humanity, can be extremely high, and
the result achieved, disastrous: the wish to find light may result in the
most catastrophic darkness. After all, even the members of the Nazi party
believed in their noble mission and perceived themselves as revolutionaries.
Berengarten clarifies this point in the poem ironically entitled 'Hail
Victory,' associated with hexagram 58 兌 (*Dui*), 'Joying. Enjoying':
"They staged vast processions / of party-followers to smile, clap, / march,
stamp, cheer. Mystical / fervour glistened on uplifted / faces. Young and
old, this was / *their* revolution, never-before- / achieved." (58/6: 470).
Unlike Cardenal, who perceives revolution as a breakthrough to a new and
better life, Berengarten is concerned that the seeming breakthrough may
well become a breakdown, when revolutionaries proudly enjoying their
messianic role in changing the order of the world commit horrible crimes
against humanity. The poem associated with the fourth line of hexagram
43 夬 (*Guai*), 'Breaking through,' eventually asks:

Shall they be forgiven, murderous revolutionaries who *knew*
they'd change the world – yet

perpetrated atrocities?

[...]

How mourn those proclaimed
and self-proclaimed heroes and
heroines who, possessed by

childlike angelic visions of
their own inflated importance
and genius, lacked one iota

of modesty or compassion?
Without fuss or compunction,
let's tear their statues down.   ('Heroes, heroines,' 43/4: 348)

In this poem, as in many others, Berengarten reminds his readers of the
thin line separating *change* and *changing*. The action in the name of "*the
Goal*" (49/3: 395) can perhaps result in the former but not the latter.
Changing is not a 'final' state but rather a perpetual and dynamic process.
In this context, it is worth noting that for all his translations of *I Ching*
hexagram titles, Berengarten employs the gerundive '*-ing*' form, which
itself implies process rather than solid or stolid stasis. As he testifies, "In
modelling the sixty-four cluster titles, as well as the title *Changing* itself, I
have consistently deployed English words ending in '*-ing*' in order to reflect
(refract, inflect), even if only in part, the complex polysemies of Chinese
graphs that serve as hexagram names in the *I Ching*" (525). Changing,
as process, requires sensitivity, patience and, above all, listening. And like
changing, harmonizing too is not an ideal state of things to be found only
in some Biblical Paradise. Its status as a gerund itself signifies a continuously
adjusting and oscillating process between *yin* and *yang*, which slowly and
carefully can bring human life, both personal and communal, to *being-
fulfilled*. Significantly, when translating the title of hexagram 11 泰 (*Tai*),
which is interpreted as 'Peace' by Hellmut Wilhelm (25) and Richard
Lynn (205) and 'Advance' by Alfred Huang (117), Berengarten chooses
'Harmonising, Prospering.' In this process, both the *Book of Changes* and
the art of poetry – which join together in *Changing* – play a central role, as
in this poem for hexagram 48 井 (*Jing*), 'Welling, Replenishing':

Consultation
of the diagrams
is helpful
[...]

[...] *in all forms of*
measurement and modes
of harmonising.   (48/0: 384)

Although Cardenal and Berengarten view revolution in different lights, they seem to agree that there is a connection between social change and inner cultivation. For Cardenal, the quintessence of this connection is overcoming self-interest and, following the Biblical message "Love your neighbor as yourself" (Leviticus 19: 18; Mark 12: 31), reaching *union* with others. For Berengarten, guided by the *Book of Changes*, self-cultivation is the continuous transformation of the self, which allows one to experience *unity* with nature and all of humankind.

The differences between these two authors' perceptions not only reflect their cultural identities, but also affect all the focal points of their poetic and philosophical discourses. Cardenal emphasizes social justice, viewing revolution as a breakthrough. Berengarten is concerned with the dynamics of changing, emphasizing the importance of harmonizing *yin* and *yang*, and warning his readers against acting with excessive energy. What is important for him is to find 'the middle way' 中道 (*zhongdao*), as is demonstrated by repeated references to this concept in *Changing*: *zhongdao* appears as a baseline in five poems (see *CH*: 74, 82, 83, 90, 258, and also the note on 538).

For Berengarten, then, the *Book of Changes* offers a way of bringing together the deep desire for a brighter future and the understanding that changing needs to arise from within. Changing is an ongoing process, an ongoing revolution occurring first and foremost in the depth of one's heart in the reality of the present moment:

Now

is time for this same primeval
struggle while deploying subtler arts –
magnanimous vision and patient

open heart   ('Embracing the waste land,' 11/2: 90)

References

Berengarten, Richard. 2016. *Changing*. Bristol: Shearsman Books.

Cardenal, Ernesto. 1993. *Cosmic Canticle*. John Lyons (trans.). Willimantic, CT: Curbstone Press.

Cohen, Jonathan. 2009. "Introduction: *Songs of Heaven and Earth*." In Ernesto Cardenal, *Pluriverse: New and Selected Poems*. Jonathan Cohen (ed.). New York: New Directions, xi-xxii.

Cohen, Leonard. 2019. "Happens to the Heart." *Thanks for the Dance*, Columbia Records and Legacy Records.

Epstein, Helen C. 2017. "America's Secret Role in the Rwandan Genocide." *The Guardian* (12 September). Online at: https://www.theguardian.com/news/2017/sep/12/americas-secret-role-in-the-rwandan-genocide

Gwin, Peter. 2014. "Revisiting the Rwandan Genocide: How Churches Became Death Traps," *National Geographic* (2 April). Online at: https://www.nationalgeographic.com/photography/proof/2014/04/02/revisiting-the-rwandan-genocide-how-churches-became-death-traps/

Huang, Alfred. 2010. *The Complete I Ching: The Definitive Translation*. Rochester, VT: Inner Traditions.

Ivanhoe, Philip J. (trans.). 2002. The *Daodejing* 道德經 of Laozi 老子. Indianapolis, IN and Cambridge: Hackett Publishing.

Jimmerson, Ellin Sterne. 2009. "'In the Beginning – Big Bang': Violence in Ernesto Cardenal's *Cosmic Canticle*." In Hawkins Benedix, Beth (ed.). *Subverting Scriptures: Critical Reflections on the Use of the Bible*. New York: Palgrave Macmillan, 129-147.

Li, Chenyang. 2014. *The Confucian Philosophy of Harmony*. London and New York: Routledge.

Lynn, Richard John. 1994. *The Classic of Changes: A New Translation of the I Ching as Interpreted by Wang Bi*. New York and Chichester, NY: Columbia University Press.

Merton, Thomas. 1965. *The Way of Chuang Tzu*. New York: New Directions.

Ooi, Samuel Hio-Kee. 2014. *A Double Vision Hermeneutic: Interpreting a Chinese Pastor's Intersubjective Experience of* Shì *Engaging* Yìzhuàn *and Pauline Texts*. Eugene OR: Pickwick Publications.

Sandoval, Jessie (trans. and ed.). 2017. *From the Monastery to the World: The Letters of Thomas Merton and Ernesto Cardenal*. Berkeley, CA: Counterpoint.

Scholem, Gershom. 1955. *Major Trends in Jewish Mysticism*. London: Thames and Hudson.

Shaughnessy, Edward L. 2016. 'Preface' to Berengarten, *Changing*. Bristol. Shearsman Books, xiii-xiv.

Warner, Harriet. 2004. 'The Butterfly Hunter.' *The Independent* (18 July), Online
at:https://www.independent.co.uk/news/world/africa/the-butterfly-
hunter-553266.html

Wilhelm, Hellmut and Richard Wilhelm. 1995. *Understanding the I Ching: The
Wilhelm Lectures on the* Book of Changes. Princeton, NJ: Mythos.

Wilhelm, Richard. 1977 [1950]. *The I Ching or Book of Changes*, trans. into
German, and rendered into English by Cary F. Baynes. Princeton, NJ:
Princeton University Press.

OWEN LOWERY

Conflicts, Parallels and Polarities
in Richard Berengarten's *Changing*

In an essay on the composition of *Changing*, Richard Berengarten describes a project stretching over decades, which involved both "heuristic and iterative" approaches (RB 2017). *Changing* emerged as the result of the author's immersion in the *I Ching*, viewing the Chinese classic as a way of thinking about life, death, and the human relationship with universality or wholeness. Berengarten has explained that his exploration of the *I Ching* forms part of a wider relationship with "Jungian thinking and practice", including the concept of the *unus mundus*, "the holistic principle of the Self" and the *coincidentia oppositorum*. [1]

For Berengarten, the correlation of these philosophical ways of thinking incorporates *polarity*, *continuity* and *centrality*. This last factor is embodied in "the Chinese graph 中 *zhong*", which

> [...] possibly develops from the image of an arrow going through the centre of something (bull's-eye?). The graph is used to mean *centre*, *inside*, *middle*, etc, and also appears in the word for China itself as the 'central kingdom', as well as in phrases for the 'central way' of Daoism and the principles in Chinese medicine." (RB, email, Oct 30, 2017)

Clearly, this orientation towards centrality also implies a belief in the importance of *balance* and *wholeness*, both of which are essential to Chinese medicine. This way of thinking is reflected in certain bidirectional aspects of the Chinese language itself, for example:

---

[1] These ideas are fundamental to Jung and the terms occur frequently in his writings. See especially *Mysterium Conjunctionis*: 457-553. Jung derived the term *coincidentia oppositorum* ['conjunction of opposites'] from the philosopher Nicholas of Cusa, '*De Docta Ignorantia*' (1440).

One of the unusual features of the Chinese language is that verbs of communication were originally bidirectional. 'Buy' and 'sell' were both written with the same word and may even have been pronounced the same, as were also 'give' and 'take', 'explain' and 'understand,' 'offer' and 'enjoy,' and countless other such words. Still today in modern Chinese 'lend' and 'borrow' are expressed with the same word, the direction of the transaction determining its sense. (Shaughnessy x)

This essay will explore some of these key motifs in *Changing* by pinpointing their occurrences in several clusters of poems, and correlating them.

❧

Consistent with these emphases on balance, continuity and energetic flow is the equilibrium of the first poem that emerged in Berengarten's creative encounter with the *I Ching*, '*Two lakes, joined*' (58/0: 464). He wrote this short piece immediately following an *I Ching* divination on August 30, 1984 (524). Berengarten clarifies that the poem is a response to hexagram 58, formed from the doubling of the trigram *Dui* (☱), and focuses on the visual suggestivity of the trigram itself:

> This trigram's form could even be said to visually suggest a cross-sectional diagram of water in a vessel, if the single broken yin line above is taken to indicate either a body of water itself or two opposing banks, firmly held by the two supporting yang lines, indicating a solid container beneath. (RB 2017)

What is more, this patterning also suggests further balances between polarities, which connects '*Two lakes, joined*' with major themes in many of Berengarten's works. Masculinity and femininity, life and death, conflict and peace, speech and silence, and individuality and universality – these are juxtaposed and balanced throughout *Changing*. And this set of polarities, in turn, reflects his interests in Daoism and Jungian philosophy.

One example is the sequence entitled 'Following', which was first published in the daring and challenging *Book With No Back Cover*. Commenting on the poem 'The Nonplussed Pleasures of Love' as it appeared in that book (RB 2006: 16), Tan Chee Lay notes the "interdependence of I/you, life/death, and human/creature" and the degree to which "the movement of time is not viewed as a one-way flow from the past to the future" (Tan 269). This observation prompts Tan to consider continuity in the poem, which we can also relate to the Jungian concept of 'synchronicity', understood as "meaningful coincidence [...] a falling together in time, a kind of simultaneity" (Jung, *CW* 8, para 840). Indeed, Tan echoes Berengarten's own observations, quoted above:

> [A] philosophical connotation of the interdependence of life and death in Berengarten's poetry is reminiscent of the Buddhist perception that life and death constitute but one continuous cycle (and hence the two conditions are not mutually exclusive but interdependent). And this mutual I/you reliance is also parallel to the Taoist understanding of Yin and Yang. (Tan 270)

Tan goes on to points out that the two polarities of *yin* and *yang* do not simply co-exist but interact in mutual dependency:

> And this mutual I/you reliance is also parallel to the Taoist understanding of Yin and Yang – in every Yin (black), Yang (white) exists, and vice versa, as illustrated by the white/black dot in the larger portion of black/white respectively in the Taoist *Taiji tu* (literally, 'Diagram of the Supreme Ultimate'). (*ibid.* 270)

This pattern of relationships is reflected in the statement-poem of the mini-sequence 'Joying, Enjoying', where the very existence of the two lakes relies on their continuing contact:

> *When two lakes join*
> *together they*
> *do not dry up.*   (58/0: 464)

Moreover, the two entities are parts of a single totality, each incomplete without the influence of the other:

> *One draws the other*
> *through constant*
> *self-replenishing.*   (*ibid.*)

Equilibrium is achieved in formal terms through the final stanza's repetition of the trope "two lakes, joined" which is echoed from the poem's first line. And since the hexagram on which this poem is based embodies what Berengarten refers to as 'Joying, Enjoying' (58: 463), it is apparent that balance, equilibrium and connectivity are to be celebrated. They are the constituents of "Joyousness" itself (58/1: 464). We should note, however, that Berengarten admits:

I wrote the first short poem that eventually became part of *Changing*, but with no thought of it leading anywhere other than to its own quick completion.   (RB 2017)

While this statement suggests that thematic continuity in *Changing* is not a given, the underlying presence of the *I Ching* is pervasive, despite the variations in meaning and association between different hexagrams and Berengarten's interpretations of them.

ↁↂ

These variations are plentiful, however, which in itself reflects the all-encompassing nature of the *I Ching*. In the 450 poems *of Changing*, each of the sixty-four hexagrams inspires one 'statement-poem', followed by six 'response-poems', which in turn explore aspects of both the hexagram and the 'statement'. This organisation lends itself to more unfolding or proliferation of the type of correspondences that occur between the elements of '*Two Lakes, joined*'.

Similarly, the opening 'statement-poem' of the whole book, '*Heaven*' finds its inspiration in the hexagram 'Initiating', which in turn generates binary pairs like "heaven over heaven" and "heaven under heaven". Also represented in the base-line to this poem are Chinese characters, which are translated as *sublime, accomplish, further*, and *persevere* – a grouping of four that itself suggests equilibrium. The poem begins with an expression of balance, suggesting, perhaps, that in the beginning there was not simply light, but equilibrium too: that is, a coexistence of polarities and a mutual dependence of forces. In this respect, similarity between '*Heaven*', and 'Joying, Enjoying' is clear from the outset:

> *Heaven over heavens*
> *heaven under heavens*
> *when and where do*
>
> *you ever stop?*   (1/0: 4)

This opening poem in itself, I suggest, contains the implication that this perfect balance is unending and self-replenishing, as the two polarities nurture one another, again echoing "the Derwent" and "the Ladybower" of '*Two Lakes, joined*'. Furthermore, '*Heaven*' addresses polarities such as beginning and finality, and individuality and universality, which in turn generate further contrasting pairs. Since the individual is part of the macrocosm, *"mind can't conceive"* the exact nature of the universe itself, with its complex of oppositions, antagonisms and contradictions, such as *"blazing blackness"*, *"white dark"*, *"black brilliance"* and *"endlessness in beginninglessness"*.

Indeed, these themes recur throughout Berengarten's poetry. Stefano Maria Casella refers to 'Tree' as a means of communication between the "hugest regions of the skies" and "the smallest and humblest aspects of nature" (Casella 2016: 170). Tessa Ransford identifies "a shamanistic experience of at-one-ment with nature" in 'Croft Woods' (Ransford 2016: 54). In the final tercet of *'Heaven'*, these connections are resolved in lexical and structural 'entanglement' (see Barad 2007: 71):

> *nothing everything*
> *destroying generating*
> *everything nothing*   (1/0: 4)

By entangling and then reversing the phrases "nothing everything" and "everything nothing", the alternation of the first and final lines here reflects the relationship between the polarities within the 'Supreme Ultimate' itself, and does so in a way that corresponds with the concept of wholeness, which embeds both the individual and the universal. For the quantum physicist David Bohm, the distinction between thinking in terms, on the one hand, of separateness, division and fragmentation (which he refers to as the Cartesian order) and, on the other, of wholeness, universality, flow and continuity, typifies the differing approaches of Western and Eastern philosophies (Bohm xi). Throughout *Changing*, the latter approach is particularly evident, as in the response to the *I Ching's* very first hexagram. Indeed, Berengarten dedicates the third poem in this suite to David Bohm (1/3: 7; and see 535).

Continuity and correspondence are equally apparent in the relationship between the initial statement-poem, *'Heaven'*, and further reflections on this theme. Thus, in the first of the response-poems, 'Bending Light' (1/1: 5), universal forces are represented by "stars", that "pull and bend / light like archers". Antagonisms are created, or reflected, along with empathic connections, between the first-person speaker, and a "nocturnal cat'" both equally "[p]ushed / and pulled by gravities", and both confronted by the same immensities: "skies" [...] that 'eventually whirl / into nothings, into holes of / sheer nothing". The second response-poem, 'What Zhang Zai thought' (involves a similar relationship between the individual and the universal, as the eleventh century philosopher and astronomer Zhang Zai becomes a part of the world around him, and

> quietly forgot about time and
> mortality and himself awhile
>
> as he soaked himself into
> and through things. (1/2: 6)

In the next poem, 'Cohering, inhering', we find similar issues to those confronted by Zhang Zai. These are now faced by an implicit first-person speaker, perhaps the poet in the act of creating and organising this book. The main preoccupation here is how to

> keep everything
> (every thing) in mind
> in its entirety, and
>
> still focus entire on
> *this*? (1/3: 7)

The problem remains one of understanding: of accepting that one is unable to perceive or comprehend wholeness because one is a mere part of it, while yet finding a sense of acceptance in the recognition that this balance only becomes possible once harmony has been achieved between the individual and the universe:

> [...] may the same quiet
>
> patient appetite for
> order cohere, inhere
> in this, in here. (*ibid.*)

Clearly, this kind of recognition also encompasses our relationship with language, words and communication, and demands that we award due consideration to every word that we use, as in Berengarten's playful punning on 'inhere', and 'in here'.

In the response-poem 'Oscillating', the connection with Bohm's conceptualisation of wholeness, and of flow rather than fragmentation, is made more explicit still, with Berengarten defining an essential aspect of the universal:

This constant flow

between *notness*
and *isness* becomes and is
all ways key.   (1/4: 8)

Then, what we understand and come to know through our relationship with the universal, is effectively described in 'Absolute', as is the continuity between end and beginning:

Absolute beginning
and final end of all
ends and beginnings.   (1/5: 9)

The closing image of an egg here represents a state that is "incessantly changing / yet changeless", a condition that is not merely embryonic and in transformation but also intact and 'rounded' in itself.

That this affinity between the individual and the universe can lead to perturbation, as well as a sense of harmony and balance, emerges in the next poem in this mini-sequence, 'Light fills and fails'. Here, repetitions inherent in the villanelle form contribute to anxiety, as the speaker is unable to separate his own small identity from the "swirling", all-encompassing passage of time, and everything that it brings and takes with it:

Terror has been unleashed. We're easy prey
to swirling hordes of phantoms day concealed.
Light fills and fails. It hovers, spills away.
How foil this overflow? How stall the day?   (1/6: 10)

The final poem in this sequence, 'Supreme Ultimate' (1/7: 11), returns to the structure of six tercets that is used for all but two of the poems in *Changing*. With this re-established pattern, order returns, and this too is one of entanglement and continuity. Here, the theme of "Endless beginningless / heaven" recurs as infinite "dimensions / [...] replicating, / self-swallowing / interbreeding", as both the origin and the end of "unemptiable fecund / sources overspilling".

☙

What happens, though, when this wholeness fails or fractures? How is this possibility presented in *The Classic of Changes* and in Berengarten's

136

Changing? For the set of poems 'Peeling' (23: 183-190), we find that there is considerable interest in the past, alongside everything that retrospection can reveal, not only about the human condition in general, but also about the human capacity for cruelty, conflict and atrocity. The statement-poem, '*Concerning archaeology*' (23/0: 184) describes the process of uncovering or unpeeling layers of time, which reveals evidence of an "*old battlefield*", "*a cat's jaw*", and a fossilised "*nautiloid, black / limestone, / 400 million years old*". However, it is not so much these details that are significant, as what we make of them:

> [...] *Meanings*
>
> *that moan in dross*
> *and memorabilia demand*
> *magnified attention.*   (*ibid.*)

Disturb the surface of time, and look behind the order and balance of the 'Supreme Ultimate', and the memory of our inhumanity resurfaces, including in the opening response-poem to hexagram 23, 'We thank our Führer'. The poem, without embellishment, and recorded as reportage, describes the treatment of Jewish people in Vienna in "March 1938", the manner in which "middle class specimens" were made to "clean streets / and scrub pavements decorated with / Schuschnigg posters and slogans", while being beaten and kicked, "especially / older and feebler ones if they stumbled or collapsed". The understated tone underlines deliberate cruelty:

> [...] The Jews were forced
>
> to work with bare hands onto which
> acid was poured. Meanwhile Viennese
> citizens stood by jeering and laughing
>
> and occasionally breaking into roars
> of delight [...]   (23/1: 185)

The words of these Viennese citizens haunt us through time, upsetting any sense of balance, reminding us that the potential for inhumanity and atrocity remains, however much the passage of time may seemingly 'protect' us from such events:

> [...] "Work for the
> Jews at last! At last work for the Jews!

We thank our Führer for finding
work for the Jews. We thank our dear
Führer for finding work for the Jews."   (*ibid.*)

In the second response-poem, 'The forensic archaeologist's testimony'
(23/2: 186), another atrocity is recorded, this time "in the area of Nyamata Church", where "atrocity was so widespread" that "gang-rape" was
"systematically / organised" and "men with / HIV waited their turn till
last." Even more disturbing is the detail of "a particularly large coffin"
containing the body of a woman, who "had been raped / with a sapling"
and "buried [...] with the tree inside her".

Similarly, in the third response-poem, 'After the massacre', the past
harbours dark and uncomfortable truths: in this case that of another
murdered young woman, symbolic of countless other victims, and
represented only by her jewellery:

>   [...] A silver chain
>
> surrounded several
> joined vertebrae, reported the
> bespectacled young forensic
>
> archaeologist, wearing
> a blue *hamsah* medallion
> around her slender throat.   (23/3: 187)

In the next poem of this sequence, 'Language Palazzo', communication
and civilisation have been lost, adding to the sense that our values are
fragile and our equilibrium is dynamic rather than static:

> The Language Palazzo
> caved in. Meanings
> collapsed to rubble.
>
> In the Hall of Great
> Welcomes, monuments
> crashed and splintered.
>
> A precious library
> housed on the *piano nobile*
> tumbled into vaults.   (23/4: 188)

As Norman Jope suggests, the themes of death and "entropy" are linked in Berengarten's books, including *The Blue Butterfly* and *Under Balkan Light* (Jope 7). He proposes that there is a "many-faceted dialogue" between Berengarten and 'Master Death' (*ibid.* 21). His implication is that Berengarten is just as aware of chaos and disorder as he is of order and wholeness. Yet perhaps this involvement too can be understood in terms of the 'Supreme Ultimate', provided that we accept that chaos and disorder are part of its dynamic equilibrium. If this is so, it may be that balance can – or will ultimately – restore itself, despite the horrifying human potential for conflict, war and atrocity.

This is the implication of response-poems 5 and 6 in the 'Peeling' suite. In the former, despite the cynicism of a "prime-minister" creating a photo opportunity out of a meeting with a "two year / old child" in a "refugee camp", the obvious crisis has nevertheless resulted in regrowth, for the birth of this child points clearly towards survival and perhaps even healing. And in the final poem in this group, the hope of restoring meaningful communication is affirmed, as well as the will to bring it about:

Our job is to foster and grow

(a) coherent language, little
by little, in patience, in respect.   (23/6: 190)

This is the means by which it becomes possible to "reaffirm the dignity / of the dead", and "*through* words", to express what had been "unsaid, unsayable" and so to "mend and change the real, / regrow and rebuild hope."

☙

Even the past, then, is mobile rather than static, fluid rather than constant. For it is part of the same continuum as the present and the future, and hence can also be interacted with, reinterpreted and reassembled. Thus, the overriding nature of universality is a dynamic equilibrium, which allows for change to occur within the wholeness to and in which we all belong.

The significance of change is reinforced at several points in *Changing*, including poems that relate to the second hexagram, 'Responding, Corresponding' (2: 13-22). Two-way influence is again in evidence here, for example between that of the earth, as a "*crusted ball of lava balanced on / one invisible axis*" and (2/0: 14) the "immeasurable law" of "Change" itself (2/3: 17), according to which "everything every- / where is constantly / on the move", as in

> [...] [t]his light playing
> swaying, straying, spraying
> across these
>
> clouded hills.   ('A yellow lower garment', 2/5: 19)

Indeed, life itself is conceived of as part of this perpetual flux, as in the sequence of poems based on and inspired by the third hexagram, 'Beginning' (3: 23-30). Here, perception of small details allows the poet to recognise and discover, as if for the first time, the miraculous process in which life cracks open the seed or seedling which *"opens, pushes up and down, / down and up"* *"powered"* by

> *nano-changes by latent pre-*
> *patterned responses to chemical-*
> *physical signals and triggers.*   ('Seed, seeding, seedling', 3/0: 24)

Understanding life as part of a bi-directional or even multivalent equilibrium facilitates *"epiphany"* and enables us to accept and rejoice in the *"extraordinary miraculousness / of* [...] *this thisness, / this entire matter of living"*. However, the same fluidity also manifests itself as the antagonistic relationship between life and death, closure and beginning, in the third-person portrayal of a woman torn between grief and hope at the end of the old year, and the possibilities offered by the new one. On the one hand, the "deaths of two friends / haunt her", while, on the other, the New Year is likened to

> wind on a Japanese
>
> mountain, a market,
> in a warm country, a new
> world I don't recognise.   ('January-end already', 3/1: 25)

Among the possibilities offered by such a broadened perspective, and the belief in life as part of a universal continuum, is that of connectivity, such as the moment when a woman phones her mother from her car, on her mother's birthday, to tell her that she has just found out that she is pregnant:

> I'm pregnant,
> she told her mother on
> her mother's birthday.   ('Hearing the other smiling', 3/2: 26)

The result is shared emotion through the connection between the two women, their maternal bond:

> In and through
> the silence at each
>
> end of the line
> both women heard
> the other smiling.   (*ibid.*)

So strong is this connection that we can even associate it with Jung's theory of synchronicity.[2] At a quantum mechanical level, synchronicity makes it possible for connections to occur between what may at first appear to be entirely separate entities and phenomena:

> In this flow, mind and matter are not separate substances. Rather, they are different aspects of one whole and unbroken movement. In this way, we are able to look on all aspects of existence as not divided from each other. (Bohm 13)

In this instance, Bohm envisages "universal flux", the connective principle of wholeness, as a "flowing stream" (*ibid.* 61-62), a conduit between entities, with these entities acting as "an ever-changing pattern of water vortices, ripples, waves, splashes, etc., which evidently have no independent existence as such (*ibid.* 62).

☙

That we are also part of this continuum, and that the whole experience of *Changing* is too, becomes apparent in the final suite, 'Before crossing over' (64: 511-518). Having made our journey so far with the poem's multiple voices, at this point, right at the end of the book, we find ourselves being prepared and preparing for a *new* experience-rather than for any simple or obvious act of 'closure'. In the statement-poem ('*Fire-tail*',

---

[2] "In the course of his research into the collective unconscious, he [Jung] had noted numerous occasions when he had experienced coincidences

> [...] so meaningfully connected that their 'chance' occurrence would represent a degree of improbability that would have to be expressed by an astronomical figure.

They must consequently, he believed, 'be connected through another principle, namely the contingency of events: the principle of 'synchronicity'." (Inglis 4)

64/0: 512), we are presented with a fox on a riverbank, which is "*not really ready to cross such a / broad flooded river*". The creature is considering "*taking a fat reckless / plunge*", but oscillates between decision and indecision. The final tercets advise caution, combined with the assurance that "*there'll be more chances later*". But the clear warning, "*No / harm done. Not yet*" goes unheeded, for in the sequel response-poem, 'Fox (again) on river-bank', the wrong decision is taken:

> [...] now
> you've really gone and done it,
> taken your big brave plunge,
>
> got ducked under water
> way over your head.   (64/1: 513)

The question is: has the fox – and have we – learnt from the experience? Are we now able to "think through seasons / and tides, get wise to things" (*ibid.*)? If so, we may be in a position to understand the difference between the "rat-light" of a torch, shedding light on "angles not glimpsed in centuries", and real "seeing!" as explained in the second response-poem (64/2: 514).

The third response-poem, 'Eyes open forward' underlines the importance of wisdom through true vision: so that we are prepared, like the implicit first-person speaker of this poem, to "keep / eyes open forward, / peripheries sharpened",

> alert for whatever, for /
> the next, and afternext,
> for the unexpected.   (64/3: 515)

This rediscovered simplicity leaves us "like children / about to cross The Road, / looking both ways, ready" (64/4: 516). The personal address in the penultimate tercet, 'Say, old friend", may perhaps be read as an invitation, partly to the reader and partly to any one of those poetic voices who have particularly influenced Berengarten, and partly to anyone who has made the same journey. And if we too are able to follow a similar path, our prize may well be the 'Alchymical Perle', that is, in achieving balance between simplicity and complexity, both of which

> [...] keep

opening out into each
other, interpenetrating,
blurring, irradiating.   (64/5: 5I7)

Only in the final response-poem, 'Brightness diffusing' (64/6: 518), do we
seem to achieve a relative point of calm and perhaps, even, epiphany. Here
the landscape is decidedly Mediterranean, and probably Greek, implicitly
recalling Seferis. This setting is established in almost Homeric images:
"Sunlight bronzes sea"; the season is "Mid-October, still warm", and "[o]
live leaves' undersides / [...] flicker / across sandy hill groves". Completion
and fulfilment are further suggested by images such as "harvested",
"sunflower heads", the light on "oleanders and cypresses", and the swelling
of "[p]rickly pears". Here, "[i]t all coheres, no question, / as do these notes
of mine." In this scene we find a balance, a universality, to which all things
belong, including the poet's own voice or voices, the voices of the past, for
example that of Seferis, and ourselves as readers – so much so that we have
time for communion, contemplation and companionship, as we take up
the final invitation:

Come sit at the table
out here on the balcony.
Drink a glass of wine.   (*ibid.*)

REFERENCES

Barad, Karen. 2007. *Meeting the Universe Halfway: Quantum Physics and the
    Entanglement of Matter and Meaning*. Durham, NC: Duke University Press.
Berengarten, Richard. 2011. *For the Living: Selected Longer Poems 1965–2000*.
    Exeter: Shearsman Books.
———. 2016. *Changing*. Bristol: Shearsman Books.
———. 2017. 'Divination, Derivation and Tinkering (some notes on the
    composition of *Changing*). (Unpublished).
Bohm, David. 2002. *Wholeness and the Implicate Order*. London and New York:
    Routledge Classics.
Burns, Richard. 2003. *Book With No Back Cover*. London: David Paul.
Casella, Stefano Maria. 2016. 'Roots and Rings: Under the Shade of Richard
    Berengarten's "Tree"'. In Jope *et al.* (eds.). 2016. *The Companion to Richard
    Berengarten*. Bristol: Shearsman Books, 164-174.

Inglis, Brian. 1990. *Coincidence: A Matter of Chance – or Synchronicity?* London: Hutchinson.

Jope, Norman. 2016. 'Introduction: Everywhere Centre'. In Jope *et al.* (eds.). 2016. *The Companion to Richard Berengarten*. Bristol: Shearsman Books, 1-8.

Jope, Norman, Derrick, Paul Scott, and Byfield, Catherine (eds.). 2016. *The Companion to Richard Berengarten*. Bristol: Shearsman Books.

Jung, C. G. 2014 [1955]. 'Synchronicity: An Acausal Connecting Principle'. In *The Structure and Dynamics of the Psyche, Collected Works*, vol. 8. London: Routledge and Kegan Paul, 417-552.

——— . 1991 [1963]. *Mysterium Coniunctionis: An Inquiry into the Separation and Synthesis of Psychic Opposites, Collected Works*, vol. 14. London: Routledge and Kegan Paul.

Ransford, Tessa. 2016. 'Love's Integument: The Poetry of Richard Berengarten'. In Jope *et al.* (eds.). 2016. *The Companion to Richard Berengarten*. Bristol: Shearsman Books, 48-58.

Shaughnessy, Edward B. 2016. 'Preface'. In Berengarten, Richard, *Changing*. Bristol: Shearsman Books, ix-xix.

Tan, Chee Lay. 2016. 'Cross-cultural Numerology and Translingual Poetics: Chinese Influences on the Poetry of Richard Berengarten'. In Jope (eds.). 2016. *The Companion to Richard Berengarten*. Bristol: Shearsman Books, 266-282.

ELEANOR GOODMAN

Changing in the Political
and Domestic Spheres

What should one make of the *I Ching*, that book that announces its own transient and molting nature in its very name, the *Book of Changes*? Evidently, it is a book intended for divination, whether by means of coins, yarrow stalks, or bibliomancy. It is also a representation of various states of being in the world, from the micro to the macro, from grand metaphysical hierarchies to social and political relationships, to how *qi*, or roughly speaking, energy, resides in and flows through the body to affect the mood, attitudes, and actions of an individual. What is more, it is a book of advice, on how to navigate the world and relate to other people, institutions, and situations. One's appreciation of the book and one's 'use' for it change over time, depending on need and interest. And since its function and purpose vary according to the needs of the person consulting it, it might be said to be self-transforming. It is not a book merely to be read, but to be lived.

Richard Berengarten has a long and complex relationship with the *Yijing* – or the *I Ching*, as it is romanized in the most famous Western translation and commentary by Richard Wilhelm (into German) and C. F. Baynes (into English from that German). Berengarten also uses the Wade-Giles transliteration for the title:

> I first came across the *I Ching* in 1962, when I was a nineteen-year-old undergraduate studying English at Cambridge: that is, just over fifty-four years ago at the time of writing this. It has fascinated me ever since and has constantly pulled me back into it. Like many others in my generation, I began to consult the book for divination and intermittently kept up the practice for many years [...].
>
> The *I Ching* operates transversally to sequential linearity. It cuts across both logical and narrative modes, intersecting them by applying a mode of thinking and perception – and hence also, by invoking a way of being – that is irreducibly synthetic, correlative, resonant, and poetic. (*CH,* "Postscript": 523)

Although *Changing* is conceived as "a composite poem made up of many small poems" (521), given the considerable span of time and the obvious commitment that have gone into its making, it also represents a way of living – and living with – the *I Ching*. Indeed, *Changing* is closely patterned on the structure of the Chinese classic. It provides a poem for every change-line in each of the sixty-four hexagrams, along with a subtitular referential gloss at the bottom of each page, and what Berengarten calls a 'head-poem,' which serves to introduce the flavor of the following six poems belonging to that hexagram. These head-poems range from the casual, even chatty tone of "*On a slow train between Cambridge and King's Cross*" (9/0: 72) to the more formal "*Consultation of the diagrams*" (48/0: 384) and the more exotic-leaning "Things, brimming" (55/0: 440). This very wide range of mode, tone, and diction is one of the book's many strengths.

Although Berengarten clarifies that *Changing* is a poetic homage to the *I Ching* and not "a translation or a commentary" ("Postscript": 521), it is interesting and illuminating to compare his renderings of hexagram-titles with the English texts of leading translators. "On a slow train between Cambridge and King's Cross" belongs to hexagram 9, whose title Berengarten designates as "Small Blessing, Possessing." Here, Wilhelm/ Baynes has "The Taming Power of the Small" and David Hinton, in his recent translation, has "Delicate Nurturing." As this variation shows, mutability and the potential for diverse interpretations are both inherent in the ancient Chinese.

As for *Changing* itself, the book also reflects the multifariousness of life as lived. It is exalted and exhausting, dirty and graceful, far-reaching and familial. The best of Berengarten's poems – and there are many excellent examples – pulse with living energy and lived experience. Take, for example, "Wild strawberry":

Cling to the rock
as if you were the root
of a wild strawberry

clasping tendrils
among crannies in
the cliff-face

over lake-waters,
and hang your leaves
direct from heaven

in a nook where
daylight and darkness
both nourish you

and no huge winds
reach, where you've all
time and space

to grow and lead
your own sweet red
wild strawberry life.   (27/5: 221)

This poem corresponds to the fifth changing line in the hexagram
"Nourishing," which Wilhelm/Baynes explicates as "Turning away from
the path. / To remain persevering brings good fortune. / One should not
cross the great water" (Wilhelm/Baynes 110). To persevere, to cling to the
rocks and nooks that support and protect, to be receptive and in some ways
passive (this is a *yin* line, in the position in the hexagram that corresponds to
speech and self-promotion) in order to prepare the groundwork for further
growth and understanding – the reader is led not just to that conclusion
but also to that sensation by the cautious, considered language of the
poem. Many of the poems in this book admirably mirror the emotional
movement of the changing line, which is no easy feat.

The last lines of "Wild strawberry" are reminiscent of "The Summer
Day" by Mary Oliver, who expresses a similar urge, as she negotiates the
shifting relationships between nature, the human heart, and the ineffable
sense of spirituality inherent in the world:

I don't know exactly what a prayer is.
I do know how to pay attention, how to fall down
into the grass, how to kneel in the grass,
how to be idle and blessed, how to stroll through the fields
which is what I have been doing all day.
Tell me, what else should I have done?
Doesn't everything die at last, and too soon?
Tell me, what is it you plan to do
With your one wild and precious life?   (Oliver 60)

In the *I Ching*, however, the concern is not with 'prayer' (to a deity), but
with the act of attention itself, which implicitly includes an attentiveness
to the forces that govern the world and the self. One main divergence
here is that Oliver is all too human in the midst of the summer day:

she is an observer set apart from the natural scene that she also inhabits. Berengarten, by contrast, takes a step closer to the objects of observation themselves: while his "you" is not exactly a strawberry plant ("Cling to the rock / *as if* you were the root / of a wild strawberry"), his poem hangs on the simile of behaving like one. The poet urges the addressee – who is perhaps himself – to behave in the natural world not from the remove of human distance, but rather as an integral part of it. Even so, irrespective of differences in their angles of approach, Oliver and Berengarten both emphasize the individuality of any given existence, whether it be that of a human or of a "wild strawberry."[1]

In the context of the heavy interpretative structure and Confucian overlay of the *I Ching* in its current incarnation, the sense of individuality and even uniqueness carried by each divination presents a fascinating puzzle. One of its abiding mysteries is how it appears to speak to specific circumstances, and to a specific reader or diviner, at any given moment across history, and within the span of an individual lifetime. Yet the hexagrams themselves, in a literal sense, are the same for everyone: the same pages present to each reader, or to the same reader upon each opening. The same advice is given. But inherent in the structure of the book is the opportunity for many different 'unfoldings,' which can be followed through the changing lines. This gives each instance of divination a sometimes-disconcerting specificity, and this quality is mirrored in the often deeply personal – and deeply touching – poems found in *Changing*.

Perhaps because of this sense that it speaks to each person individually and directly, the *I Ching* sometimes gives the diviner the feeling of consulting a wise sage. In *Changing,* Berengarten at times exhibits a similar authority and authenticity. Some poems read uncannily like a description of the time in which we now find ourselves living. Take the poem in this section of "Collusion" from the hexagram "Stagnating, Decaying":

Rottenness spread
so normally, so spiced
and glazed with reason

most believed it inevitable
and universal. Few noticed
this was no product of

---

[1] *Editors' note*: For a separate yet interestingly coincidental comparison between Berengarten and Oliver, see Paul Scott Derrick's essay above (51-68).

'wild' nature, or natural
'law', but of cultivated
controlled operations

but profiteers and complicit
acolytes.   (12/2: 98)

Clearly, this poem could fit *any* period, from the intrigues of the Warring
States period in China to the current political tension in the world today.
Yet the language is precise, impersonal, and this emphasizes one of the
insights found in Berengarten's work, namely that such grand themes as
these necessarily dissolve into the intensely personal.

For the same hexagram, the final poem of this set, entitled "A
Sacrifice," reads:

What fact or factor
determines who'll be a hero
with the blind courage

to lead, by design
or impulse, and against
all odds of chance, who'll

be ready to follow him
and who'll, rather, stay at home,
be swallowed up by ruin,

victimise others, murder
by rote or proxy, flee into
exile, fatten and get rich,

mine chaos, exploit it –
and who'll go down giving
his own life, own death,

to save another, a stranger, like
Maksymilian Kolbe, Auschwitz,
1941, for Franz Gajowniczek.   (12/6: 102)

This masterful movement from grand concepts such as 'hero' and 'courage'
down to the horrifying and painful detail – of the Polish friar Maksymilian
Kolbe, and the prisoner at Auschwitz Franz Gajowniczek – speaks to the
control that is maintained throughout this book. The facts are given plainly,
without explanation, and yet it is very clear what is being referenced and

what the emotional and political stakes are. Further, this poem is a reminder of how vitally important it is that each one of us remember the moral significance of what to those with little sense of history might seem distant actions and decisions, and even far-fetched and incomprehensible ones. Here, when all is said and done, what is revealed consists of no more than the names of two men at the site of a mass atrocity: the one active, the other passive, the former sacrificing himself, the latter being allowed to live on.

References to the Second World War and the Holocaust appear throughout *Changing*. Berengarten's applications of the *I Ching* to modern events and interpretations in the light of modern concerns and beliefs point bot only to the remarkable timelessness of the *I Ching* but also to the timeliness of *Changing*, as the world seems to begin to forget the lessons of violence it managed to learn only tenuously over the course of the twentieth century.

"A sacrifice" also reminds us of an issue that is repeatedly explored in the *I Ching*. Since rulers make decisions, how and on what grounds should leaders make correct decisions, bearing in mind that these will inevitably affect individuals, families, and communities? Indeed, the intense *personal* moral responsibility that this question implies is one of the *I Ching's* fundamental underpinnings: how does one properly deal with the possession of power, with respect to one's intimates, as well as with one's colleagues and fellow community members?

❧

There are also moments of true intimacy in the book, where Berengarten turns his gaze more directly toward the beloved. One beautiful instance occurs in the set for hexagram 22, "Grace Adorning," in the poem "Concerning light and her," which features lines like these:

> She gathers light
> in her arms and on
> her shoulders, in
>
> her belly and
> breasts, and over her
> forehead and eyes.
>
> Wrists, knuckles,
> thumbs and fingers
> of light entwine her.   (22/3: 179)

150

In Wilhelm/Baynes the change-line, which is at play in this poem, is translated as: "Nine in the third place means: / Graceful and moist. / Constant perseverance brings good fortune" (92). The "moist" here means watery, a surface that can reflect light easily. Indeed, in David Hinton's beautiful translation, he translates the same moving line as: "In such elegance, such glistening, good fortune is inexhaustible, is indeed unending" (Hinton 45). The glistening is here in Berengarten's poem as well, in the light that gathers on and adorns the woman, who is presumably a lover, given how closely she is observed. The delicious specificity – belly, breasts, forehead, eyes – point the gaze, while the "wrist, knuckles, thumbs, and fingers" are not human hands as we might at first imagine, but emanations of light that envelop the figure. The poetic touch here is sensual and delicate, both powerfully direct and figurative.

While much of *Changing* addresses the wider sphere, perhaps because the *I Ching* itself appears primarily to address the political and larger social worlds, several sections do delve into the 'dailyness' of life. The set of poems addressing hexagram 37, under the title "Dwelling, Householding" is one such moment, where the reader's attention is focused down onto and into the 'ordinary', especially in "Lara's garden in August":

> Drove Arijana through Friday
> rush-hour to stay the weekend
> with Lara in her new house
>
> in St. Albans. Jelena arrived
> from work and we sat and drank
> elderflower cordial and
>
> chilled white wine in the long
> garden and looked at old photos
> and chattered about
>
> family things, nothing in
> particular. [...]   (37/1: 297)

"Pleasures so / simple they're almost / incommunicable" – is this not the essence of family, of the "nothing in / particular" that constitutes our everything? The skilful line-breaks and confidence in the breath of the poem tune us in to the rhythm of our own lives, as well as to the resonant accuracy of the poet's phrasing.

☙

Other lessons earned hard over the last century include those involving the roles women can and should be able to play in the world. In the Wilhelm/Baynes translation of the "Dwelling, Householding" hexagram, rendered as "The Family" in their earlier text, Confucian overtones, combined with an overriding assumption of patriarchal inheritance, cannot be ignored (145):

Six in the second place means:
She should not follow her whims.
She must attend within to the food.
Perseverance brings good fortune.

The wife must always be guided by the will of the master of the house, be he father, husband, or grown son. Her place is within the house. There, without having to look for them, she has great and important duties. She must attend to the nourishment of her family and to the food for the sacrifice.

Hinton avoids gendering the line, saying merely: "Don't set out imagining distant destinations. Stay home, and you can push through to completion, for the nourishment of the abiding center is inexhaustible in bringing forth good fortune" (Hinton 37). Similarly, in his poem for this line, entitled "Ownership," Berengarten resists foisting traditional household roles onto his readers:

The house you rent
or own owns you.
You are guest

of its walled interior
that welcomed you when
you were a stranger.

The conifer's hundreds
of thousands of days
and the millions

of nights slept by stone
that were poured
into the hard

building of wall,
pillar, lintel, roof
antedate and anticipate

you, present
occupier, sitting
here at your ease.   (37/2: 298)

Rather than reinforcing a patriarchal view of the family, here Berengarten elegantly turns the emphasis toward the "present occupier," who is at home and comfortable. This kind of reticence is essential to *Changing* as a whole: it involves neither a wholesale acceptance of the *I Ching* nor any kind of simple rewriting of it, with all its historical blemishes and limitations. In any case, the 'standard' Chinese version of the *I Ching* that has come down to us is ambiguous in many cases as to gender and specific interpretation – which is, of course, part of its usefulness as a divinatory text. What is more, Berengarten's poem appears not to insist upon a 'right' course of action, but rather to delineate a way of being. The householder is beholden to his or her property: it must be cared for and consistently maintained, and the relationship is symbiotic rather than unidirectional. The house offers the shelter necessary for survival, but it itself must be lived in if it is to become a living, lived-in home. The key is not who does the cooking and cleaning, but that the house's occupants are there, in it and protected by it, at their ease, in its space, with each other.

Berengarten writes evocatively of unity and human connectedness, but just as strongly of dissolution: twin themes that are arguably the basis of the *I Ching* itself. He does so often with a remarkable musicality, as in "Past zenith," for the ominous sixth change-line of hexagram 11 泰, which he entitles "Harmonising, Prospering":

Mould stains steps
and spiral stairways.
Gleaming water

wears away what
was glass and glaze.
Great halls fall.

Take heart. Time
to admit pattering
of inevitable fate.   (11/6: 94)

Here, the expert play of consonance and assonance, the movement from "gleaming" to "glass" to "glaze," and then from "great" to "heart": here and throughout the book, a formidable poetic ear is at work. These poems are as much artistic statement as they are expressions of lived experience. The tone is rich, mature, and generous throughout, but also personal and personable. Berengarten's *Changing* is a window onto how an ancient text and tradition can be lived, studied, interpreted, and re-envisioned in the present moment. As such, it makes a significant contribution to larger and deeper conversations and should be read alongside other fruitful grapplings with an endlessly rich and mutable text.

REFERENCES

Berengarten, Richard. 2016. *Changing*. Bristol: Shearsman Books.

Hinton, David (ed. and trans.). 2015. *I Ching: The Book of Change*. New York: Farrar, Straus and Giroux.

Oliver, Mary. 1992. *House of Light*. Boston, MA: Beacon Press Books.

Wilhelm, Richard and Baynes, Cary F. (trans.) 1977 [1951]. *The I Ching*, Princeton, NJ: Princeton University Press.

LUCAS KLEIN

Lakes and Mountains:
Richard Berengarten's *Changing* via the
transnational and translational *I Ching*

"Octavio Paz, Allen Ginsberg, Jorge Luis Borges, and Charles Olson, among many others, wrote poems inspired by its poetic language," writes Eliot Weinberger. "Fritjof Capra in *The Tao of Physics* used it to explain quantum mechanics and Terence McKenna found that its geometrical patterns mirrored the 'chemical waves' produced by hallucinogens. Others considered its binary system of lines a prototype for the computer." Weinberger is referring, of course, to the *I Ching*, China's Bronze Age "Classic of Changes." He continues:

> Philip K. Dick and Raymond Queneau based novels on it; Jackson Mac Low and John Cage invented elaborate procedures using it to generate poems and musical compositions. It is not difficult to recuperate how thrilling the arrival of the *I Ching* was both to the avant-gardists, who were emphasizing process over product in art, and to the anti-authoritarian counter-culturalists. It brought, not from the soulless West, but from the Mysterious East, what [Richard] Wilhelm called 'the seasoned wisdom of thousands of years.' It was an ancient book without an author, a cyclical configuration with no beginning or end, a religious text with neither exotic gods nor priests to whom one must submit, a do-it-yourself divination that required no professional diviner. It was a self-help book for those who wouldn't be caught reading self-help books, and moreover one that provided an alluring glimpse of one's personal future. It was, said Bob Dylan, "the only thing that is amazingly true." (Weinberger 2016: 145-146)

To Paz, Ginsberg, Borges, Olson, Dick, Queneau, Mac Low, and Cage can now be added Richard Berengarten. His *Changing* is the newest work to write into and out of the methodology of the *I Ching*; it may also be the most ambitious. And yet the ambition of *Changing* is counterbalanced with the understated everydayness of many of Berengarten's poems, like the interplay of *yin* and *yang* 陰陽 in a hexagrams' broken and unbroken lines. Weinberger's essay provides a helpful lens and filter through which to view *Changing*.

Berengarten mentions that he "came across the *I Ching* in 1962," as "a nineteen-year-old undergraduate studying English at Cambridge"; that the first poem he wrote "out of" the *I Ching* was on August 30, 1984; and that he was "beginning to entertain the idea of writing a collection based on the *I Ching*" by the nineties (*ibid.* 523-525). So not only have these ambitions served him for over fifty years, but, since writing the first poem of the book, he has published, by my count, at least nine other books of poetry, not to mention his prose and the collections he's edited.

And yet look at the first poem he wrote chronologically, titled '*Two lakes, joined*', in the set 'Joying, Enjoying':

> *Two lakes, joined,*
> *one above the other*
> *along the same river:*
>
> *Upstream, the Derwent*
> *and, below,*
> *Ladybower.*
>
> *When two lakes join*
> *together they*
> *do not dry up.*
>
> *One draws the other*
> *through constant*
> *self-replenishing.*
>
> *Upstream, the Derwent*
> *and, below*
> *the Ladybower.*
>
> *Joyousness:*
> *two lakes, joined,*
> *one above the other.*   (58/0: 464)

This piece, Berengarten explains, "was based on a divination," and "articulated itself quickly and effortlessly through composition into its particular form, with little need for restructuring or rewriting" (524-525). The poem comes across as sexual yet not lustful, and therefore loving but not Romantic (there is a Derwent in Wordsworth's Lake District, but here the Derwent and Ladybower are man-made lakes in the Peak District) (561). Overall, the poem is one of *joy*: indeed, that is the gloss Berengarten gives at the bottom of the page:

joy [...] *on joy*

Not that *Changing* doesn't include poems more emblematic of its drive to encompass swathes of reference and experience. The thirty pages of notes at the end of the book attest to this scope and inclusiveness, Bronze Age China to Paul Robeson and Joan Baez; from Woody Guthrie (*"The night before // he was executed, Joe telegraphed / Big Bill Haywood: 'Don't waste / time in mourning. Organize"*) to Edmond Jabès ("Singular, unique *you*, // final piece in its puzzle, / end-cog, wired connection / completing its circuit, // switching it on, off, on, / you open and close the book / with no back cover");[2] from Thomas Malory ("And when Sir Bedivere had / thrown the sword in the lake, an / arm and hand rose up straight / from the waters and grasped it) to Theodore Adorno's comment about "no poetry after Auschwitz" ("I shall find words, my / own, after, despite *and* because / of this. *And* speak of it. / … Whatever your intent, your // words invite barbarism / to root in nothing-saying. / Failure is not of or in // language, but small trust / and short vision. Our task lives / in words. Not outwith them"); and from quoting Cesar Vallejo while riffing on Matthew Arnold (*"Calor, Paris, Otoño, ¡cuanto estío / [Heat, Paris, autumn, so much summer]* – / and then turned pages and read // *C'est la vie, mort de la Mort!* – / and that was even finer than fine. / Poetry is a criticism of death.") to collating Blaise Pascal and Shakespeare's Caliban in the lines "The grandeur of / these infinite spaces / gives delight and / hurts not" (56, 141, 157, 293, 333, 445).

And there is of course ambition in the heightened pitch of many of the poems:

Josh's fossil turned out
a nautiloid, black limestone,
400 million years old.

---

[2] *Editors' note*: in this line, RB references his *Book With No Back Cover* (2003). See also 176 and 316-317 below.

Air in these lungs
is thick with crumbled
shit dust. Meanings

that moan in dross
and memorabilia demand
magnified attention.   ('Concerning archaeology', 23/0: 184)

Or here, where the texture of the language is as onomatopoeically and alliteratively loaded as Anglo-Saxon verse or Ezra Pound's "Canto 1":

Ballasted angled keels,
hewed smooth-curved hulls to
sit stable in water, caulked

carvel planks, lengthened
bowsprits, hoisted masts further
forward, slung neat jibs   (*'Sloop-building'*, 42/0: 336)

But more common are plainspoken statements with philosophical implications, for example, *"A lake on a mountain"*:

A mountain presses
up, pushes its presence
to rear, bucking

against gravity. So
when a lake forms on
a mountain, opposed

forces meet and
merge in fine self-
checking balance.   (31/0: 248)

Which is to say, the book's greatest ambition may well be to stay as accessible as the everyday.

This "quotidian" ambition of *Changing* also gives it an internal tension. If this is an embodiment of the *I Ching's* yin and *yang*, it is at once the result of the poem's – and, I think, Berengarten's – greatest influences, which are the poetics of Octavio Paz and Ezra Pound. Pound, of course, was not only, in T.S. Eliot's words, "the inventor of Chinese poetry for our time" (Eliot 1928) with *Cathay*, his 1915 translations of medieval Chinese poetry, but also one of the progenitors of the by-now-long tradition of writing Chinese culture in poetry in English.[3] Pound is, unsurprisingly, referred to many times throughout *Changing*, from the last line of the epigraph ("it coheres all right": Pound 1970: 27) to the final poem ("Brightness diffusing," 64/6: 518): "It all coheres, no question, / as do these notes of mine". Another Poem, titled "Hail Victory," i.e. *Sieg Heil* (58/6: 470) is targeted against Pound's "The Return": "these were the 'Wing'd-with-Awe', / Inviolable" (Pound, 1928: 85). But while Berengarten clearly opposes the Fascist in Pound, he emulates his erudition.

The Paz in *Changing* is perhaps the more interesting case. "Of all the poets I have known personally," Berengarten has written elsewhere, "Octavio Paz has had the strongest and most lasting effect on me" (RB 2017) – and it shows. They met in Cambridge in 1970, when Paz was writing *The Monkey Grammarian* (whose main character, the simian deity Hanumān, is also incarnated as Sun Wukong 孫悟空 in the Ming-dynasty *Journey to the West* 西游記). While Pound has his focus on the luminous detail, Paz is the gentler poet, and his influence lends *Changing* its understated tenderness – even without being cited as often (or, indeed, because he is not cited as often).

Nor should Paz's relationship to China be overlooked as a contiguous and deeply connected wellspring for Berengarten's involvement in the *I Ching*. Weinberger has catalogued some of Paz's expressions of China:

> Throughout the 1960s and 1970s, translations of Chinese and Japanese poets. *East Slope* [*Ladera este*, 1969], arguably his best book of poetry, takes its title from the Sung Dynasty poet Su Shih, who wrote under the name Su Tung-p'o (East Slope). The pages on Taoism and Chinese eroticism in *Conjunctions and Disjunctions* [*Conjunciones y disjunciones,* 1969]. [...] In the 1970s and 1980s, short essays on Tu Fu, Wang Wei, Han Yu, and other Chinese poets. [...] In 1989, Duo Duo, the young Chinese poet avidly read by students demonstrating in Tiananmen Square, remarks that his favorite poet is Octavio Paz. (Weinberger 1992: 35)

Weinberger adds that Paz "never indulged in Orientalism" (see Said 2003). Alongside Duo Duo's interest in Paz, there is also the contemporary Chinese-language poet Yang Lian whose long poem *Yi* is also based on the *I Ching* and, according to its translator Mabel Lee, bears many similarities

---

[3] As I've written elsewhere (Klein 2018), Eliot's remark about Pound as inventor ended up being less about *Cathay* than it was a testimony to a career of creating an English into which Chinese could be incorporated. See, also Saussy, Stalling and Klein 2008.

to Paz's poetics in "Sunstone." (Lee 1997).[4] An example of one of Paz's most 'Chinese' poems is "Concord":

Water above
Grover below
Wind on the roads

Quiet well
Bucket's black Spring water

Water coming down to the trees
Sky rising to the lips   (Paz 2012: 273)

Weinberger points out that this short poem "takes its first two lines from the *I Ching* (the 28th hexagram, Ta Kuo: 'The lake rises above the trees: The image of "Preponderance of the Great." Thus the superior man, when he stands alone, is unconcerned, and if he has to renounce the world, he is undaunted.')" (Weinberger 1992: 35). Paz wrote this poem in 1968, two years before Berengarten met him. "In 2014," Berengarten writes, he discovered that "Octavio had been exploring the Chinese *Book of Changes* as early as 1958." Serendipitously, the two "had been following similar explorative approaches into the *I Ching* [...] but by independent routes." Berengarten concludes: "To Octavio, then, what is called chance is just one of the modes through which our perception registers the inherent coherence and connectivity of things" (RB 2017).

But if Paz never indulged in Orientalism, has Berengarten done so? And is *Changing* indicative of what Timothy Yu has said about "white writers praising Chinese culture while ignoring Chinese people"? Weinberger's line above, about "the seasoned wisdom" from "the Mysterious East," implies that nearly any vision of the *I Ching* would have its Orientalist aspects. While *Wikipedia* introduces Berengarten as "a British poet, translator and editor," it also states that he prefers to think of himself "as a European poet who writes in English." Here, several further questions arise. First, is such cosmopolitanism not a pose that overrides locality and real borders, which he can afford by virtue of a passport he doesn't admit to? Second, since the allusions I have traced above are all of Western literature, in writing from the *I Ching* is he extracting value from Chinese heritage *only* for the exclusive use of a separate tradition in the West?

---

[4] For a related discussion on Yang Lian's *Yi*, see Klein 2018: 68-109. Connections such as these ramify: Berengarten and Yang Lian are friends and have appeared together at several literary events in Cambridge.

My answer is no. Orientalism is real, but reflexive accusations of Orientalism for nearly any engagement with a cultural other are too easy. For one thing, Berengarten points as frequently to scholarship on China and the *I Ching* in its earlier contexts as he does to European and American reference points. The sources for his knowledge about the *I Ching* are not only from the earlier Wilhelm tradition but also from such present-day scholars as Edward L. Shaughnessy (who also provides *Changing* with its preface) and Richard J. Smith, as well as innumerable Chinese friends and acquaintances who have guided him in his journeys. Their not being included above among illustrations of *Changing*'s breadth represents no more than a selection of references based on the likely readership of this book. In addition, Berengarten's acknowledgement of his living Chinese sources not only makes the *I Ching* more contemporary but also avoids the typical Western construction of China, which is to make *itself* the standard-bearer of modernity while relegating China to antiquity.

Weinberger reminds us that according to the ancient Chinese tradition of the *I Ching*'s mythic origins, Fu Xi discovered that "the patterns of nature" – namely the markings on birds, rocks, and animals, the movement of clouds, the arrangement of the stars – could be "reduced to eight trigrams, each composed of three stacked solid or broken lines, reflecting the *yin* and *yang*, the duality that drives the universe. [...] From these building blocks of the cosmos, Fu Xi devolved all aspects of civilization – kingship, marriage, writing, navigation, agriculture – all of which he taught to his human descendants." Of course, "The archaeological and historical version of this narrative is far murkier":

> In the Shang dynasty (which began circa 1600 BCE) or possibly even earlier, fortune-telling diviners would apply heat to tortoise shells or the scapulae of oxen and interpret the cracks that were produced [...]. Where the hexagrams came from, or how they were interpreted, is completely unknown. (Weinberger 2016: 140-141)

For centuries, much of the story of the *I Ching* has already been international: the movement westward includes not only the registry of writers this essay starts with, but also many earlier ones, for "the *I Ching* was discovered in the late seventeenth century by Jesuit missionaries in China [...]. Leibniz enthusiastically found the universality of his binary system in the solid and broken lines." Later, "Richard Wilhelm's 1924 German translation of the *I Ching* and especially the English translation of the German by the Jungian Cary F. Baynes in 1950 [...] transformed the text from Sinological arcana to international celebrity." The German edition gave general terms to "specifically Chinese referents," as well as "scores of footnotes noting 'parallels' to Goethe, Kant, the German Romantics, and the Bible." In this way, by being presented through the lens of a "Jungian, metaphysical version of chance," the Wilhelm/Baynes version became a text that wrote the merging and melding of times and cultures (Weinberger 2016: 142, 145).

చౌ

Changing, of course, is an elaboration of the *I Ching*, not a translation. Berengarten explains: "My hope is that this book will be read first and foremost as a poem, or gathering of poems, in its own right and for its own sake" (521). Nevertheless, as Weinberger suggests, insofar as "the *I Ching* is a mirror of one's own concerns or expectations […] like one of the bronze mirrors from the Shang dynasty, now covered in a dark blue-green patina so that it doesn't reflect at all," (Weinberger 2016: 151), we can also draw the same conclusion about the reflections and refractions, the clarities and opacities, of *Changing*. The book is both encyclopedic and linked to many other works of poetry, as well as to art, ritual, history, philosophy, and mythology. It can also be read either cover to cover, or else be "dipped into at random, the way one reads E. M. Cioran or Elias Canetti." (Weinberger 2016: 147). I recommend dipping into it, even perhaps consulting it as you might an *I Ching* translation.

Hexagram 52 (*Gen* 艮) is one of the eight 'doubled' trigrams. It consists of two 'mountains' ☶, one above the other, designated as ䷳. For this hexagram, Berengarten deploys the title "Stilling," and the first poem in this set of seven involves climbing a mountain.

He left his city,
walked out past
wind-battered scanty

fields carved vertiginous
in terraces, sheds wedged
against hillside rills

nestling perilous on
edges and past these
higher still where

scant trees grew,
to a cloud-smothered
mist-wreathed hut

on a gorse-spattered
plateau. Friend, he said
on arrival, I bring you

no gift, either of inheritance
or of adequate skill. None
the less, here I am.   ("*He left his city,*" 52/0: 416)

The poem starts to narrate what seems like the prototypical Chinese hermit at the moment of becoming, but Berengarten's mist-wreathed mountain is in fact a plateau, spattered with gorse – a flower native to western Europe. Perhaps the mountain on mountain takes place not far from the "*Two lakes, joined,*" above, from which *Changing* grew? And here, rather than pursuing perfect solitude, Berengarten's hermit meets a friend. In its way, then, this poem, like every poem in *Changing*, is a microcosm – both of the book in which it takes its part and of its relationship to the *I Ching*: two mountains conjoined, as if reflecting each other across the surface of a lake, rippling with differentiation, and y*et al*ways returning to each other in stillness.

Yin and *yang* are not only the broken and solid lines of *I Ching* hexagrams, or the feminine and masculine, respectively, or the out-of-the-ordinary and the quotidian; they are also, in their earliest definitions, the north side of a body of water or south face of a mountain (*yang*), and the south side of a body of water, or a mountain's face (*yin*). And even when they are still, they are always changing.

REFERENCES

Berengarten, Richard. 2016. *Changing*. Bristol: Shearsman Books.

————. 2015 (July 8). "Octavio Paz in Cambridge, 1970: Reflections and Iterations." Online at: http://fortnightlyreview.co.uk/2015/07/octavio-paz/

Eliot, T.S. 1928. "Introduction." In Pound, Ezra. *Selected Poems*, xvi.

Fenollosa, Ernest and Pound, Ezra. 2008. *The Chinese Written Character as a Medium for Poetry: A Critical Edition*. Saussy, Haun, Stalling, Jonathan and Klein, Lucas (eds). New York: Fordham University Press.

Hinton David (trans.). 2015. *I Ching: The Book of Change*. New York: Farrar, Straus and Giroux.

Klein. Lucas. 2018. *The Organization of Distance: Poetry, Translation, Chineseness*. Leiden and Boston, MA: Brill.

Lee, Mabel. 1997 "Discourse on Poetics: Paz's Sunstone and Yang Lian's [Yi]." In Lee, Mabel and Hua, Meng (eds.), *Cultural Dialogue and Misreading*, Broadway, NSW: University of Sydney World Literature 1, *Wild Peony*, 86-99.

Minford, John (trans.). 2014. *I Ching: The Essential Translation of the Ancient Chinese Oracle and Book of Wisdom*. New York: Viking.

Paz, Octavio. 1981. *The Monkey Grammarian*. Lane, Helen R. (trans.). New York: Seaver Books.

——————. 2012. *The Poems of Octavio Paz*. Eliot Weinberger (trans. and ed.). New York: New Directions.

Pound, Ezra. 1915. *Cathay*. London: Elkin Mathews.

——————. 1928. *Selected Poems*. London: Faber & Gwyer.

——————. 1964. "Canto 1". In *The Cantos of Ezra Pound*. London: Faber and Faber, 7.

"Richard Berengarten." *Wikipedia*. Online at: https://wiki2.org/en/Richard_Berengarten

Said, Edward W. 2003 [1978]. *Orientalism*. London: Penguin Books.

Shaughnessy, Edward L. (ed.). 1996. *I Ching, The Classic of Change: The First English Translation of the Newly Discovered Second-Century B.C. Mawangdui Text*. New York: Ballantine Books.

——————. 2013. *Unearthing the Changes: Recently Discovered Manuscripts of the Yi Jing (I Ching) and Related Texts*. New York: Columbia University Press.

Smith, Richard J. 2012. *The I Ching: A Biography* Princeton, NJ: Princeton University Press.

Weinberger, Eliot. 1992. "Paz in Asia." In *Outside Stories: 1987-1991*. New York: New Directions.

——————. 2016. "The *I Ching*." In *The Ghosts of Birds*. New York: New Directions.

Yang, Lian. 2000. *Yi*, Lee, Mabel (trans.). Copenhagen and Los Angeles, CA: Green Integer.

Yu, Timothy. 2016 (April 9). "White Poets Want Chinese Culture Without Chinese People." *The New Republic*. Online at: https://newrepublic.com/article/132537/white-poets-want-chinese-culture-without-chinese-people.

Rico Sneller

Spirit and Word: Berengarten's *Changing* and Jewish Prophecy

Writing is the anguish of the Hebraic *ruah*, experienced in solitude by
human responsibility; experienced by Jeremiah subjected to God's dictation ("Take thee a roll of a book, and write therein all the words that I
have spoken unto thee"), or by Baruch transcribing Jeremiah's dictation
(Jeremiah 36: 2,4); or further, within the properly human moment of
pneumatology, the science of *pneuma*, *spiritus*, or *logos* which was divided
into three parts: the divine, the angelical and the human. It is the moment
at which we must decide whether we will engrave what we hear. And
whether engraving preserves or betrays speech.

Jacques Derrida (1967: 19)

INTRODUCTION

We know that the Jews were prohibited from investigating the future
(*Zukunft*). The Torah and the prayers instruct them in remembrance
(*Eingedenken*), however. This stripped the future of its magic, to which
all those succumb who turn to the soothsayers for enlightenment
(*Auskunft*). This does not imply, however, that for the Jews the future
turned into homogeneous, empty time. For every second of time was
the strait gate through which the Messiah might enter (*eintreten*).

With these words the German-Jewish philosopher Walter Benjamin
concludes his *Historical-Philosophical Theses* of 1940 (264). In this short
treatise, Benjamin makes a case for what could be called 'Messianic time',
or a Messianic conception of time. For being ever-imminent, this Messianic
time cannot be predicted. It is of note that, according to Benjamin, to the
Jews foretelling of the future is neither logically nor physically impossible;
the attempt is, rather, nefarious, since it focuses on what is vacuous and
vain. The appropriate attitude, Benjamin holds, is one of remembrance
(*Eingedenken*: 'commemoration'). The conventional English translation

here cannot fully render this German neologism, since it lacks the preposition 'in' (*ein*). *Eingedenken*, therefore, seems to involve a process or activity that enigmatically corresponds to the Messiah's arrival, that is, it implies going *into* (*en*tering) the moment *out of*, or, *through which* the Messiah can also enter (*eintreten*).

In this essay, I want to explore Richard Berengarten's *I Ching*-inspired work in the light of two key motifs in the Jewish prophetic tradition: רוח (*ruah*, 'spirit') and דבר (*dāvār*, 'word'). I will be drawing here on the well-known study of this tradition in *L'Essence du prophétisme* by the French-Jewish scholar and philosopher André Neher. In this book, Neher confronts the Jewish prophetical tradition, ranging from its conception of time and the cosmos to its cultural and religious environment in Egypt and Mesopotamia. This confrontation between substance and context results in an antithetical relationship. It is not my aim here to assess the validity and limits of this polarity. Instead, by exploring the two aforementioned prophetic key notions, 'spirit' and 'word', I will aim to cast some light on Berengarten's poetry and poetics. By taking into account the significant polysemy of *any* word, in whichever language it occurs, I hope to reduce any discursive pretensions that are liable to arise in the course of any such prose commentary. And a still bigger risk, I believe, would be to 'essentialise' *Judaism*, and so to 'define' Berengarten's poetry as 'Jewish' poetry. In my view, for which arguments will necessarily be preliminary in the limited space available here, the Jewish tradition itself exemplifies the main challenge to any such essentialising. That is to say: what is Jewish cannot be pinpointed, since it is always changing and itself consists of self-transcendence. Derrida writes:

> Mais l'identité à soi du Juif n'existe peut-être pas. Juif serait l'autre nom de cette impossibilité d'être soi. Le Juif est brisé et il l'est d'abord entre ces deux dimensions de la lettre: l'allégorie et la littéralité.
> Derrida, 'Edmond Jabès et la question du livre' (1967: 112)[1]

Moreover, to whatever extent Jewish motifs and ideas may be identifiable outside the Jewish tradition, it does not make sense either to isolate them or to attempt to root them in ethnicity. Imagery of 'mingling' and 'inter-breeding' in the poem 'Harvesting (2)' might well imply such a view:

---

[1] "But perhaps the identity of the Jew doesn't really exist. So 'Jew' might well be another name for the impossibility of being oneself. The Jew is split – split in the first instance between the two dimensions of the letter: the allegorical and the literal" (trans. Anthony Rudolf, an English translator of Edmond Jabès, with RB).

In fields on fire
one flame fuels five,
all of which seed,

breed, bleed, into
each other instantly,
constantly.   (12/1: 97)

Therefore, rather than incarcerating Berengarten's writing within a con-
ceptualised 'Judaism' or 'Jewishness', I would like, modestly, to read his
work as a contemporary perpetuation of ancient Jewish traditions, and
to follow the hypothesis that these traditions 'echo' through his oeuvre.
The explicit and relatively widespread references to Judaic themes and
Jewish history in *Changing* [2] will thus serve to function as pointers and eye-
openers, not as furnishers of 'proof'.

WIND, SPIRIT

According to André Neher, the Hebrew word רוח (*ruah*, 'wind', 'spirit') is
a key term that characterises the Biblical prophetic tradition. The prophet
is a "man of spirit" (*ish ha-ruah*). *Ruah*, or 'the' *ruah*, inspires people; and
those invested with *ruah* are possessed by it in abundance. This means
that *ruah* is transmissible. Contrary to plausible interpretation, however,
ruah is by no means a 'ghost' or 'ghostly'. [3] Thus, instead of envisaging
and interpreting *ruah* as an entity that one comes across accidentally, for
example in thunder, lightning or rain, the Hebrews experienced *ruah*
differently. In Neher's interpretation, they rather conceived of it as a

---

[2] See, for example: 'Warsaw Ghetto April-May 1943' (39/5: 317) in the suite
'Struggling, Stumbling'; references to Belsen, Majdanek and Auschwitz in 'Darkening' (36: 287-294), and poems that recall Biblical narratives, such as 'Working for Laban' (11/5: 93) and *'Moses'* (33:0/ 264), and rituals such as 'Building a
Tabernacle' (28/1: 225). References to Jewish mystical traditions are also much in
evidence: for example: *tikkun*, explicitly in *'Tikkun*, Majdanek' (36/6: 294) and,
implicitly, in '(A) coherent language' (23/6: 190), as well as in the 'Thirty-six just
men' (34/5: 277), and many others.

[3] In one of Berengarten's poems, a ghost appears who has "no / instrument to play"
('Ghost, revisiting', 61/5: 493); while in another, the ghost is "as / yet breathless"
('Thank you ghost', 38/4: 308). However, in the latter poem, the ghost's envisaged
presence is needed not only for poetry but for the *word itself*: "Without / you no
poem / and indeed no / word."!

"substantial disposition", that is, as an encounter, or mode of encountering, which, despite its experienced alterity, nevertheless belongs to the human condition. In other words, *ruah*, even though it *differs* from what constitutes the human, responds or corresponds to a human being by calling that individual back to his or her position on earth (Neher 85ff).[4] To pursue this point further through paradox: *ruah* is a mystery with which a human being is *at all times and already* familiar. Thus, *ruah* is a principle of *life*, not in the mere biological sense, but in the sense of an *experienced* or *lived* life, a life one is *aware* of.

This intimate, felt, and necessary connection of *ruah* with life, or awareness of life, mitigates the exclusive position of those reportedly invested with *ruah*, such as Moses' successor Joshua, who "was filled with the spirit of wisdom [*ruah chochma*]" (*Deuteronomy* 34:9), or King David ("from that day on the Spirit of the Lord [*ruah YHWH*] came powerfully upon David" (*I Samuel* 16:13). What is more, in examples such as these, the powerful descent of *ruah* reminds us of the blowing of the wind. "La *ruah* des prophètes," Neher interestingly observes, "n'est pas distincte de la *ruah* du monde ou de la *ruah* des hommes profanes, ou, plutôt, elle n'avait de fondement qu'en elles. L'esprit que plus tard on appela saint était, à l'époque biblique, l'esprit tout court." He continues: "Cette situation, c'était pour l'homme, tout d'abord, de posséder lui-même une *ruah*, c'est-à-dire : de *vivre*."[5] In other words, the mystery of prophecy is a full-blown *human* mystery, one that does *not necessarily* isolate the prophet from his fellow human beings – even though in practice this is often the case. On the other hand, Neher concludes, an encounter with *God* is a necessary condition for (the) *ruah* to vitalise or revitalise man and so to *become* a prophet. In any case, (the) *ruah* does not appear to be informed by an inherent teleology that would articulate it in meaningful speech.[6] Perhaps it could be said that the nature of the *ruah* – which becomes 'despondent'

---

[4] This theme is reminiscent of Kierkegaard's distinction between *repetition* and *memory*, or *transcendence* and *immanence* (in *The Concept of Anxiety*).

[5] "The *ruah* of the prophets is no different from the *ruah* of the world or the *ruah* of profane people; or rather, it has its foundation in them. The spirit that later would be called holy was in Biblical times 'just spirit'. For a man, to be possessed of a *ruah* means to be *alive*." Neher, 89 (my translation, RS). Of course, when it comes to English translation, the cloudy polysemic borders between 'being possessed of' and 'being possessed by' should not be ignored either.

[6] And see also: "il n'y a pas de relation *magique* entre Dieu et le prophète. Dieu n'est pas l'obligé du *nabi*" (Neher 96). ("There is no *magical* relation between God and the prophet. God is not obliged to the *nabi*.")

when isolated – is one of re*sponse*, re*spondence*, if not *correspondence*. The power of logic compels us to assume the precedence of the word, which calls out to a person through the co-respondence of *ruah*, initiates an oscillatory relationship that *subsequently* erases its outspoken origin *as* an origin. Inspiration propels it, sublating or sublimating the source that first allowed its presence or manifestation. The 'pneumatic' response or reply disseminates the verbal origin.

Since the theological history of the Western world, combined with extensive etymological analysis, has familiarised us with the concept of 'spirit' and all its concomitant notions and distinctions, it hardly seems possible to return to a pre-theological polysemy of *ruah*, as 'wind', 'spirit', 'breath'. The cognate word *r̊ah* means 'smell'.[7] Interestingly, in *Changing*, not only is the 'wind' a crucial motif; but the *word* also enhances polysemy, thereby perpetuating *both* the polysemy of the word *ruah and* polysemy itself – as if 'ruah', before meaning or signifying something or anything, were itself the beginning of polysemy. Since it is my hypothesis that Berengarten's *I Ching*-inspired poetry can be meaningfully read in the light of the Jewish prophetical tradition, here I will continue to dwell on the polysemy of *ruah* and so aim to avoid neglect of its *cosmic* dimension. This approach, I hope, may also have the triple advantage of (1) liberating the notion of *ruah* from unnecessary spiritualisation; (2) exempting prophecy from a naïve, linear conception of time ('foretelling the future'); and (3) shedding at least some light on *Changing* – whether as a Sino-Jewish *prophetology*, or possibly even as a modern form of *prophecy* (that is, if such a distinction has any meaning).

While *ruah* opens the narratives of creation in *Genesis* ("In the beginning God created the heavens and the earth. Now the earth was formless and empty, darkness was over the surface of the deep, and the *Spirit* of God was hovering [*merachèfet*] over the waters." *NIV*; my italics, RS), the first and third suites of poems in *Changing* – (1) 'Initiating' and (3) 'Beginning' – repeat these initiating movements in their own way. The second suite is

---

[7] In his parallel discussion of Hegel's philosophy and Jean Genet's writings, Jacques Derrida similarly associates spirit (*Geist*) with smell, albeit not always with pleasant ones: "l'essence de la rose, c'est sa non-essence: son odeur en tant qu'elle s'évapore. D'où son affinité d'effluve avec le pet ou avec le rot." ("The essence of the rose is its non-essence: that is, its smell, insofar as it evaporates. Hence, as effluvium, its affinity with a fart or a burp." (Derrida 1974: 69; emphasis added). Similarly, the polysemic word *qi* (trad. 氣; simp. 气) appears in expressions such as 臭氣 (*chou qi* 'bad smell, smelly breath'). Bad smells or breath also occur in *Changing*: see 'Push me, said the girl' (54/0: 432). On *qi* 氣, see also table III, 349 below.

meaningfully entitled 'Responding, Corresponding'. Together and cumulatively, both these suites re-evoke the matching verbal motifs and images of *Genesis*. Here we find both *heaven* ("*Heaven over heavens / heaven under heavens / when and where do / you ever stop?*" – 1/0: 4) and *earth* ("*you seething and proliferating surface / you forested and river-fed and windblown / time-space of human origins and ends*" – 2/0: 14). We also find *paradise* ("You paradisal particle of star", "you tabulated Eden" – *ibid.*); and *beginning*, for example "Absolute beginning / and final end of all ends / and beginnings" – 1/5: 9). Similarly, in 'Supreme Ultimate' (1/7: 11) we find "Endless beginningless / heaven holds everything / including astronomical // creation and demise / of universes into and out / of nothing." And in the preceding poem, 'Light fills and fails' (1/6: 10), albeit indirectly and implicitly, we find the contrasted images of "vast spools of shadow" and light that "hovers, spills away". In this poem, is it possible that there may even be the suggestion of a shadowy *spirit* hovering over the waters? What is more, if my equating of *ruah* with the experience of human *response* and/or *correspondence* be accepted, then perhaps the title of the second suite ('Responding, Corresponding') may itself be evocative of 'the spirit', even if equally indirectly.

In the light of the poem 'Light fills and fails' in the first suite, together with its evocation of the waters ("this dark flood") that unseal "chaos", cause a shipwreck, an observation made by Neher is of particular interest. In his explanation of the key prophetic notion of *ruah*, he points out that, in the first verses of *Genesis*,

> la *ruah* divine est encore décrite comme un fluide; le verbe est même très expressif: la *ruah plane* sur les eaux, elle étend ses ailes, tel un oiseau. Mais cette *ruah* originelle, détachée du chaos et veillant sur lui, n'est pas seulement fluide vital, mais source de vie. Cette révélation première de Dieu au monde, le premier reflet que le monde eut de Dieu. Elle est comme l'annonce, le germe, des révélations futures.[8]

In the context of Neher's comparison of the spirit to a bird brooding eggs, Berengarten's description of the ship splitting in two due to the "dark

---

[8] "[…] the divine *ruah* is still described as a fluid; even the verb is very expressive: the *ruah hovers* over the waters, it spreads its wings, like a bird. But this original *ruah*, detached from the chaos and watching over it, is not only a vital fluid, but the source of life. It is the first revelation of God to the world, the first reflection the world has received from God. It is, as it were, the announcement, the germ, of future revelations." Neher, 88 (my translation, RS).

flood" of original chaos becomes particularly meaningful; it is "[c]rushed like an egg".[9]

It is only to the extent that the *ruah* is fluid – is breath – that its presence in the poem quoted can be assumed. For, if it had been solely 'spiritual', i.e., 'immaterial', chaos would have prevailed. But it does not do so, at least not in *Changing*, as also appears from 'The force that fills and empties', a parallel poem that strongly resembles 'Light fills and fails' in both form and in content, since both are villanelles:

> Come friend, sit with me. Drink this wine, I pray,
> and break bread, though around us chaos raves.
> The force that fills and empties things of day
> *holds* all our love, yet wipes that love away.   (2/6: 20; my italics, RS)

The broken *bread* of friendship amidst chaos reminds us, by near-homophony, of the *breath* hovering over that same chaos. It could even be maintained that the *breaking* of the bread in 'The force that fills and empties' (2/6: 20) resembles the splitting of the ship's mast in 'Light fills and fails': "The mast has split in two beneath salt spray. / Crushed like an egg, it sinks. Its sides must yield" (1/6: 10). This association, if taken as far as identification, might well alarmingly entail a mutual implication for the covenant of friendship, or love, in the destruction of its vessels. However, despite its destructiveness, "[t]he force that fills and empties things of day / *holds* all our love" even though it is wiped away (2/6: 20; my italics, RS).[10]

---

[9] See also the image of 'heaven's dimensions' "interbreeding" ("*breed*", "*brood*", "*bread*", "*breath*", "*break*" in 'Supreme Ultimate' (1/7: 11). 'Flood' is also a recurrent motif in *Changing*, for example in 28/6: 230. Water, however, can also be or become contained in a well, as in the suite 'Welling, Replenishing': see 'From underground streams' (48/3: 387) and 'Well, inexhaustible' (48/6: 390). Through this sequence, the poet moves between 'floods' and 'wells'; and in 'I lower my question', he draws up "water-wisdom" (48/5: 389). On the relation between a breaking egg and a brain haemorrhage, see 'Broken blur, crimsoned', where "[a] blood-vessel in my / head bursts. A black sun / breaks like an egg" (13/1: 105). Interestingly, the union of love is "unbreakable", as is water: "Sounded, fathomed // by eyes, breaths, hearts, / signed in words and silences, / bonds unbreakable" ('As water', 8/1: 65).

[10] In Lurianic Kabbalah, the creation of the world is equal to its own Fall; humans are called upon to mend the world (*tikkun olam*). The motif of *tikkun olam* itself occurs explicitly in several poems in *Changing*: see note 4 above. See also Fine, chs. 6 and 7.

The earlier cosmic connotations of *ruah* may also differ markedly from currently prevailing tendencies to intellectualise or psychologise the various concepts of 'spirit'. Nevertheless, such ancient connotations and connections do dominate *Changing*. To the extent that *wind* and *storm* are frequent motifs,[11] both as physical and psychical phenomena, the creative, creatively inspiring "Spirit of God hovering over the waters" (*Genesis* 1:3) is never far. Take for example *Blowing, Billowing*, the most wind-laden and wind-possessed suite in the entire volume (57: 455-462). As if invited by the linguistic alliteration of the combined bilabial plosive with the lateral (*b*, *l*), expanding into the repeated *-owing*, this title in itself already implies the presence of the wind hovering or drifting over the waters.[12] The opening poem, '*What's that whirring*', explicitly associates 'wind' and 'spirit':

> *What's that whirring*
> *in the guttering? Only*
> *the wind muttering.*
>
> *And that clattering*
> *above the ceiling? Your spirit*
> *staggering and reeling.*   (57/0: 456)

Further on in the same poem, these sounds are even connected to "*[t]he breath / of Death*" and "*[y]our soul / breaking its casement*". If we ignore any law of causality or subject/object distinction, here the synchronistic vision associating "wind" with "spirit" implies a holistic world-view of nature and psyche that is rooted and routed in *correspondences*.

Erosion of a purely a-cosmic psyche by the inspiration of the wind also takes place in 'Wind's paths'. In this poem, the creative inspiration flowing through the poet's veins cannot itself be codified: "The wind's paths / can't be written. Neither / ink nor blood will // code the wind" (57/5: 461). One might even ask if ink and blood themselves, *before* clotting, are not indistinguishable from or, at least, identifiable with the wind. Biblical echoes resonate here, for example: "If [God] withdrew his spirit (*ruho*) and breath (*nishmato*), all humanity (*kol basaar*, lit. 'all flesh') would perish

---

[11] For the motifs of storm and thunder, see particularly the suite 'Shaking, Quaking' (51: 407-414). For a further study of *ruah* as wind, especially storm-wind, see also Sneller 2018.

[12] See also 'Scattering', which opens with the line "Wind's knife cuts waves" (59/1: 473), and the image of "*wind-ravaged / waves*" in 'Fabric of the human orgasm' (44/0: 352).

together and mankind (*adaam*) would return to the dust" (*Job* 34:14f).[13]

Nonetheless, in 'Wind across grass', Berengarten clarifies that "[y]ou can't watch the wind, only / wind's effects" (19/1: 153). And even though it is transient, and despite the statement that "soon I'll have / become invisible" ('Wind's paths', 57/5: 461), the wind cannot dispense with my living it out, or writing it out in poems. As is evident in the preceding poem, the wind not only inspires life and poetry, but also asks *questions*.[14] Yet, these cannot be answered by any book, not even the poet's:

> [...] At the end
> of every good argument
> containing many
>
> interesting matters, at
> least one question always
> gets left behind. This
>
> book of yours may
> be done. But this question
> outlasts your book.   (*'Hah!* replied the wind', 57/2: 458)

Word

In his discussion of Hebrew prophecy, André Neher identifies a second key term: רבד (*dāvār*, 'word'). *Ruah* and *dāvār*, 'spirit' and 'word', are always connected, Neher adds. However, whereas *ruah* still contains a certain ambiguity or fluidity, *dāvār* is without ambiguity. Being exterior, the 'word' has a certain objectivity or solidity of its own.

I would like to add that, like *ruah*, Hebrew *dāvār* is liable to similar 'metaphysical' misinterpretations. Other than meaning 'word' (*Wort*, *parole*, *woord*), *dāvār* is not purely lingual, since it can signify *both* 'word' *and* 'thing' or 'object'. Like Greek *logos*, *dāvār* precedes a certain Platonic distinction, predominant today, between 'language' and 'being'.

The greater objectivity of *dāvār* as compared to *ruah* does not diminish the fact that both words arouse the human subject's (prophetic) nature,

---

[13] Referenced by Neher, 91; and see also *Job* 27:3ff and *Psalm* 104:29ff.

[14] In this respect, here the wind resembles the ghost in another poem, 'Ghost, revisiting': "But you prefer // to ask questions of me" (61/5: 493). However, the questions here are only "[a] test".

whether by frightening or enchanting it. "[L]a parole, à l'égal de l'*esprit*", Neher writes, "est pathétique."[15] Nevertheless, while *both* spirit *and* word are transcendent, the power of the latter to reside within the material (phenomenal) world, and so to affect it as an immanent and active presence, is stronger. "'Is not my word (*devari*) like fire,' declares the Lord, 'and like a hammer that breaks a rock in pieces?'" (*Jeremiah* 23:29, *NIV*) Indeed, when *dāvār* belongs to or emanates from God, it can signify an *order*, i.e. a command or 'commandment'; and when it pertains to man, an *act* or *action*. "[L]a *ruah* ne peut que planer sur le chaos, mais la *parole* l'organise."[16] It is also noteworthy here that a Biblical passage that configures the prophet's reaction to the Divine Word deploys the same verb as in *Genesis* 1:3 in depicting the movement of the spirit 'hovering – *merachèfèt* – over the waters': "My heart is broken within me; all my bones tremble (*rachefu*)" (*Jeremiah* 23:9, *NIV*). The Jewish-Moroccan Bible translator André Chouraqui renders this verse as "tous mes os couvent", alluding to the brooding of a bird; while the Jewish-German philosophers Martin Buber and Franz Rosenzweig deliver the German translation as: "all meine Gebeine flattern". *Flattern* ('to flutter') likewise indicates the movement of a bird's wings. Indeed, the subliminal associative links between trembling and hovering are brought out clearly in the image of *fluttering*.

On the other hand, there are occurrences where the transcendence of the *word* is mitigated by its previous digestion by the prophet: "When your words (*devarècha*) came, I ate them; they (*devarècha*: 'your word') were my joy and my heart's delight" (*Jeremiah* 15:16, *NIV*).[17] In any case, Neher concludes, "la parole transmise n'est pas homogène à la parole reçue. La même parole, captée par le prophète, prend un sens nouveau lorsque le prophète l'énonce."[18]

In interpreting Neher's analysis of רוח (*ruah*) and דבר (*dāvār*) in Biblical prophecy, I would argue that both these words function within closely related and indeed overlapping 'fields' of meaning in relation to one single and cohering phenomenal continuum. What is more, both signify the presence of an otherness that is always experienced powerfully and intensely,

---

[15] "[T]he *word*, like the *spirit*, is rich in feeling." Neher, 105 (my translation, RS).

[16] "[T]he *ruah* can only hover above the chaos, but the *word* organises it." Neher, 109 (my translation, RS).

[17] Examples given by Neher, 104, 105.

[18] "The transmitted word is not homogeneous with the received word. The same word, captured by the prophet, takes on a new meaning when it is articulated by the prophet." Neher, 109 (my translation, RS).

and often sharply or strikingly. However, while *ruah* as 'spirit' may unite, the precise and often incisive power of *dāvār* as 'word' (whether it comes across as hard as a hammer or as sweet as honey) introduces *distinction*, *personhood*, and the possibility of addressing the other *as* other.

Here I set aside the question whether any sharp distinction exists between prophetology (theory about prophecy) and prophecy itself. If there *is* one (which I doubt), Berengarten's poetry hovers over the edges of both.[19] Not only does it highlight the simultaneous rise, arousal and arrival of *word* with *otherness*, but it also testifies to *its own* transmission of this *word*. The suite 'Following', for example, opens with '*Rules*' – which perhaps itself reminds us of the strand in *dāvār* that pertains to 'commandments': "*to submit your / habitually warring / and undisciplined // spirit in willing / modesty to what / needs to be done*" (17/0: 136). Another poem in the suite, aptly entitled 'Other voices', also explores the transmission of words, via 'inner speech', between an *I* and a pluralised *you*, who bear "strong / kinship with" each other:

> I bear strong
> kinship with these other
> voices, not mine,
>
> that speak inside my
> head and heart and here
> more truly than any
>
> I might even call
> my own. These voices
> that have no
>
> mouth except in
> your mouth, no breath
> but in your own

---

[19] See for example lines from 'The stone carver': "And hard- // edged borders be-tween / stone and air were easy / tracks for her hands // to cross" (38/5: 309). This motif of the *transversing*, *transgressing*, and *transcending* of demarcations is found elsewhere too, for example: "borders and edges [...] simultaneously // flow into one / another, merge, / blend, bond" ('Dark gates of things', 14/5: 117). The suite 'Travelling' explores these themes, too, in lines such as "Today we remain / borderers, go-betweens" ('Borderers', 56/1: 449), and "we, boarders, borderers" ('Elsewheres', 56/5: 453).

lungs' breathing, tell
me where to go, what
to do, and how.

I follow straight
without complaint
or grief.   (17/2: 138)

Here, interestingly, the 'you' whose mouth and breath are referred to, is
not specified. It could be anyone, and therefore perhaps *ought* not to be
specified. Furthermore, lest a temptation should arise to try to identify
this 'you', another of the poems in the same suite reminds the reader of
the impossibility of doing so, even though here the 'you' is "singular" and
"unique" – that is, *tu* not *vous*. The poem, entitled 'You' deserves equally
to be quoted in full:

The book is constantly
being written. Made though
it may be (*will be, has been*),

always there's a fault in it,
some minor imperfection,
fissure, sliver, gap, crack –

into and through which
you enter, whoever you may be.
Following, you fill, you fulfil

the book. You straddle it,
leap into it and complete it.
Singular, unique *you*,

final piece in its puzzle,
end-cog, wired connection
completing its circuit,

switching it on, off, on,
you open and close the book
with no back cover.   (17/5: 141)

Remarkably, the 'fissure' or 'crack' that allows (the) *you* to enter, (the) *you*
who fill(s) or fulfil(s) the book, also reminds us of two poems already quoted
above: 'Light fills and fails' and 'The force that fills and empties' (1/6: 10
and 2/6: 20 respectively). Both poems are concerned with a *breaking*: that

176

of the ship in the former and of bread in the latter. I propose here to re-read these poems in the *light* of the last quoted poem, 'You'. What the wreck of a ship, bread of friendship, and a fissured text have in common is that they all allow entry to *you* – whoever such a person might be. Only (the) *you* can complete the book. Ultimately, as in *'What the book said about itself'*, one has no choice but to "*sit and wait / in a patience within patience / without praise or hope // for meanings to grow / like ferns unscrolling from / cracks between lines*" (20/0: 160). Sit and wait like a bird brooding its eggs, one might be inclined to add.

What is more, these fissures and cracks also remind us of the broken and unbroken lines of the hexagrams of the *I Ching*, not to mention the cracks in the shells of turtles and shoulder blades of oxen; for prior to the method of divination involving yarrow stalks and consultation of the *I Ching*, the ancient Chinese practised plastromancy and scapulimancy. Thus, in 'Lines broken and unbroken', we find: "So too we / carved necessity and made / patterns of our own // and from their cracks / and fissures drew lines / unbroken and broken." (20/6: 166) Among the objects that suggest "lines / unbroken and broken" are "eggs", "bark", "waves" and "winds".

Even though the "patterns of our own" that are created out of necessity's "cracks and fissures" are in need of one or other *you* to complete the book, can't they also be compared to the prophetic transmission of the Word? The prophet, whether shocked or delighted by the 'swallowing' of the divine Word, transmits what he has received, though inevitably altering its intent. The poet, by transmitting "other voices" that surface through the fissures of his life, tries to make sense of them. These patterns are his own, as they consist of both *his* suffering (a broken ship) and *his* friendships (broken bread). According to the poem entitled 'Patterns of our own', creating these patterns imitates nature: they derive from "gradual wind-markings / on disappearing clouds", "light's striations on water", and "tracks made by animals, / birds, spiders, insects, worms / in sand, dust, mud, clay –". And this poem continues: "observing these high / and low with eyes peeled / we learn to copy // and with fingers mark / patterns of our own in shell, / wood, clay, hide, stone" (20/1: 161).

Here, we return once again to the first two poems in *Changing*, which were quoted at the beginning of this essay. For the "sand, dust, mud, clay" and "wood, clay, hide, stone" of 'Patterns of our own' are strongly reminiscent of the "[r]ock, mud, clay" that "swirl as vast spools of shadow are unreeled" in 'Light fills and fails' (1/6: 10). What is more, in the companion piece, 'The force that fills and empties' (2/6: 20), we also discover this force's "[s]tirring breath, blood and bones", as "it spurs my clay / to build the buttresses and architraves / that hold our love, yet wipes it clean away." So, here we have sand, dust, mud, clay, rock, breath, blood, and bones – all of which are stirred by "the force that fills and empties". This force commands the poet-prophet – whose blood and bones may be trembling (*rachefu*) – to create "patterns of his own", and could well be identical with (the) *you* – the "singular, unique *you*" – that "straddle[s]" it (like the spirit *hovering* [*merachèfet*] over the waters), "leap[s] into it and complete[s] it". The trembling ('stirred') bones of the poet-prophet are mirrored by the 'straddling' of (the) *you*, as if in mutual cooperation:

> You, perfectly
>
> I have foreseen
> you reading this be-
> fore you were ever
>
> conceived. And
> so for sure I recognise
> you, perfectly. How
>
> and how long this
> lives depends now
> and ever on you.
>
> On the other side of
> this page *I* lurk as well
> behind your eyes.
>
> Seek me nowhere.
> Whoever or whatever I
> was dissolves. All
>
> that's left is this, in
> your eyes, ears, mouth,
> heart, mind, spirit.   (53/6: 430)

In *Jeremiah*, we read: "'Is not my word like fire,' declares the Lord, 'and like a hammer that breaks a rock in pieces?'" (23:29). Similarly, in some of the poems in *Changing*, it is as if the solid exteriority of the divine *word* received by the prophet were melting in the poet's mouth. Or as if the severity of prophecy, propelling the transcendent *word*, were reiterating how it all began: with the spirit of creation hovering over the waters, brooding upon them, flapping its wings. What is more, "[w]hen your words came, I ate them; they were my joy and my heart's delight" (*Jeremiah* 15:1). Indeed, it is as if the necessary requisite for any such prophetic or poetic swallowing and digestion were *time itself* – in just the same way that the successful hatching of an egg needs 'to take time'. What both processes require is *incubation*; and, in the cases of prophecy and poetry, this comes about through preparative pondering, in 'dream-time':

> Human speech   surfaces
> from oceanic language first
> through dreaming.
>
> Phonemes   root and
> grow on binary distinctions
> built in the mouth's cave.
>
> Speaking   the quick
> exterior human dialogue
> opens now in now.
>
> Writing   miming speech
> through time throughout it
> makes it monumental.
>
> Lettered   word and
> ideogram spatialising history
> treat and draw time as field.
>
> Poetry   inner speech
> pouring from such stores
> roams earth and vast skies.[20]   ('Ground, grounds, store', 26/6: 214)

In the preceding paragraph I mentioned the statement in *Jeremiah* that in the mouth of the prophet, the divine 'word' can be as hard as a hammer shattering or cracking a rock, and the need for (poetic-prophetic) digestion to mitigate it. "Patterns of our own" are to be "carved" into "necessity", as if in shells, bones, or stones. The poem 'Working for Laban' suggests that

---

[20] This poem is connected to another entitled 'Ground', in which the process of composition itself "engenders poetry as / hope, as act, as ground- // base of firmed world" (14/2: 114). The presence of "hope" here in turn correlates indirectly with 'Light fills and fails': "No hoop of faith or stave of hope can stay / the chaos that this dark flood has unsealed. / Light fills and fails. It hovers, spills away" (1/6: 10). Note in particular the alliterative patterning of in *hoop*, *hope*, *hovers*, and of *stay*, *stave*.

the promise of a *kiss* can enable one to lift a stone: "And he lifted // the stone, and kissed her." (11/5: 93)[21] or a *dream* ("He went out from that stony place / where he had dreamed of the ladder"). Or – we could add – a *poem*. When Buber and Rosenzweig render the verse from *Jeremiah* into German – "'Is not my word [...] like a hammer that breaks a rock in pieces [*yefotsēts sāla*]?'"– they do so as follows: "Ist meine Rede nicht so: [...] gleich einem Schmiedehammer, der Felsen zerspelt." Now *zerspellen* is an unusual German synonym for *zerspalten* ('to split'), and etymologically cognate with the English verb 'to spell'.[22] And just as the shards of a cracked rock may teach us to mark out or delineate the patterns of our own life – "with eyes peeled[23] / we learned to copy // and with fingers mark / patterns of our own in shell, / wood, clay, hide, stone" ('Patterns of our own', 20/1: 161), so also the letters of a word, in combination with the spaces between them, may enable us to write prophetic poetry: "Lettered   word and / ideogram spatialising history / treat and draw time as field" ('Ground, grounds, store') – and, moreover, thus enable us to *get a life*. What is more, I am inclined to read the final stanza of this poem as an account of poetry's creative activity, by virtue of its allusion to the hovering spirit: "Poetry   inner speech / pouring from such stores / roams earth and vast skies." Indeed, the absence of any attempt to "treat and draw time as a field" may induce "disappointment on a wry // embittered face", as in 'Marcello', where the 'disappointed' person is compared to "a fluttering creature wafted / on every wind" that moves "only / when prompted" (57/3: 459).

Conclusion

"the correct turning of antennae towards origins" (48/0: 384)

I started this essay by quoting Walter Benjamin's renowned statement about the Jews being forbidden to investigate the future – whether or not

---

[21] *Isaiah* 6:6ff describes how the prophet Isaiah is called by God's angelic kiss.

[22] As is well known, *to spell* not only indicates the action of reading or reciting the letters in a word, but also has both magical and numinous connotations, as in expressions such as 'to weave a spell, to cast a spell'. In Dutch, *voorspellen* means 'to predict', 'to foretell' or 'forecast'.

[23] This image is reminiscent of Robert Musil's 'man without qualities' (*Der Mann ohne Eigenschaften*): See also: "Outwardly lacking an I, / though being all eye" ('Ordinary', 5/1: 41).

it is actually possible to foretell the future. The logic of this prohibition, according to Benjamin, is not based on the assumption of an entirely empty, homogenous time. On the contrary, the Messiah may arrive, and he may so do at any moment. What is more, the arrival of the Messiah infinitely exceeds what any reading of the future might conceivably offer. To adopt a word deployed by the French philosophers Deleuze and Guattari, it *de-* or *re-territorialises* all our hopes, predictions, and expectations.

By starting out from the hypothesis that it makes sense to read the *I Ching*-inspired poetry of *Changing* in the light of the Jewish prophetical tradition, I have turned to the analysis of this tradition by the Franco-Jewish philosopher André Neher. He distils this tradition to two major motifs, *spirit* and *word*. Drawing on the polysemy of the Hebrew words *ruah* and *dāvār*, I have followed their trajectories into some readings and interpretations of *Changing*. Their pursuit has offered various insights, which not only put the notion of 'prophecy' into a somewhat different perspective, but also recast the practice of *I Ching* consultation, and even that of divination in general. For, according to such a view, it is neither necessary nor inevitable that divination should turn one's attention to foretelling, or for that matter, towards 'the future' or futurity, but rather, if anything, *back* towards a reorientation in the here-and-now. Indeed, Berengarten hints at this kind of specific, attentive, and active refocusing in the present in several poems, for example '*Consultation of the diagrams*':

Consultation
of the diagrams
is helpful

in the construction
of hypotheses, buildings
and voyages,

in the precise
locating of wells, mines,
bridges, towers, mirrors,

in alleviating
insomnia and fears
of death,

in the correct
turning of antennae
towards origins

and in all forms of
measurement and modes
of harmonising.   (48/0: 384)

The closely connected poem '*I Ching*' ends by maintaining that the companionship of the Chinese sourcebook has kept the poet's "feet still / grounded rooted / in *this here now*" (48/4: 388).

Is it a coincidence that the Biblical passage quoted above – in which God's word is compared to a hammer breaking rocks (*Jeremiah* 23:29) – is directed *against false prophets*? The passage continues as follows:

> "Therefore," declares the Lord, "I am against the prophets who steal from one another words supposedly from me. Yes," declares the Lord, "I am against the prophets who wag their own tongues and yet declare, 'The Lord declares.' Indeed, I am against those who prophesy false dreams," declares the Lord. (*NIV, Jeremiah* 29:30ff)

All English translations that I have been able to consult read *I am against*. The Hebrew text itself, however, is much more interesting, especially in the light of the conclusive emphasis of Berengarten's: "feet still / grounded rooted / in *this here now*." The thrice-repeated phrase *I am against* has taken on even richer and fuller meanings in contemporary Jewish philosophy – for example, in Rosenzweig and Levinas. Yet, here they are pronounced by God: *hinneni* – "here I am", or, more literally, "see me!"[24]

> "[E]very second of time was the straight gate through which Messiah might enter."

REFERENCES

Benjamin, Walter. 2007 (1968). 'Theses on the Philosophy of History'. In *Illuminations. Essays and Reflections* (Zohn, Harry, trans.) New York: Schocken Books.

Benveniste, Émile. 1966. *Problèmes de linguistique générale*. Paris: Editions Gallimard. English version, 1971. *Problems in General Linguistics* (Meek, Elizabeth Mary, trans.). Miami, FL: University of Miami Press.

Buber, Martin and Rosenzweig, Franz. 1985 (1958). *Die Schrift. Verdeutscht von Martin Buber gemeinsam mit Franz Rosenzweig*, Bd. 1 and 3. Darmstadt: Wissenschaftliche Buchgesellschaft.

---

[24] Chouraqui translates: *me voici contre les inspirés*.

Chouraqui, André. 1989. *La Bible*. Paris: Desclée de Brouwer.

Deleuze, Gilles and Guattari, Félix. 1972. *L'Anti-Œdipe. Capitalisme et schizophrénie*. Paris: Minuit.

Derrida, Jacques. 1967. *L'écriture et la différence*. Paris: Seuil. English version, 2001 [1978]. *Writing and Difference* (Bass, Alan, trans.). London and New York: Routledge.

――――. 1974. *Glas – Que reste-t-il du savoir absolu ?* Paris: Galilée. English version, 1986. *Glas* (Leavey, John P. Jr. and Rand, Richard, trans.). Lincoln NE and London: University of Nebraska Press.

Fine, Lawrence. 2003. *Physician of the Soul, Healer of the Cosmos. Isaac Luria and His Kabbalistic Fellowship*. Stanford, CA: Stanford University Press.

Kierkegaard, Søren. 1980. *The Concept of Anxiety* (Thomte, Reidar *et al.*, eds. and trans.). Princeton, NJ: Princeton University Press.

Neher, André. 1983 [1972]. *L'essence du prophétisme*. Paris: Calmann-Lévy.

Sneller, Rico. 2018. 'Benjamin's Angel in Light of Jewish Mysticism'. In Kasten, M. (ed.), *Benjamin's Figures: Dialogues on the Vocation of the Humanities*. Nordhausen: Bautz.

PART 3

In the Wake of C. G. Jung

RODERICK MAIN

Poetry, the *I Ching* and Synchronicity: Reflections on Richard Berengarten's *Changing*

In his erudite and illuminating 'Postscript' to *Changing*, Richard Berengarten states that the *I Ching* served him not only as a source for his poem, both its 'compositional structure' and many of its themes, but also as 'a ground for poetry' more generally (525). He notes in particular how the *I Ching*[1] underwrote his use of a variety of '"connecting" principles' (526) and in relation to this he makes the following, to my eyes, pregnant statement:

> As for associative, analogical or correlative thinking, sometimes also known as 'correlative cosmos-building', this is not only the mental foundation for poetry, ritual and magic in all societies, but specifically underpins the holistic vision of the universe that runs through all traditional Chinese thought – most evidently so in Daoism. It also gives rise to C. G. Jung's theory of synchronicity, which is itself rooted in the *I Ching*. (*ibid.*)

Among other things, Berengarten seems to be implying here that Carl Gustav Jung's (1875–1961) concept of synchronicity (1) is a modern expression of correlative thinking and, as such, both (2) underpins a 'holistic vision of the universe' and (3) provides 'the mental foundation for poetry, ritual and magic'. These three far-reaching implications could be important for understanding not only Berengarten's *Changing*, as well as poetry more generally, but also the cultural significance of Jung's concept of synchronicity. In this essay I shall focus on the first

---

[1] Like Berengarten (*CH* 521 note 1), I use Pinyin to transliterate Chinese terms, except in the case of the *I Ching*, for which I use the more familiar Wade-Giles transliteration.

part of the third implication: the possible relevance of synchronicity for poetry. Such a focus seems particularly justified in view of Berengarten's acknowledgement that synchronicity is one of the factors that both motivates and underpins his own poetry and informs his view of the task of contemporary poetry more broadly.[2] In order to explore the relationship between synchronicity and poetry I shall first clarify what Jung meant by synchronicity, including what the concept entails philosophically, and then attempt a reading of one cluster of seven poems in *Changing*, with the concept of synchronicity in mind.

SYNCHRONICITY

Jung defined synchronicity in several ways and illustrated the concept with a wide range of examples (Main 2004: 39-47). On the one hand, synchronicity was for Jung a kind of experience – 'meaningful coincidence' (Jung 1952: §827)[3] – in which an inner psychic state is connected with an outer physical event not causally but through the meaning that the events jointly express. In such meaningful coincidences, the connected physical event may be perceived either simultaneously with the psychic state or only later because it occurs at a distance or in the future (Jung 1951: §984; 1952: §§850, 855). Jung's examples include, among others: the case of a patient who was telling him her dream about being given a jewel in the form of a scarab beetle, when an actual scarabaeid beetle appeared at his consulting room window (Jung 1951: §982; 1952: §§843, 845); the story of how Emanuel Swedenborg, in a visionary state, described the course of a fire hundreds of miles away in Stockholm, all the details of which were subsequently confirmed (Jung 1951 §983; 1952: §912); and an anecdote told to Jung by a friend, who dreamed of certain scenes and events unfolding in a Spanish city he had never visited, which then occurred exactly as in the dream when the friend did visit the city shortly afterwards (Jung 1951: §973).

On the other hand, synchronicity was for Jung the principle – 'an acausal connecting principle' – that explained why these kinds of experiences occur (Jung 1952). He argued that this principle was 'intellectually necessary'

---

[2] See Nikolaou and Dillon 90, 98, 110-114; Burns 1981: 32-38; Berengarten 2008; 2015: 25-31; 2020.

[3] *Editors' note*: Use of the paragraph symbol § is standard practice for citations from Jung's *Collected Writings*.

(*ibid.* §960), to account for meaningful coincidences (*ibid.* §967); and he suggested that synchronicity and causality stood in a relationship of complementarity to each other as principles of explanation (*ibid.* §§960-61, 963).

Deeply informed by Jung's studies and practical experience of the *I Ching*, the concept of synchronicity can be seen as a modern Western formulation of correlative thinking (Jung 1930, 1950; Main 2004: 77-79),[4] inasmuch as both concepts connect events: (1) independently of external causation; (2) by interpreting events as parts of a larger whole (that is, as 'a pattern' with 'meaning'); and (3) by discerning associations, correspondences, or coincidences among the events. Both synchronicity and correlative thinking, in their different ways, attempt to capture the basic idea of acausal connection through 'meaning'.

Jung considered that the concept of synchronicity opened up 'a very obscure field which is philosophically of the greatest importance' (Jung 1952: §816), for it implies a range of subsidiary ideas that are deeply at odds with mainstream modern thought in the West. The most prominent of these are the notions of acausality and objective meaning. *Acausality* is the idea that events can come into being or can be connected among one another without causal determination (*ibid.* §§818-821, 965). This notion further implies, as Jung's examples of synchronicity illustrate, that under certain psychic conditions there can be a *relativity of space and time* (*ibid.* §840), making it possible to gain knowledge of spatially and temporally remote events without the need for sensory transmission of information. Jung called such knowledge, unconditioned by the ego and consciousness, '*absolute knowledge*' (*ibid.* §§912, 923, 931, 948).

Jung's main argument in relation to meaning was that it was not merely a subjective factor – 'just a psychic product' or 'anthropomorphic interpretation' (*ibid.* §§915-916) – but could be objective. While he was aware of the extreme difficulty, perhaps even impossibility, of proving the reality of *objective meaning* (*ibid.* §915), he nonetheless reiterated that meaning, or, more cautiously, 'that factor which appears to us as "meaning"' (*ibid.* §916) could 'exist outside the psyche', 'outside man', and that it was 'self-subsistent', 'transcendental', and 'a priori in relation to human consciousness' (*ibid.* §§915, 942, 944). For Jung this objectivity

---

[4] On correlative thinking, see also Smith 32-36. Jung did not use the expression 'correlative thinking', or any German equivalent, but tended to refer more broadly to 'Chinese thinking' or the 'Chinese mind'. See Jung 1930: §§75, 85; 1950: §968 *et passim*; 1952: §924.

of the meaning expressed in synchronicities stemmed from his belief that meaning itself is rooted in archetypes, which he saw as structuring factors of the collective unconscious that are universal, numinous, psychophysically indeterminate (or 'psychoid'), and knowable only when expressed symbolically as archetypal images (*ibid.* §§840-841, 845, 964).

The connection of events through synchronicity implies that the same pattern of meaning can express itself in both psychic and physical events and thus reveals a sense in which at a deeper level those events form a *psychophysical unity* (*ibid.* §915), pointing, Jung argued, towards a fundamental 'unity of being' (*ibid.* §960), which he later came to call the *unus mundus* or 'one world' (Jung 1955-56: §662). Finally, the possibility of transcendental meaning and the unitary nature of reality revealing themselves in empirical psychic and physical events suggests that synchronicity expresses, however momentarily, a *harmony between transcendence and immanence* (Main 2007: 53-55).

Synchronicity and Poetry:
A Reading of (48) 'Welling, Replenishing'

The notions embedded in the concept of synchronicity – acausality, relativity of space and time, absolute knowledge, objective meaning, psychophysical unity, and harmony between transcendence and immanence – can help in attuning to the resonances between synchronicity and poetry. In very general terms, acausality articulates the essential creative moment of poetry. Indeed, one of Jung's pithier definitions of synchronicity was 'acts of creation in time' (Jung 1952: §965; also §§967-968). As for the notions of relativity of space and time and of absolute knowledge that are implied by acausality, these are evident in the ability and license of the poetic imagination to draw its material from any place or period and to articulate insights based on direct intuition. As Jung's writings show, together these notions also allow for the occurrence of radically anomalous events and altered states of consciousness (*ibid.* §§830-840, 846-857, 924-936) – the kinds of events and states that have contributed to legendary images of the poet as diviner, magician, or shaman.

The notion of objective meaning, which for Jung was collective and numinous, aptly expresses the qualities of universality and emotional intensity that can attach to poetic insights. Meanwhile, the psychophysical unity through which objective meaning expresses itself is implied in various aspects of poetry: for example, in the attribution of animate qualities to inanimate objects, in the portrayal of emotions through an 'objective correlative' (Eliot 107-108) and in the many subtle ways in which heterogeneous domains of form and content, or sound and sense, can correspond to one another. Finally, the harmony between transcendence and immanence that represents the deepest level of unity revealed by synchronicity has its parallel in the conception of poetry as a means of affirming and expressing the numinous while remaining grounded in quotidian realities.

However, rather than discuss the connections between poetry and synchronicity at a general level, in the remainder of this essay I should like to explore these connections by using the concept of synchronicity, with its various philosophical implications, as a lens through which to read closely one cluster of poems in *Changing*. Of the 450 poems that comprise *Changing*, I have chosen to comment on the seven in the cluster (48) 'Welling, Replenishing' (383-390), which are based on hexagram 48 of the *I Ching*, 井 *Jing* ('The Well', Wilhelm 185-188). I have been influenced in this choice both by Berengarten's identifying the motif of the well as the symbol that for him has most come to represent the *I Ching* itself (526-527) and by his presenting this cluster of poems as homage to Jung (555-556). I also happen to think that the cluster contains some particularly fine poetry.

As for all but two of the clusters in *Changing*, 'Welling, Replenishing' comprises seven poems, each of eighteen lines arranged in six tercets.[5] I shall comment on the poems in the sequence in which they occur.

'CONSULTATION OF THE DIAGRAMS'

The first, italicised poem, which Berengarten refers to as the 'head-poem', reads as follows:

Consultation
of the diagrams
is helpful

in the construction
of hypotheses, buildings
and voyages,

---

[5] The first and second clusters include an eighth poem, reflecting that the first two hexagrams of the *I Ching* have an extra line-reading.

in the precise
locating of wells, mines,
bridges, towers, mirrors,

in alleviating
insomnia and fears
of death,

in the correct
turning of antennae
towards origins

and in all forms of
measurement and modes
of harmonising.   (48/0: 384)

As can be seen immediately, this poem consists of a single, long but orderly sentence describing a variety of ways in which consulting the hexagrams of the *I Ching* can be helpful (ll.1-3). The ways are predominantly practical but cover physical (ll. 4-9), psychological (ll. 10-12), and spiritual (ll. 13-15) concerns. The concluding tercet generalises the idea that the utility of the hexagrams applies to all tasks involving the creation of measure and harmony (ll. 16-18).

Berengarten explains in his 'Postscript' that each head-poem of a numbered cluster 'is related thematically to its corresponding hexagram title and statement in the *I Ching*' (525). In the present case, however, there is no textual basis in the *I Ching* itself for relating the hexagram title of 'The Well' to the content of the head-poem, namely, use of the *I Ching*. Rather, the thematic relationship depends, aptly enough, on the 'symbolic resonance' between the well and the *I Ching* (526), an association that appears to be Berengarten's innovation, at least in the extent to which he has elaborated it.

An immediately striking feature of this head-poem is its understated, matter-of-fact tone and practical focus, which are in tension with the – from a modern viewpoint – extraordinary claims being made for the act of consulting the *I Ching*. For all of the ways in which consultation of the diagrams is said to be helpful in order to achieve the eminently rational objectives of 'measurement' and 'harmonising' involve the operation of divinatory, intuitive, or, as Jung called it in relation to synchronicity, 'absolute' knowledge, transgressing the usual strictures of time, space, and causality.

Also striking is the poem's comprehensive (albeit concise) coverage of content. As noted, the poem covers concerns that are variously physical ('construction [...] locating' [ll. 4,8]), psychological ('alleviating' [l. 10]), and spiritual ('turning [...] towards origins' [ll.14-15]). And within each tercet the phenomena mentioned reach out orthogonally from one another to capture different dimensions of experience: the 'construction' in lines 4 to 6 is of things abstract ('hypotheses'), concrete ('buildings'), and transitional ('voyages'); the 'precise locating' in lines 7 to 9 is of objects that effect various conjunctions: between ground and underground ('wells', 'mines'), one side of separated space and another ('bridges'), ground and sky ('towers'), and actual and reflected reality ('mirrors'); and the 'alleviating' in lines 10 to 12 is, first, of the inability to escape consciousness ('insomnia'), and then, contrastingly, of the dread of losing consciousness forever ('fears of death'). In the penultimate tercet (ll. 13-15) only one act of 'correct turning' is mentioned, but this simplification is also fitting since what is being referred to here is, as I read it, the finding of fundamental spiritual orientation ('turning of antennae / towards origins'), an idea arguably picked up in the final poem of the cluster.

The comprehensiveness so pithily evoked in this poem can be seen as a microcosm of the comprehensiveness of *Changing* as a whole, as well as of the *I Ching* itself. According to the *Dazhuan* ('The Great Treatise'), one of the early commentaries integrated into the canonical *I Ching*, 'The Changes is a book vast and great, in which everything is completely contained. The tao of heaven is in it, the tao of the earth is in it, and the tao of man is in it' (Wilhelm 351-352). Inspired by and following the structure of the *I Ching*, *Changing* as a whole is similarly encompassing in the range of subject matter covered by its 450 individual poems. The *Dazhuan* goes on to explain that the comprehensiveness of the *I Ching* stems from its being in a relationship of correspondence with 'heaven and earth', 'the four seasons', 'sun and moon', and 'the supreme power' (302). As Willard Peterson puts it, the *Dazhuan* would have us 'imagine, or perhaps believe, that the *Change* actually is a formal and processual duplicate of the realm of heaven-and-earth' (Peterson 1988: 225). In other words, the *Dazhuan* appears to be claiming that the workings of the *I Ching* move synchronistically in harmony with the movement of the cosmos as a whole. The correspondence of *Changing* with the *I Ching* and of '*Consultation of the diagrams*' with *Changing* charges this individual poem, and the cluster of which it is head, with the full potency of a synchronistic relationship.

193

1. 'Who drinks from an old well?'

The remaining six poems of 'Welling, Replenishing' relate in turn to the six line-statements of the corresponding hexagram in the *I Ching*, and they bear the numbers 1 to 6 in addition to their individual titles. The first of these numbered poems opens with the image of a dried up and abandoned well (ll. 1-3). The central twelve lines depict a society in which administrators, lawyers, politicians, and property owners have all become corrupt, causing ordinary citizens to emigrate (ll. 4-15). The poem ends by asking whether it is possible to find a dowser, presumably in order to rediscover the well or an alternative source of replenishment:

> [...] Can
>
> we find a dowser
> with forked hazel
> or willow branch?   (48/1: 385)

Unlike the head-poem, this first numbered poem begins thematically very close to the corresponding line-text of the *I Ching*. 'One does not drink the mud of the well. No animals come to an old well', reads the line-text (Wilhelm 187). 'Our well has dried / up. Not even birds / circle or settle here', read Berengarten's opening three lines. At this point, the poem abruptly shifts to an account of how society has been corrupted. This connection between the well and society is not without warrant in the *I Ching*. As Berengarten notes in his 'Postscript', the kind of well represented in hexagram 48 is that of the ancient Chinese 'well-field' (*jing tian*) system of social organisation, according to which 'fields or farms were divided into nine equally sized square areas, with eight families tilling one outer area each, while the ninth, the central one that belonged to the feudal overlord [and contained the well], was cultivated by all eight families' (*CH* 526, quoting Fung 10-13; Wilhelm 185-186). The Chinese character for 'well' 井 (*jing*) is a stylised representation of this arrangement of fields, whose 3 x 3 grid has itself been characterised as 'a sub-set of correlative thinking' (Peterson 1986: 659, reviewing Henderson). In this context, the implied correlation between the dried-up well abandoned by the birds and the corrupt society abandoned by its members seems apposite and natural enough.

The final lines introduce another seemingly abrupt change of topic in the poem: 'Can // we find a dowser / with forked hazel / or willow branch?'

But again this shift makes sense in terms of the cluster's emerging symbolism and correlative logic. The dried-up well symbolises a lack of access to intuitive wisdom, and without such wisdom society becomes corrupt. The renovation of society depends on renovating the well, that is, restoring access to intuitive wisdom. For this someone is needed – a 'dowser' (or diviner) – who has sufficient intuitive technique to be able to locate the lost source of water (or 'water-wisdom', as the fifth numbered poem will put it later). Given how deeply based *Changing* is on the divinatory text of the *I Ching*, it is easy to identify the needed intuitive technique, in at least one of its expressions, as poetry. The dowser-diviner, again in at least one of its expressions, would then be the figure of the poet. In implying this equation between diviner and poet Berengarten is not alone. In his 1974 lecture, 'Feeling into Words', Seamus Heaney, distinguishing technique from craft, characterises the former as involving the poet's 'discovery of ways to go out of his [or her] normal cognitive bounds and raid the inarticulate' (Heaney 19). He continues:

> If I were asked for a figure who represents pure technique, I would say a water diviner. You can't learn the craft of dowsing or divining – it is a gift for being in touch with what is there, hidden and real, a gift for mediating between the latent resource and the community that wants it current and released. As Sir Philip Sidney notes in his *Defence of Poesy*: 'Among the Romans a Poet was called *Vates*, which is as much as a Diviner …' […] The poet resembles the diviner in his ability to make contact with what lies hidden, and in his ability to make palpable what was sensed or raised. (*ibid.* 20)

In basing a long poem on what is undoubtedly the world's most revered book of divination, Berengarten seems to be affirming, as powerfully as could be wished, the status of the poet as *vates*.

A last thing to note before leaving 'Who drinks from an old well?' is that not only has the wellhead ceased to flow, but so, correspondingly, has the rhythm of the verse. Where the head-poem consists of a single sentence governed by one main verbal phrase ('is helpful'), this poem includes seven sentences and ten main verbs in the same number of lines.

2. 'Sometimes they answer'

The second numbered poem returns to the diagrams of the head-poem, though without referring to them other than through the pronoun 'they'.

The poem describes various ways in which, in the poet's experience, the hexagrams have sometimes operated at a tangent to conscious intention: providing answers when no question has been asked (ll. 1-3), outright disregarding the questions asked (ll. 4-6), or answering unformulated and unsuspected questions behind the questions consciously asked (ll. 7-18).

> Sometimes they answer
> even though I've asked
> no question.
>
> Sometimes they say
> nothing, and appear to
> smile and look away.
>
> Or else they stare, like
> the dead, through me
> towards infallible sky
>
> as quietly they pick
> out question *behind*
> question, before even
>
> any thought lurking under
> images and their nuances
> or timbres has arisen
>
> let alone right words
> to articulate thought have
> discovered me and opened.   (48/2: 386)

What immediately stands out about this poem is its personification of the hexagrams, which are the subject of all the main verbs: they 'answer', 'appear to / smile and look away', 'stare, like / the dead', and 'pick / out question *behind* / question'. They have autonomy and intentionality in relation to the person consulting them.[6] For linear diagrams in a book

---

[6] The sense of being related to by the *I Ching* as if by a person is a common experience among those who consult the oracle. The translator and commentator John Blofeld, for example, recounts that 'The first time I did this [consulted the *I Ching*], I was overawed to a degree that amounted to fright, so strong was my impression of having received an answer from a living breathing person' (26). For his part, Jung, when performing the consultation related in his foreword to the Wilhelm/Baynes translation, deliberately 'personified the book' in a manner that he believed to be 'strictly in accordance with the Chinese conception'

to exhibit personality in this way breaks down the normally assumed separation between the physical and psychic, 'getting rid', as Jung claimed synchronicity does, 'of the incommensurability between the observed and the observer' (Jung 1952: §960). What normally maintains the perspective of the separate observer is a dominant ego, yet here it is precisely the ego's intentions that are bypassed or thwarted. And not only has the expected object, the book, become the subject, but by the end of the poem the expected subject, the poet or inquirer, has become the object: it is not that the poet discovers the thoughts and words in which to formulate a question, but the thoughts and words 'have discovered' the poet.

Nor is it only the normally assumed relationship between the psychic and the physical that is subverted in this poem. So too is the normally assumed understanding of time as flowing straightforwardly from past to present to future, inasmuch as the oracle seems to know what the inquirer will ask before even the inquirer knows; to the *I Ching* the future seems somehow already to be present. The uncanny dimension in which such relativisation of time and such unconditioned knowing ('absolute knowledge') can take place is evoked by the image of the hexagrams staring '*like / the dead,* through me / towards *infallible* sky' (ll. 7-9, emphasis added). The understanding stemming from this dimension is non-representational, deeper than 'words', 'thoughts', 'images', and the 'nuances' and 'timbres' of images – a characterisation that evokes Jung's formulations of the irrepresentable archetype itself (as distinct from representable archetypal images), the 'psychoid' archetype, which he saw as the source of the objective meaning expressed in synchronicity.

The concluding lines of the poem – 'right words / to articulate thought have / discovered me and opened' – express the idea that, although the poet is the object of discovery by the words (that is, by the intelligence of the *I Ching*), it is only after that discovery that the words open; however objective the meaning expressed by the oracular pronouncement may be, the poet or inquirer, the 'me', even though de-centred, is necessary for its emergence. In an interview with Sean Rys in 2012, Berengarten had the

---

(1950: §975; see also RB 2016: 1, 534), and he received a response 'as though the *I Ching* itself were the speaking person' (Jung 1950: §977). I thank Richard Berengarten for recalling Blofeld's account to my attention. Berengarten has also pertinently noted in this connection that 'the intimate experience of *hearing a personal voice* that is markedly "other" corresponds to *poetic inspiration* (Muse, Muses) and *theophany* (e.g., the voice of God that appears to prophets in the Old Testament)' (personal communication).

following to say, with reference to his earlier poem *The Blue Butterfly*, about the role of the ego in synchronistic experiences:

> I would say that the transcendent experience of synchronicity that we've been talking about in relation to the making of this poem [*The Blue Butterfly*] didn't abolish ego-consciousness but, on the contrary, first consolidated it and strengthened it. My conclusion, then, is that identity, far from being obliterated, gets more firmly rooted, consolidated (grounded) and deepened through this kind of experience. (Nikolaou and Dillon 140)

This is a view that will receive powerful expression later in 'Welling, Replenishing', especially in the fourth and sixth numbered poems.

3. 'FROM UNDERGROUND STREAMS'

Standing at the centre of the cluster, this third numbered poem provides a vivid description of the hard, physical, co-operative work of restoring the well (ll. 1-16). It concludes by envisaging the repaired well's unprecedented capacity for storing water (ll. 16-18).

Where the previous poem focuses exclusively on the *I Ching*, the present poem focuses exclusively on the well. Its tone, like that of the head-poem, is literal and matter-of-fact. Unlike the head-poem, though, it depicts, in detail, just one enterprise – the restoring of the well. The picture it creates is vividly realised, with sound and rhythm perfectly matching sense in the descriptions of the activities of the workers, the equipment they use, the waste matter that has been choking the well, and the restored well itself. The diction, predominantly Anglo-Saxon rather than Latinate, is heavy with consonants and diphthongs. There is also a density of main verbs: 'clambered', 'let down', 'dredged up', 'Hauled out', 'Separated', 'Hammered', 'Deepened and widened'. And one can almost feel the materiality and earthiness of the objects named: 'ladders and ropes', 'shovels, sieves, / buckets, poles, mallets', 'mud and waste', 'rich stinking vegetable stuff / and rotten wood', 'clay', 'fields', 'brackets', 'walls'. As in the first numbered poem, there are seven short sentences that move with a slow, effortful rhythm. The rhythm only becomes more fluent in the concluding lines describing the capacity of the repaired well 'to hold more / water pooled from underground / streams than ever before' – the abundance of water evoked by the rapidly accumulating water words ('water', 'pooled', 'streams').

Although there is nothing internal to this poem to suggest that it should be read symbolically, its position within the cluster makes it inevitable to read it as a symbol of the *I Ching* and of all that the *I Ching* has come to represent in *Changing*. The restored well could thus stand for a renewed relationship to intuitive thinking – including correlative thinking, synchronicity, and poetry – a more holistic way of knowing, such as might help to mend the corrupted society depicted in the first numbered poem. The hard physical work so vividly conveyed by the present poem could be seen as symbolic of the effort needed to access and secure a stable relationship to such thinking, especially in a culture where intuitive thinking is not highly valued. And the depths of the well fed by the underground streams readily correspond to the collective unconscious and its currents that, in the Jungian framework, are the source of intuitive wisdom.

Seeing the present poem as an answer to the first numbered poem is facilitated by the parallels in their subject matter (a well in need of repair), in their rhythm (slow and effortful), and in the way they both strike a more forward-looking and optimistic note in their concluding three or four lines. There is also an interesting connection to the theme of ego-identity from the second numbered poem. In 'From underground streams', the first person plural pronoun is used at the beginning to introduce the activities described: 'We clambered down [...]', 'We dredged up [...]'. Thereafter, however, the pronoun is dropped: 'Hauled out [...]', 'Separated [...]', 'Hammered in [...]', 'Deepened and widened [...]'. It is as though the sense of self has been supplanted or transcended, or at least forgotten about, by absorption in the sheer activities. There is arguably, too, a subtle foreshadowing of subsequent poems in the cluster, especially in the repeated use of the prepositions 'down', 'up', 'in', 'out', suggesting connection and interchange between levels of reality (above and below, transcendent and immanent) and between dimensions of experience (inner and outer, psychic and physical) – themes that are elaborated in what follows.

4. '*I Ching*'

In '*I Ching*', another fluent, single-sentence poem, the poet personifies the divinatory book, addresses it intimately (ll. 2-3), and offers a laudatory enumeration of its extraordinary qualities (ll. 4-13). The poem ends with a double paradox: the act of 'plumbing' the well that is the *I Ching* enables the poet to 'soar' (ll. 14-15), yet in soaring the poet remains securely 'grounded' (ll. 16-18).

Comprising a mere forty-two words and shorn of articles, this is the sparest poem in the cluster. Yet it powerfully expresses, as I read it, several major aspects of the vision of *Changing*, especially as this relates to synchronicity. First, the personification of the *I Ching* in the second numbered poem is even more in evidence, as now the poet is in direct relationship to the book, addressing it intimately as 'friend, companion / and spirit-guide' (ll. 2-3). As in the earlier poem, this transgression of the usual modern view that would maintain an ontological division between physical artefacts (such as books) and psychic qualities (such as spiritual wisdom and capacity for relationship) points to the idea of a unitary psychophysical reality, which is one of the key implications of synchronicity.

Second, the qualities praised in absolute terms in lines 4 to 6 – 'always trustworthy, / never diffident / never irrelevant' – express that the *I Ching* has been experienced as affording access to a kind of knowledge that would be beyond the powers of human consciousness to produce on its own. What is evoked is the 'absolute knowledge' that for Jung is implied in the occurrence of synchronicity.

Third, the paradoxical formulations in lines 7 to 9 – 'solid yet flowing / firm yet yielding / radiating images' – primarily allude to the *I Ching*'s unbroken and broken lines and their creative expression in the trigrams and hexagrams with their associated texts. These generative ('radiating') images of the *I Ching*, internally charged by the interplay of opposites and capable of manifesting in both psychic and physical contexts, are equivalent to Jung's archetypes, the factors underpinning the objective meaning disclosed in synchronicity.

Fourth, in lines 10 to 13, the terms 'self-replenishing' and 'inexhaustible', met already in the base-line to the head-poem but accompanied now by 'fathomless' and 'ever-fresh', evoke ideas of acausality, creativity, transcendence, and eternity. Yet, no sooner have they done so than, seamlessly, the main clause in the closing lines of the poem balances this move towards transcendence with an equally emphatic expression of immanence: 'in plumbing you / I soar // feet still / grounded rooted / in *this here now*' (ll. 14-18; emphasis in original). The repetition of rhythm, absence of connective, and deepening in meaning of 'grounded rooted' and the triplet of stressed and italicised monosyllables '*this here now*' make absolutely clear that the mysterious operations of the *I Ching* do not entail forsaking what William Blake called, in a phrase often invoked by Berengarten, 'the minute particulars'.[7]

---

[7] The phrase appears in *Jerusalem*, Plate 55, ll. 48–53, 60–6. See Blake 745-746. For Berengarten's uses of the term, see Nikolaou and Dillon 52, 84, 86.

5. 'I LOWER MY QUESTION'

The penultimate poem of the cluster celebrates the abundant wisdom that can be accessed by consulting the *I Ching* (ll. 1-9), explicitly symbolised by the well:

> I lower my
> question on a rope
> of thought.
>
> I draw up
> water-wisdom. It
> flows everywhere.
>
> I drink from a fund
> of deep light. Could
> wine be sweeter?   (48/5: 389)

The poem also expresses the poet's readiness to accept the oracle's responses with gratitude and humility, whether the responses are negative or positive (ll. 10-18):

> If its taste is bitter
> then I swallow it. Its
> bitterness is me.
>
> Is it sweet? Then
> I'm thankful – but
> keep aloof from
>
> drugs coiled in
> sweetness. These ways
> I come and go.   (*ibid.*)

Like the first and third numbered poems, this poem is concerned with ethical implications of the *I Ching*. In 'Who drinks from an old well?' there is a correlation between the well being dried-up and society being corrupt, with the implication that restoring the well (symbolically, the *I Ching* and the kind of thinking that underpins it) could help to mend society. In 'From underground streams', the laborious task of restoring the well has been taken up and carried through successfully, creating an abundant source of replenishment – symbolically, the implication is, as well as literally. The fifth numbered poem now describes a responsible, balanced way of using this resource: appreciating what it gives, without either avoiding negative ('bitter') outcomes or one-sidedly identifying with positive ('sweet') outcomes. Taken together, these three poems presuppose an ethical dimension to the order of objective meaning that reveals itself in divinatory and synchronistic events.

In 'I lower my question,' the synchronistic unity of psyche and matter expressed by the *I Ching*'s being symbolically equated with the well is explicit in the phrases 'a rope of thought' and 'water-wisdom', which combine in single images the psychic ('thought', 'wisdom') and the physical ('rope', 'water'). That the water-wisdom 'flows everywhere' expresses the idea that normal spatial limitations, like normal temporal limitations, can be transgressed by divinatory insights. And the phrase 'I drink from a fund / of deep light', which combines the mundane act of drinking with an image evocative of mystical realisation, recalls the harmony between transcendence and immanence so powerfully articulated in the preceding poem.

6. 'WELL, INEXHAUSTIBLE'

This final poem in the cluster is another single-sentence poem, which this time unfolds towards its end without even a main verb. It again addresses the *I Ching*, symbolised by the well, in laudatory terms. This praise is followed by a series of powerful metaphors through which a vivid picture of the well emerges (ll. 3-14). The poem concludes with the image of a star reflected at the bottom of the well (ll. 15-18).

In this poem, the personification that we have seen in the second and fourth numbered poems returns even more emphatically. The *I Ching*, symbolised by the well, is not only directly addressed but also attributed a 'face' (l. 4), a 'mouth' (l. 6), and a 'gaze' (l. 7); and organic and animate features are attributed more widely: heaven and earth are ascribed 'skin and core' (ll. 13-14) and the sky a 'forehead' (l. 17). Besides this conjunction of the psychic and physical, other unions of usually opposed ideas are also evoked. In the lines, 'generous // secret, open face / of Underworld' (ll. 3-5), what normally withholds gives and what is normally inaccessible is open and scrutable – paradoxes reinforced by the deft juxtaposition 'secret, open'. The 'rounded mouth // and level gaze' (ll. 6-7) simultaneously build the picture of the round, still well and suggest the *I Ching*'s encompassing powers of expression and imperturbable wisdom. The next pair of metaphors, 'polished mirror and / porthole of night' (ll. 8-9), depict further the smooth, black surface of the water at the bottom of the well, preparing for the concluding lines of the poem and at the same time evoking ideas of scrying and of seeing through from our cabined existence to an oceanic vastness beyond.[8]

The idea of connection between different levels of reality continues in the lines that conclude the encomiastic invocation of the *I Ching*/well: 'silvery cord / and vertical pipe / invisibly joining // heaven and earth's / skin and core' (ll. 10-14). The 'silvery cord' is what links the spirit to the body in Ecclesiastes 12:6-7, or the astral body to the physical body in accounts of astral projection within Western occultism and studies of out-of-body experiences (Muldoon and Carrington) – associations that are appropriate enough in an invocation that by this point has become almost ecstatic. Calling the well a 'vertical pipe' highlights the idea of conveyance from one level to another, and the extremes between which the conveyance and invisible 'joining' take place are both cosmic ('heaven and earth's' – also suggesting above and below) and intimate ('skin and core' – also suggesting outer and inner). Taken together, all these images of conjunction and unity create an overwhelming sense of wholeness, an impression encapsulated by the image of the well itself, which in this poem emerges unequivocally as circular, mandalic.[9]

Following the fourteen lines of address to the *I Ching*/well, the poem ends with four lines of which the first three begin with prepositions of location ('*beneath* these eyes // *in* your reflection / *on* the sky's forehead –' [ll. 15-17, emphasis added]), which rapidly focus attention in the fourth and last line on a single point, the concluding words and image of the poem – 'a star' (l. 18). In this marvellously realised image of a single star reflected in the bottom of the dark well, the farthest-away object is located in the lowest visible depth, perfectly expressing again the idea of harmony between transcendence and immanence.

The second and third numbered poems hint that engagement with the divinatory process of the *I Ching* is capable of drawing a person into a process of personal transformation. The fifth numbered poem extends this idea by highlighting the ethical dimension of consulting the oracle. This

---

[8] On the polished mirror, see also Blofeld 31. I thank Richard Berengarten for sharing this reference.

[9] For Jung the mandala was the symbol *par excellence* of wholeness, and could refer to not just psychological wholeness, the self, but also cosmic wholeness, the *unus mundus* ('one world'). See Jung 1955-56: §662.

final poem presents a further, perhaps culminating stage of personal transformation. Where first-person pronouns have appeared in all the previous poems of the cluster except the head-poem, here the phrase 'these eyes' is the only hint of the poet's subjectivity. The phrase is included as a single though by no means central element in a wider field in which subjectivity and objectivity are combined, where the well is addressed in the second person ('*your* reflection') and the sky is personified (has a 'forehead'). At the focal point within this subjective-objective field appears a star. In a poem that makes such sparing use of articles and in a phrase from which even the expected main verb ('is') has been omitted, the decision to use the indefinite article 'a' is deeply significant. The particularity brought into focus by engagement with the *I Ching* and all that it symbolises is not '*the* star' but '*a* star' – one realised entity among many potential such entities, an 'individual'. Of course, the individual that might be symbolised by the star is not the poet's or inquirer's ego, which, displaced from centrality, is, as we have seen, merely part of the observing totality. In terms of Jung's thought, the star – or rather, the star and the circle of well-water in which it manifests: a centre and a circumference – here would likely be a symbol of realised wholeness, psychologically of the self, but also, cosmologically, of the *unus mundus*, the unitary nature of reality as a whole.

It is interesting to compare this poem, the last in the cluster, with the head-poem, the first. Both consist of a single, long sentence celebrating the range and power of the *I Ching*. However, whereas the head-poem is practical in focus, matter-of-fact in its use of language, and understated in tone, the final poem is mystical in focus, richly metaphorical in its use of language, and ecstatic in tone. As already noted, the expressions 'self-replenishing' and 'inexhaustible – which for Berengarten appear to be the essence of the correlation between the *I Ching* and the (restored) well – are buried in the base-line in the head-poem, while in the final poem they are the opening words. Finally, while both poems stand out from the others in the cluster for not including any first-person pronouns, in the head-poem the effect is of impersonality, while in the final poem it is rather of 'trans-personality', that is, of a field that includes but also transcends ordinary personality.

Conclusion

In his 'Postscript' to *Changing*, Berengarten discusses the special significance for him of hexagram 48, 井 *Jing* ('The Well') as a symbol of the
I Ching as a whole; and he concludes his comments with the hope that
his poem, like the well, might *'reflect and echo itself* to a reader while it
is being read, and so enable the reader to reflect *on* it', as well as 'reflect
and echo (*and* enable the reader to reflect on) the material it integrates,
the processes of its own making, and its own "deep" source, the *I Ching*'
(527, emphasis in original). In this essay I have aimed to read the poems
specifically associated with hexagram 48 in the spirit of these statements
by the poet. What I have seen and heard from my gazing and calling
into this well suggests to me that Berengarten's insight that correlative
thinking – and by implication its modern expression as synchronicity – is
foundational for poetry stands up to scrutiny and indeed is a perspective
that can generate considerable illumination both in theorising about
poetry and in analysing actual poems. Of course, Berengarten's interest
in Jungian psychology and synchronicity, his having based *Changing* on
the *I Ching*, and my having chosen to analyse a cluster of poems that is
explicitly linked to both Jung and the *I Ching*, have all facilitated these
observations about the relationship between synchronicity and poetry. But
such facilitation, I would argue, only reflects that this relationship is part
of what *Changing*, as both a visionary poem and an *ars poetica*, purposely
expresses. Through the comprehensive range of its subject matter and the
insightful and generative connections of its poetry, *Changing* advocates a
holistic, creative vision of reality, in which reality can be divined, read, and
written poetically, and in which poetry can be productively envisioned as
a form of 'applied' synchronicity.

References

Berengarten, Richard. 2008. *The Blue Butterfly* (second edition). Cambridge:
Salt Publishing.

———— . 2015. *Notness: Metaphysical Sonnets*. Bristol: Shearsman Books.

———— . 2016. *Changing*. Bristol: Shearsman Books.

———— . 2020. 'A Synchronistic Experience in Serbia'. In *Holism: Possibilities
and Problems* (eds. Christian McMillan, Roderick Main, and David
Henderson). London and New York: Routledge, 154-169.

Blake, William. 1977. *The Complete Poems*. Alicia Ostriker (ed.). Harmondsworth, UK: Penguin.

Blofeld, John (trans.). 1991. *I Ching: The Book of Change*. London: Arkana.

Burns [now Berengarten], Richard. 1981. *Ceri Richards and Dylan Thomas: Keys to Transformation*. London: Enitharmon Press.

Eliot, Thomas Stearns. 1953. 'Hamlet [1919]'. In *T. S. Eliot: Selected Prose* (ed. John Hayward). Harmondsworth, UK: Penguin, 104-109.

Fung Yu-Lan. 1983. *A History of Chinese Philosophy*, vol. 1. Bode, Derk (trans.). Princeton, NJ: Princeton University Press.

Heaney, Seamus. 2002. *Finders Keepers: Selected Prose 1971-2001*. London: Faber and Faber.

Henderson, John. 1984. *The Development and Decline of Chinese Cosmology*. New York: Columbia University Press, 1984.

Jung, Carl Gustav. 1930. 'Richard Wilhelm: In Memoriam'. In *Collected Works*, vol. 15, *The Spirit in Man, Art and Literature*. London: Routledge and Kegan Paul, 1966, 53-62.

——— . 1950. 'Foreword to the "I Ching"'. In *Collected Works*, vol. 11, *Psychology and Religion: West and East*, 2nd ed. London: Routledge and Kegan Paul, 1969, 589-608.

——— . 1951. 'On Synchronicity'. In *Collected Works*, vol. 8, *The Structure and Dynamics of the Psyche*, 2nd ed. London: Routledge and Kegan Paul, 1969, 520-531.

——— . 1952. 'Synchronicity: An Acausal Connecting Principle'. In *Collected Works*, vol. 8, *The Structure and Dynamics of the Psyche*, 2nd ed. London: Routledge and Kegan Paul, 1969, 417-519.

——— . 1955-56. *Collected Works*, vol. 14, *Mysterium Coniunctionis: An Inquiry into the Separation and Synthesis of Psychic Opposites in Alchemy*, 2nd ed. London: Routledge and Kegan Paul, 1970.

Main, Roderick. 1997. 'Synchronicity and the *I Ching*: Clarifying the Connections'. *Harvest: Journal for Jungian Studies* 43(1), 31-44.

——— .2004. *The Rupture of Time: Synchronicity and Jung's Critique of Modern Western Culture*. Hove and New York: Brunner-Routledge.

——— . 2007. *Revelations of Chance: Synchronicity as Spiritual Experience*. Albany, NY: State University of New York Press.

Muldoon, Sylvan, and Carrington, Hereward. 1969. *The Phenomena of Astral Projection*. London: Rider.

Nikolaou, Paschalis, and Dillon, John (eds.). 2017. *Richard Berengarten: A Portrait in Inter-Views*. Bristol: Shearsman Books.

Peterson, Willard.1986. Review of *The Development and Decline of Chinese Cosmology*, by John Henderson. *Harvard Journal of Asiatic Studies* 46: 657-674.

———. 1988. 'Some Connective Concepts in China in the Fourth to Second Centuries B.C.E.'. *Eranos* 57: 201-234.

Smith, Richard J. 2008. *Fathoming the Cosmos and Ordering the World: The Yijing (I-Ching, or Classic of Changes) and Its Evolution in China*. Charlottesville, VA: University of Virginia Press.

Wilhelm, Richard (trans.). 1968. *The I Ching or Book of Changes* (third edition). Rendered into English by Cary Baynes. London: Routledge and Kegan Paul.

SHEN HEYONG

Poetry, Heart and Soul:
Richard Berengarten's *Changing*

詩言志，心有靈犀

As poetry expresses aspiration, so the heart communicates the spiritual. [1]

For more than two thousand years, the *I Ching* 易經 has been considered the first of the Six Confucian Classics and the manifestation of the Way (Dao 道), that is, the harmonious natural order. The "Literature" section of the *History of the Han Dynasty* (*Hanshu, Yiwenzhi* 漢書,藝文志) identifies the moral orientation of each Classic, and the overarching importance of the *Changes* in particular:

> The *Book of Music* for the harmony of gods and the embodiment of benevolence; the *Book of Songs* for uprightness of words and the uses of righteousness; the *Book of Rites* for brightening the body, all the brighter to see; the *Book of Documents* for the widely heard, so that knowledge may also be known; and the *Spring and Autumn Annals* for judging things, as the symbol of trust. These five books cover the five common ways, but the core and original source of them all is the *Book of Change*. Therefore, the *Book of Change* is the most important of all the Classics. This in turn means that the *Book of Change* itself is the core of culture, including the wisdom of the spirit and of the heart. (Ban 34)

The *I Ching*'s moral authority derives primarily from its reputation as a book of wisdom that reflects the patterns and processes of the cosmos,

---

[1] *Editors' note*: The first part of this statement presents a definition of poetry which appears in several ancient contexts (see 209-210 below, esp. note 3). The second is a popular Chinese saying about love and friendship. Placing these two together is the author's original (and imaginative) combination.

the natural Way. On the back cover of an edition of the Wilhelm/Baynes translation of the *I Ching*, we find this idea: "The *I Ching*, or *Book of Changes*, represents one of the first efforts of the human mind to place itself in the universe." Richard Berengarten joins this long tradition of philosophical inquiry, scholarly exegesis, and poetic inspiration. Indeed, his choice of the character 'Dao' 道 (the Way) for his Chinese name, Li Dao (李道), suggests his ongoing effort to use the *Changes* as a means of exploring the mysterious, infinitely complex connections that unite the realms of Heaven (*Tian*, 天), Earth (*Di*, 地) and Man (*Ren*, 人).

The title of his book, *Changing*, may be translated into Chinese in several ways: for example: *Bianhua* (變化, old script; 变化 new script), which can express a range of meanings, including 'change, variation, modification, fluctuation, substitution', and possibly 'transformation'; and *Zhuanhua* (轉化, old script; 转化, new script), which can mean 'change, transformation, exchange, conversion, cyclic change'.[2] *Changing* not only articulates the wisdom and inspiration of the *I Ching* but also witnesses its mystery and fascination. C. G. Jung called the images of the *I Ching*'s hexagrams "readable archetypes" (Jung 1976: 584). *Changing* embodies these archetypal images and their rich, polysemous meanings.

"Poetry expresses aspiration." So says Wei Hong's 'Great Preface' to the *Shijing* (*Book of Songs*). The statement continues with an expansion: "Poetry expresses aspiration. In the heart reside aspirations. Speaking (them) out is poetry." (《诗言志。毛詩大序曰：詩者、志之所之也。在心爲志。發言爲詩。》)[3]

In the second of these pronouncements, an early connotation of the character 志 *zhi* ('aspiration, ambition, will'), was 'intention, meaningful intention'. Xu Shen's *Shuowen jiezi* 說文解字 (lit. "Discussing Writing

---

[2] *Editors' note*: These last senses ('conversion' and 'cyclic change') may well suggest 'diametrical reversal'. This meaning is very close, if not identical, to the idea conveyed by Aristotle by means of his term περιπέτεια (*peripeteia*), in his analysis of tragedy (*Poetics* 11: Loeb edn. 64-65). This kind of change, i.e. of a situation into its direct opposite, is accounted for in the structure of the *I Ching*. It occurs when every line in a hexagram is a 'change-line': i.e. when all *yin* lines transform into *yang*, and vice-versa. In the context of tragedy, Aristotle notes that περιπέτεια always produces ἀναγνώρισις (*anagnorisis*, 'recognition or discovery'.)

[3] The first sentence also appears as part of a longer statement in the ancient *Book of Documents*: 《尚书,虞书，舜典》：《言志，歌永言，声依永，律和声。》 ("Poetry expresses aspiration; and this expression is perpetuated in singing, accompanied with variation in tunes, harmonised through rhythm or melody." See also 208 above, note 1.

and Explaining Characters") was written during the Han Dynasty to serve as a dictionary. This text contains an entry that, roughly translated, reads: "Follow the tone of the heart and *zhi* ('advance, go forward'). *Zhi* means the heart advancing."

Since the core-text of the *I Ching,* the so-called *Zhouyi,* meaning the 'Zhou Changes', was compiled or composed "most probably, during the last two decades of the ninth century, B. C." (Shaughnessy 49), etymological exploration of its Chinese characters and of their components yields profound historical insights, and these inform our current interpretation. An ancient form of the character 志 *zhi* looks like this:

The upper part of this graph means 'advance, go forward', and the lower, 心 *xin,* meaning 'heart', frequently occurs as a 'radical' (i.e. a basic semantic indicator) in Chinese words. The upper graph represents a seed growing out of the earth. The combined graph, then, clearly presents the image of *a seed emerging from the heart.* Thus, traditional Chinese psychology may be said to imply that, first, the heart is the 'seedbed' of aspiration; and, second, *seed* and *heart* share a common motif: that of a 'natural core'. Indeed, the Chinese word 芯 *xin* ('core') contains the radical graph 'heart' 心 *xin* beneath not one but two growing seeds, which yields 艹 *cao,* the 'grass' radical. So the motif of 'the core of the core' invokes the forms of both heart and natural organic vegetal growth. Confucius construes this nexus to indicate nothing less than the essential quality of *benevolence* or *kindness* (*ren* 仁), that is, of *being-human* and *being-humane,* all of which underpin his noble conception of the 人 *ren* ('person, human being'). Herein lies the first principle of Confucianism.

Overall, then, we can interpret the formative image and symbolic meaning of 志 *zhi* ('aspiration') as 'the sprouting of the seed of the heart', and we may legitimately interpret this graph in English to imply the composite idea of 'heart-motivated intention' or 'will activated by heart-felt desire.'

Significantly, in *Changing,* the image of the heart is to be found in many varied contexts:

[…] voices, not mine,

that speak inside my
head and heart […]   ('Other voices', 17/2: 138)

[…] *heart healed by living*
waters, eyes and ears
sky-filled, star-rooted […]   ('*Young Arthur*', 19/0: 152)

[…] by following the heart's
paths and injunctions – to
reaffirm […] dignity   ('[A] coherent language', 23/6: 190)

[…] *to anyone else's*
deepest and most
heartfelt words […]   ('*We thirst but drink too little*
                                             water', 47/0: 376)

Similarly, the heart appears in several titles:

'With their whole hearts'   (29/3: 235)

'Unpredictable heart'   (31/5: 252)

And also in 'base-lines'

resonances […] *from the heart's core*   ('We wash things', 15/2: 122)

approaching […] *big-hearted*   ('At Dragon Gate', 19/6: 158)

returning […] *noble-hearted*   ('Under the bridge', 24/5: 197)

From this quick survey of a key term in Berengarten's *Changing* viewed through the lens of Chinese etymology, the themes of the ancient *Book of Songs* are again made manifest. *Poetry expresses aspiration. Aspiration resides in the heart. Speaking out is poetry. Poetry is the heart speaking.* This pattern of interconnections is already implicit in the Chinese graphs themselves. This is to say: the Chinese characters *themselves embed inner archetypal images.*

While studying the *I Ching*, C. G. Jung learned the Chinese characters that designate the hexagrams' names. In the *Red Book*, he writes: "One would like to learn this language, but who can teach and learn it? Scholarliness alone is not enough; *there is a knowledge of the heart that gives deeper insight.*" (Jung 2009: 233; emphasis added). Blaise Pascal writes:

"Le cœur a ses raisons, que la raison ne connaît point" ("The heart has its reasons, of which reason knows nothing," *Pensées* 277). Echoing Pascal – again in *The Red Book* – Jung responds: "Scholarliness belongs to the spirit of this time, but this spirit in no way grasps the dream, since the soul is everywhere that scholarly knowledge is not." (*op. cit.* 2009: 233).

દ્ગ

Speaking out is poetry. Poetry is the language of the heart. Poetry expresses aspirations. The heart possesses tacit understanding. This is the theme that Richard Berengarten explores in *Changing*. While reading his 'Tree' (RB 2011a) and *The Blue Butterfly* (RB 2011b), I have also responded to this same resonant quality – engendered by "the heart's tacit understanding".

The many meanings of the *I Ching*, especially for Depth Psychology, concern not only the telling of fortune or misfortune but also the rinsing (purifying, cleansing) of the heart, and its (re)awakening. As an archetypal image, the beat of the heart resonates not only in relation to the human world ('the very pulse of things'), but equally in and for everything else on earth and in heaven – that is, in and for the *Dao*. As Hexagram 24, 復 *Fu* ('Returning'), says: "Returning, to see the heart of heaven and earth" (Fu: 142-143).

Changing is Richard Berengarten's poetic exploration and celebration of the *I Ching*. Here, a "return" to deep connections, which necessarily involves "the heart's tacit understanding", is constantly evident. In this context, hexagram 4 (蒙 *Meng*), which is formed from the trigram *mountain* ☶ (艮 *Gen*) over *water* ☵ (坎 *Kan*), is worth attention. *Meng* is rendered by Wilhelm/Baynes as 'Youthful Folly' (Wilhelm: 20), and by Berengarten as 'Bringing up' (*CH* 31).[4] Berengarten introduces his set of seven linked poems, with the magical picture of a child counting (4/0: 32). Then, a poem entitled 'Himself at the centre' responds to the hexagram's first line:

---

[4] *Editors' note*: Wilhelm (1967: 20) explains in a footnote that by the words "fool" and "folly", he means "immaturity of youth and its consequent lack of wisdom rather than stupidity". In all the poems in this cluster except one ('Dependence veiled', 4/3: 35), Berengarten avoids this possible misunderstanding by interpreting this hexagram through poems that explore the world of children and childhood, rather than youth or youthfulness in the wider sense.

So first he drew a building
with himself and his family
in it and he wrote *home*.   ('Himself at the centre', 4/1: 33)

The themes of home and childhood are central to Berengarten's treatment
of this hexagram. Interestingly, here too the formation of the Chinese
characters reveals a connection between 家 *jia* 'home, family' and 蒙 *Meng*.
This connectedness is immediately evident in the identical lower part of
the two graphs, both of which contain the graph 豕 *shi*, 'pig' – a symbol of
nourishment and well being. *Meng* 蒙 displays the upper radical consisting
of two small sprouts growing (艹 *cao* 'grass'), which we have already seen
in 芯 *xin* ('core') – while in *jia* 家 ('home, family'), the 'roof' radical 宀
appears over 豕 *shi*, 'pig', a combination that is quickly readable as a symbol
of protected, protective, stable nurture and upbringing.

Not only do these related images indicate commonality, but the
poems of *Changing* – at least from my point of view and so far as my own
response to them is concerned – are attuned to these implicit connections,
because "the heart possesses tacit understanding" – *because the poet intuits
connectivity*.

For the 'nine in the second place' of the *Meng* hexagram, Wilhelm
interprets the old *yang* line as: "To bear with fools in kindliness brings
good fortune" (Wilhelm/Baynes 22). By contrast, the poem that Berengarten devotes to this hexagram-line tells of an event at a poetry workshop
in an English primary school, when "a nine-year old boy / called Shane
stood up and // read the poem he'd been / making." After this, everyone
fell quiet, and

[…] in that silence we
were held in an almost palpable
ring of awe, made by

Shane's words rippling
on and through air into our
ears, until one child

put hands together
and started clapping and
everyone joined in.   ('In the primary school', 4/2: 34)

The basic structure of the hexagram 'Bringing up' is that *yang* follows
yin. The outer *yang* lines nearly (though not entirely) hold and contain

the *yin*. Overall, the function of 蒙 *Meng* is to comment on nurturing the young. Well reflected in Berengarten's poems, the motifs clustered in hexagram 4 combine the theme of 'growth from the heart' with the need for 'safe and secure protection'. This combination expresses the meaning of family upbringing, of educating and nourishing children.

ɛ⅋ɔ

On January 3, 1957, in a letter to Michael Fordham, Jung wrote:

> The experience you had with the *I Ching*, calling you to order when trying to tempt it a second time, also happened to me in 1920 when I first experimented with it. It also gave me a wholesome shock and the same time it opened wholly new vistas to me. I well understand that you prefer to emphasize the archetypal implication in synchronicity. (Jung 1973: 343)

I think what Jung had in mind here was the hexagram 'Bringing up'. The image for the hexagram in Richard Wilhelm's translation is:

> A spring wells up at the foot of the mountain:
> The image of YOUTH.
> Thus the superior man fosters his character
> By thoroughness in all that he does. (Wilhelm/Baynes 20-21)

In 2006, we held the 2nd international conference of Analytical Psychology and Chinese Culture. Afterwards, we made a trip to Mount Tai, to Spring City in Jinan, and to Qufu, the home city of Confucius.[5] That night in Qufu, I had a dream in which a voice called out: "A spring wells up at the foot of the mountain. That's what *Meng* means." When I woke up, the connections were immediately clear to me: a spring, Spring City; the mountain, Mount Tai; and *Meng* ('Upbringing') and Confucius, the enlightened educator. This dream vividly brought home to me the real and living presence of this hexagram's archetypal image in the psyche.

ɛ⅋ɔ

Poetry expresses aspiration. A seed grows from the heart. The heart possesses tacit understanding. In the wake of C. G. Jung, Richard Berengarten's poems

---

[5] *Editors' note*: Jinan (济南) is also called '泉城' (the City of Springs), for its abundance of springs.

manifest many of the themes of Analytical Psychology. Consider the poem *'Way Down'* in the context of the image and meaning of hexagram 29, *Kan* 坎, which Wilhelm entitles 'The Abysmal (Water)' (Wilhelm/Baynes 114), and Berengarten, 'Falling (in a Pit)' (231):

> *If all ways are*
> *gifts, named or unnamed,*
> *downwards may yield*
>
> *dark treasure,*
> *though it is called*
> *unnameable, being*
>
> *so swift sweep-*
> *ing in arrival, no*
> *recognizance can*
>
> *prepare the heart*
> *for batterings there*
> *to be endured.*
>
> *From retrospects*
> *you'll know later*
> *were no accidents,*
>
> *courage. What is*
> *yet indecipherable, you*
> *will mark and name.*　　　　　　(29/0: 232)

This poem implies that an inevitable downward movement is being experienced by its addressee – a breakdown perhaps? The speaker, though, after saying that "the heart" will "endure" the "batterings" that will need to be faced in the depths – in which "dark treasure" may also be found – finally invokes "courage", thereby offering *encouragement*. The word *courage* itself derives, via French *cœur*, from Latin *cor*, 'heart'.

Structurally, hexagram 29 reduplicates the trigram for 'water' ☵, just as the contrary and complementary hexagram 30 does for the trigram 'fire' ☲. The Chinese name for both the trigram 'water' ☵ and its doubling hexagram is 坎 *Kan* and, for the trigram ☲ and its corresponding hexagram, 'fire', 離 *Li*. Interestingly, in *I Ching* tradition, when the pure primary *yin* principle ☷ (redoubled as hexagram 2, 坤 *Kun*) is manifested in the phenomenal world of human experience, it transforms into 'water', in the same way as the contrary *yang* principle ☰ (reduplicated as hexagram 1, 乾 *Qian*) is manifested in the phenomenal world by transforming into 'fire'. And since *Qian* is the image of 'heaven' and *Kun* of 'earth', so 'fire' is to 'heaven' as 'water' is to 'earth'. Thus analogy and parallelism (equivalence) both come into play here. These quaternary correspondences and transformations are mapped in the diagram below, together with the English names for these hexagrams given by both Wilhelm and Berengarten.

TRANSFORMATIONS AND CORRESPONDENCES						
	TRIGRAM	HEXAGRAM (DOUBLED TRIGRAM)		CHINESE NAME AND MEANING	HEXAGRAM NAME IN ENGLISH	
	Form	Form	Number		Wilhelm/ Baynes	Berengarten
Pure Yang	☰	䷀	1	乾 *Qian* Heaven	The Creative	Initiating
transforms	↓	↓	↓	↓	↓	↓
in the phenomenal world	☲	䷝	30	離 *Li* Fire	The Clinging	Clinging
Pure Yin	☷	䷁	2	坤 *Kun* Earth	The Receptive	Responding, Corresponding
transforms	↓	↓	↓	↓	↓	↓
in the phenomenal world	☵	䷜	29	坎 *Kan* Water	The Abysmal	Falling into a pit

I Ching: some patterns of 'elemental'
transformations into the phenomenal world [6]

---

[6] In a similarly elegant counterpoint, the *I Ching*'s two final hexagrams, numbers 63 (既濟 *Ji Ji*, ䷾) and 64 (未濟 *Wei Ji*, ䷿), present *both* possible combinations of 坎 *Kan* 'water' ☵ and 離 *Li* 'fire' ☲. In the former, 'water' ☵ appears over 'fire' ☲, and in the latter, vice-versa. The contrastive titles of these two hexagrams are rendered into English respectively as 'After Completion' and 'Before Completion' by Wilhelm/Baynes (244 and 248), and as 'After crossing over' and 'Before crossing over' by Berengarten (503 and 511).

To conclude her book entitled *Sandplay: A Psychotherapeutic Approach to the Psyche*, Dora Kalff, a student of C. G. Jung and the founder of Sandplay Therapy, also deploys the image of water falling to the lowest possible level:

> The many-sided psyche expresses itself in images and dreams. To access the psyche's creative center, we must try to understand this symbolic language. When we are able to understand the language of symbols, a transformation of the psyche is effected. [...] All in all, the course of psychic development can best be compared with flowing water. A commentary in the *I Ching* says: *It flows on and on, and merely fills up all of the places through which it flows; it does not shrink from any dangerous spot nor from any plunge, and nothing can make it lose its own essential nature. [...] It remains true to itself under all conditions.* Thus likewise, if one is sincere when confronted with difficulties, the heart can penetrate the meaning of the situation. And once we have gained inner mastery of a problem, it will come about naturally that the action we take will succeed. (Kalff 140; emphasis added)

A similar plea for sincere (heartfelt) intent is evident in Berengarten's key-poem for hexagram 29, quoted above. Retranslated into Chinese, Kalff's emphasis on water-flow in the *I Ching* might well suggest that a good working principle for Jungian therapy is 用心 *yongxin*. This term, which again includes the 'heart' graph 心 *xin*, could be back-translated as 'attentiveness to your heart', 'confidence in your heart', and 'trusting and following your heart'.

The heart-motif is further embedded – and embodied – in the Chinese character 愈 *yu*, meaning 'healing', which brings together the composite image of a boat, along with the tools for making or repairing it, and (again) the heart 心 *xin*. An older version of this graph shows the heart clearly:

The boat is depicted on the left-hand side of the upper part, and the tools on the right. With this image of the Chinese character for 'healing' in mind, the modern word *therapy* (derived from Greek θεραπεία) undergoes a fascinating and gentle transformation. Rather than indicating 'cure' – and still less, 'defence' or 'prevention' – the implicit subliminal image of *yu* is one of 'sailing' or 'riding on water'. In Chinese, then, the motif underlying Jungian therapy may be construed variously as 'a voyage for the heart', 'the heart going on a voyage', and even 'a voyage on (and in) the heart (as containing vessel)': that is, 'a voyage that relies (depends) on the heart'.

Berengarten's emphasis on the heart's conviction and on 'whole-heartedness' appears frequently in *Changing*. As already mentioned, the title of the third poem in his treatment of hexagram 29 is 'With their whole hearts' (29/3: 235). According to Kalff, as she ponders the same hexagram: "When confronted with difficulties, [only] the heart can penetrate the meaning of the situation."

❧

Poetry expresses aspiration. As if a seed in the heart were sprouting. The heart has tacit comprehension. In Chinese, following the principles of the *I Ching*, this phenomenon may be termed 'heartfelt influence'. This is how the poems of *Changing* affect me.

For hexagram 31 (咸 *Xian*), Wilhelm/Baynes has the title 'Influence (Wooing)' (122). Berengarten has 'Reciprocating', which extends the idea to 'mutual influence' rather than any subject-object implication. Here, the poet deploys the constituent trigrams *lake* ☱ and mountain ☶ both to open his own reflections and as a guide to them, repeating the phrase '*A lake on a mountain*' as the hexagram's base-line (247) and as title for the opening poem (248). In this poem, he expresses not only the presence of water, but also its constant pressure downwards, to find the "deepest possible / places" in impermeable rock.

> *Massing water*
> *presses down, finding*
> *lowest outlet. A lake*
>
> *collects, builds*
> *in deepest possible*
> *places, soaks*
>
> *into permeable*
> *ground to pool on*
> *impassable rock.*
>
> *A mountain presses*
> *up, pushes its presence*
> *to rear, bucking*

against gravity. So
when a lake forms on
a mountain, opposed

forces meet and
merge in fine self-
checking balance.   (31/0: 248)

We have already noted that hexagram 4, 蒙 *Meng* ('Bringing Up') is formed from the trigram mountain ☶ over water ☵. In that hexagram the 'solid' rests upon the 'liquid', which suggests foundations that are as-yet-unstable, fluid. This uncertainty fits well with the delicate theme of a child's upbringing. Here, however, in the treatment of hexagram 31, the 'watery' element rests upon a far firmer base: the liquid compliance of the lake is safely contained by the unyielding quality of "impassable rock", while the lake-water "supplies moisture to nourish the mountain" (Huang 265). The two "reciprocating" components mutually "influence each other". They are in harmony. The poem's final word is "*balance*".

ຝ

The image of a lake on a mountain reminds me of the story of C. G. Jung and 'Mountain Lake'. In 1924, at the age of forty-nine, Jung travelled to America, where he visited the Taos Pueblos Indians in New Mexico. He befriended their chief, whose name was Ochwiay Biano (Mountain Lake). Jung asked him why he thought white people were all mad.

> "They say that they think with their heads," he replied.
> "Why of course. What do you think with?" I asked him in surprise.
> "We think here," he said, indicating his heart.
> I fell into a long meditation. […] This Indian had struck our vulnerable spot, unveiled a truth to which we are blind. I felt rising within me like a shapeless mist something unknown and yet deeply familiar. (Jung 1963: 233-234)

ຝ

The 'Commentary on the Decision' in the Wilhelm/Baynes version of hexagram 31 (咸 *Xian*) contains the statement: "INFLUENCE means stimulation" (Wilhelm/Baynes 541). As we have seen, the word *influence* translates the Chinese hexagram name 咸 *Xian*. A similar back-translation of the word *stimulation* yields the Chinese word 感 *gan*. A side-by-side glance at these two graphs, 咸 and 感, immediately shows an intimate etymological connection: for the latter, *gan*, consists of two components: 咸 *xian* ('influence') in the upper position and 心 *xin* ('heart') below. So *gan* means not only 'stimulation' but 'heartfelt influence'.

In his version of hexagram 31, entitled 'Mutual Influence', the Daoist Alfred Huang analyses the relationship between 咸 *Xian* and 感 *gan* as follows:

> When the ideograph for heart, *xin*, appears underneath *xian*, then *xian* becomes *gan*. According to Confucius's Commentary on the Decision, *xian* should be *gan*. If we consider the whole context of this *gua* [hexagram], *gan* makes more sense. It has been suggested that the ideograph for heart might have been left out in the ancient text. In ancient Chinese writings, a radical or root of a complicated character was frequently left out. (Huang 264; italics added)

An early form of the character *gan* looks like this:

Huang's and Wilhelm's correlations of *xian* and *gan* confirm not only Confucius but also the entry in the *Shuowen Jiezi* (Han dictionary), which states that *gan* means "moving the heart. Its sound follows the heart and *xian*".

Once again, the heart is the core. Rather than merely indicating 'stimulation', the early meaning of *gan* might well be construed as 'mutual influence via the heart', 'hearts reciprocating', and 'touching each other (or one another) through (or by, or by means of) the heart'. What is more, by being 'centred' and 'grounded' in the creaturely world, the motif 'mutual influence' is not only widened and deepened, but also vividly personalised and particularised in human experience. Combining Chinese and English resonances together yields the motif of 'sympathetic or empathetic flow via the living heart'.

Despite these arguments, it should also be borne in mind that the presence of the character 咸 *xian* as a hexagram title – that is *without* 心 *xin*, the heart symbol, rather than as 感 *gan* – could well be construed to embody a more subtle point: 'influence' in a sense not only more fundamental and elemental than the heartful sincerity of the individual human being but also entirely *beyond* and *exceeding* the human — that is, *influence of a cosmic order*. This reading is implicit in the Wilhelm/Baynes text:

> Heaven and earth stimulate each other, and all things take shape and come into being. The holy man stimulates the hearts of men, and the world attains peace and rest. If we contemplate the outgoing stimulating influences, we can know the nature of heaven and earth and all beings. (*op. cit.* 541)

℀

In Chinese tradition, *gan* usually appears in a pairing with yet another complementary word, 應 *ying*, simplified today as 应. Notably, the traditional script for this character includes the heart-graph 心 *xin*, though this has been lost in the modernised version. Here is an early form of the *ying* 應 graph, with the heart in the lower right corner.

The core meaning of *ying* is 'responding, (answering, complying, agreeing) from the heart'. It is related closely to hexagram 61, 中孚 *Zhong Fu*, translated as 'Inner Truth' (Wilhelm/Baynes 235) and by Berengarten as 'Inner Trusting' (487). Trust means reliance on truth, as the *Oxford English Dictionary* confirms: it defines *trust* as '[f]irm belief in the reliability, truth, or ability of someone or something; confidence or faith in a person or thing, or in an attribute of a person or thing" (*OED* online). Berengarten's first poem for this hexagram, 'Ring of truth', deploys the two constituent trigrams, 'wind' (巽 *Xun*) and 'lake' (兌 *Dui*), whose forms are directly counterposed (☴ *Xun* above and ☱ *Dui* below):

> *Wind over lakes*
> *whips still water*
> *in shimmerings* [...]   (*'Ring of truth'*, 61/0: 488)

In the *I Ching*, two images appear in the commentary for this hexagram's second line:

> A crane calling in the shade.
> Its young answers it.

I have a good goblet.
I will share it with you.   (Wilhelm/Baynes 257)

Both these images, one belonging to the natural world and the other to the human, delicately imply heartfelt mutual influence, wholehearted trust, heart-to-heart responsiveness, sympathy and empathy.

The former image has to do with instinctual parenting among wild creatures and the latter with warm human conviviality. The motif of sociably sharing wine occurs in many of the foremost Chinese poets, including Tao Yuanming and Du Fu. The juxtaposition of these images here shows their intimate relatedness within the overall order of things (the Great Dao); and both separately and together, they embody the spirit of 感應 *ganying*. Notably, in both of these graphs, the heart radical emphasises feeling and intuition, even though this connection has been lost in one of the recent simplified characters (感应). And while, at its simplest level, the phrase 感應 *ganying* means 'stimulus and response', it is never merely 'mechanistic'. As its etymology clarifies, it has a considerably more profound echoic value, implying a wide range of associated aspects of an integral worldview: *resonance, vibratory harmony or consonance, analogical correspondence, correlative thinking, correlative cosmos-building, and holistic coherence.* These motifs are central not only to Berengarten's involvement with the *I Ching* but also to the overall context, intention and scope of his oeuvre.

As for the intuitive faculty, the *I Ching* was a source of profound inspiration for C. G. Jung, especially in his gradual development of an 'intuitive method' of analysis. Jung often relied on what he described as "mantic methods" and "the intuitive technique *for grasping the total situation* which is so characteristic of China, namely the *I Ching* or *Book of Changes*" (Jung 1960, *CW* 8: §863):

> The *I Ching*, which we can well call the experimental foundation of classical Chinese philosophy, is one of the oldest known methods for grasping a situation as a whole and thus placing the details against a cosmic background – the interplay of Yin and Yang. (*ibid.* §863)

These remarks resonate with 'the psychology of the heart', as expressed in hexagram 31. They embody the inner meanings of both 'inner trusting' and 'inner truth'. Jung was deeply attuned to the images and meaning of this hexagram.

ೲ

The Chinese character 易 *Yi* or *I* – which is the first component in the title *I Ching* or *I Ching* – is richly polysemic and has several interpretations, some of which even appear to compete contradictorily. One of its ancient forms – which is close to the design on the cover of *Changing* by the calligrapher and poet Yu Mingquan, looks like this:

One interpretation of this graph is that it represents the sun tailing the moon beneath it: that is, a composite cosmic symbol of *yang* and *yin*. At least three further layers of meaning are ascribed to 易 *Yi*, all of which cohere with this interpretation.

1. *easy and simple*. This ancient idea implies, first, that the *I Ching*'s meanings, like the sun and moon, are 'there for all to see'; and, second, 'to see, you only have to look'.[7] Just as sun and moon are immediately apparent in an unclouded sky, so the *Yi* too is a 'natural phenomenon'.

2. *change, transformation*. Like the sun in its path from sunrise to sunset, and in its changing seasonal positions in the sky, and like the moon waxing and waning, the *Yi* manifests the subtle interplay of *yin* and *yang*, and the movements of *qi* (energy).

3. *eternal constancy and durability*. Though the configurations of the *Yi* are subject to change, and its applications potentially infinite, this change is itself governed by constant, unchanging law, like the regular pathways of the sun and moon through the sky – and like the Great Dao itself. The unchanging law is *everything is subject to change*.[8]

In the *I Ching* itself, the third of these motifs receives particular focus in hexagram 32, 恒 *Heng*, translated as 'Duration' (Wilhelm/Baynes 126) and 'Enduring' (*CH* 255). Berengarten's treatment in his key poem, 'Between is and not', elegantly states the theme of eternal constancy and durability:

---

[7] *Editors' note*: This theme, however, is taken up, contradictorily, by Berengarten in a sonnet in his series, 'On synchronicity': "When you no longer look, it's then you see." (RB, *Notness*, 2015: 27):

[8] See also the poem 'Change' (2/3: 17), which re-iterates this: "The one // common inhering / condition that never / changes is Change."

That which is
nameless and formless
is, by definition, not.

Its condition being
not-being, what-it-is
is what-is-not.

It can't be approached
or encompassed, because
what-it-is is not.

Nor can its notness
be present, because it
contradicts isness.

Yet though absent, by
mere dint of being called,
notness is ever-present.

In continuous interplay
between isness and notness
arises this. Enduring.[9]   (32/0: 256)

Here, the intricate and paradoxical counterposing of *yin* and *yang* in the "continuous interplay" of "*notness*" and "*isness*" is clearly the movement of the Dao itself. However, precisely what the word "*this*" means is uncertain. Could it be "this poem"? Or could it apply to *any* particular "this" or "thisness" (Latin *haec, haecceitas*) being experienced in the here-and-now? Perhaps its identity has been deliberately left open for the reader to 'fill in'. But this is not quite the end of the poem. Between full stops, the final word "*Enduring*" reiterates that the ephemeral nature of the "*this*", which embodies change itself, is what endures.

An early form of the graph 恒 *Heng* ('Enduring', 'Duration') includes the heart (once again). It appears on the left, accompanied on the right by a boat navigating between two horizontal lines, perhaps suggesting shores or river-banks, with the upper possibly symbolising heaven and the lower, earth:

---

[9] *Notness* is also the title of a collection of 100 sonnets (RB 2017). The words *notness* and *sonnets* are anagrams.

In its earliest known form, the graph presented images of a heart with the sun and the moon. The original meaning may well have combined both the changing motions of sun and moon over earth and across day and night, with the durable and reliable constancy, year in year out, of their eternal cycles. Once again, the presence of the heart instils and focuses an intimate, personal dimension into the composite image, making the human being 'at home' in the macrocosmic order.

❧

In a letter dated October 25, 1935, marked *Anonymous*, and sent to a 'Mr. N.', Jung writes:

> The technique and wisdom of the *I Ching* is something so subtle that it needs the refined culture of an age-old Eastern education to understand it truly. [...] What we need is a psychological education so that we slowly become able to understand the *I Ching*. [...] If I understand anything of the *I Ching*, then I should say it is the book that teaches you your own way and the all-importance of it. [...] I'm a jealous lover of the *I Ching*. (Jung 1973: 200-201)

Jung also expresses his feelings about the *I Ching* in his essay 'Richard Wilhelm: In Memoriam':

> Anyone who, like myself, has had the rare good fortune to experience in association with Wilhelm the divinatory power of the *I Ching* cannot remain ignorant of the fact that we have here an Archimedean point from which our Western attitude of mind could be lifted off its foundations. It is no small service to have given us, as Wilhelm did, such a comprehensive and richly coloured picture of a foreign culture. What is even more important is that he has inoculated us with the living germ of the Chinese spirit, capable of working a fundamental change in our view of the world. We are no longer reduced to being admiring or critical observers but find ourselves partaking of the spirit of the East to the extent that we succeed in experiencing the living power of the *I Ching*.
>
> (Jung 1966, *CW*15: §1018)

Further, at the close of his foreword to Wilhelm's translation of the *I Ching*, Jung writes:

> The *I Ching* does not offer itself with proofs and results; it does not vaunt itself, nor is it easy to approach. Like a part of nature, it waits until it is discovered. It offers neither facts nor power, but for lovers of self-knowledge, of wisdom – if there be such – it seems to be the right book. To one person its spirit appears as clear as day; to another, shadowy as twilight; to a third, dark as night. He who is not pleased by it does not have to use it, and he who is against it is not obliged to find it true. Let it go forth into the world for the benefit of those who can discern its meaning.
>
> (Jung 1970, *CW* 11: §78)

Like Jung, Richard Berengarten is one of the modern discoverers – or, rather, rediscoverers of the *I Ching*. As he has said, and as we can experience when reading *Changing*, the *I Ching* expresses a "correlative" way of experiencing the world, in that it "specifically underpins the holistic vision of the universe that runs through all traditional Chinese thought. [...] Above all, the *I Ching*'s ambiguities and necessary openness to polysemic interpretation are inherently poetic" ('Postscript': 526). And he continues: "Mention of dream reopens a fuller dimension. The *I Ching*'s original mantic purpose was to unlock the mysterious secrets of time, to peer into the future, and to interpret the apparently unfathomable patterns of destiny" (*ibid.*).

This insight reveals that Berengarten's understanding is closely akin to that of Analytical Psychology. In his address to the Kulangsu International Poetry Festival (2016), Berengarten provided a coda to this point: "Poetry, which is based on breath (on rhythm, on *qi*, on inspiration) gives us needed space and time to absorb and assimilate these changes."

Changing is not only replete with images but, as I hope I have shown, like the *I Ching*, its main source, it is intricately and intimately patterned on the combined constancy and delicate fragility of the human heart. A reading of Richard Berengarten's *Changing*, like that of the *I Ching* itself, conveys far-reaching meanings. For change, simplicity and endurance, the three basic qualities of the *I Ching*, are those of this poetic work. *As poetry expresses aspiration, so the heart communicates the spiritual.* With this essay, I convey my respect and gratitude to Richard Berengarten and his *Changing*: both to the author and to the book.

REFERENCES

Aristotle. 1999 [1995]. *Poetics*. Halliwell, Stephen (trans.). Cambridge, MA and London: Harvard University Press, Loeb edns. XXIII.

Ban Gu. 1990. *Hanshu Yiwenzhi* 漢書‚藝文志 ('History of the Han Dynasty, Record for Art and Literature'). Zhengzhou: Zhongzhou Classics Publication.

Berengarten, Richard. 2011. 'Tree'. In *For the Living: Selected Longer Poems, 1965-2000*. Exeter: Shearsman Books.

———. 2011. *The Blue Butterfly*. Bristol: Shearsman Books.

———. 2015. *Notness: Sonnets*. Bristol: Shearsman Books.

———. 2016a. *Changing*. Bristol: Shearsman Books.

———. 2016b (October 21). 'Imaginationalism: an extract from a longer statement'. Kulangsu Island, Xiamen: Address to the Kulangsu International Poetry Festival. Online at: http://www.zgshige.com/c/2016-10-22/1955283.shtml

———. 2017a. 'A Forest of Trees'. *Margutte*. Online at: http://www.margutte.com/?p=22640&lang=en

———. 2017b. 'Tree, a Video'. *Margutte*. Online at: http://www.margutte.com/?p=25449&lang=en.

Fu Huisheng (trans.). 2008. *I Ching, the Zhou Book of Changes*. Changsha: Hunan People's Publishing House.

Huang, Alfred. 2004 [1998]. *The Complete I Ching: The Definitive Translation by the Taoist Master*. Rochester VT: Inner Traditions.

Jung, C. J. 1960. 'Synchronicity: An Acausal Connecting Principle'. In *The Structure and Dynamics of the Psyche* (*Collected Works*, vol. 8). Hull, R. F. C. (trans.). Princeton: Princeton University Press, Bollingen Series.

———. 1963. *Memories, Dreams, Reflections*. Jaffé, Aniela (ed.); Winston, Richard and Clara (trans.). London: Routledge and Kegan Paul.

———. 1970. 'Foreword to the *I Ching*'. In *Psychology and Religion: West and East* (*Collected Works*, vol. 11). Hull, R. F. C. (trans.). Princeton. Princeton University Press, Bollingen Series.

———. 1966. 'Richard Wilhelm: In Memoriam'. In *The Spirit in Man, Art, and Literature* (*Collected Works*, vol. 15). Hull, R. F. C. (trans.). Princeton, NJ: Princeton University Press, Bollingen Series.

———. 1973. *Letters*, vol. 1, Gerhard Adler (ed.); Hull, R. F. C. (trans.). Princeton, NJ: Princeton University Press, Bollingen Series.

———. 1976. *Letters*, vol. 2, 1951-1961. Gerhard Adler (ed.); Hull, R. F. C. (trans.). Princeton, NJ: Princeton University Press, Bollingen Series.

———. 2009. *The Red Book*. Shamdasani, Sonu *et al.* (eds. and trans.). New York: W. W. Norton and Company.

Kalff, Dora M. 2004. *Sandplay: A Psychotherapeutic Approach to the Psyche*. Cloverdale, CA: Temenos Press.

Oxford English Dictionary (online).

Pascal, Blaise. 1670. *Pensées*. Paris: Guillaume Desprée.

Shaughnessy, Edward L. 1983. *The Composition of the "Zhouyi"*. (PhD thesis, Stanford University). Ann Arbor, MI: University Microfilms International.

Wei Hong. 1979. 'Great Preface' to *The Book of Odes*. (Thirteen Classics Explanatory Notes and Commentaries). Beijing: Zhonghua Publishing House.

Wilhelm, Richard and Baynes, Cary F. (trans.). 1967 [1951]. *The I Ching, or Book of Changes*. Princeton, NJ: Princeton University Press, Bollingen Series XIX.

Xu Shen (Han Dynasty). 2013 [1978]. *Shuo Wen Jie Zi* 說文解字 ("Discussing Writing and Explaining Characters"). Beijing: Zhonghua Publishing House.

PART 4

CHANGING
AND THE *I CHING*:
POEISIS AND THE *DAO*

MIKE BARRETT

Positive and Negative Capability:
I Ching and the Poet

OVERVIEW AND METHOD

I have foreseen
you reading this be-
fore you were ever

conceived.   ("You perfectly," 53/6: 430)

My first encounter with the *I Ching* was eighteen years before the time of writing this essay, while preparing for a trip to China as part of an education delegation from Missouri. I threw coins and read hexagrams with the help of a book whose tone was self-help. I found a more authentic version in a text I bought in China, *The Illustrated Book of Changes* by Yan Li, an illustrated version of the *Zhou Changes*. The gnomic language in the text – "Plain white clothing. Not bad" (Yan 154) – captured the essence of imagist poetry, that "intellectual and emotional complex in an instant of time" (Pound online), while also functioning as a meditative prompt, in a similar way to Tarot Cards, Buddhist koans, John Dee's hieroglyphs, or Kabbalistic figures.

The poet who deploys the *I Ching* in the process of composition may engage a vatic role, recalling Sidney's statement: "Among the Romans, a poet was called *Vates*, which is as much a diviner, foreseer, or prophet" (Sidney 106). Shelley, too, in his "Defence of Poetry" echoes this theme:

Poets [...] were called in earlier epochs of the world legislators or prophets: a poet essentially comprises and unites both these char-acters. For he not only discovers those laws according to which pre-sent things ought to be ordered, but he beholds the future in the present [...] (Shelley 781)

The Blakean Bard, "who Present, Past, and Future sees" (Blake 37) enacts this same vatic function. Throughout this essay, when I refer to the 'diviner-poet', I mean the poet who conducts the *I Ching* divination procedure and responds with poetry. The diviner-poet, in this respect, is both *vates* and *maker*.

The *I Ching* itself may be regarded as a semiotic system applicable to *all that is, could, and should be*. The diviner-poet, working with intention and guided by meditation, composes a question. Meditation necessarily precedes formulation of the question – it reduces the 'self' or, at least, that part of the 'self' that is conditioned by subjective responses to the phenomenal world. Meditation, then, releases these responses, so that, localized in the body's here-and-now, the diviner-poet may attend more deeply to the present.

A random procedure – whether gathering yarrow stalks, throwing coins, or transforming situations into numbers – operates on this semiotic system and generates either a single hexagram or a sequence of two hexagrams in answer to the diviner-poet's question. The hexagram is a topological function that projects those pertinent aspects of what *is, could, and should be* for the diviner-poet to consider and respond to. S/he will also consult judgments, predictions, and prescriptions, accumulated and selected from the past and integrated into the text of the *I Ching*. The ground for the entire procedure is an assumption that *immutable laws govern mutability*. Out of this process, the diviner-poet makes a poem.

By examining this procedure, I derive eight emergent properties of the *I Ching*:

> It is semiotic.
> It is kinesthetic.
> It is esthetic.
> It is ethical.
> It is civic.
> It is mathematical.
> It is cosmic.
> It is hermeneutic.

In this essay I will discuss Richard Berengarten's *Changing* by analyzing it in relation to this procedure and these properties.

1. *It is semiotic*

> [...] these
> marks, this residue
>
> constantly dissolving
> and recrystallizing, this
> efflorescence. ("A shimmer of leaves," 10/3: 83)

In some sources, the *I Ching* results from *inductive* reasoning – sages observed the comings and goings of things to derive a system of signs. For example, in the cluster "Watching":

> mountain-shapes in mist,
> textures of fur, skin, and hair,
> light's striations on water,
>
> tracks made by animals,
> birds, spiders, insects, worms,
> in sand, dust, mud, clay –
>
> observing these high
> and low with eyes peeled
> we learned to copy
>
> and with our fingers mark
> patterns of our own in shell,
> wood, clay, hide, stone. ("Patterns of our own," 20/1: 161)

Harmony with Hopkins's *inscape* is heard here – the deep-down tune in things, source of their *haecceitas*, perpetually expressed to the attentive observer. The account of Fu Hsi developing the eight trigrams is similarly narrated:

> [...] looking up, [he] contemplated the images *(xiang)* in the sky and, looking down, the markings *(fa)* on the earth. He observed the patterns *(wen)* on birds and animals and their adaptations to the earth. From nearby, he took hints from his own body [...] then he began to make the "eight trigrams" of the *Book of Changes* to pass on the model symbols *(xianxiang)* to later times. (qtd. in Gu 263)

The origin of the trigrams is also defined *deductively*, as an axiomatic transmission from heaven. Berengarten's "Changing into Beautiful" begins: "What the book says of itself / is that first of all came numbers / taking forms of straight lines" (20/3: 163). In this version, the origin is a formal system assumed to be anterior to the existence of natural phenomena. Thus, whether derived from observation or intuited from 'eternal forms', the *I Ching* functions as a semiotic system to encode phenomena and transmit that code into the future.

In his essay "The *Zhouyi* (Book of Changes) as an Open Classic: A Semiotic Analysis of Its System of Representation," Ming Dong Gu argues that it is an "open book amenable to appropriations and manipulations by people of any doctrine, religious belief, or moral standard, and its openness comes from it being a semiotic system whose principle of composition warrants unlimited interpretations" (Gu 258).[1] In Berengarten's *Changing*, the *I Ching* is applied to peoples of many historical periods, cultures, and doctrines: Old Testament Jews, modern European Jews, Russians, Serbs, Moroccans, Poles, Rwandans, Chinese, English (Medieval and contemporary), Classical and modern Greeks, *et al.*

The sixty-four hexagrams form the base-signifiers of this semiotic system. The trigrams themselves assume multiple, polysemous roles: for example, the trigram ☱ *Dui* 兌, signifying 'lake' or 'marsh', might become a cloud, young girl, body part, or meteorological condition. Gu calls a hexagram's multiplicative signifying potential its "representational capacity" (*ibid.* 265). This capacity increases geometrically when trigram is stacked on trigram to form a hexagram. The diviner-poet is thus able to transform metaphoric interpretation into metonymic substitution: the youngest daughter in one hexagram takes the form of a lake in another. In Berengarten's poems generated by hexagram 31, *Xian* 咸, which he renders as "Reciprocating," the upper trigram *Dui* is a lake, a young lover, a frustrated plan, a *hamsah*.

The linguistic commentary accrued over time is added to the computable system of hexagrams: "the hexagram images constitute a system of symbols while the hexagram and line statements form another system of linguistic signs" (*ibid.* 265). Hellmut Wilhelm finds these linguistic signs to be archives of folk wisdom, incorporating both Confucian and Taoist themes, wherein can be found the *I Ching*'s "real value" and "its comprehensiveness and many sidedness" (Wilhelm, H. 1995a: 51). Gu elaborates:

> First it is a network woven with both visual and verbal signs. Second, the symbolism of a sign is polysemously designated. Third, the

---

[1] *Editors' note*: For Gu Ming Dong's essay on *Changing*, see 89-106 above.

signs relate to each other in indeterminate relationships on multiple levels. Fourth, the network is amenable to different but equally valid interpretive strategies. Last…the system has a tolerant quality that permits new views to be assimilated into it as new components.

(Gu, *op. cit.* 275)

Berengarten's *Changing* is a twenty-first century assimilation. Its design enacts further significations. The foot of every page holds what Berengarten calls a "base-line," a set of words or phrases which functions not "merely as a by-product of the poem's design but as an integral part of its content […] to echo, reinforce, support, strengthen, contextualize, complement, qualify, offset, develop, ramify, interpret, self-reflect, reflect upon and/or comment upon the main body of the poem" (RB 2018).

The *I Ching* itself allows multiple significations by clearing "a hermeneutic space constructed with imagistic or verbal signs capable of generating unlimited interpretation" (Gu, *op. cit.* 259). Berengarten calls this hermeneutic space "A reading of now":

A reading of now
and its tails and hooks
antennae and entrails

roots and routes
tendrils and crannies
. webs and branches

[…]

questions and quests
imminent and immanent
pitfalls and strands

and movements of
this to its end here is
posited, is posted.   (15/5: 45)

The poet observes the world through its sign systems, "its roots and routes / […] webs and branches," in order to "posit" and "post" the reading, which joins 3,000 years of previous positions and posts.

Information systems require channels through which messages pass. Although the *I Ching* may signify endlessly and prompt the poet's insight, the poet must become a clear channel so that insight may be transmitted:

You have to sit and wait
in a patience within patience
without praise or hope

for meanings to grow
like ferns unscrolling from
cracks between lines.   (*"What the book said about itself,"* 20/0: 160)

2. *It is kinesthetic*

'I' dissolves. 'I' keeps
on dissolving.   ("Tracks to stars and back," 25/4: 204)

In order to see, the poet seeks clarity. How does this happen? Sit and wait
until the self dissolves – the poet has clarified here. Images in *The Illustr-*
ated Book of Changes depict sages, male and female, in Taoist meditative
postures. In some, they meditate; in others, they sit in front of yarrow
stalks, scrolls, or with hexagrams hovering above their heads. These images
reflect the *I Ching* procedure as meditative practice, stilling the body and
quieting the mind.

Taoist or Buddhist meditation guides emphasize the importance of
posture during meditation. Proper posture ensures that the body rests on
a firm foundation. The kinesthetic and proprioceptive senses, secure in the
balance of the body in space and time, become less active, calming the
nervous system. But as the body settles, the mind must quieten too. If not,
mind stirs body in a negative feedback loop:

Eyes down-inclining,
I entered in here-now,
in their intertwining

What might interfere
or come undermining
but a host of sincere

wanderings of thought
commenting and resisting
on this *must*, that *ought*,

clamouring, insisting,
till skin and muscles fought
and clarities kept misting?   ("Must, ought," 33/3: 267)

Even though the narrator has begun meditation with the proper posture, the frontal lobe, with its "musts" and "oughts," agitates the kinesthetic, "till skin and muscles fought." The poem's *aba / cac / ded / ede / fgf / gfg* rhyme-scheme reinforces the tangling of mind and body in disquietude.

Among the sages in *Changing*, Shi Jing represents a contemporary meditation model. In the poem "In Epping Forest," we see Jing meditate under an oak. When a boy asks, "Oy, aintcha cold, mister?" Berengarten writes, "Smiles open and spread / through him, then join up / a single smile" (33/6: 270). Mind and body united and clear, Jing smiles with his entire nervous system.

Berengarten employs hexagram 52, 艮 *gen*, mountain over mountain, which he calls "Stilling," to narrate the process of the 'I' dissolving, of brain circuitries becoming "unconditioned" (Austin 116), under the guidance of Shi Jing.

The commentary in the *Illustrated Book of Changes* to line 1 of hexagram 52 "Stilling" reads: "Stopped to look at your feet. Right – this is the right moment to make a long-term plan" (Yan 359). When we stand, we connect to the earth with the soles of our feet. The commentary implies: "Your connection to the earth is secure; now consider what's beyond this path." In Berengarten's response, the sitting narrator isn't yet ready to look down because his head is busily insecure:

> I settle slowly, mind
> top-heavy turbulent giddied
> not yet ready to look down
>
> let alone gaze into deep
> nothing.   ("Meditation at Hourn Farm," 52/1: 417)

Shi Jing's bowl-bell that calls meditators to attention is the subject (and object) in poems 2, 3, 4, and 6 of "Stilling." The bowl-bell is emblem of the meditator's ideal mind: dissolved of the filling ego, the bowl sits ready to receive:

> [...] Lacking
> hope or desire, bowl-bell
> has no views on things,
>
> no opinions, options or
> ideas, and sits or seems to
> sit in perfect rounded
>
> silence.   ("Gatekeeper," 52/2: 418)

Its tone when struck – which is reminiscent of Hopkins's "bow swung" that "finds tongue to fling out broad its name" (Hopkins 1587) – is unique to each bowl. If it is not empty, its tone is distorted. Only an empty bowl can hold everything:

> [...] What happens
> is nothing. Everything
>
> fills to the brim with
> absolute nothing. That's what
> empties (into) everything.   ("Nothing happens," 52/5: 421)

As already suggested above, the *I Ching* procedure can be seen as a meditation session. The diviner-poet meditates until a question emerges; then, much like handling prayer beads, the poet's hands are occupied in a familiar patterned movement while throwing or picking up yarrow stalks and contemplating the question. When the hexagram is generated, s/he meditates on it, much as a Zen Buddhist meditates on a koan, in order to respond. This meditation session never really ends. Once activated, the kinesthetic sense recalls the poet to a balanced body and clear mind, and s/he is thereby enabled to act propitiously. Berengarten likens this process to replenishment that requires a kinesthetic act – lowering and lifting a bucket from a deep, clean well:

> I lower my
> question on a rope
> of thought.
>
> I draw up
> water-wisdom.   ("I lower my question," 48/5: 389)

By practicing the *I Ching*, the narrator is able to "draw [...] wisdom". This over-brimming is akin to the "spontaneous overflow of powerful feelings": it only works for one who has "thought long and deeply" (Wordsworth 160).

3. *It is esthetic*

> light changing
> on surfaces

is delight, is
glory, the unique
common miracle [...]   ("Adhering, Inhering," 55/1: 441)

As the previous section explains, the ego dissolves through meditation, then the channels of reception open. Clear perception then reveals the numinous in nature. In the essay "An Unexpected European Voice," Paul Scott Derrick comments: "[Berengarten's] poems could be described as the hymn of the praise of things" (Derrick 157).[2] *Changing* adds to the hymnal.

For Berengarten, things collect and connect, for example a *"Cox's Pippin"*:

I bring you the very
sweetest apple in the whole
world, from an orchard

in England. Its pips
rattling in their pods recall
spring rain scattering

on greeny rivers. Red
umber and gold clouds
on its shiny skin bring

back misted dawns
and bronze sunsets   (*"Cox's Pippin,"* 26/0: 208)

This apple is multidimensional. Time and space give its form. The poem is rich in sound quality. For example, "shiny skin bring / back misted dawns / and bronze" and the repetition of nasal /n/ in "shiny," "skin," and "dawn." The /br/ chime rides along the sprung rhythm of "bring / back misted dawns." This melopoeia is sweet like a Cox's Pippin.

Things derive blessings from local conditions, as does art. "A Singer from County Clare" is the poem for the first line of hexagram 25 (无 妄 *Wu Wang*, rendered by Berengarten as "Untwisting"), consisting of the trigrams *thunder* ☳ (震 *Zhen*) under *heaven* ☰ (乾 *Qian*). The Wilhelm/ Baynes version translates these trigram names as, respectively, "The Arousing" and "The Creative." In Berengarten's poem, local conditions tune the timbre of the voice:

---

[2] *Editors' note*: For Paul Scott Derrick's essay on *Changing*, see 51-68 above.

[...] its brindling by sun
and cloud on sward, its
tough difficult farms

tucked in sallow nooks
among karst mountains
flecked grey and black,

its goose ponds and mud,
its angles of slopes between
dune-marram and ocean [...]

("A singer from County Clare," 25/1: 201)

Creativity grows locally. As in "Cox's Pippin," the sound is rich: the network of consonant echoes in "brindling," "sun," "cloud," and "sward." The assonance of "karst" and "farm" conjoins, before another measure of consonantal sounding begins in the next stanza.

In Berengarten's esthetic, beauty is light-fed and night-rested, sky-born and earth-swaddled – channelling the grace that moves through everything.

Under hills this
grace flows
through everything.

Chestnut and oak
bud, green
earth's carpet.

Red tulip petals
scatter. A blue
butterfly hovers.   ("*Under hills,*" 22/0: 176)

Noah Heringman, scholar of Romantic literature, names this kind of poetry "nature at home" (*n.p.*). After reading *Changing*, a reader could easily describe the 'nature at home' with Berengarten in Cambridge: its flora and fauna, its weather, the casting of its light.

Throughout Berengarten's oeuvre, the sign of natural grace is light. That visible form of energy illuminates our sense and fuels us:

Always light above and
light's inflections most

> keenly inject glory
> through tunnels in
> tissues behind eyes.   ("*Water in the stone jug*," 10/0: 80)

Derrick aptly writes, "the poet [Berengarten] has become – in Emerson's famous phrase – a transparent eyeball, trembling with the power of a blinding glory that grants him a second sight" (Derrick 156). In Berengarten's response to hexagram 35 (晉 *jin*), consisting of the trigrams *fire* ☲ (離 *Li*) over *earth* ☷ (坤 *Kun*) which he entitles "Dawning," the sun is heaven's gift and arouses the earth to life. Light clings to things the way earth clings to heaven:

> How light and things
> trust each other. Unshakably.
> Light everyday loves
>
> things so much it sticks
> to, passes through, lingers
> over, surrounds
>
> all. Light adheres, inheres
> everywhere, there, here in
> here.   ("Light and things," 35/3: 283)

4. *It is ethical*

> It's light that
> most demands to be
> affirmed against
>
> death [...]   ("Towards my window," 30/4: 244)

The *I Ching* is often deployed as a guide to deciding on the action proper to changing circumstances. Therefore, it calls the diviner-poet to an ethical as well as an esthetic response. Alfred Huang notes that the Confucian School uses the *I Ching* in a daily, practical way (Huang 111); and Richard Wilhelm calls it a rulebook for the art of living (Wilhelm, R. 224). This dimension is evident in Berengarten too. His response to the first line of hexagram 10 (履 *Lü*), *sky* over *lake* (which, following Wilhelm, he calls "Treading"), models the kinesthetic component of the ethical:

hands washed and open
breath clear, regular,

feet slightly apart, knees
and shoulders unstressed,
supple eyes prepared

to take in all angles,
ears filtering slightest
sounds – all of which

accumulate to a poised,
coiled, sustained alertness –
so treading on anything is

delicate as a small bird's
footprints on snow, a sturdy
bee's on stamens.   ("Spread white rushes," 10/1: 81)

The position of the body here recalls *tai chi* posture and the poem dic-
tates that attentiveness is the essence of careful treading. This poem may
be compared to *The Illustrated Book of Changes*, which contains a tiger
motif: "Tread lightly because you don't know what you may step on"
(Yan 64). Berengarten's concluding analogies are precise, and procreative:
"a small bird's / footprints on snow, a sturdy / bee's on stamens."

The Confucian commentary indicates that only a righteous moral state
will allow the diviner-poet to see accurately: "But if you are not the right
man / the meaning will not manifest itself to you" (qtd. in Wilhelm, H.
1995a: 85). Berengarten provides practical tips for achieving this state:

[...] Best
to read, walk

a little, meditate,
exercise – breathe in this
present, for there

is no other – keep
body and mind clear as
'one' can, say little,

be cheerful or at
least act it [...]   ("Readying, steadying," 47/4: 380)

In addition, live modestly:

> From now on self
> will be surrounded
> by a very few
>
> loved and familiar
> objects and still fewer
> impossible desires.   ("Tidying up, clearing out," 60/4: 484)

Like the Kabbalah and hermetic worldviews, the *I Ching* positions the human being in a microcosmic/macrocosmic relationship to the cosmos (Wilhelm, R. 203). The ethical is achieved by following the balance of heaven, as signed by natural phenomena:

> *Rules that govern*
> *the gathering of rooks*
> *into creaking colonies,*
>
> *V formations of geese,*
> *vastness of herring shoals,*
> *bees' mouth-shapes*
>
> *to particular flowers,*
> *also govern patterns of*
> *your mortal time* […]   (*"Rules,"* 17/0: 136)

The final ethical dimension that I will discuss here is found in the Hebrew word *tikkun* ('mending, restoration, restitution'), which connects *Changing* to the Kabbalistic tradition (545). Many of these poems, both those directly addressing Jewish tradition and history and those concerning other peoples, apply *tikkun* to a world sorely in need of this remedy:

> Our job, to clean
> air, protect unkempt wild
> hidden spaces twined
>
> in forest lights, where
> nest-singing birds that
> chorus like angels […]   (*"Tikkun*, Majdanek," 36/6: 294)

Changing itself is an act of *tikkun*.

5. *It is civic*

Malcolm didn't register
how indelibly and ineradicably
were inscribed their interests

in models and infrastructures
of obsolete systems [...]   ("Old rot," 18/4: 148)

In the same way that the *I Ching* proposes a micro/macro relationship between the individual human being and the cosmos, so also civil society relates to heaven. In an essay applying the principles of the *I Ching* to economic globalization, Wang and Kelly write:

> From the insights provided by Chinese culture, the process is not only geopolitically global but cosmic, through the unity of heaven, earth, and humanity, symbolizing the harmonious relationship between all strata. This means that the human component – be it individual, state (through its government), or the international system – finds harmony with both heaven (Yang: the moral universe, related to justice and ethics) and earth (Yin: the source of nourishment, related to economics, environment, governance.
>
> (Wang and Kelly 247)

To be sure, the *yin / yang* polarity can be applied to any current political or economic circumstance, but the *historical* grounding of the *I Ching* complicates any such application. For example, *The Illustrated Book of Changes*, with its roots in the Zhou dynasty, is replete with images of taking prisoners for human sacrifice. Clearly, metaphorical transformation is required to derive contemporary civic instructions from these Bronze Age practices.

Furthermore, auspicious or inauspicious judgments are often made by determining whether *yin* and *yang* are in their appropriate position (Huang 100-108). In China, for more than two millennia, the *I Ching* has functioned as a rhetorical 'instrument' to maintain the social *status quo*. In *The I Ching: A Biography*, the historian Richard J. Smith explains: "The *I Ching* provided a cosmologically grounded justification for the social and political hierarchies of Imperial China from the Han period through the Qing" (Smith 219). Thus we can see how "issues of the day affect an exegete's reading of a classic, and how an exegete's reading of a classic helps to shape the direction of public debate" (Hon 15).[3]

––––––––––––––

[3] *Editors' note*: For the essay on *Changing* by Tze-ki Hon, see 257-262 above.

One civic thread that runs through *Changing* is a continuation of Berengarten's previous project in *The Manager*. Late-stage capitalism is embodied through vignettes peopled by characters living under its strains. For example, we meet Antonino, a Mafioso hitman (40/6: 326); the widow of Magistrate Parving-Potts (54/1: 433); Julie, negotiating her adolescence (45/3: 363); and an isolated celebrity, Samantha (45/6: 366). Similarly, we encounter interns and managers, an NGO worker named Chiara (18/1: 145), and Julius, a wealthy, dull scion (6/3: 51).

Three main themes emerge from a survey of these characters. First, people become inured to the stench of greed and economic corruption:

> Rottenness spread
> so normally, so spiced
> and glazed with reason
>
> most believed it inevitable
> and universal. ("Collusion," 12/2: 98)

Second, self-absorption dulls perception:

> Brisk, confident, but blind
> in assumptions and certainty,
> Jo screws up nearly every
>
> time she moves [...] ("An apprentice," 18/3: 147)

Third, the practice of *tikkun* is a powerful antidote to the Zeitgeist: "Plant saplings, shrubs, bushes" (18/1: 145).

Another civic thread that runs through *Changing* occurs in Berengarten's response to hexagram 29 (坎 *Kan, water* over *water*), which he calls "Falling (in a pit)." In *The Illustrated Book of Changes*, this hexagram shows soldiers falling into a deep man-made trap. The positive and negative outcomes of that circumstance are set out in the line-readings. Berengarten's first poem introduces us to three Moroccan political prisoners, Ali Bourequat and two of his five brothers, Bayazid, and Midhat. They are imprisoned in Tazmamart, "a disused tank barracks / beneath Atlas Mountains," where they are held in "cells, three meters by two / pitch dark" (29/1: 233).

> If they lie down
>
> they'll never get up
> or out of this desert hole
> where four winds meet. ("Where four winds meet," 29/2: 234)

The prisoners hang on to their lives and each other by sharing memories:

'So long as we

had nothing at all,' says Ali
'our memories clothed us, who
were spiritually naked.'   ("With their whole hearts," 29/3: 235)

This poem recalls the work of the contemporary Korean poet Ko Un, whose series *Ten Thousand Lives* began when Ko was a political prisoner. He kept sane in isolation by recalling, in detail, every person he had ever encountered. Ko's poetry and Berengarten's account of the Moroccan prisoners highlight the life-sustaining nature of social memory.

When the prisoners are finally released eighteen years later, the prisoner Ali, while walking a beach in Scandinavia, affirms:

I'm sharper in awareness
of injustice from knowing

unbounded strength far
beyond hate. We were dead
and we came back. Now

delivered, I savour
unique moment's breath
night and morning.   ("By a Scandinavian sea," 29/6: 238)

I have noted how an "exegete" interprets hexagrams as a mode of political discourse. Hexagram 29 has also been interpreted in light of administrative law (Smith 219). How, then, does Berengarten's exegesis of that same hexagram shed light on *Changing*'s civic dimensions? First, whereas in the past, Chinese interpretation of the hexagrams has tended to reinforce social order, Berengarten's main concern is in *justice* over *order*. Second, in writing about the Muslim Ali and his two brothers, Berengarten has taken a population currently 'othered' by European and American nationalists and portrayed them with humanity and dignity. The reader identifies with their courage and their fate. Third, his exegesis ends optimistically, matching the optimism of his work in general. Last, Berengarten has been called a European poet writing in English. His poems in *Changing* indicate that he is a *world* poet writing in English.

6. *It is mathematical*

First came number
out of both nature and
our own minds…

'Numbers are instantly
available for every

counting operation,
like spirits that can be
conjured up at will.'   ("First came number," 20/2: 162)

In his book on the *Plum Blossom Anthology*, Da Liu observes that the Chinese character 算 *suan* means both 'to predict' and 'to calculate' (Liu xi). The idea of exegesis as 'calculation' speaks to a foundational assumption of divining with the *I Ching*: *immutable laws govern mutability*. The universe is deterministic and its determinism can be expressed mathematically:

What the book says of itself
is that first of all came numbers
taking forms of straight lines

like fingers, which gradually
folded in upon themselves
being and denoting

pattern in inner and
outer worlds […]   ("Changing into beautiful," 20/3: 163)

Berengarten here reflects on the role of numbers in the *I Ching*: they *inhere* in the pattern of things. He embodies that numeric foundation in the form of *Changing*: every poem is composed of six stanzas re-enacting the structure of the hexagrams themselves.

Berengarten and Liu both reflect a kind of mathematical Platonism wherein mathematics is not merely an accurate calculus for modeling the cosmos but, rather, *the cosmos itself is ordered mathematically*. In addition, Huang states that numbers represent the motions between heaven and earth (Huang 23). By digging deeper into this assumption, we can further analyze this calculating process.

The random mathematical operation that generates a hexagram reduces all cosmological (macrostate) determinations to those that apply to the diviner-poet. Perhaps the contours of the present are disclosed through the random operation – like iron filings aligning themselves with an unseen electromagnetic field, or the role of observation in quantum mechanics: upon observation, all possible microstates (i.e. a macrostate) collapse into one *that is the case*. The random operation provides an observable scale to a cosmic measure:

> As the universe
> keeps all measures
>
> and all in measure,
> and each thing main-
> tains its own seams,
>
> stains, marks, patterns,
> edges, pleats, horizons –
> may the same quiet
>
> patient appetite for
> order cohere, inhere
> in this, in here.   ("Cohering, inhering," 1/3: 7)

For Berengarten, then, the pattern "inhering" in a hexagram, uncovered in the present, signifies a coherent cosmic design, reproduced in the poem itself.

Nearly every introductory text on the *I Ching* in a Western language alludes to the story of Leibniz and one of the first Jesuit missionaries to China, the Frenchman Joachim Bouvet, who introduced the German mathematician to the sixty-four hexagrams. This episode is compelling to enthusiasts because it implies the *I Ching's* comprehensive accuracy. Two mathematical aspects of the *I Ching* drive this implication. First, the foundation of the entire system is *binary*. Liu relates *yin* and *yang* to positive and negative charges in atomic particles. Computational systems run on binary code. Matter/antimatter and energy/dark energy are also binary systems. Second, the *I Ching* requires *combinatorics*. This is the mathematical branch that governs the behavior of elements when combined in a finite set, such as trigrams and hexagram. Combinatorics is also used in molecular biology. Sergey Fedotov's essay "Simple Association of the Genetic Code with Hexagrams of the Book of Changes" applies the structure of the hexagrams to the codons that compose DNA.

However, these applications could be interpreted as properties of the *I Ching*'s adaptable semiotic system rather than revealing 'true' cosmic measure. This idea can be demonstrated by considering the two nuclear or inner trigrams (or 'core *gua*') in each hexagram. Huang discusses the importance of these for interpreting the *I Ching* (Huang 144). Because of the way these trigrams are chosen (the 4th, 3rd, and 2nd line for the lower nuclear trigram; and the 5th, 4th, and 3rd line for the upper), only sixteen possible hexagrams can result from among them. This is by combinatory rule.

Now, if one takes the core of the core by applying the same procedure to these sixteen, one is left with only four hexagrams: the 1st, 2nd, 63rd, and 64th (in the Wilhelm/Baynes version, respectively named "Initiating", "Responding", "After crossing over", and "Before crossing over"). Then, if one proceeds to extract the core of the core of the core, "Initiating" will continue to initiate and "Responding" to respond. However, "After crossing over" will turn into "Before crossing over" and vice-versa, and go on doing so, *ad infinitum*. Therefore, a mathematical necessity becomes a fundamental truth about the cosmos – heaven and earth are eternal, with everything in between perpetually coming or going. The *combinatoric* becomes the *cosmic*.

7. *It is cosmic*

Without the Platonic mathematical assumption, there is another way to think about cosmic coherence, for "Spaces / comets, stars, galaxies, / quasars, supernovae"

> [...] stretch around,
> among, within
>
> us who, being
> on earth, thereby
> reside in heaven,
>
> among heavens,
> made of the same
> heaven-stuff as they.   ("Heaven-stuff," 55/5: 445)

There is no separation between heaven and earth in this real sense; everything was one thing at the Big Bang, and everything has been changing ever since.

Studying physical laws that govern the mechanics of these heavenly bodies as they change is to study formal systems nesting into other formal systems:

> [...] *coherence*
>
> *of all separable discrete*
> *entities in a grand design,*
> *the ways they all fit,*
>
> *how fitting it all is, how*
> *suitable, at all levels, from*
> *the most tractable forms*
>
> *threaded on the known and*
> *probable to apparently least*
> *significant hidden strings.*   ("*Order in grand design*," 14/0: 112)

Jack Spicer had a good line about the fit and finish of the universe. In a letter to Robin Blaser he wrote, "Things fit together. We knew that – it is the principle of magic" (Spicer 164). *Changing* operates on the same principle.

Last, we may bring the locus of discussion back to where the design of the universe is continually revealed and reckoned – the now. We don't *see* mathematical laws themselves; we see their manifestations. In the present, coherence manifests through, and inheres in, change:

> [...] every-
> where is constantly
>
> on the move through-
> out spacetime, just as
> reciprocally spacetime
>
> itself is always on
> the move through
> things. The one
>
> common inhering
> condition that never
> changes is Change.   ("Change," 2/3: 17)

8. *It is hermeneutic*

> [...] in plumbing you
> I soar
>
> feet still grounded
> in *this here now*.   ("*I Ching*," 48/4: 388)

Surely the previous seven engagements proceed from the hermeneutic
moment, the reading of divinatory clues and commentaries. As mentioned, Berengarten calls this process "A reading of now" (5/5: 45). His
title accurately designates the hermeneutic of *Changing*: "this *now*, / *this*
knowing, this *nowing* / for poems" ("In his wake," 21/2: 70). The diviner-
poet in this respect is seer and maker, reading the *is*, *could*, and *should be* in
the present, and inscribing its changing forms in poetry. Like the *I Ching*
itself, poetry is made from responding and initiating.

The *yin* poet is a microcosm open to macrocosmic possibilities. Shao
Yung, eleventh century author of the *Plum Blossom Anthology*, defines a
sage in this manner:

> The sage is a person by means of his one single mind to observe
> myriad other minds, by means of his own single body to observe a
> myriad other bodies, by means of a single (external) object, a myri-
> ad of other objects [...] (qtd. by Liu xiii)

The poet's receptive state recalls Keats's "negative capability," which he
defines as "when a man is capable of being in uncertainties, Mysteries,
doubts, without any irritable reaching after fact & reason" (Keats 863).
Berengarten is certainly sage enough to practice this receptivity, as evid-
enced in the enormous scope of subject matter and variety of narrative
locales *Changing* inhabits. Negative capability is necessary for a creative
response, but makers *make*, and making takes initiative: "the superior man
keeps himself vital without ceasing [...] and to enrich his virtue to sustain
all things" (Huang 88). This creative vitality I call "positive capability"; it
is *yang* in making. *Changing*, the result of a fifty-year relationship with the
I Ching, is a testament to the positive capability of Berengarten.

In poetic composition, in general, both these orientations are always
involved. But poetic composition is recursive, and finding a scale fine-
grained enough to determine the exact order of negative and positive
capabilities is impossible:

This is where we start
every time – in purposeless
potential, in a *before* so far

'back' 'behind' all other
befores, it can't really be counted
as being *in* time of any kind,

let alone pertaining to or
belonging to time. Its *isness* –
meshed so tight and sheer

into its *notness* that neither
is extricable from the other –
yields a pointless point

neither passive nor active
neither *this* or *that* but both –
point of departure [...]   ("Being simple," 2/7: 21)

Berengarten's 'base-line' for the above poem includes the phrases "unhewn block" and "uncarved wood", represented by the Chinese character 樸 *pu*. The extended meaning of *pu* is 'pure and simple. But *pu* can only be "unhewn" or "uncarved" if it is already *meant* for hewing and carving. This point of departure opens the way for poetic composition, in which the poet becomes *yin* and *yang* merged in the process of making. It is as if the poet were an entangled quantum particle – both initiating and responding in a single state.

Changing is a work hewn out of the accrual of presence and a sagacious response to our anxious age. In "The Spirit of Art According to the Book of Changes," Richard Wilhelm writes:

> How are we able to rescue the spiritual heritage from the vulgarity pressing in on us from all sides? Art that succeeds to solve this problem of human kind is good art. Such art passes on spirit and flame kindled in the heart and it will continue to kindle, propagate, and guard the sacred fire, so that it may continue to burn.
>
> (Wilhelm R. 232)

Changing is the kind of art that Wilhelm calls for. It initiates and responds with vitality and optimism. It sends the reader 'back' into the present, 're-patterned' in spirit. In its own words, *Changing* is a book

[...] fit for, capable of examining,
expressing, understanding, *in*
and *through* words, what had

been unsaid, unsayable [...]

so that it may

[...] mend and change the real,
regrow and rebuild hope.   ("[A] coherent language," 23/6: 190)

Acknowledgements

Grateful thanks to the editors for their careful reading, to Seido Ray Ronci for insight into the meditative sequence of the *I Ching*, and to Tim Langen for assistance with combinatorics.

References

Abrams, M.H. (ed.). 1986. *The Norton Anthology of English Literature* (5th edn., vol. 2.) New York: Norton.

Austin, James H. 1998. *Zen and the Brain: Toward an Understanding of Meditation and Consciousness*. Cambridge, MA: The MIT Press.

Berengarten, Richard. 2011 *The Manager*. Bristol: Shearsman Books.

———. 2016. *Changing*. Bristol: Shearsman Books.

———. 2018. "Modelling Base-Lines: Connectivity and Grounding" (*n.p.*).

Blake, William. 1986. "Introduction." In Abrams, 37.

Derrick, Paul Scott. 2015. *Lines of Thought*. Valencia: Biblioteca Javier Coy d'estudis nord-americans.

Fedotov, Sergey. 2016. "Simple Association of the Genetic Code with Hexagrams of the *Book of Changes* (*I Ching*)." *Cardiometry* 9, 32-43.

Gu, Ming Dong. 2005. "'The *Zhouyi* (Book of Changes) as an Open Classic: A Semiotic Analysis of its System of Representation." *Philosophy East and West* 55(2): 257-282.

Heringman, Noah. 2015. "Notes on *Recto Verso*" (*n.p.*).

Hon, Tze-Ki. 2005. *The I Ching and Chinese Politics: Classical Commentary and Literati Activism in the Northern Song Period, 960-1127*. Albany, NY: State University of New York Press.

Hopkins, Gerard Manley. 1986. "As Kingfishers Catch Fire." In Abrams, 1587.

Huang, Alfred. 2000. *The Numerology of the I Ching*. Rochester, VT: Inner Traditions.

Keats, John. 1986. "Letter to George and Thomas Keats." In Abrams, 862-863.

Liu, Da. 1979. *I Ching Numerology*. New York: Harper and Row.

Ningchuan, Wang, and Yunxiang Kelly Chen. 2014. "The Dialogue of Civilizations: How the I Ching Can Help Understand the Relationship Between Globalization and Anti-Globalization." *Globalizations* 11(2): 239-253.

Pound, Ezra. 1913 "A Few Don'ts by an Imagiste." *Poetry Foundation*. Online at: www.poetryfoundation.org/poetrymagazine/articles/58900/a-few-donts-by-an-imagiste

Shelley, Percy Bysshe. 1986. "A Defence of Poetry." In Abrams: 781.

Sidney, Sir Philip. 1983. *Selected Prose and Poetry*. Madison, WI: University of Wisconsin Press.

Smith, Richard J. 2012. *The I Ching: A Biography*. Princeton, NJ: Princeton University Press.

Spicer, Jack. 2008. *My Vocabulary Did This to Me: The Collected Poetry of Jack Spicer*. Middletown, CT: Wesleyan University Press.

Un, Ko. 2005. *Ten Thousand Lives*. Brother Anthony *et al.* (trans.). Los Angeles, CA: Green Integer Press.

Wilhelm, Hellmut. 1995a. "The Trigrams and the Hexagrams." In Wilhelm and Wilhelm, 47-62.

———. 1995b. "The Ten Wings." In Wilhelm and Wilhelm, 83-100.

Wilhelm, Richard. 1995. "The Spirit of Art According to the Book of Changes." In Wilhelm and Wilhelm, 194-235.

Wilhelm, Richard and Baynes, Cary F. (trans.). 1965 [1951]. *The I Ching, or Book of Changes*: London: Routledge and Kegan Paul.

Wilhelm, Richard and Wilhelm, Hellmut. 1995. *Understanding the I Ching*. Princeton, NJ: Princeton University Press.

Wordsworth, William. 1986. "Preface to Lyrical Ballads." In Abrams, 155-170.

Yan, Li. 1997. *The Illustrated Book of Changes*. Beijing: Foreign Languages Press.

Tze-ki Hon

Well, Inexhaustible: Spring, Inexhaustible On Richard Berengarten's 'Welling, Replenishing'

As a metaphor for the power of nature, water appears in different ways in different traditions. It is "the great flood" in the Epic of Gilgamesh of Mesopotamia and the Story of Noah of the Old Testament. It is "a flowing river" in Greek philosophy ("No one ever steps in the same river twice") and in classical Confucianism ("Such is its passing, is it not? It ceases neither day nor night"). It is "a well of water" in the Gospel of St. John ("a well of water springing up into everlasting life") and in the *I Ching* ("In the well there is a clear, cold spring, from which one can drink"). In its various guises, water can be violent and destructive, benign and nurturing, hidden and enriching.

In the *I Ching*, the motif of "a well of water" appears in hexagram 48 (井 *Jing*, "Well"). Following hexagram 47 (困 *Kun* "Oppression / Exhaustion"), *Jing* is full of hardship and danger, suggested by the two trigrams that make up the hexagram: ☴ (巽 *Xun* "wood") below, and ☵ (坎 *Kan* "water", or a bucket of water) above. The authors of the Judgment (one of the *Ten Wings*, the earliest commentaries) solemnly warn readers that despite relentless efforts, no substantial result will be achieved if one is in the situation of *Jing* ("It neither decreases nor increases"). Worse still, in *Jing*, one will face severe challenges in achieving one's goal: "If one gets down almost to the water, and the rope does not go all the way, or the jug breaks, it brings misfortune" (Wilhelm 1967: 185).

If we look at the line statements, *Jing* tells a similar story of hardship and danger. In lines one and two (counting from the bottom), the well is desolate because it has been idle for a long time. It is full of mud at the bottom (line 1) and the jug that carries water to the surface is broken (line 2). Things begin to change in lines 3 and 4 when the well is cleaned up (line 3) and strengthened with lines of new stones (line 4). Yet, despite the renovation, the well remains useless because "no one drinks from it" without a jug to bring up water. Finally, fresh water is brought up to quell the thirst of the people. But, as lines 5 and 6 tell us, the challenge is to make certain that fresh water is continuously brought to the surface "without hindrance." In the end, the tone of *Jing* remains dark and somber. "Supreme good fortune" will come only when there are concrete results (Wilhelm 1967: 187-188).

By a stroke of genius, Berengarten captures the paradox of *Jing* – being at once full of potential and full of danger – with two simple words "Welling, Replenishing" (48: 383-390). In gerund form, these words imply continuous effort, deep-seated commitment, and the will to succeed despite setbacks and disillusionment. Together, these combined qualities symbolize the long, treacherous process of cleaning the well, firming up its walls, enabling the underground water to flow, and above all, bringing fresh water, bucket by bucket, from the bottom of the well to the top.

Departing slightly from the line statements, Berengarten sees the challenge of *Jing* as particularly severe at the beginning rather than at the end. In the first three numbered poems in this set, he compares the burden of cleaning the well to a person's self-doubt – similar to Moses's question of "Who am I?" in Exodus and Hamlet's "To be or not to be" soliloquy in Shakespeare's *Hamlet*. Speaking from the perspective of a well-cleaner, Berengarten keeps asking "Who drinks from an old well?" Daunted by the heavy burden of cleaning an old well, the speaker's self-doubt is real and inevitable because the obstacles seem insurmountable ("Our well has dried / up. Not even birds / circle or settle here"); support is lacking ("Our clerks have been / corrupted by one regime / after another. Even // lawyers and judges / have sold out"); and resources are scarce ("Can // we find a dowser / with forked hazel / or willow branch?" 48/1: 385). Yet, even though the prospect is bleak, there seem to be promising signs for the future ("Sometimes they answer / even though I've asked / no question"); so there appears to be hope in a hopeless situation ("Sometimes they say / nothing, and appear to / smile and look away" 48/2: 386).

The paradox of *Jing* is the gap between what is and what will be. On the surface, the old well is useless; but it is full of potential, waiting to be tapped. Opportunity is available; but the question is how to turn the potential into reality and how much work is needed to complete the task. To Berengarten, the biggest challenge in *Jing* is not external but internal. The critical moment in *Jing* appears when the cleaner decides to replenish the well and to bring fresh water up to the surface. Once this decision has

258

been made, there is no return. The task must be completed despite hardship, setback, disillusionment and dissatisfaction. Here, Berengarten is at his best, using poetic language to express – vividly and powerfully – the cleaner's commitment to finishing the tedious and filthy task.

We clambered down ladders
and ropes. Workmates at the top
let down shovels, sieves,

buckets, poles, mallets.
We dredged up a mountain
of mud and waste fallen

in and mulched down
there over years. Hauled out
rich stinking vegetables stuff

and rotten wood. Separated
it from clay to fertilise fields.
Hammered in new

stepping brackets and
handles as we relined walls.
Deepened and widened

entire cavity to hold more
water pooled from underground
streams than ever before.   (48/3: 387)

For Berengarten, the process of replenishing the well is a test of the will. Each step in cleaning the well is an expression of one's commitment, and each step in fortifying the well is an externalization of the will to succeed.

But when fresh water is finally drawn up from the replenished well to quell the thirsty people, the cleaner's success is both personal and communal. It is not only the triumph of the will of the cleaner, but also a great service to the community, who need fresh water in order to live. To Berengarten, this communal significance is even more important than any sense of mere personal achievement. And precisely for this reason, he regards the "well of water" not only as the theme of *Jing*, but also as the central motif of the entire *I Ching*. In what seemingly is an abrupt change in focus, in the rest of 'Welling, Replenishing' Berengarten stops discussing the refurbishing of a well and turns his attention to the meaning of the *I Ching* itself.

Fifty years my
friend, companion
and spirit-guide

always trustworthy,
never diffident
never irrelevant

solid yet flowing
firm yet yielding
radiating images

self-replenishing
inexhaustible
fathomless

ever-fresh well –
in plumbing you
I soar

feet still
grounded rooted
in *this here now*.   (48/4: 388)

This abrupt change in focus makes the poem unique and profound. It no longer follows the original line statements of *Jing*. Instead, Berengarten embarks on a heartfelt meditation on the meaning of the *I Ching* itself. Like a well, the *I Ching* enables its readers to reflect on who they are by asking questions dear to their heart; like a well, the *I Ching* also nourishes its readers by providing them with thoughtful advice, heart-warming encouragement, and careful suggestions; and, like a well, the *I Ching* gives life when it is needed most. As such, *Jing* can be used as a guide to the *I Ching*, and even, indeed, as an encapsulation or symbol of its entirety, teaching readers how to use this Chinese classic to cope with fear and anxiety in life. So that readers recognize this point fully, Berengarten opens this set with a head-poem entitled 'Consultation of the Diagrams', suggesting how helpful the practice is "in the construction / of hypotheses, buildings / and voyages" or "in the correct / turning of antennae / towards origins" (48/0: 384). For careful readers, the "diagrams" in this poem will be understood to refer to both the sixty-four hexagrams of the *I Ching* and the six lines of *Jing*. This double signification makes this opening poem both intriguing and enlightening, because it openly encourages readers to look attentively at *Jing* as a unit of innerly coherent meanings in its own right, as well as an encapsulation of the entire *I Ching*.

Indeed, the hexagram *Jing* is an appropriate and powerful symbol of the *I Ching*, because it puts emphasis on the give-and-take, the trial-and-error, between the reader and the text. Berengarten tells us that when we, as readers, lower our questions "on a rope / of thought" into the well, we "draw up / water-wisdom" and "drink from a fund / of deep light." The "water-wisdom" may be auspicious or inauspicious, encouraging or discouraging. But the point is not whether this water-wisdom is "sweet or bitter," but what we learn from it (48/5: 389). As a "self-replenishing and inexhaustible well," Berengarten reminds us, the *I Ching* is even more resourceful:

> Self-replenishing
> and inexhaustible
> well, generous
>
> secret, open face
> of Underworld, with
> rounded mouth
>
> and level gaze –   (48/6: 390)

Here, the capitalized word "Underworld" has an implicit suggestion of pagan mythologies, as in the Greek Hades, whose great queen, Persephone, embodies the motif of fertility and renewal. The Underworld in Berengarten's line is clearly also a fund, a resource for new life. The new life comes from a conversation with the *I Ching*, or better yet, a conversation with the ambiguity, contingency, and uncertainty of life. In realizing that we are powerless in facing a world that is ever-changing, we transmute our fear and anxiety into the motivation to adapt and respond to our surroundings. In this sense, *Jing* clearly and simply invokes one of the essential qualities of fresh water. For by flowing, water in itself symbolizes flexibility, fluidity, and above all, moving in accord with changing circumstances.

In his poetic address to the *I Ching* (48/4: 388), Berengarten compares it to an "ever-fresh well," which prompts us to be more firmly "grounded, rooted / in *this here now*." And if we link "*this here now*" to the *I Ching*, we find yet another meaning of "a well of water." Rather than suggesting that we seek help from without (such as from a divine power), the *I Ching* asks us to take command of our own fates in *this here now*. By focusing on what is happening in the here-and-now, we are able to diminish, partially if not fully, our fear and anxiety in an ever-changing world. Accordingly, in the 'Postscript,' when explaining his aims in writing *Changing*, Berengarten returns to the image of the well as a metaphor of life:

> If any single motif or symbol in the *I Ching* has most come to represent the *I Ching* in my own mind, it is that of the well (hexagram 48). [...] In the same way that looking down into a well filled with water under sunlight facilitates visual reflection – not to mention mental reflection (on heights, depths, and their relative perspectives) – and just as calling down into a well sets up echoic resonance, so my hope is that *Changing* may both, *reflect and echo itself* to a reader while it is being read, and so enable the reader to reflect *on* it, just as I also hope it may reflect and echo (*and* enable the reader to reflect on) the material it integrates, the processes of its own making, and its own 'deep' source, the *I Ching*. (527)

Just as the fresh water of a replenished well must be brought up to reach thirsty people, so too the goal of reading the *I Ching* is not only to transform its readers, but also to enable them to effect change in the world around them. For this reason, as suggested in the sixth line of *Jing*, "supreme good fortune" comes only when concrete results have been secured for the community, not just for a few sensitive souls. Thus, the key to being at ease in an ever-changing world means taking appropriate action to achieve definite results in changing our surroundings – be it vis-à-vis our family, our neighborhood, or our extended community – or all three. In Berengarten's words, we must plant our feet deeply and firmly in "*this here now.*"

References

Berengarten, Richard. 2016. *Changing*. Bristol: Shearsman Books.

Wilhelm, Richard and Baynes, Cary F. (trans.). 1967. *The I Ching or Book of Changes*. Princeton, NJ: Princeton University Press.

Geoffrey Redmond

The Literary Geometry of
Richard Berengarten's *Changing*

In my contribution to this collection of essays on Richard Berengarten's remarkable long poem, *Changing*, I will focus not on content by itself, interesting as that is, but rather on the literary significance of its distinctive structure. My analysis might be termed a study in literary geometry, as it is the mathematical properties of the hexagrams that give a distinctive character to this Chinese classic. While the seeming cosmological meanings of the hexagrams have been at the forefront of consideration, their literary function has received less attention.

The *Book of Changes* is not only one of the world's strangest ancient classics: it has also been one of its most fertile. Berengarten's *Changing* serves as an instance of the fecundity of the *I Ching* in inspiring new ideas, nearly 3,000 years after its initial compilation. This occurred relatively early in the development of literacy, when the descriptive power of written language was limited. Over the ensuing long duration, the laconic textual fragments that make up its earliest layer, referred to as the *Zhouyi,* have been read in increasingly complex ways. Not all commentators have been able to resist the temptation of imposing new meanings under the pretense of knowing what the book "really" meant. It is the distinctive six-line diagrams, or hexagrams, basically unchanged over the millennia that, I suggest, account for its persistence in human consciousness. (Technically there were slight alterations in how the lines were written; at some point the notion of changing lines was introduced, yet the hexagrams are clearly the same as those in the earliest extant manuscript, which is held by the Shanghai Museum and dated to c. 300 BCE.)

I base my observations on the *Zhouyi*, the earliest text layer, as it has been reconstructed through the work of Chinese philologists, beginning in the last century. My own translation draws upon these earlier reconstructions. These meanings differ considerably from the later ones, which are based on

Confucian philosophy and familiar from the Wilhelm/Baynes translation (1951). The most important English works based on restoration of early meanings are those of Richard Kunst (1984), Richard Rutt (1996), and, of course, Edward L. Shaughnessy (2014), author of the Preface to *Changing*.

The structure of the *Book of Changes*, based on the hexagrams, is distinctive; no other of the world's ancient classics, apart from those derivative of the *I Ching*, organizes texts upon a geometric template. (There are other texts with diagrams but these serve as illustrations, not organizing systems.) Without the hexagrams, the *I Ching* would merely be another collection of often banal divinatory responses, not always more profound than those of fortune cookies. While the hexagram structure is in a sense a Procrustean bed, it is also the underlying genius of this so far timeless classic.

In accord with mathematical set theory, groups of six items, each of two possible values (solid and broken; later *yang* and *yin*) self-generate sixty-four possible arrays. As a cosmological model, the geometric completeness of the six-line sets suggests the completeness of the cosmos, which provides the metaphysical fascination of the hexagrams.

As I explain in my own translation (Redmond 2017), this array provided a structure that permitted organization of the heterogeneous fragments that constitute the judgment and line texts (2017). When the early meanings are considered, thematic unity in the *I Ching* exists only in brief passages, not in the text as a whole. Yet such was the prestige of the text that it was always assumed to be coherent.

⁊

The essence of poetry is imagery. Some poems tell a story or develop a consistent theme, but some do neither. Images or themes can follow one another without obvious connection or, may be unintelligible without a thick tome of explanatory notes. This is the case with Ezra Pound's *Cantos*, for example. Although such modernist works are not to be dismissed, interest in Pound's work seems to be waning, in part because of his Fascist politics.

Poetry also depends on inspiration; images, ideas, phrases, may arise in the poet's mind independently of one another. Manuscripts, and especially print, require a sequence in time and space, for poetic images need to be organized. This was much less the case in pre-literate times when oral material could be, and routinely was, reordered. Once transmission and diffusion required writing, the creator had to submit his or her material to a constraining system, although free within this to follow inspiration.

Richard Berengarten has adapted the hexagram system to his contemporary poetry-making. Like the *I Ching*, *Changing* was composed gradually, though over decades rather than centuries, but held together by the same hexagram system as the ancient classic. Some of the greatest works of Western literature similarly impose order under a system somewhat external to the narrative. In the *Odyssey*, for example, all sorts of strange creatures and events are connected because Odysseus encounters them during his epic voyage to reach his home. The voyage or journey functions as a device to connect these oddities. Another example is Dante's *Commedia*, a compilation of descriptions of the *post-mortem* fate of famous people. Like Odysseus, the figure of Aeneas in Virgil's *Aeneid* provides seeming continuity. Ultimately, this long poem is organized not only by religious themes but also by a mythical geography of the realm beyond death. In assigning persons to locations, its structure is similar to the *ars memorativa*. Some long poems lack even this degree of structure, Ezra Pound's *Cantos* being a modern example. It is divided into different "cantos" but these are thematic only to a limited degree.

I hope it is clear that I am not faulting Berengarten's *Changing* for lacking conventional thematic structure; rather I want to suggest that it has a *different* organizational structure than a narrative poem such as, for example, Byron's *Childe Harold's Pilgrimage*. As with the *Book of Changes* itself, different portions of *Changing* will resonate at different times, depending on the reader's current life-situation. In either case, reading in a random order can at times unveil mental patterns that have not yet reached consciousness.

Walter Ong, the great scholar of the development of literacy, points out that the linear organization of material only became necessary with the development of writing, particularly printing, which was constrained to produce standardized versions to a far greater degree than manuscript culture (314 *et passim*).

Efforts of various savants to discover an overt or covert mathematical pattern in the various hexagram orderings have convinced no-one but themselves.[1] There are two common sequences based on line-patterns, but

---

[1] *Editors' note*: It is worth noting here that there is a highly respected and complex Chinese tradition of exploring mathematical patterns in the *I Ching*, which goes back at least two thousand years – from its early embodiment in *yinyang* binary theories to a great many other forms of sophisticated numerical constructions.

these do not correlate with any system of meaning. In the so-called King Wen or received arrangement, hexagrams are paired with their inverse when possible; solid is replaced with broken and vice-versa. Hexagram sequencing is discussed in more detail in Rutt (102-118) and in Redmond and Hon (147-169).

Ordering the hexagrams seems to have been simply for convenience. While Shaughnessy provides evidence from the Shanghai Museum bamboo strips that the hexagram sequence of this version may have been similar to the transmitted one, the Mawangdui manuscript order is quite different (Shaughnessy 47-53). Since this recently discovered version was written on silk, its sequencing must have been intentional. In contrast, the process of writing on bamboo strips involved no absolute need for a fixed order. The strips were bound together with leather thongs, which could break or wear out; so rearrangement, whether deliberate or accidental, must have been common. Given the very limited evidence available, we cannot reconstruct an "original" sequence, and there may well not have been one. Given that the ordering principle of the hexagrams is essentially random – that is to say, variable rather than fixed – we can feel free to access them in any order that serves our own purposes. Perhaps the commonest mistake made by beginners approaching the *I Ching* for the first time is to try to read it in a fixed order, as one would, say, a novel, or non-fiction monograph. This can only result in confusion, since the texts were compiled to be read in response to a specific query.[2] The *I Ching* is organized as a reference book, almost like a manual or a dictionary.

I would propose the same method for reading Berengarten's *Changing*, although I do not know if he would agree. You can pick a poem based on coin toss or other traditional method, then ponder what it might mean to you in relation to your current life situation – or just let your thoughts flow from it.[3] This may seem odd at first as by force of habit we tend to seek thematic organization, yet it provides the reader with opportunities for serendipity. Nothing prevents one from beginning

---

[2] *Editors' note*: Geoffrey Redmond's discussion of sequencing in the *I Ching* exactly reflects Berengarten's early intention to publish *Changing* as a 'loose-leaf' collection of sixty-four folios. These were to be shuffled into any order, like a pack of cards. The entire set of sixty-four would have been presented as a 'book-in-a-box' (RB, email to Paschalis Nikolaou, 1 March 2021). For more on this plan vis-à-vis *form* and *content*, see 315-317 below.

[3] *Editors' note*: The suggestion offered here has actually been put into practice by Alan Trist and Bob DeVine. See 286-306 below.

at the beginning and proceeding onward, of course. (Personal disclosure: when reading a new book, particularly a complex scholarly one, I usually begin by opening at random until I find a passage that strikes my interest at that moment. I may or may not end up reading the whole book, but somehow, perhaps because of the years I have spent grappling with the *Zhouyi*, this works for me.)

Although we imagine otherwise, an individual's life is only a narrative in retrospect. The human mind seeks to put events into a purposeful pattern, thus conferring meaning to them. Rather than providing a ready-made narrative, the *I Ching* provides fragments that are made into a narrative only during divination. Mysteriously, for the inquirer, the act of fitting these snippets into such a narrative often clarifies situations. Elsewhere, I have discussed possible explanations for how divination might work (Redmond and Hon 19-36).

While I avoid making metaphysical claims, many people tell me that divination in one form or another has been helpful in their lives. Poetry can work in a similar way: instead of absorbing the reader as does a novel, it can offer images, themes, and situations that the mind is free to make of what it will. A long poem like *Changing* is particularly suitable for this, given its great variety of images and its arrangement by hexagrams, by means of which lines (or rather, in this case, poems) can be selected by coins or other random means.

As an example, I will consider 4.1, the first line-text of hexagram 4, *Meng*, translated as 'Youthful Folly' in the Wilhelm/Baynes translation and as 'Neophytes' in mine. A theme of this hexagram is how to deal with the young and immature, generally with a punitive tone. Here is Wilhelm/Baynes:

> To make a fool develop
> It furthers to apply discipline.   (Wilhelm/Baynes 22)

My version:

> In teaching neophytes, it is beneficial to use physical punishment.
> Use scolding to restrain before, in order to lead to remorse. (2017: 83)

And here is Berengarten in *Changing*:

> The project that term
> was community. The boy
> was asked to draw

himself at the center
then radiate lines out to all
things he was part of. (4/1: 33)

I offer my own interpretation; no doubt other readings would be equally valid. The meaning of the Chinese text is unpleasant to modern sensibility; even in Wilhelm/Baynes' usually benign translation, the raising of children involves harsh discipline. Berengarten's poem casts yet another light on the process: the child is motivated by exploring the richness of his multiple connections to others and, by implication, his responsibilities to them. I would even go so far as to suggest that this is a Confucian reading, which stresses the individual's relation to society. The poem does not endorse the *I Ching*'s advice but suggests an entirely different way to look at the process of education.

I give this example to suggest how traditional ways of using the *I Ching* can be adapted to *Changing*, so that it can be the basis of a practice. We also see that Berengarten's poem is not a paraphrase of the Chinese classic but extends it in multiple directions. This has been the nature of *I Ching* commentaries from Wang Bi (226-249 CE) to the present (see Richard J. Lynn's translation, 1994). My way of reading *Changing* is as a counterpoint to the *I Ching*, no doubt because the *Book of Changes* has been a preoccupation of mine for more than three decades; others, of course are free to find their own ways.

Perhaps the greatest mystery of the *Changes* has been its capacity to continuously inspire fresh insights. Richard Berengarten continues this great tradition.

References

Kunst, Richard Allen. 1985. *The Original "I Ching": A Text, Phonetic Transcription, Translation, and Indexes, with Sample Glosses*. PhD thesis, University of California at Berkeley. Ann Arbor, MI: University Microfilms International.

Lynn, Richard John. 1994. *The Classic of Changes: A New Translation of the I Ching as Interpreted by Wang Bi*. New York: Columbia University Press.

Ong, Walter J., 2004. *Ramus: Method, and the Decay of Dialogue: From the Art of Discourse to the Art of Reason*. Chicago, IL: University of Chicago Press.

Redmond, Geoffrey and Tze-ki Hon. 2014. *Teaching the I Ching (Book of Changes)*. Oxford: Oxford University Press.

Redmond, Geoffrey. 2017. *The I Ching (Book of Changes): A Critical Translation of the Early Text*. London: Bloomsbury Academic.

Rutt, Richard. 1996. *The Book Of Changes (Zhouyi): a Bronze Age Document*. Richmond: Curzon.

Shaughnessy, Edward L. 2014. *Unearthing the Changes: Recently Discovered Manuscripts of the* Yi Jing (I Ching) *and Related Texts*. New York: Columbia University Press.

Wilhelm, Richard (ed. and trans. into German). 1951. *The I Ching or Book of Changes*. Baynes, Cary F. (trans. from German). London: Routledge and Kegan Paul.

TAN CHEE LAY

In the Philosophical Sphere of the *I Ching*: A Quick Stylometric Look into Richard Berengarten's *Changing*

Even a quick and simple glance at the white cover of Richard Berengarten's *Changing* is fascinating. Against this background, the ancient pictogram 易 (*Yi*) is painted in concise strokes of black ink.[1] To me, this pictographic character suggests the form of a bird flying, a suitable connotation for the ever-changing nature of time and space as perceived from within the perspective of the fleeting existence of a human being. The English word *Changing* has a double nature, for it can be construed either as a present participle or as a verbal noun (gerund). In either case, the image of the wings of a bird in flight might well symbolise transitory and transformative movement in and through space-time.

Claimed to be one of the most ambitious poems ever written outside the Chinese language in connection with the *Book of Changes* or *I Ching* (*I Ching*), *Changing* represents a unique reading experience for me. Since I am a Chinese speaker who, as a student, read the original *I Ching* text in an almost traditional manner in the Chinese department of a university in Taiwan, Richard Berengarten's book feels both oddly familiar and curiously

---

[1] *Editors' note*: The spirit of *Yi* (易, 'Change') proposes connectivity in contiguity and involves infinite variation. The cover image for *Changing* is by the contemporary Chinese calligrapher and poet Yu Mingquan, who has provided a different calligraphic rendering of the same character for our book of essays. For *Changing*, the written character is based on an extremely ancient calligraphic form; for our book, on a more recent but still ancient form, from the Song Dynasty. The cover design for both books is by the Cambridge graphic artist Will Hill.

strange to me. It is familiar because the text and structure of the *Book of Changes*, which are the direct sources of inspiration for Berengarten's poem, are subjects that have been studied and scrutinised by generations of Chinese scholars over the ages; and these are integral to the most formative aspects of my cultural and literary background. Yet the approaches and styles of Berengarten's literary creation, which both adhere to and depart from the text of *The Book of Changes* itself, are so refreshingly unfamiliar for any Chinese scholar-reader that his interpretations might equally be said to be novel and reinvigorating.

With regard to the former aspect, the *Book of Changes* consists of a total of sixty-four hexagrams. Each hexagram is made up of two sets of three broken or continuous lines (trigrams). With their corresponding commentaries, *in toto* they represent a coherent attempt to emulate the entirety of the universe. Indeed, by combining and recombining the many variations and permutations of these figures (384 in all, i.e. 64 x 6), they are meant to embody – or mirror – the circularity (or cyclicity) of human life and fate. Berengarten's book fully recreates this oriental philosophical aim in such a way that it both 'envelops' his own multicultural interpretations and contextualises his inspiration within the multiple and complex traditions of Chinese culture. In his 'Postscript', Berengarten writes:

> I have modelled *Changing* closely on the *I Ching* by replicating and adapting its architectonic patterns at various levels of compositional structure. At the micro-level [...] each poem has six stanzas and each stanza consists of three lines. In this way, the forms of both hexagram and trigram are implicitly re-presented (re-called, re-embodied, reduplicated, replicated, etc.) in each poem's *mise-en-page*. (*CH* 525)

Evidently, form ('pattern') is important to Berengarten. Of the 450 poems in this book, all but two contain six tercets. While the tercet itself directly echoes the three-line structure of the trigrams in the *Book of Changes*, similarly the number of stanzas in each poem fully replicates the number of lines in a hexagram. In this way, rather than being a mere source of inspiration, the *Book of Changes* has been closely 'followed' in *Changing*, not only with regard to content but also in the 'modelling' or 'patterning' of its *mise-en-page*. In this way, Berengarten has added an innovative poetic and artistic dimension to his philosophical interpretation, which enriches and augments its apparently timeless and universal appeal in a way that is entirely original. Both these aspects of Berengarten's poem – the traditional and the innovative – are clearly due to the fact that he has spent fifty years interacting with the *I Ching*, so much so that his poetry is steeped in its traditions.

∾

Within these parameters of classical Chinese tradition and personal poetic innovation, we can quickly and easily establish that in *Changing*, Berengarten's own personal voice and foci of attention are not only portrayed but fully evident through his highly individualised poetic language. One way of deciphering his specific concerns and individual responses to *The Book of Changes* is by exploring the entire body of his text by means of an analysis of the count, variety, choices and frequency of words. By deploying the online digital corpus system, *Textalyser* (http://textalyser.net/index. php?lang=en#analysis) to calculate and analyse results, we are able digitally to generate the following outcomes:

Table 1: Statistics of *Changing*, derived from *Textalyser*

Total word count	37,923
Number of different words	8,324
Complexity factor (lexical density)	21.9%
Readability ("Gunning-Fog Index"): 6 = easy; 20 = hard	6.8
Total number of characters	239,307
Number of characters without spaces	181,311
Average syllables per word	1.59
Sentence count	2,836
Average sentence length (words)	13.6
Readability (alternative) beta: in general, 100 = easy; 20 = hard; optimal = 60-70	58.3

From the above table, we see that of a total of more than 37,000 words in the book, Berengarten has used more than 8,000 different words. Here, the machine is only able to determine a relatively simple and direct *complexity factor* of the text, which is to take the total word count

(37,923) and to divide them by the number of different words that occur (8,324). This results in a complexity percentage of 21.9%. This feature is sometimes also called *lexical density*, which is defined as the total number of words in the book divided by the number of lexical words (or content words). In this case, by utilising a mode of intervention and calculation that is purely mechanical, every single word, including *non-representational* words such as articles, prepositions, conjunctions, and others that are more grammatical (syntactic) in nature and function, is taken into consideration for the calculation. Of course, we also have to note the special characteristics of poetry, among which is the fact that every single word counts and is important in this highly dense and concise genre. In such a context, and even more so than in other genres, I believe it is also important that non-lexical words should be counted, in order to determine the complexity factor.

In the case of *Changing*, a complexity factor of 21.9% is not especially high. Just to obtain a preliminary idea, we can make a simple comparison with another poet with whom we are familiar, for example, William Carlos Williams. Williams' *Paterson*, for instance, a long poem in four parts, has 3,592 different words out of a total word count of 13,380 words, which works out as a complexity factor of 26.8%, and a readability of 7.4, as compared to Berengarten's 6.8 (the higher the index, the lower the readability). While these two cases may not be fully compatible, we could roughly deduce that each of Berengarten's words appears about five times while Williams' appears about four times. Consequently, might we be able to infer that the use of many identical or similar words is a deliberate strategy of Berengarten's, not only (as noted above) in terms of his explicitly professed aim to "re-present" the "forms" of the *I Ching* "[…] in each poem's *mise-en-page*", but also in reproducing some of the repeating aspects of the lexicon of the *Book of Changes* itself? Repetition, after all, is a key element in poetry, at all levels from the phonemic (rhyme, assonance) to the lexical; and in lyrical poetry, just as in song, the refrain (or chorus) has a complex function. It is noteworthy, for example, that the verbs used in the above quotation "re-presented (re-called, re-embodied, reduplicated, replicated, etc.)" are highly similar to some of those in the following poem, whose subject and title is, precisely, "(A) coherent language":

> Our job is to foster and grow
> (a) coherent language, little
> by little, in patience, in respect.

[…] following the heart's
paths and injunctions – to
reaffirm the dignity

of the dead, and reclaim,
recall, rediscover – or find for
 the first time (a) language

fit for, capable of examining,
expressing, understanding *in*
and *through* words, what had

been unsaid, unsayable, and
so mend and change the real,
regrow and rebuild hope   (23/6: 190)

Related to the complexity factor, of course, is the readability or *Gunning-Fog Index* of the text, which for *Changing* stands at 6.8. This figure, obtained from a weighted average of the number of words per sentence and the number of complex words, renders Berengarten's text as highly readable: 6 is considered easy, and the most difficult text can go up to 20 on the Gunning-Fog index scale.

As a form of triangulation to confirm the relatively high readability of Berengarten's text, we further see that the average number of syllables per word is only 1.59, which means that there is a far higher proportion of words of one and two syllables than any other. Besides the higher likelihood of simpler and direct words in *Changing*, words with fewer syllables may be more likely to portray a 'faster' rhythm. To justify such an argument, the following table shows the frequencies of both syllable count and word length. From Table 2, it is clear that words of one syllable have an extremely high frequency, of almost 58%, and that words of one syllable and two syllables, considered together, make up an overwhelmingly large proportion of the entire text of *Changing*: that is, more than 87%.

Table 2: Syllable and Word Counts in *Changing*

Syllable count	Word count	Frequency
1	21,114	57.5%
2	10,891	29.7%
3	3,489	9.5%
4	1,029	2.8%
5	173	0.5%
6	25	0.1%
8	1	0%

Subsequently, Table 3 further confirms that, the highest frequency for word-lengths is words of three, four and two characters respectively, and that this makes up over 52% of all words in *Changing*. Words containing over 10 characters have frequencies of less than 1% each.

Table 3: Word Length in *Changing*

Word Length (characters)	Word count	Frequency
3	7,738	19.7%
4	7,048	18%
2	5,652	14.4%
5	5,120	13.1%
6	3,800	9.7%
7	3,347	8.5%
8	2,176	5.5%
9	1,405	3.6%
1	1,316	3.4%
10	913	2.3%
11	381	1%
12	174	0.4%
13	86	0.2%
14	42	0.1%

While longer words in English tend to be derived from Latin or Greek and often belong to more 'intellectual', 'educated', and 'professional' registers, poets writing in English, possibly including Berengarten, frequently advocate using simpler and more easily communicative language. For example, in the 'Prologue' to his play *Every Man in His Humour*, Ben Jonson advocates "language such as men do use" (2009); and Wordsworth in his 'Preface to *Lyrical Ballads*' argues for "a selection of the language really used by men" (1993).

Next, we delve further into the specific words used, and produce the frequency table of word types in the complete text of Berengarten's *Changing* in Tables 4 and 5.

Table 4: Frequency table of words in Berengarten's *Changing*

Word	Occurrences	Frequency	Rank
and	1582	4.2%	1
the	986	2.6%	2
in	833	2.2%	3
of	791	2.1%	4
to	680	1.8%	5
a	626	1.7%	6
on	361	1%	7
you	302	0.8%	8
is	259	0.7%	9
or	252	0.7%	9
he	232	0.6%	10
this	231	0.6%	10
it	227	0.6%	10
i	221	0.6%	10
for	219	0.6%	10
as	215	0.6%	10
with	215	0.6%	10
his	214	0.6%	10
all	195	0.5%	11

her	183	0.5%	11
our	180	0.5%	11
we	171	0.5%	11
at	168	0.4%	12
not	167	0.4%	12
from	165	0.4%	12
out	162	0.4%	12
by	161	0.4%	12
no	160	0.4%	12
she	150	0.4%	12
your	147	0.4%	12
one	146	0.4%	12
they	142	0.4%	12
him	82	0.3%	N/A
hers	4	0.01%	N/A

An examination of Table 4, opposite and above, reveals several possibly significant facts. First, the few words that Berengarten has utilised most frequently from his vocabulary-base include, in the following order, *you, he, it, I, his, her, our, we, she, your* and *they*. From these high-frequency pronouns, might it be suggested that there is a strong tendency in the poems to be 'relationship-oriented' and even 'intimate' and, along with this, that a major concern in the poem has to do with personal interactions?

The pronouns *we* (subject), *us* (direct or indirect object), *our* and *they*, all indicate plurality, while *you* and *your* may be either singular or plural, according to context. The prevalence of the first, second and third persons plural *we, our, us, they*, and perhaps *you* and *your*, could perhaps indicate a primary concern for social issues of the masses – which is very much in keeping with the earliest use of divination in Chinese history, even before the *I Ching* existed, when diviners applied intense heat to induce cracks in tortoise plastrons and ox-shoulder bones. The evidence of inscriptions on these oracle bones suggests that when rulers consulted diviners they did so mainly on social issues (Knightley: 25).

Another interesting feature we see here is 337 occurrences for the words *she, her* and *hers*, by comparison with 528 occurrences for *he, him* and *his*. This yields a ratio of 1:1.57 of feminine pronouns to masculine ones. If we take subject pronouns *she* and *he*, with 150 for the former and 232 for the latter, the ratio is nearly 1:1.55. While masculine pronouns are more frequent, Berengarten's interest in representing the perspectives and experiences of women as subjects is evident.

> [S]he hasn't yet caught up even
> with this year's beginning,   ('January-end already', 3/1: 25)

> I'm pregnant,
> she told her mother on
> her (mother's) birthday.   ('Hearing the other smiling', 3/2: 26)

Both of these passages relate to the third hexagram, 屯 (*Zhun*), which Berengarten translates as 'Beginning' (3: 23). Here, Berengarten portrays the perspectives and experiences of female subjects and voices at the beginning of a new year, thus emphasising Mother Nature / Mother Earth and the beginnings of all life in birth. second of the above extracts is from a poem entitled 'Hearing the other smiling': a daughter is talking, privately, about being pregnant, to her own mother. The intimacy of the situation is evident in the base-line, which, as elsewhere, serves as a metatext: "after ten years // she conceives" (3/2: 26). The parenthesis in the phrase "her (mother's) birthday" clarifies that the timing of this conversation itself celebrates the recurrence and continuation of life and implies the cyclicity of human fate, since life always returns to the starting point: birth.

Next, following the same model as in Table 4 above, Table 5 lists a small selection of words that specifically reveal semantic content in *Changing*. Most of these are nouns: these will clearly reveal patterns of imagery which themselves indicate dominant and/or recurrent motifs or themes in Berengarten's long poem. Of the 11 terms chosen, the last 8 are also the names of the trigrams of the *I Ching*:

Table 5: Selected high-frequency images or 'imagems'

Word	Occurrences	Frequency	Rank
Time	117	0.3%	13
Light	94	0.2%	14
Nothing	84	0.2%	14
Wind	77	0.2%	14

Water	56	0.1%	15
Heaven	47	0.1%	15
Fire	44	0.1%	15
Mountain	35	0.1%	15
Earth	29	0.1%	15
Thunder	29	0.1%	15
Lake	25	0.1%	15

The eight primary trigrams, which are the core 'building units' in the *I Ching*, must inevitably play a key role in *Changing*, even if here they are not explicitly presented as contrasting pairs: *heaven / earth, mountain / lake, thunder / wind*, and *water / fire*. Even so, the multiple patterns created by the interplay of these elements is imaginatively captured in Berengarten's long poem, through a multitude of complex and varied relationships with one another. The typical functions attributed to each of these configurations evidently include many traditional motifs, for example: thunder instigates; wind scatters, water (as rain) irrigates; fire (as sunlight) warms; mountains steady; lakes please; heaven rules; and earth stores (Ziporyn: 244-245).

While all these polysemic themes are fully evident in *Changing*, in Berengarten's text these eight elements take on still more manifestations and proliferations, which include multiple literal, symbolic, and abstract meanings, connotations, and associations. Hence, in *Changing*, thunder not only booms in a storm but is also the sound 'borne' by victors; wind not only scatters but also infiltrates; water can be either dangerous or life-enhancing and soothing; fire can either smoulder slowly or blaze fast, fuelling more flames; mountains may represent obstacles as much as achievements; a lake may signify not only serendipity but also flooding, which "rises above the trees" (28/1: 224); heaven is, perhaps surprisingly, not only almighty and transcendental, but also immanent and all-embracing; and earth, though motherly, life-giving and nourishing to all, is nonetheless equally the 'storehouse' for the slaughtered, the dead, and decay.

Let's take a closer look at one of these eight trigrams, 巽 (*Xun*), 'wind' ☴. In *Changing*, the word *wind* has the highest frequency of all these eight elements (77 occurrences; and this does not of course include many related words, such as *breeze, draught, gust*). In the *I Ching*, while *wind* can embody the strength of dispersing and scattering movements, it can also infiltrate (and even 'dissolve') its influences into other parts of nature, and do so too – literally, metaphorically and symbolically – into both human and metaphysical domains (Ziporyn: 245). Both these aspects are explored and configured in *Changing* – the motif of dispersal, for example, in 'Fields frost', and of infiltration, merging and re-emerging, in '*Against clouds*':

> [...] That

> dour music is the wind
> blowing down from
> northern deserts.   ('Fields frost', 2/1: 15)

> *Then wind's puckered*
> *mouth spread hints of*
> *almost-words through*

> *the tree's entire body,*
> *reiterating them with*
> *each renewed gust.*

> *Then wind dissolved,*
> *letting leaves speak to*
> *themselves, without*

> *thanking its disposers,*
> *three parts droppletted,*
> *four parts ash.*   ('*Against clouds*', 5/0: 40)

To further explore the semantic 'bundling' of such high-frequency words – and thus to reveal what we might well think of as dominant themes in *Changing* – we could possibly look at related image-clusters, or *imagems*, as Berengarten calls them (RB 2013: 26; and RB, letter to author: 4 Nov 2019). This word *water* occurs 56 times, in addition to which many others are also present which either belong to or are associated with the same imagem or 'word cloud', for example: *river, rain, wet, flow, pool, sea, ocean, current, stream, drop, drip, wash, drink, drank, lake, marsh, canal, mud, lagoon, mist, soak*, and so on. Notably this list includes both nouns and verbs. Examining such imagems and their relationships, we see that water not only flows and irrigates as mentioned above, but that it can also impose its presence powerfully and forcefully, and destroy:

> [...] Rain
> lashed and slashed soil,

> rivers burst, mists rose,
> fields lay soaked.   ('Relief', 40/1: 320)

Rain on rain, storm
on storm, flood on
flood.   (*'The lake rises above the trees',*
                                                      28/0: 224)

Evidently, imagems involving the element of water are often deployed by Berengarten to signify a variety of 'flows', whether spatial or temporal or both. So the flow is not only through space but also through time:

[C]an you see
how, here, across grass, time
may *flow* backwards too, as
floods of was and will-be inter-
penetrate, the unpredictable

unlikely casual tomorrow [...]   ('Wind across grass', 19/1: 153;
                                                      emphases added)

But we needed markets.
And love and war like water *flow*
unnoticed in quiet places.   ('Wall', 46/6: 374; emphases added)

Furthermore, in addition to *flow*, water-imagems have yet another function: they blend and bond the natural and the human, stasis and motion, and the word and silence. Thus, apparently disparate elements come together in a unison, a seamless and harmonious unity. This theme is beautifully elaborated in several poems, for example:

When you are I come together,
We join in a union, blend in a unity,
Flow in a unison.   ('As water', 8/1: 65; emphasis added)

Border and edges
Among things [...]

flow into one
another, merge,
blend, bond.   ('Dark gates of things', 14/5: 117
                                                      emphasis added)

These motifs of *flowing* and of *merging*, *blending* and *bonding*, of course, connect both *wind* and *water*.

A further point that is clarified by this short exploration is that all the eight trigrams in the *I Ching*, combine connotations that are both 'positive' and 'negative', both 'life-enhancing' and 'destructive'. This oppositional quality is of course inherent in all such symbols. In *Changing*, Berengarten explores their binary potentials to the full.

❧

Besides the nouns that indicate the eight elemental trigrams, some of the other words with the highest frequencies in this book are *time* (117 times), *light* (94 times) and *nothing* (84 times). We will probably not be surprised to note that these three words have strong philosophical implications, many of which Berengarten actively explores both in *Changing* and elsewhere.

First, the word *time* is a key concept that is inherent in the *Book of Changes*, for change necessarily involves motion in and through both time and space. In fact, 'time' – or rather 'transition', 'transitoriness' or 'transience' – which is often referred to as the continuous flow of *qi* 'energy' – is crucial to an understanding of *Changing*. *Qi* is the agent of interactions between nature (including time) and humans (receivers/perceivers of time), so as to maintain balance and harmony in the natural, physical and philosophical dimensions of the world – which, of course, include the realm of poetry and poems.

As for the condition and concept of *nothingness*, this has never ceased to fascinate thinkers and philosophers in the East. In Chinese, 无 *wu* ('nothing', 'nothingness', 'no', 'none', 'without') is a core theme in both the *Book of Changes* and Daoist thinking. It is also a key component of the compound 无常 *wuchang* 'impermanence', which is fundamental in forming the philosophical notion of 'ephemerality, transience, transitoriness'.[2] In fact, the Daoist belief is that 'nothingness' is the foundation of all things and happenings, as first witnessed by Lao Zi in his *Daodejing* (Liu: 38-40). Interestingly, Berengarten's book of sonnets, published a year before *Changing*, is entitled *Notness*, a coinage which is an anagram of the word 'Sonnets'. This book also explores the concept of nothingness, especially when he testifies that "the so-called 'core' of *isness* is *notness*, just

---

[2] 无 (simplified) or 無 (traditional) *wu* is also a component of the phrase 无为 / 無為 *wuwei*, which Berengarten often cites in *Changing*. He notes that it means 'without doing, without action', 'without being, without becoming', and adds "This key concept in Daoism, which is reflected in Chinese, Japanese and Korean martial arts, is also translated as 'effortless action'" (*CH* 553). See 349 below.

as at that of *notness* is *isness*: a never-ending dance" ('Afterword', RB 2013: 85). In the context of time, the 84 occurrences of the word *nothing* in *Changing* is telling. Here are just two of many passages that focus on this triple theme of nothingness, *isness* and transience:

> Sometimes you catch a
> (the) moment, you really do,
> don't you? But then, what
>
> was it – dust, a nothing,
> or figment of a nothing?   ('Dusts', 38/6: 310)

> a learning consisting
> of unlearning. What happens
> is nothing. Everything
>
> fills to the brim with
> absolute nothing. That's what
> empties (into) everything.   ('Nothing happens', 52/5: 421)

Thinking more deeply, we can deduce that the idea of "nothing", or of a "figment of nothing" – which is even more of a *nothing* than *nothing* – is in fact the "something" ('isness') that inspires the poem. What is more, in the 0/1 binary or base-2 mathematical system of the *I Ching*'s hexagrams, the broken line (or *zero-nature* that counterpoises the *oneness* or *fulness* of the solid line) itself represents 'nothingness'. In both of the poems just quoted, a fleeting moment is both as full as a "nothing" and as empty as a "something". Yet it is precisely in these moments (or in such *scintillae* of dust) that we can catch meaning and thoughts that make our lives fuller and more meaningful.

ↀ

The above stylometric analysis of the vocabulary of Berengarten's *Changing* has enabled glimpses into his strategies in composing this poem: simple, direct and highly readable, yet containing a wealth of philosophical profundity. Are there perhaps more general points to be drawn here? For example: that truth-telling is often simple; that depth of insight does not necessitate abstruse or recondite terminology; and that wisdom often resides in 'open secrets'?

What is more, many of the poems in *Changing*, including those quoted above, might almost appear to have been written during 'gaps between passing moments' – fanciful though such an idea may be – that is, in such a way as to 'catch' or at least 'glimpse' nuanced aspects of the fleeting, transitory nature of change itself. In Berengarten's ambitious poem, thoughts and feelings of the utmost delicacy are traced or hinted at. And inevitably, such subtleties in themselves equally indicate the delicacy of Berengarten's relationship with the *Book of Changes*. Like an ancient Chinese scholar, he consults or explores the *Book of Changes* in a personal, intimate way, with respect not only to major actions and dramatic or important events but also to the relatively humdrum matters and textures of day-to-day living, with all its minor activities and processes.

On a personal note, as a doctoral student in Cambridge in the mid-2000s, I had the privilege of visiting Richard Berengarten's study once every other month for two years. I saw first-hand his rich and varied collection of books and materials on and about the *Book of Changes*. In the postscript of his book, he writes: "I first came across the *I Ching* in 1962, when I was a nineteen-year-old undergraduate studying English at Cambridge: that is, just over fifty-four years ago at the time of writing this" (523). Furthermore, long before *Changing* was published, Berengarten was consulting the *I Ching* and making 'deep' use of it when composing other texts, including the opening and closing poems in *The Blue Butterfly* (see 3 and 111). And during our correspondence in 2007, when I was preparing an earlier essay on his writings (Tan 2010; 2011), he sent me some thoughts on the influence of Chinese culture on his life and work, including the following note:

> I even found myself consulting the *I Ching when actually composing poems*. This was a wholly organic and natural development from the 'personal' kind of consultation. [...] This means that the *I Ching* has often helped me to articulate poems in a way that I think is correct and appropriate. I may be wrong, but my own belief is that this also means that these poems enter a 'mode of being' and a 'form' that is not merely rooted in my own subjectivity and opinions, but in a 'wider'/ 'deeper' / 'higher' ('trans-subjective', 'intersubjective') field.
>
> (RB, letter to author: October 5, 2007)

Berengarten's account of this aspect of his poetics confirms that *Changing* is not only fully rooted in the *I Ching* itself but also steeped in the Chinese classic's wider, deeper and higher spheres of influence.

REFERENCES

Berengarten, Richard. 2011. *The Blue Butterfly*. Bristol: Shearsman Books.

_____ . 2013. *Imagems*. Bristol: Shearsman Books.

_____. 2015. *Notness*. Bristol: Shearsman Books.

_____. 2016. *Changing*. Bristol: Shearsman Books.

'Biography'. Online at: http://www.berengarten.com/site/Biography.html (website no longer available).

Huan, Zhang Yu and Rose, Ken. 1973. *A Brief History of Qi*. Brookline MA: Paradigm Publications.

Jonson, Ben. 2009. *Every Man In His Humor*. Online at: https://www. gutenberg.org/files/5333/5333-h/5333-h.htm

Liu, JeeLou. 2012. *Neo-Confucianism: Metaphysics, Mind, and Morality*. New York: Wiley Blackwell.

'Richard Berengarten'. *Wikipedia*.

Tan, Chee Lay. 2010. 'Cross-Cultural Numerology and Translingual Poetics: Chinese Influences on the Poetry of Richard Berengarten'. In *A Delicate Touch: Essays on Chinese Influences and Chinese Genres*. Singapore: The Singapore Centre for Chinese Language, Nanyang Technological University; with McGraw Hill Education, 1-18.

_____. 2016 [2011]. 'Cross-Cultural Numerology and Translingual Poetics: Chinese Influences on the Poetry of Richard Berengarten. In Jope, R., Derrick, Paul S., and Byfield, Catherine, E. (eds.) *The Companion to Richard Berengarten*. Bristol: Shearsman Books, 266-282.

Textalyser. Online at: http://textalyser.net/index.php?lang=en#analysis

Wordsworth, William. 1993. 'Preface to *Lyrical Ballads*'. Online at: https:// www.bartleby.com/39/36.html

Ziporyn, Brook. 2012. *Ironies of Oneness and Difference: Coherence in Early Chinese Thought; Prolegomena to the Study of Li*. Albany, NY: SUNY Press.

ALAN TRIST AND BOB DEVINE

The Zen of the Tao:
Journeys Along the Ridgepole

The Way is unimpeded harmony;
Its potential may never be fully exploited.
It is as deep as the source of all things:
It blunts the edges,
Resolves the complications,
Harmonizes the light,
Assimilates to the world.
Profoundly still, it seems to be there:
I don't know whose child it is,
Before the creation of images.
                    Lao-tzu, *Tao Te Ching*

The *I Ching* consists of layered mythic, shamanic and philosophical statements and concepts, in a corpus of written texts developed over hundreds,
perhaps thousands of years. Its original purpose was divination, and it is
still an immediately usable working oracle, offering guidance interpretable
at many different levels. Richard Berengarten's long poem, *Changing*, or
"gathering of poems", as he elegantly calls it ('Postscript', 521), is a significant addition to the literature on the Ching,[1] the poem's main source. This
essay tells a story of how some of these new poems have worked to enhance
consultations of the old oracle by two of its long-term students.

---

[1] We prefer to use the more intimate term the Ching, with neither italics nor
quotation marks, rather than the slightly cumbersome *I Ching*, to suggest that,
as the book becomes a friend and familiar with use, the text appears to be alive
and *animated* – an experience of many who consult the oracle, for example C. G.
Jung: "Why not venture a dialogue with a book *that purports to be animated?*"
('Foreword', in Wilhelm/Baynes: 1968: xxvi. See also Jung 1958: 594, para. 976;
and *Changing*, 534 (7).

Brimming and Bracing (Trist)

The occasion of my first meeting with Richard in 1961 magnified the meaning of chance by its ritual and ceremonial context. To be matriculated into a lifetime's membership of a Cambridge college is a formal event befitting its gravitas of expectation and promise. At the celebratory dinner in Pembroke's hall, we sat opposite each other at the long oak tables, and thereafter our undergraduate lives were entangled. As our correspondence has developed following the publication of his masterwork, our entanglement seems to be of the quantum kind, as marvellous connections across time and space have arisen, as will be seen.[2]

For the first time in many years, during his poetry reading tour of the United States in 2012, Richard and I met in the San Francisco Bay Area, where I had been living since 1970. On this occasion, Richard presented me with a screenprint version of his 365-line chant-poem 'Tree' (1988); we visited a 'cathedral' redwood grove in Samuel P. Taylor State Park – and from then on, an arboreal theme was present in our lives. The redwoods of the Bay Area are close to the southern end of the West Coast's temperate rainforest, which stretches from Alaska to Monterey Bay. Then, five years later, in 2017, at a time when I was moving house to a location 500 miles north, on the coast range of the Oregon Coast – and in that same coastal rainforest – the incidents underlying the writing of this essay began to unfold. And at that point, the Ching gradually emerged as an increasingly explicit factor in the continuing entangled branchings of our lives. What is more, as will be seen, the motifs of *wood*,

---

[2] Two quantum-entangled particles cannot be understood independently. "The consequences of entanglement – a particular type of acausal quantum correlation – belong to the most surprising and counter-intuitive effects of physics and our physical understanding of the world. Furthermore, entanglement endows quantum theory with a holism and a peculiar kind of non-locality which is in complete contrast to the reductive nature of classical physics…. [I]n order to explain the quantum correlations arising from entanglement in a classical setting, non-local influences seem to be unavoidable" (Filk 109). The book containing Filk's paper explores the current implications of the work undertaken by C. G. Jung and Wolfgang Pauli in their search for a unified theory of being, especially in the context of Jung's theory of synchronicity and these two thinkers' collaboration and correspondence – the former a psychologist and the latter a physicist (see Jung and Pauli 1955; Jung 1960; and Meier 2001). Further, the 'blinking' on and off of photons, as described in quantum mechanics, is a close analogue of the absence and presence of consciousness, as understood in Taoism.

trees and *poles* in this story came to assume a force and energy entirely of their own.[3]

☙

Those of us who came of age in the 1960s had the benefit of easy access to the world of Chinese classics, and much else of the world's literature, through the then fairly new medium of the paperbound book, which was to be found and read in coffee shop bookstores. You did not have to know what you were looking for, as would, say, a scholar in a library; it fell into your hands. In those newly born and self-informing communities, it was unusual not to find a worn copy of the *Ching* on someone's bookshelf. While over the years my record of appeals to the oracle has been haphazard, like the shadows of clouds moving across mountains, and not disciplined by orderly strata of recollection, the text, transmuted through one English version or another, has never been far from reach; a friend, stern, kind and reliable, trustworthy, in turn enigmatic and straightforward. And I learned with *Changing* that Richard, too, has long been a dedicated student.[4]

And here's where the leaven of chance began to rise: at the moment of this book's publication, I happened to be involved in a deep study of the use of the *Ching* for parallel personal issues, together with an artist friend of mine, Bob DeVine, another lifetime student of the oracle and fellow-follower of the Tao. Soon we found ourselves being drawn into a conversation around *Changing*,[5] which, though neither a translation nor a

---

[3] Richard's long poem 'Tree' was partly inspired by his first visit to Muir Woods, another redwood grove in the Bay Area, in 1979. In the online *Albero Project*, versions of 'Tree' are being published in an increasing number of languages, together with ancillary and associated texts, photos, paintings, and a video (see Berengarten 2017). "Hopefully this tree will become a spinney, then a wood, then a forest, attracting all manner of life to it" (Berengarten, email to Alan Trist, April 4, 2018).

[4] As Bob DeVine writes later in this essay, *Changing* is a "river of poems", one for each hexagram, and every line found in the Chinese classic: 450 poems in all.

[5] We felt as though suddenly thrown into the Taoist tradition of *qingtan*, 'witty discourse', exemplified by the third century 'Seven Sages of the Bamboo Grove': "Seven Taoist scholars, musicians, and writers seclude themselves in a bamboo grove outside the capital, where they drink wine, engage in the witty Taoist discourse called *qingtan*, and enjoy a simple life of writing poetry and manuals of Taoist mysticism" (Bincsik 6).

commentary, has a matching organisation to the Ching. The unexpected result was that, for us, *Changing* immediately became another source to work with, along with the seven translation texts we were already consulting between us.[6]

In the following story, it's important to bear in mind Berengarten's caveats regarding *Changing*. Bob's reference to it as "a river of poems" is apt, for it reflects the author's conception of *Changing*, noted in his postscript, as "a single work, a composite poem made up of many small poems [...] to be read first and foremost as a poem, or gathering of poems, in its own right and for its own sake". Here, while Berengarten affirms that *Changing* is rooted in, structured by, and inspired by the Ching, he is unequivocal that "it is not a translation or a commentary" (521). While one would normally be properly constrained by this authorial intent and statement of limitation, *Changing* happened to 'fall into our hands' while we were already in the Land of Ching, becoming part of an intensifying synchronistic field then developing; and nothing could have prevented it from becoming an auxiliary text – not a primary oracular text, but an evanescent co-respondent in the timeless web of the Tao, just as if it had actually been *made* for 'easy' reference thanks to its parallel organisation and structure to the Ching itself.[7] I will return to this point later in this story, for it too shows the Way, but I must ask for the author's – and perhaps also the reader's – forbearance, in that we didn't read *Changing* primarily as a long poem as he had intended, but entered it, rather, as both the Ching and the Tao directed, and as our own story unfolded.

℘

When, some months after the book's publication, Richard wrote to ask if, as regular, long-term users of the Ching, Bob and I might like to collaborate on an essay on *Changing* for a forthcoming volume, providing, so to speak, a working perspective, we both embraced the idea.[8] Fatefully, as it turned out, we decided that, as a case in point, we would both throw the coins that very night and go from there. I have always consulted the

---

[6] Wilhelm 1968 [1951]; Blofeld 1965; Cleary, 1986 and 1987; Walker, 1992; Karcher, 2003; and Hinton, 2015.

[7] Interestingly, and perhaps paradoxically, one of the various meanings of the Chinese word '*I*' (易) in the name *I Ching* (易经) happens to be 'easy'.

[8] Richard Berengarten and Alan Trist, personal correspondence, June 7, 2017 and November 28, 2017.

Ching with a specific question or situation in mind, based on the theory once received from a commentary that it would enhance the specificity of the reply. Yet I have also doubted this claim, for even though it is likely to focus the mind, the web of the Tao is surely too complex, intricate and subtle, and language itself too clumsy, arbitrary and inflexible, to allow any 'particular' to be genuinely illuminated. So I asked Bob how he thought our various histories of the moment would play into any guidance the Ching might offer. "Don't worry about that," he said, "but rather concentrate on the question of the moment, our collaborative task." We were both to be very surprised, for the oracle had other ideas.

Holding in mind the question of how best to proceed, I threw Hexagram 28 (*Ta Kuo*, 大過), with changing lines in the fourth and sixth places. This is variously rendered as 'Preponderance of the Great' in Wilhelm/Baynes, 'Great Traverse' in Karcher, and 'Vast Beyond' in Hinton. But in whatever way the various English translators characterise the condition, the image of a "sagging ridgepole" presides. As Karcher puts it, "This figure marks a dialogue between structure, the house and the ridgepole as the social structures that support and constrain us, and the process of becoming a true individual" (Karcher 234).

But before I could address these matters in relation to the *consciously* intended purpose of this consultation, which was how to approach the writing of this essay, I was overwhelmed by a feeling that the Ching itself – in accord with the Tao, as always – had redirected the focus of my question to the current condition of stress in my own life: the ridgepole was indeed sagging and the oracle seemed to be saying, "Address this personal matter, now!" This was a stunning result, as if a statement demonstrating that the inner need for prioritisation had been issued by an 'objective authority' somehow selecting itself out from among the infinite plethora of nested foci within the net of being – and positing a reordering of the quantum entanglement.

I think this interpretation of mine came about because, primarily, all the English translations of the traditional text are full of images of rising water and housing instability. At this time, I was living in the actual reality specified in the oracular text, as I travelled between two houses, both with building construction going on, just as the creeks were rising and the hoarfrost lingering in the hollows with the onset of winter. In pointing out the parallelism here, I mean to focus on specific external correspondences with the texts, for the purpose of illustrating by dynamic example a central feature of 'live' experience with the oracle: the *synchronistic quality of contextualising events*. These correspondences can be discerned through the thinned veil of the Tao: the field of their action appears to arise in *response* to the casting of the oracle itself, which is, of course, an intentional act.[9] This correlative parallelism will become clearer in quotations from Berengarten's poetry below.

At the same time, internally, "bracing the ridgepole" means seeking resolution and integration of self and relationships, perhaps at a point of crisis. The Ching carries a warning about overstepping bounds in the process of integration, which is brought to light in Hexagram 28, as becomes apparent in all English renderings of the fourth and sixth changing lines, e.g. Wilhelm/Baynes:

Nine in the fourth place means:
The ridgepole is braced. Good fortune.
If there are ulterior motives, it is humiliating.

Six at the top means:
One must go through the water,
It goes over one's head.
Misfortune. No blame.   (Wilhelm/Baynes 113-114)

And Cleary, in *The Taoist I Ching*, renders the text and commentary of the changing line 4 of Hexagram 28 as follows:

The ridgepole is raised; good fortune. There is another shame. Great yet able to be small, the mind equanimous, the energy harmonious – this is like the ridgepole being raised and not crumbling. [...] One should not be too yielding anymore, because if yielding is excessive it will damage firmness, and the great path will be impossible to complete – one will become a laughingstock [...]   (Cleary, 1986: 122)

At this point, in contemplation of the meaning of this counsel, in turning to *Changing* I found a powerful poem whose theme is reconstruction and ridgepole-shoring. As Berengarten pursues this theme metaphorically in

---

[9] The debate over mechanism is never-ending. Some say the Ching works by magic, some say serendipity, some say future science. "The *I Ching* hexagrams embody change in a schematic form, so they allow us to locate ourselves in the unfolding of change. This requires that you use [...] yarrow stems or coins to perform a 'chance' procedure. We call it a chance procedure, but it is in fact a distilled moment in the process of change, and so it allows you to find the hexagram relevant to your situation" (Hinton 2015: xi). One could say that chance, for the *I Ching*, is a portal offering a glimpse into the workings of the Tao, the Way of Heaven, the Cosmos at large.

'Quake', he first takes us deep into the interior of the Earth, then to its "mantle", and then morphs the metaphor to "bracing" the house:

> Our roof may fall in. Panic
> multiplies – too fast for response,
> too sudden for remedy.
>
> Growls, roars, tremors
> between tectonic plates. Cracks
> in earth's mantle.
>
> How shall we avoid yet
> another calamity? Foundations
> need scaffolding.
>
> deepening, shoring, and
> roots of pillars, drilling like
> teeth. Diagonal trusses
>
> and cross braces will
> buttress frame and shell.
> Nor shall we rely
>
> on others to get
> these tasks done. We'll see
> to them ourselves. Now.   (28/4: 228)

The methodical work recommended in this poem, starting with the "foundations" and working upwards, specifies that developing inner firmness involves attention to detail. Was I now beginning to find initial bearings for my own personal journey, which the Ching was bringing to notice by redirecting attention *through* Richard's poem? And although the intricacies of my own psychological journey in regard to these emergent patternings are beyond the scope of this essay, the poignancy of seeking to build a studio apartment at one end of the ridgepole and a home in the heart of my partner at its other end brimmed with personal meaning. The metaphoric ridgepole of the text in fact stretched 50 miles on the ground. As I moved back and forth between its end-points, the words of the hexagram matched the conditions of the wintry journey, the dangers of flood and storm, and the strains of the inner work.

"Mists submerge the trees. Great Traverses" (Karcher 236)[10]

My partner at the time, on reading a draft of this essay and my struggles to understand Hexagram 28, replied:

> I think it's *all* about the inner work. The metaphors of ridgepoles, mists, water over your head and moving through it speak to that. The building projects are serendipitously active at either end of the journey you refer to as the ridgepole. The ridgepole, however, is the binding, the stabilizing element, and refers to the solidifying of your internal process, the Tao, and the holding together of these elements of your life; the mists and waters are the amorphous difficulties, obstacles and challenges. To quote Richard: "… this slow laborious scrabbling / from one secured mark / to the next …"; and I'd say the Tao isn't hooked on the external thorns of the brambles – perhaps that's why it cut through the generalities to your particulars.[11]

Meanwhile, Berengarten's poems for the conditions of Hexagram 28 had brought the story into inescapable focus by exactly reflecting the situation 'on the ground'; and, as the oracle's drama continued to unfold, Bob, on hearing that the Ching had not directly answered my question but instead given cogent advice in regard to my particular existence, responded:

> The more I have thought about your observation on your casting of the *I Ching* and arriving at the crisis of the sagging ridgepole, Hexagram 28, and its morphing into the winds of successful change, Hexagram 57, I find your conclusion most accurate. I do believe that the issue of the houses … is this moment's concern for you, and maybe the river of poems by Richard will aid you in penetrating the winds of change that stir in your soul, as you have so expressed. They may be the boat across the Great River. Look at his poem for

---

[10] Both this photo and the following one were taken by Alan Trist while journeying 'along the ridgepole', Coast Range, Oregon, Winter 2017.

[11] Sandy Duveen, personal correspondence, January 9, 2018.

the sixth line of the ridgepole's sag, it's as if he witnessed the stables of your labors. ... I was dumbstruck by that timely poem.

I'll let the remarkable applicability and eloquent precision of Berengarten's "river of poems" carry the story forward from here, referring especially to the external correspondences, which I am calling the *synchronistic field*. This is the point at which unequivocal reference to *Changing* finally took over and I gave in to reading my throw, in part, through its lens. What also became apparent was the opportunity this experience presented, to demonstrate the 'speaking' of the poems themselves as an illustration, or perhaps filter, of the Ching's synchronistic power.

Berengarten's title for the suite for Hexagram 28 is 'Overbrimming'. The initial poem, '*The lake rises above the trees*', described the conditions prevailing during a time that, for me, coincided with deepening winter. Aside from weather, this poem spoke to the actual new building work that was being undertaking: stables for horses, fences, and drainage.

Rain on rain, storm
on storm, flood on
flood. Won't it ever

Stop? The only way
forward is this clumsy
paddling, this careful

wading, weighed down
by too much baggage,
and then this slow

laborious scrabbling
from one secured mark
to the next. No time

to contemplate gifts or
horizons, let alone dream
or think. Every muscle,

bone, corpuscle, must
be put to work, getting
past and through.   (28/0: 224)

The 'fit' is uncanny. And 'Floods', Berengarten's poem for the changing line at 6, was even more exactly and aptly descriptive:

Roads at hills' feet swirl
and in valleys' lower dips
cross-currents carve

runnels down
to our river, swollen five
times normal width.

Thick sludge swirls,
fast moving, covering
tree trunks, whose

greeneries swish away.
We've stabled our horses
on higher land, but

our cows, marooned
in corners of sodden fields,
cluster wherever small

pockets of green have
not yet gone under. We
can't cross the river.   (28/6: 230)

"We can't cross the river."

No, we can't, and here's the rub. The flood catches us up short; we're in the deep Ching of myth and metaphor, where pointers to individuation and enjoinders to self-correction are invoked as necessary conditions for 'success'. As I write this, the crossing is still under way and, as ever, there's procrastination on the banks, for the river has a fast and furious flow.

But like the "gentle, penetrating winds" in various English translations of Hexagram 57,[12] to which the changing lines of 28 were pointing, Berengarten's head-poem for the situation, '*What's that whirring*', in the cluster 'Blowing, Billowing'. provided the right mood and tone, and a necessary stance of noticing, to enable the crossing:

> *What's that whirring*
> *in the guttering? Only*
> *the wind muttering.*
>
> *And that clattering*
> *above the ceiling? Your spirit*
> *staggering and reeling.*
>
> *And that sighing*
> *in the eaves? The gale that*
> *frets and grieves.*
>
> *And that rattling in*
> *the chimney? The breath*
> *of Death, your enemy.*
>
> *And that whimpering*
> *in the rafters? The wind's*
> *weepings and laughters.*
>
> *And that rattling in*
> *the basement? Your soul*
> *breaking its casement.* (57/0: 456)

Here the house itself speaks, literally and metaphorically. *I heard it.* How fortunate to have found such a perfect lyric in this net of chance, its own completeness magnified by the contextual fit; as if the poem itself, like the wind, were moving around the house in a timeless universe, witness to the inner questing within. "Breaking the casement" proceeds, *I feel it*; a new journey comes into being – "staggering and reeling", we begin. All must cross the river, including the marooned cows of 'Floods' (230). Who are these cows? Are they not us? Marooning ends when the land is

---

[12] Hexagram 57, 巽 *Sun*: in Wilhelm, 'The Gentle (The Penetrating, Wind)'; Blofeld, 'Willing Submission, Gentleness, Penetration'; Walker, 'The Penetrating, Wind'; Cleary, 'Wind'; Karcher, 'Subtle Penetration, Spreading the Fates'; and Hinton, 'Reverence'.

dried by the wind, *pneuma*, the breath of clarity ... leading to movement, "firm but flexible".

༄

The sources and consequences of poetry, whether from the ancient East, as in the Ching texts, or newly from the West, as in *Changing*, are 'without dimension', at least in terms of the ways in which we experience and interpret space and time in the material world.[13] But it's precisely through and into this world that poetry constantly resurfaces, springs up, breaks out, and burgeons forth anew – always alive, and sometimes numinous.[14] The Zen of the Tao arises as we notice it; the Ching reflects an unfolding vision. And just as poetry is always entangled in time, so the Tao is eternally pointed and repointed in and through poetry. In quantum mechanical terms, if two particles can be entangled in the space/time continuum, can two poems, authored in different eras on different continents, be joined in the web of the Tao?

As I have suggested, it could of course be debated whether or not an ancient corpus of oracular utterances such as the Ching is 'poetry' in quite the way that Berengarten's consciously crafted verses so clearly are. But it's reasonable to suppose that a Muse is common to both the ancient divination text and this modern poetic artefact. Both originate from deep layers of being and becoming. Both speak out of personal and communal history and cultural experience: that is, out of both an individual and the collective unconscious.[15] Both discover (uncover) the universal in the particular,

---

[13] For another account of such entangled poetic 'eternity', see Michael Schumacher's account of Allen Ginsberg's mediation of William Blake (Schumacher: 94-99).

[14] For a sustained use of the expression "burgeoning forth" see David Hinton's exposition of Taoist philosophy through the lens of Chinese landscape painting in *Existence* (2016).

[15] Throughout this essay, the influence and concepts of C. G. Jung are present, especially in such terms as 'individuation', 'collective unconscious', 'synchronicity', and 'self'. At a eulogy that Jung gave at Richard Wilhelm's memorial service in 1930, he said that Wilhelm "[...] inoculated us with the living germ of the Chinese spirit and we found ourselves partaking of the spirit of the East as we experience the *living power* of the *I Ching*. It is capable of working a profound transformation of our thought. [...] I heard from him in clear language the things I had dimly divined in the confusion of the European subconscious. I received more from him than from any other man" (Jung 1966: 55, para. 78, emphasis added; see Karcher 1999: 60-83; Goulding 170-186; Stein 209-222).

and bridge (connect) and rebalance (repoint) the two. Both embrace correspondence between microcosm and macrocosm as their guiding principle. Both are inspired by *something beyond ordinary knowing*.

I believe that the story told here, in our personal account of the Ching's action in time, is a testament to the powers and beauty of the ancient Classic. I also believe that this story has literally *incorporated* Berengarten's *Changing* – even if *and* because, not by our conscious choice, but rather by the magically natural way in which this book 'fell' into the laps of Bob's life and mine, at a particular time and a particular place: that is, *synchronistically*. For while *Changing* professes to be no more than "a poem, or a gathering of poems" – at least in our case, its 'mode of falling', or *be*falling, inevitably transformed it into an auxiliary to the oracle, into its expressive variant, and even its valid representation: attributes that were triggered initially by its identical structure with that of the Ching.

As is well known, an author's conscious intentions can never encompass *all* the ways in which a book is likely to be read. Our own *active* way of reading *Changing* has involved applying it both symbolically and literally to our own lives; and to my mind this suggests a valid way of revealing the inner inspirations and meanings of Berengarten's poems too.[16]

---

[16] In his forward to Richard Wilhelm's translation of the *I Ching*, Jung remarks: "Wilhelm [...] has made every effort to open the way to an understanding of the symbolism of the text. He was in a position to do this because he himself was taught the philosophy and the use of the *I Ching* by the venerable sage Lao Nai-hsüan; moreover, *he had over a period of many years put the peculiar technique of the oracle into practice.* His grasp of *the living meaning of the text* gives his version of the *I Ching* a depth of perspective that an exclusively academic knowledge of Chinese philosophy could never provide" (Jung 1968, xxii, emphasis added). Jung, as an approach to writing his forward, framed it with book-end consultations of the Ching, and proceeded by analysis of those two coin-throws. We too, in the writing of this essay, have used a similar active reading of *Changing*: the interpretations we make in this essay of our consultations of the Ching are informed by the experience of long use. These parallels notwithstanding, our efforts, of course, pale in comparison to Jung's analytical powers and Wilhelm's knowledge of Chinese language and philosophy.

The Tiger Path (DeVine)

As fate would have its way, I decided to keep a diary of all my castings of the Ching from January 2017 into 2018 and was able to pinpoint the first hexagram I threw at the time of reception of the gift of *Changing* from Alan. My initial question concerned my projected move into a new house as a single person for the first time in thirteen-plus years. I had just broken up from a long relationship with a woman I loved, and all that was clear to me at the time was the fact that our previously shared journey was, inevitably, now transforming into two quite separate paths.

The *Ching* responded to my inquiry for wisdom and guidance in this new adventure, delivering Hexagram 10, 'Treading',[17] with changing lines in the second and fourth places. This led to Hexagram 42, 'Increasing'.[18] The dominant image and message of Hexagram 10 is the care needed when finding oneself "treading on a tiger's tail". While this image has many meanings, associations and applications, most obviously connected with danger, it is specifically to do with the weak (– –) approaching the strong (—) in the territory of the latter.[19]

After reviewing the standard texts, I approached *Changing* to understand its relationship to the Ching's counsel. In Berengarten's

---

[17] Hexagram 10, 履 *Lü*: in Wilhelm, 'Treading (Conduct)'; Blofeld, 'Treading, Conduct'; Walker, 'Treading (Conduct)'; Cleary, 'Treading'; Hinton, 'Walking'; and Karcher, 'Treading / Mating with the Tiger'.

[18] Hexagram 42, 益 *Yi*: in Wilhelm, 'Increase'; Blofeld, 'Gain'; Walker, 'Increase'; Cleary, 'Increase'; Hinton, 'Enrichment'; and Karcher, 'Augmenting / The Blessing'.

[19] Regarding the yin (– –) and yang (—) lines, variously imaged as 'weak and strong', 'yielding and firm', 'female and male', Hellmut Wilhelm writes: "[In the *Book of Changes*] the whole order underlying the world and life is imaged in two lines charged with spiritual meaning. These lines are an embodiment of the orbit of change and of the two poles that determine it. It is important to think of this representation as very concrete. Today we tend to speak of 'symbols' in such a context [...]. In a magical world view, however, such as the one that has left its impress on the oldest strata ..., a thing and its image are identical." He continues: "The system of linear complexes that make up the hexagrams develops naturally and logically from the imagery of the divided and undivided lines." This is a process which constructs eight trigrams and then sixty-four hexagrams, classically described in the *Tao Te Ching* as, "Tao gave birth to the one, the one gave birth to the two, the two gave birth to the three gave birth to the ten thousand things" (Wilhelm, 47-49).

head-poem for the hexagram 'Treading', entitled *'Water in the stone jug'*, the beauty of the image is achieved differently, by expressing the upper trigram (*Qian* ☰, or 'Heaven' in the classic texts) as 'light', and the lower trigram (*Dui* ☱, or 'The Joyous, Lake'), simply as 'contained water'. The image of dancing light on water was now apparent, as the manner of treading needed to move forward in my situation. It was then I remembered that 'Fire' (*Li* ☲) is indeed the lower nuclear trigram,[20] as stated in Richard Wilhelm's translation (Wilhelm 435).

Reflections off water
in the stone jug on our table
wander over walls

doodle across ceiling
because of noon breeze
and pool and still

above our fireplace.
Always light above and
light's inflections [...]   (10/0: 80)

When I entered *Changing*, considering it primarily as an 'epic poem', I realised that one of the main ways in which Berengarten connected his texts to the ancient Chinese text was through his footers or 'base-lines'. These occur both on each hexagram's title page and also beneath each poem. My interpretation has been that in the italicised base-line for the title-page, the left-hand notation often expresses the upper trigram, represented by the top three stanzas of a poem, while the right-hand notation often expresses the lower trigram, represented by the bottom three stanzas of a poem.

I then became aware that for 'Treading', a key to understanding Berengarten's expression of 'Heaven' (*Qian* ☰) is that the image of light is clearly evident – even if one has to discover it by pondering a little. In the footer to the introductory page for the hexagram. It reads *"a lake … flooded by sky."*

---

[20] 'Primary', 'upper', 'lower' and 'nuclear' trigrams are technical terms in the structure of *the I Ching*. The nuclear trigrams are considered the core trigrams of a hexagram, as if the hexagram were germinating outwards from its seed and then growing into its finalised version, with the addition of the first and sixth lines. The lower nuclear trigram is composed of lines 2, 3 and 4, and the upper nuclear trigram of lines 3, 4 and 5. Lines 3 and 4 are regarded as the 'still point' of a hexagram: that is, the 'two 'that becomes the 'three', and the 'three', the 'ten thousand things'.

(*CH* 10: 79). The light appears in the sky's brilliant dance that blankets the lake, so that a perfect image of the process for 'Treading' is described here: the sky doesn't sink beneath the lake's surface, it bounces between 'lord' heaven and 'lady' lake; and in this way a marriage is achieved. In this way, the italicised footers become a wonderful window into the poem's homage to the Ching itself, and onto its guiding instructions.

So *Changing* has inspired both heart and mind through poetry, in a song of faithfulness to the Ching. For me, journeying with it has become more complex, and the weave of the Tao ever more intriguing. Berengarten's imagery has proved true and my journey down the Tiger Path, successful. I now reside in a little cottage where the light of the moon and sun traverses my walls through the rippled surfaces of two beautiful, stained glass windows. I bathe in the delight of the union of sky (*Qian* ☰) and lake (*Dui* ☱).

The Role of Water Dripping (DeVine)

The wonder of *Changing* unfolded in even fuller dimensions as I entered the collaboration with Alan for this essay. Upon learning of his take on his throw of the Ching, and in light of Richard's timely, timeless poems in the cluster 'Overbrimming' for Hexagram 28, and of my simultaneous casting of Hexagram 31, 'Reciprocating', my role became clearer as co-author of this essay. I saw that I would be the element of 'water dripping' into the process of the project. My deliberations would follow the course of water's love of gravity and seep towards the granite of Alan's foundation of understanding and Richard's insightful expressions of the Ching's mysterious meanings.

As I read and reread Berengarten's poems, his fresh take on the Ching began to settle in. With his head-poem for Hexagram 31, 'A lake on a mountain' in the cluster 'Reciprocating',[21] which Hinton entitles 'Wholeness', a deeper understanding of the hexagram occurred to me: of the coupling of 'Lake' (*Dui* ☱) and 'Mountain' (*Gen* ☶), with 'female' above and 'male' below. The top three stanzas describe the lake's formation as descending in movement, implying that the lake's wholeness, its coming

---

[21] Hexagram 31, *hsien*: in Wilhelm, 'Influence (Wooing)'; Blofeld, 'Attraction, Sensation'; Walker, 'Influence (Wooing)'; Cleary, 'Sensing', in *The Buddhist I Ching*, 'Sensitivity', in *The Taoist I Ching*; Karcher, 'Conjoining / Uniting in Spirit'; and Hinton, 'Wholeness'.

into being, is not yet realised.

*Massing water
presses down, finding
lowest outlet. A lake*

*collects, builds
in deepest possible
places, soaks*

*into permeable
ground to pool on
impassable rock.* (31/0: 248)

This process of completion unfolds in the next stanzas with the mountain's upward heaving. The beauty of wholeness is realised in the last stanza:

A mountain presses
up, pushes its presence
to rear, bucking

against gravity. So
when a lake forms on
a mountain, opposed

forces meet and
merge in fine self-
checking balance. (*ibid.*)

The lake's formation takes place within and without the mountain through the meeting of the 'gentle' above and the 'firm' below. The lake is created only after a "fine self-checking balance". It might even be surmised that a kind of 'consciousness' on the part of and within nature itself is doing its work for the lake to come into being, a supposition that posits a kind of teleonomic (purposeful) directedness in nature. What is more, this motif of 'reciprocating' through lake-formation spoke to my collaborative relationship with Alan; my role as 'water dripping' had now become clear. This essay is the 'Lake' that we have been forming.

In contrast, however, in 'Overbrimming', Hexagram 28, the movement also follows the direction of the primary trigrams, but with the 'Lake' (*Dui* ☱) above pushing both downward to the point where it passes its bounds, and then rising above the trees or collapsing ridgepole. These energies will be tamed by the wind's stubborn, lateral movement in Hexagram 57 ('Blowing, Billowing', *Xun*). We now see the theme of what Alan calls "brimming and bracing" in terms of the forces of stabilisation that occur both in Hexagram 28, 'Overbrimming', and in Hexagram 31, 'Reciprocating'. In the latter poem, stabilisation takes place *only* through a process of the natures of water and stone meeting each other half-way, that is, in their respective forces moving downward and upward, and so shaping the attainment of the lake.

As I peek at the nuclear trigrams of hexagram 28, I see that the upper and lower trigrams both embody 'the Creative' (symbolised by *Qian* ☰ 'heaven'). This suggests that the day-by-day renewal of the originary principle of the 'Creative' (as embodied in hexagram 1) spells out how the overbrimming of the river and the stress on the timber bridge of the ridgepole *in themselves form the path to resolution*. By following the wind's method of effectiveness, that is, its continual blowing in one direction, the example of the Creative is followed: it renews itself day after day, and thus parallel paths are followed, so that the renewal of deliverance is achieved.

Berengarten's poems bring the image of these mysterious workings of the Tao brilliantly to light. The wonders of the synchronistic web of the Ching and *Changing*, unfolding in time and in varied life paths, can be clearly glimpsed in the story told here. This is a most rewarding experience. The poems stay true to the spirit of the Ching and both reflect and inflect the structure of the trigrams. Berengarten's stanzas are aligned to their natures, and so *Changing* is a sound boat in which to cross the Great River called Change.[22]

❧

We have come a long way with *Changing*. It has served us both well vis-à-vis several personal issues at times of major change in both our lives. What is more, it has provided a powerful and fresh voice for understanding the ancient texts of the *I Ching*. Our hope is that the story told here of how we entered the poems and profoundly resonated with them 'in real life' will add to their own life to come; and that *Changing* will be internalised by its readers and become active in them. Nothing is as constant as change, it is

---

[22] Pao-t'ung, eighth century student of Shih-t'ou, Patriarch of Japan's Soto Zen sect, says: "The sutras say to cross a river we need a raft, but once on the other shore, we no longer need it. If a person resolves to find their true source and plumbs the depths of reason and nature, they will see their original face and instantly awaken to what is unborn. This is to reach the other shore" (Red Pine 34).

said, like the wind "blowing, billowing". Its great agent, the Tao, is always working on us as individual human beings, nudging us to listen and learn.[23]

> Great Nature has another thing to do
> To you and me; so take the lively air,
> And, lovely, learn by going where to go.

(Theodore Roethke)

REFERENCES

Berengarten, Richard. 2016. *Changing*. Bristol: Shearsman Books.

———. 2017. 'The Albero Project'. *Margutte*. Online at: http://www.margutte.com/?p=23972&lang=en.

Bincsik, Monika. 2017. 'Japanese Bamboo Art: The Abbey Collection'. *Bulletin of the Metropolitan Museum of Art* (Spring issue). New York: The Met.

Blofeld, John (trans.). 1968. *I Ching (The Book of Changes)*. New York: E.P Dutton and Co.

Burns, Richard. 1988. 'Tree,' screenprint by Carol Wheeldon. Linton: Chilford Hall Press.

Calaprice, Alice (ed.). 2005. *The New Quotable Einstein*. Princeton, NJ: Princeton University Press.

Cleary, Thomas (ed. and trans.). 1986. *The Taoist I Ching*. Boston, MA: Shambhala.

———. (ed. and trans.). *The Buddhist I Ching*, 1987. Boston, MA: Shambhala.

———. (ed. and trans.). 1998. *The Essential Tao*. Edison, NJ: Castler Books.

Filk, Thomas. 2014. 'Quantum Entanglement, Hidden Variables, and Acausal Correlations'. In Altmanspacher, Harald and Fuchs, Christopher A. *The Pauli-Jung Conjecture*. Exeter: Imprint Academic.

Gandhi, Mahatma. 1999. '153. General Knowledge About Health [XXXII] 12. Accidents: Snake-Bite' (*Indian Opinion*, 9 August 1913). In *The Collected Works of Mahatma Gandhi* (electronic book: 98 volumes). New Delhi: Publi-

---

[23] "We but mirror the world. All the tendencies present in the outer world are to be found in the world of our body. If we could change ourselves, the tendencies in the world would also change. As a man changes his own nature, so does the attitude of the world change towards him. This is the divine mystery supreme. A wonderful thing it is and the source of our happiness. We need not wait to see what others do" (Gandhi, 241). "The world as we have created it is a process of our thinking. It cannot be changed without changing our thinking" (Einstein, in Calaprice: 279).

cations Division Government of India. Vol. 13: March 12, 1919 – December 25, 1920.

Goulding, J. 2015. 'The forgotten Frankfurt school: Richard Wilhelm's China Institute'. *Journal of Chinese Philosophy I Ching*, 1-2 (March -June 2014).

Hinton, David (trans.). 2015. *The Book of Change*. New York: Farrar, Strauss and Giroux.

——. 2016. *Existence, a Story*. Boulder CO: Shambhala.

Jung, C. G. 1960. 'Synchronicity: An Acausal Connecting Principle'. In *The Structure and Dynamics of the Psyche* (*Collected Works*, vol. 8). R. F. C. Hull (trans.). London: Routledge and Kegan Paul.

——. 1966. 'Richard Wilhelm: In Memoriam'. In *The Spirit in Man, Art, and Literature* (*Collected Works*, vol. 15). Hull, R. F. C. (trans.). London: Routledge and Kegan Paul.

——. 1968. 'Foreword'. In Wilhelm, Richard, 1968 (see below).

——. 2001 [1958]. *Psychology and Religion: West and East* (*Collected Works*, vol. 11). Hull. R. F. C. (trans.). Hove: Routledge.

Jung, C. G. and Pauli, W. 1955. *The Interpretation of Nature and the Psyche*. Hull, R. F. C (trans.). London: Routledge and Kegan Paul.

Karcher, Stephen. 1999. 'Jung, the Tao and the Classic of Change'. *Harvest: Journal for Jungian Studies* 45(2).

——. 2003. *Total I Ching: Myths for Change*. London: Piatkus, imprint of Little Brown.

Meier, C. E. (ed. and trans.). 2001. *Atom and Archytype, The Pauli/Jung Lerters 1932–1958*. Princeton, NJ: Princeton University Press.

Pine, Red (trans.). 2004. *The Heart Sutra*. Berkeley, CA: Counterpoint.

Roethke, Theodore. 1975. 'The Waking', in *The Collected Poems of Theodore Roethke*. New York: Anchor Books / Doubleday.

Schumacher, Michael. 1992. *Dharma Lion: A Biography of Allen Ginsberg*. Minneapolis: University of Minnesota Press.

Stein, M. 2005. 'Some reflections on the influence of Chinese thought on Jung and his psychological theory'. *Journal of Analytical Psychology* 50(2).

Walker, Brian Browne (trans.). 1992. *The I Ching or Book of Changes*. New York: St. Martin's Press.

Wilhelm, Richard (trans. from Chinese into German; and into English by Cary F. Baynes). 1968. *The I Ching or Book of Changes*. London: Routledge and Kegan Paul.

Wilhelm, Hellmut, and Wilhelm, Richard. 1995. *Understanding the I Ching: the Wilhelm Lectures on the Book of Changes*. Bollingen Series LXII and XIX: 2. Princeton, NJ: Princeton University Press.

PASCHALIS NIKOLAOU

Some Constants of Change

PATTERNS OF INFLUENCE AND AFFINITY

After nearly thirty years of continuous incubation, intermittent and inter-
rupted work, experimentation with form and presentation, and occasional
hints, glimpses and premonitions through other collections, Richard
Berengarten's *Changing* was published by Shearsman Books in 2016. Any
reader handling the book first meets Will Hill's bold and minimalist cover
design. This incorporates a modern recreation of an ancient version of the
Chinese graph for 'change' by the contemporary calligrapher and poet Yu
Mingquan. Thanks to this design, a reader is invited to entertain shapes
and systems of language and to plunge into ways of being, thinking and
seeing that differ markedly from long-established Western models. Nor is it
even certain that this rather abstract-looking design is in fact an ideogram.
To a Western reader, at first sight, it might even seem to be entirely abstract
and non-linguistic.

So even though Chinese influences have permeated all aspects of contemporary western life, from cuisine, art and film to medicine, martial arts
and technology, the simplicity of this cover design apparently betokens a
shift into 'another world'.

As a counterbalance to this point, as any reader familiar with twentieth
century Anglophone poetry knows, the entry of Chinese graphs into poems
was first broached by Ezra Pound in his *Cantos*. From Pound and others, a
rich tradition of translation of Chinese poetry into English has developed
ever since then, in the USA, the UK and Australia. But while Chinese
script is familiar enough in Anglophone countries, few people know how
to read it. To most Westerners, Chinese feels familiarly unfamiliar.

ॐ

If we consider Berengarten's *Changing* in terms of its intellectual and poetic precursors, models and influences, among the many that could be mentioned, several are dominant. These include Ezra Pound, Peter Russell, Octavio Paz, the *I Ching* itself, and C. G. Jung.

Pound is both a direct and indirect influence: the former, because in his early twenties, Berengarten read Pound's work keenly; and the latter, because in 1965, shortly after graduating from Cambridge, the young poet spent a year working as an English teacher in Venice. During this time, he lived in an apartment belonging to his first significant mentor, the English poet Peter Russell (see Burns 1996 for his memoir). Russell (1921–2003) was a dedicated Poundian, who had edited a book entitled *An Examination of Ezra Pound* (1950). Contributors included Ernest Hemingway, Edith Sitwell, T. S. Eliot, Wyndham Lewis, Allen Tate, George Seferis, and twelve other internationally distinguished writers.

In 1958, Russell's book was one among various influential factors that persuaded the American authorities to release Pound from his twelve-year incarceration in St. Elizabeths Hospital, DC. Pound then moved quickly back to Italy. Then, in 1964, Russell moved to Venice from Berlin in order to be close to Pound (see Burns 1996). Since Russell visited the aging Pound almost daily, Berengarten inevitably learned a great deal about Pound from the older English poet. Berengarten, who is Jewish, obviously had a revulsion against Pound on account of the latter's anti-Semitism, and he only 'half-met' Pound once, with Russell, at La Fenice theatre. Even so, he has consistently acknowledged Pound's importance to him as a poet. Some of these patterns of direct and indirect influence have been tracked by John Gery (2016 [2010]: esp. 147-149), who clarifies that one of the main aspects of Pound's work that Berengarten unreservedly admired was the attempt to write a huge, complex poem, *The Cantos*.

Although in structure, content and worldview, *Changing* differs radically from *The Cantos*, these two works share at least three elements: first, the fact that both are large, inclusive works; second, the strong influence of Chinese culture, thought and language; and, third, the rejection of traditional narrative as a unifying structural principle.

 confused

As for the influence of Octavio Paz, Berengarten met the Mexican poet in Cambridge in 1970. Two years later, he published his first attempt at a 'long' poem, entitled *Avebury*. He not only dedicated this work to Paz, but in its 'Afterwords' announced the influence of both Russell and Paz: "If I had not first read the former's unpublished *Ephemeron* and the latter's *Blanco* and *Sunstone* (*Piedra de sol*)," he writes, "I doubt if *Avebury* would have got written" (RB 1972: unpaginated). With respect to the genre of the long poem, both these influences on Berengarten, then, arose out of friendships formed relatively early in his poetic career. Tracing these, along with that of Pound, helps to fill in the 'deep' background to *Changing*.

On the same page, Berengarten acknowledges his debt to C. G. Jung. Then, forty-five years later, he writes a considerably more detailed memoir on his friendship with Octavio Paz (RB 2015a). This later memoir gets written around the time Berengarten completes *Changing*, while awaiting the book's publication. It includes a quotation from Paz's essay on Charles Tomlinson's paintings: "What we call chance is nothing but the *sudden revelation of relationships between things. Chance is an aspect of analogy.* Its unexpected advent provokes the immediate response of analogy" (Paz 1986: 33-34; emphasis added). Then Berengarten expands:

> My book *Changing*, a long poem rooted in the *I Ching*, explores coherences instantiated, revealed and sustained by *chance and analogy*. It should be added here, too, that the "*sudden revelation of relationships between things*" that Octavio writes about in relation to Charles Tomlinson is not only the basis of the 'correlative thinking' that underpins the claims of the *I Ching* as a book of divination, but also of Carl Gustav Jung's theory of synchronicity, of sympathetic magic in general (another area of interest of Octavio's, once again following Breton), and of the poetic experience itself, as articulated by English Romantic poets, such as Wordsworth. [...] To Octavio, then, what is called chance is just one of the modes through which our perception registers the inherent coherence and connectivity of things. (Berengarten 2015a; emphases added)

Here is a larger web of connections, all relevant to our theme. Berengarten is occupied here with the twin elements of chance and analogy that occur in all forms of correlative thinking. His ideas develop partly out of Paz's remarks vis-à-vis Tomlinson. Correlative thinking is *based* in perception of relatedness (analogy, affinity). The lines by Wordsworth that Berengarten quotes from *The Prelude* (Book 2: ll. 401-405) themselves propose that the creative discovery of *affinities* is the foundation upon which the *interminable building* of a poem is *reared*: that is, the work of the imagination, towering through poetry. Here, broadly speaking, Wordsworth's term *affinities* means *analogies*. The quotation is repeated as an epigraph to *Changing* (1).

Yet for Berengarten, correlative thinking is the key that not only forms and opens the *poetic experience*, as instanced by both Paz and Wordsworth, but also, underlies three further zones: the *I Ching*, C. G. Jung's theory of synchronicity, and sympathetic magic. (I shall explore these correlations more specifically later.) What is clear is that here Berengarten is tracing analogies among finders and discoverers of analogies in various *fields*. His correlation of these four elements (poetry, the *I Ching*, synchronicity, and sympathetic magic) is not only original itself but relevant to *Changing* in all respects.

Two more details cast light on Berengarten's friendship with Paz that are relevant to *Changing*. First in a separate essay, Paz writes in similar vein of the parallelism he perceives in Chinese poetry and philosophy:

> [P]arallelism is the nucleus of the best Chinese poems [...] [I]t corresponds to the vision of the universe of the Chinese poets and philosophers: the *yin* and the *yang*. The unity that splits into duality to reunite and to divide again. (Paz in Weinberger 2016: 50)

Here, *parallelism* is evidently a kind of analogy.

Second, in his 2015 memoir of Paz, Berengarten mentions his discovery in the previous year that the Mexican poet had been familiar with the *I Ching*. "In 2014, I discovered from a short book on the history of *I Ching* that Octavio had been exploring the Chinese *Book of Changes* as early as 1958." The book is Richard Smith's *The I Ching: A Biography* (2012: 202-204). Curiously, the date of this discovery clarifies that Berengarten hadn't been aware of Paz's interest in the *I Ching* before then. Berengarten has confirmed to me (email, 7 January 2021) that he and Paz didn't talk about the Chinese masterpiece in 1970, and also that Paz had little interest in Jung. This commonality of interest, then, marks an elective affinity rather than influence.

Even so, there were wide differences in background and context. Whereas Paz's interests in the *I Ching* were allied with his interests in French anthropologists such as Lévi-Strauss, the *Oulipo* poets and the music of John Cage, Berengarten's arrived through Jung and Richard Wilhelm.

❧

The 450 sections of *Changing* constitute by far the longest single offering in Berengarten's poetic oeuvre. An understanding and enjoyment of this work is obviously enriched by some knowledge both of the *I Ching* and of

Berengarten's relationship to it. He was first introduced to the Wilhelm/ Baynes translation in 1962. In the 1960s, this was the only English version readily available. It was regarded as the authoritative standard. For at least three decades, until the late 1990s, Berengarten relied on it exclusively for both reading and divination, by which time other translations had become available.

Despite stating in his 'Postscript' that *Changing* is primarily an independent poem in its own right (521), the poet constantly affirms his poem's dependence on the *I Ching*. This is immediately evident in three ways: first, in his discussion of the *I Ching*'s long history in his postscript (521-527); second, by his listing of nine of the many translations of the *I Ching* he has consulted (532); and third, by his invitation to Edward L. Shaughnessy – who, with Richard J. Smith, is among the half-dozen leading authorities on the *I Ching* outside China – to preface his composition. These indications point towards the absolute centrality of the *I Ching* to the entire composition of *Changing*. Irrespective of the poem's intrinsic qualities, then, our own reading of *Changing* is necessarily conditioned too by this knowledge, including our own perception of an originary text that we think of as containing poetry only in the "loosest of senses" (Shaughnessy, 'Preface': ix). Complementarily, any rereading of the *I Ching* in the light of *Changing* may well highlight our sense of the ancient text's *literary* qualities.

CORRELATIVE THINKING

In an as yet-unpublished essay 'Divination, Derivation and Tinkering: Some Notes on the Composition of *Changing*' (2021b), Berengarten provides insights into the origins and early development of the mode of composition he has adopted in the making of this poem:

> The practice that I had developed for divination in the early 1960s always involved writing. [...] I usually took notes on statement(s), image(s) and change-line(s) and, especially when I was first finding my way around the text, sometimes added my own thoughts and responses. Out of these, if the frame of mind was right, ideas and notes for a poem might emerge and occasionally, an entire poem. (RB 2021b: unpaginated, n.p.)

The first poem to surface in this way was '*Two lakes, joined*'. This occurred in the summer of 1984, shortly after a visit to the Peak District in

Derbyshire, twenty-two years after his first exposure to the *I Ching*: a long period of incubation. But then, rapidly, the poet realised that "somehow" he had "spontaneously happened upon a form":

> Since I wrote the poem immediately after (and as the direct result of) an *I Ching* divination, it's equally possible that its shape was directly influenced by the hexagram structure, even though at a sub-liminal level. The total of eighteen lines also suggested three hexagrams stacked one over another. (*ibid.* unpaginated)

After finding himself writing more poems based on the same pattern, and through a range of approaches that move beyond direct divination to a consciously planned compositional strategy, Berengarten gradually accumulates and eventually delivers a work that not only takes the *I Ching* as its starting point, but also intentionally reflects – and reflects *back upon* – the originary text. And while a number of French, English, Irish and American poets have utilised their own *I Ching* divinations to 'trigger' poems, as has the composer John Cage, Berengarten has gone one step further. For not only does he explore, meditate and expand on the details of each one of the *I Ching*'s sixty-four hexagrams (as well as on each of their individual lines) in terms of their symbolic associations and thematic resonances, but he also 'returns to source' in several other ways. For *Changing* engages, embodies and transmutes the *I Ching*'s inherent numerological patterns and formal structures, as well as, to a considerable extent, its philosophy. With regard to this last point, Berengarten's patterning system in *Changing*, which is based on non-identical repetition, implies a perspective that, on the one hand, is ancient, insofar as it embodies *correspondances* between macrocosm and microcosm, and, on the other, belongs decidedly to our own age, insofar as it embeds a version of fractal thinking.

For these reasons and in these ways, it might be suggested that while Berengarten's focus on meanings epitomises the Poundian concept of *logopoeia*, his attentiveness to layerings of variegated but repeated forms embodies both *melopoeia* and *phanopoeia* (see Pound 1964b: 25). The overall result is a composite *mimesis* in the sense in which Auerbach (1953) deploys the term.

༄

A fuller understanding of Berengarten's intentions in *Changing* is evident from his response to other modern poets' and artists' perceptions and configurations of the Chinese text. His notes on the composer John Cage's deployment of the *I Ching* are especially revealing. Berengarten regards Cage's emphasis on methods based entirely on *chance* to generate compositions as an avoidance of many of the *I Ching's* other "latent qualities and inherent potentials", particularly its structural features that are "clearly cohesive, symmetrical, binary, correlative, generative". These, according to Berengarten, are "just as 'interesting' as chance, if not more so". Berengarten goes on to argue that Cage's insistence on aleatory or random reveals

> [...] a naïve and sentimentalised western version of nineteenth century romanticism, which he *imposes* on the *I Ching*. Wordsworth, the great poet of nature, and Turner, the great painter of nature, saw pattern and order in the cosmos. [...] As far as the *I Ching* is concerned, where Cage sees uncaged randomness, I see a carefully mapped, all-embracing cosmogony consisting of subtly balanced geometrical oppositions, and including a multiplicity of caringly and carefully coded shifts and movements throughout space-time. [...] In the *I Ching*, all these elements keep constantly checking and chasing one another in a kind of eternal cosmic dance, patterned through space-time. This dance itself constitutes a cohering order in which humanity is an integrated *part* of nature (the cosmos). The meaning of the term *I Ching* is the *Book of Change(s)*, not the *Book of Chance(s)*. (RB 2021c: unpaginated, n.p.)

In another unpublished essay, entitled 'Connectivity, Grounding and Amplification', Berengarten again emphasises coherence and complexity:

> [T]he *I Ching* appears to me as a self-cohering and highly complex system, *all of whose signs are themselves signs of other signs*. [...] In the last resort, then, the base-lines in *Changing*, like this book's other structural features, as well as its entirety are meant to infer (confer, prefer, refer to, defer to) a world-view that assumes (takes for granted) *the coherence of the cosmos*. [...] And while the *I Ching's* operations are by definition unforeseeable and unpredictable, whether through the toss of coins or manipulation of sticks, the connections that it allows, admits and proliferates, form part of an *organic web of interrelated phenomena*, which naturally and inevitably incorporates not only perceptions of phenomena but also beliefs about *both* the phenomena *and* the perceptions of them. (RB 2021d: unpaginated, n.p.)

❧

Interestingly, several other poetic ventures in the course of Berengarten's career bear thematic and compositional similarities to the primary structural elements in *Changing*. As has already been suggested, sequences such as *The Manager* (2001) and, earlier, *Avebury* (1972) present twin attempts to incorporate the over-arching architecture of a possible 'narrative' while simultaneously exploring its tendency to dissolution or subversion. In both these works, a principle of *controlled indeterminacy* is evident: that is to say, the distinct prospect of an anarchic or at least non-linear reading is never far from the surface.

What most distinguishes the *I Ching* from traditional western literary texts is not only the way in which, following a divination, any interpretation of the meaningfulness of a hexagram is both unique to the occasion and wholly personalised, but also the fact that this quality is artic-ulately *predicated and predicted* by the prime function built into the *I Ching* itself: the operational intention of divination. Clearly, no divinatory text can function effectively at all without generating and enabling a specific, differentiated and, indeed, unique reading for each and every diviner, on each and every occasion that s/he 'uses' (consults) the book. So the text itself – replete with all its values, worldview, and stances on meaningful action and behaviour – functions effectively as a divination manual *by virtue of* its necessarily vast and possibly unlimited fund of potential interpretations and applications, only a tiny number of which will ever be actualised (revealed, resonated) by and through any one reader's (diviner's) participation at any particular point in space-time. This is to say: what makes the *I Ching* so effective as a divination manual is *precisely* its inclusive, fuzzy-edged *imprecision*: or, in other words, its polysemy.

By adopting the *I Ching* as his model, Berengarten has been able to take on and incorporate these core elements into his own imaginative artefact. The poet himself is acutely aware, on the one hand, that the ancient Chinese text fits well with contemporary notions of a literary text as a powerful *generator* and prolific *distributor of meanings* (plural) rather than as an 'object' that contains and carries one specific (singular) meaning. On the other, he is equally aware that far from functioning primarily in the relatively 'closed' diachronic manner of a myth or a novel, the *I Ching* operates "[…] transversally to sequential linearity. It cuts across both logical and narrative modes, intersecting them by applying a mode of thinking and perception – and hence also, a way of being – that is irreducibly synthetic, correlative, resonant, *and poetic*" (*CH* 'Postscript': 523, emphasis added). Being far less 'fixed' than either the ancient literary or religious texts that we might think of as possibly analogous to it in the West – for example the Sumerian *Epic of Gilgamesh*, the Homeric epics, or the Semitic *Bible* – the *I Ching* itself reminds us emphatically of the extent to which all texts made out of language are irreducibly polysemic. Or, to put this another way: the Ching has been *determined* (in all senses) to function best in *zones of indeterminacy*.

In *Changing*, Berengarten redeploys and redistributes the *I Ching*'s irreducible polysemy into patterns of his own. He does this vis-à-vis both form and content. For example, we encounter a mini-set entitled 'Watching' (20/159-166) which contains interesting and relevant observations on divination itself, especially in the head-piece, entitled *'What the book said about itself'*: "*Meanings lie neither / in words nor in lines but / cluster behind both.*" And this piece concludes:

> You have to sit and wait
> in a patience within patience
> without praise or hope
>
> for meanings to grow
> like ferns unscrolling from
> cracks between lines.   (20/0: 160)

Evidently, here Berengarten is partly following an idea presented in several classical Daoist texts. In any journey through and along the 'way' (*dao*), words, as mere vessels for meanings, may be discarded once whatever they contain has been imbibed, just as, later, ideas and meanings may be discarded too. This is reminiscent of the famous parable in the *Zhuangzi*:

> A fish trap is used to catch fish, but once the fish have been taken, the trap is forgotten. The rabbit trap is used to snare rabbits, but once the rabbit is captured, the trap is ignored. Words are used to express concepts, but once you have grasped the concepts, the words are forgotten. I would like to find someone who has forgotten the words so I could debate with such a person!
> (*The Book of Chuang Tzu*, Palmer *et al.* trans: 242)

So far so good, but in Berengarten's lines, a second motif is evident. For *"meanings"* (plural) are *generated* ("grow" organically) from readings "between the lines", i.e. from multiple, layered, and implicit contexts and connections rather than out of any readily evident and explicit statements. The "cracks" here, then, as well as those that surface throughout *Changing*, are *vacant spaces* (gaps, absences), through and into which, for any reader/

diviner, meanings may be mysteriously attracted and, surprisingly, arrive. In terms specific to the Daoist *I Ching*, these cracks could only be receptive *yin* elements, not active *yang*. Furthermore, third, in this poem's last line, the specific word "cracks" precisely recalls and suggests the origins of the *I Ching* itself in the first-ever known Chinese divination system during the late Shang Dynasty: the mantic interpretation of splits that appeared when intensely focalised heat was applied to holes neatly chiselled or drilled into mammalian clavicles and turtle carapaces (see Keightley 1978, 2000 and 2012). Here, then, in a passage *about* the polysemic proclivities of the *I Ching*, the poetic *technique* of polysemy itself functions locally as a methodological model that carries three distinct and specific directions of meaning and reference. Polysemy is deployed to pull all these three together, and in this way, is also used to comment reflexively on polysemy itself.

❧

As these samplings suggest, Berengarten has consistently pursued possibilities of meaning and arrangement both 'above' and 'beneath' the level of line and page. In the early stages of composing *Changing*, and crucially, in previous works such as *The Manager*, the poet has already toyed with a loose-leaf formula. For example, during a discussion of the genesis and design of this poem in an interview with Joanne Limburg, Berengarten questions traditional treatments of diachronic time, 'coherence', and notions of 'development':

> [F]or a long while, I toyed with the idea of publishing *The Manager* as a loose leaf album, in a ring-binder, or as a set of unbound pages in a box, like B. S. Johnson's wonderful novel *The Unfortunates*. The sections would then be able to be taken out and reshuffled into different orders. I still don't think this was an entirely stupid or fanciful idea. Many people, myself included, often read books of poems in random order, or even back to front. [...] But I finally rejected the idea of random or multiple sequencing. I think this was partly because I began to sense that there was some kind of pattern of movement, or change, or even (if one were to be pompous about it) 'narrative' or 'transformation' – going on in and through the book. I find it hard to intellectualise this. The feeling is still a visceral one.
> (RB and Limburg 2017: 55)

❧

An equally illuminating example of the problematisation of order is inherent in the title, contents and overall typographic design of *Book With No Back Cover* (RB 2003), a work, as the poet himself puts it, with "two beginnings, a middle, and no end – a challenge, among other things, to Aristotle's convention of time in the *Poetics*. *Book With No Back Cover* is especially relevant here, because one 'half' of it is a preliminary rehearsal for *Changing*. Here the poet makes a first attempt to gather thirty-eight of the poems that have already emerged from his readings of *I Ching* and his early ruminations on the ancient Chinese masterpiece. Even though he discards some of these in the final version of *Changing*, in *Book With No Back Cover* Berengarten's experimental attentiveness to the organic relationship between structure and content establishes an unusual and appealing *mirroring*. And the title he chooses for this preliminary selection of *I Ching* poems is 'Following', which he explains in this way:

> The standard translation of hexagram 17, 随 (*Sui*) ䷐ 'Following', supplied the title for this selection, because I felt that it actually embodied my experience in (and of) composition. I believed that I was 'following' the *I Ching* in several senses: not only treating it as a model, a pattern, a prototype, but also learning from it and, as it were, 'taking instruction' from it, whether through divination or other compositional strategies.

As for the title's resonances, the book has 'no back cover' simply because its front cover is repeated, the one version differing only from the other by being upside-down from it. There is neither *former* nor *latter* in this mode of delivery, for a meaningful reading may begin at either 'end'. And could it be that this book-shaping implicitly and intrinsically comments on *and* enacts the dual motif of Eliot's *Four Quartets*? "In my beginning is my end" ('East Coker', ll. 1, 14) and "In my end is my beginning" (*ibid.* final line).

As this discussion suggests, in the patterning and presentation of *Book With No Back Cover*, few things are entirely or merely left to chance (pun intended). Rather, an apparently fortuitous 'intuition' of connectivity – which is experienced at the time as meaningful, even if it isn't at first fully understood – is later gathered 'back' and 'up' into a consciously applied and developed motif or pattern. The perception of "meaningful coincidence" that arises here, as elsewhere, always involves discovery, recognition, *anagnorisis*. This is a point I shall return to later, in connection with the theory of synchronicity.

☙

No less interestingly, in terms of experimentation in matters of spatial design, the strong influence of Octavio Paz on Berengarten's writings, which he acknowledges in his memoir of the Mexican poet (2015), is evident in *Book With No Back Cover* too:

> Octavio was also fascinated by *the book* [emphasis added], both as concept and in its materiality and texture: on the one hand, the idea of the world and time *as* Book – a theme both very ancient and very modern – and on the other, the endless potential that books contain in themselves for variation in design, format and typography. Shortly after leaving Cambridge, he sent me a signed copy of a beautifully printed edition of his poem *Blanco*. This volume, when opened up, unfolds like a concertina as a single long sheet or scroll of paper between its two covers, implying continuity and cyclicity. *I found and continue to find this playfulness delightful, elegant, challenging and fertile. Ever since then, partly inspired by Octavio, I have been trying out similar bondings and blendings of poetic text and experimental format.* (RB 2015a; emphases added)

Even though the eventual printed realisations of *The Manager* and *Changing* are more orthodox and practical than that of *Book With No Back Cover* – that is, by comparison with the ways in which these publications were originally envisioned – the spectre of the undecided (indeterminate) text haunts all three books. Admittedly, in *The Manager* and *Changing*, these sleeping ghosts may hardly be more than subliminally sensed, if at all, by a first-time reader.

Various explorations of *correspondance* between form and content occur, then, in Berengarten's oeuvre well before we arrive at the options that *Changing* presents to the reader. As for the presentation of *Changing* itself, before this book's publication under the Shearsman imprint, Berengarten attempted to find a publisher to bring the entire work out as 'a book in a box', on the precise model of B. S. Johnson's *The Unfortunates* (1969). This attempt was almost identical to one he had first entertained about a 'loose leaf album' or binder, in connection with *The Manager*, as expressed in his interview with Joanne Limburg (315 above). For *Changing*, he at first intended each of the sixty-four sets of seven poems – each one imaging a single *I Ching* hexagram and its six lines – to be stapled as a mini-folio. The fact that these folios could be shuffled and read in any order would reflect not only the non-linear way in which any reader of any book of poems might 'browse', in any direction, but also the multitude of possible ways in which the result of a particular divination would *itself organise* both the selection and order in which any pair of hexagrams would be read.

✥

By way of further self-commentary, a poem in *Changing*, pointedly entitled 'A thing like this', introduces the specific spatial analogy of *mosaic-making* in order to amplify another aspect of Berengarten's compositional model. While the mosaic-maker (*aka* poet, composer, compositor) needs at all times to keep one eye firmly on "each parcelled / fragment" and "its unique resonances / to light and touch," the other eye needs to be allowed

> to wander over the whole
> design, its soarings and cascades,
> fractal novelties and intricate
>
> repetitions, which turn
> and tune space to music.   (17/3: 139)

Here, synaesthesia is introduced, or at least a perception of patterning that's both visual and aural ("which turn / and tune space to music"). The effective composition of a mosaic, then, depends on this dual mode of keeping "details" in balance with "the whole", so that they "correlate and intertwine". The result of this twinned vision is transformational, for

> when patterns take care of one
> another (and of you), they
>
> let you let go of all old skills
> and all old selves. Whatever you
> were falls away, irrelevant.   (*ibid.*)

So this poem concludes with a variant of the same motif of casting aside the fish trap once the fish is caught, as in the *Zhuangzi*, above. But here, it isn't fish or words that are discarded as "irrelevant", but "*all* old skills / and *all* old selves". All facets, trappings and components, then, of outworn identity are to be "let go", as mere shells and shards.

If these observations are considered together, might it not be suggested that at least one of this particular poem's themes is the way in which the poem itself gets made? And if this is so, then couldn't the theme of the making of *this* poem, by implication, resonate with that of the entire composition of *Changing*, and, indeed, of any poem?

ↂↄ

From around 2008, as Berengarten intensifies his work on his growing mass of poems connected with and arising out of his readings of the *I Ching*, he gradually discovers ever-expanding and proliferating ways in which his own operational strategies (i.e. modes and styles of work, driving motivations and obsessions, and thematic predilections and choices) mesh together with his understanding of diverse historical periods and his sense of self-placement within and among a variety of literary traditions. What's more, by virtue of being combined, these factors all return to (refer back to, reaffirm) the logic of the *I Ching* as he has perceived it from within his own poetic imperative; and together, they all congregate around the project that has emerged (emanated) from his continuing relationship with the Chinese source. The result is a multiple piling (interlayering) of reflection and self-reflexion. To put this another way: all his latent poetic energies, directives, imperatives and skills cluster around the *I Ching* like iron filings around a magnet. The *I Ching*, then, isn't merely the originary 'source' of *Changing*. It also becomes both a *strong attractor* and an *objective correlative* throughout both the writing and the reading of the poem, and a functional and necessary core around which the entire work revolves. And here, as *work* is construed both as "labour (working, effort)" and as the "product of labour (opus, oeuvre)", a reciprocal *thinking through* occurs for both writer and reader, which symphonically reflects (*and* reflects back upon) the source itself.

As an instance of this concatenating and simultaneous self-reflection and reflexivity, Berengarten is enabled to sense more and more layerings of analogy, for example:

> [...] a correlation between the theme of hexagram 50 (which in *Changing* becomes 'Cooking, Sacrificing') and the story in Herodotus of Croesus consulting the Delphic Oracle. The common motifs here are the sacrificial cauldron, the tortoise and the act of divination itself. Though these may be accidental or incidental, to me they were striking. It has often been said that the cauldron itself is *pictorially* represented in its own graph 鼎 (*ding*), which names this hexagram. It has been suggested, too, that the upper and lower constituent trigrams, 'fire' (*Li*) ☲ rising from 'wood' or 'wind' ☴ (*Xun*) represent and enact the basic process of cooking. (RB 2021b)

As I connect this statement with other works by Berengarten, my sense is that some poems written far apart in time across his career – which may at first reading appear to be widely (and even wildly) different – in fact turn out to be bound (bonded) together at varying levels and in similar ways. And here I'm thinking not so much of form, whether this is construed as outer appearance or as inner structure, but rather of the patterning of content.

Among these patterns are associations that are significantly generated by motifs that emanate from China. While these may remain unnoticed by a casual reader, as soon as one of Berengarten's works is compared with another, they become clear. His *Balkan Trilogy*, for instance, also includes several poems developed via the *I Ching*. In *The Blue Butterfly* (2006), not only do the first and final poems of the book result directly from *I Ching* divination, but they also recur, under slightly modified titles, in *Changing* ('*Decay*', 12/0: 96; and '*Under hills*', 22/0: 176). In the later book, these both appear as master-poems to mini-sets for hexagrams.

This double use of texts or, rather, this mode of *recontextualisation*, is no accident, not least because the very inception of *The Blue Butterfly* is based on synchronicity.

℃℈

Since C. G. Jung's theory of synchronicity is one of the major keys to Berengarten's *Changing*, it will be helpful here, even if only briefly, to sketch out the relevant deeper background and connections. In 1952, Jung published the first German version of his essay on synchronicity, together with an essay by his friend and colleague, the Nobel Prize-winning physicist and pursuer of the mysterious neutrino, Wolfgang Pauli, who contributed an essay on the scientific theories of Kepler. In the first English edition of this book, *The Interpretation of Nature and the Psyche* (1955), Jung's own essay bears the title 'Synchronicity: An Acausal Connecting Principle'. In this essay, he also presents his brief definition of synchronicity as "meaningful coincidence" (See Jung 1955 and 1960).

Most significant here is the fact that Jung's theory, which he developed and refined over many years, arose initially out of his own readings of the *I Ching*, in the translation of his friend Richard Wilhelm, which was first published in German in 1923. His gradual evolvement and refinement of the theory of synchronicity was initially sparked by his attempts to understand his own inner and deeply meaningful experience of the resonances between his own questions put to the *I Ching* and the responses given by the ancient text. Jung's preface to this book is preserved in all subsequent editions of the English translation too.

Berengarten first read Jung's writings as a student at Cambridge between 1961 to 1964, at around the same time that he discovered the *I Ching*. In this way, in the poet's early twenties, Jung and the *I Ching* were fortunately and organically connected for him at a formative stage in his poetic development. A comparative reading of Berengarten's writings soon reveals that synchronicity is a theme, and even a guiding principle, that runs throughout his work, often subliminally, but in recent years, increasingly explicitly. References to synchronicity and treatments of it occur in poems, essays and interviews and at conferences and seminars. Most significantly, Berengarten links and even at times *identifies* the onset of poetic inspiration itself with synchronistic experience. His essay 'A Synchronistic Experience in Serbia' (RB 2108, 2020, and 2021a) clarifies that the originary event that set in motion the entire gestation and composition of *The Blue Butterfly* and, hence, of his entire *Balkan Trilogy*, was a synchronistic experience at the site of a 1941 massacre by Nazis on the outskirts of the Serbian city of Kragujevac. In *A Portrait in Inter-Views*, he also refers frequently to synchronicity (RB 2017, index: 201). And perhaps most tellingly of all, of the hundred poems in *Notness: Metaphysical Sonnets*, ten belong to a cluster entitled 'On Synchronicity' (RB 2105: 25-31). As an example, both the instressed and inscaped patterns of 'The flows of time' are indicative of Berengarten's long-term dwelling on (and in) synchronicity:

> Nor is it just that time has different speeds
> or that its currents currently compose
> one passing river, or that this proceeds
> through past to future. It's that time-now flows
> not in some simple horizontal plane
> but dips and peaks, in spirals, wells, coils, spools,
> returning and re-gathering again
> in centripetal-centrifugal pools
> from so many dimensions and directions
> and in such varied patternings and modes,
> bearing such differing lightnesses and loads,
> incursions, repetitions and inflections,
> that what this present holds and overspills
> is all time, as it fills, empties, refills.   (*ibid*. 28)

Other poems in *Notness* manifest similar "currents", or rather, under-currents, for example: "This is where *when* itself watches tail-ends / of things implode in singularities" ('Notness, *end*', 52); "*Now*, crumbling in the vast imperative / of arrowed curves and carvings, falls like rain, / a plaintive, pliant interrogative / pouring away. Nor will *you* come again." ('*Now*, crumbling', 60); and 'Though infinitely varied, things repeat/ in rhythms, waves, expansions that they share./ with all else that's unique, beyond compare.'" ('Walking', 71). In passages such as these, Berengarten explores varying modes and qualities of our experience of time and transience. The reappearance in various contexts of themes and philosophical conceptions such as these is certainly a strategic aspect of Berengarten's oeuvre. What is more, this sometimes crystallizes in particular words that take on a talismanic quality. In just this way, the term *notness*, with all its implicit resonances from the earlier book, will itself find its way into *Changing* in four separate poems (1/4: 8; 2/7: 21; 8/2: 66; and 32/0: 256).

THE COMMON MIRACLE

Changing is replete with short poems that are rooted in the minutiae of common experience. This observation itself leads us into an apparent diversion which will eventually lead us back to Berengarten's latest long poem.

In Belgrade in 1989, the poet composes an essay about a Nazi massacre in the town of Kraljevo, Serbia, in 1941. Its title is 'A Grove of Trees and A Grove of Stones'. Like the later piece, 'A Synchronistic Experience in Serbia', this too is closely connected with the themes of *The Blue Butterfly*. Berengarten reflects on the memorial site in the town:

> Constantly the dead remind us that whatever is around us is also inside us, that the mysterious stuff we are made of is shared with all other things and beings – wind, flowers, butterflies – and *that this intimate connectedness threaded through creation really is the common miracle*. (See RB 1993: 34-39; and RB 2021a: 43; emphasis added).

The frequent recurrence of the motif of "the common miracle" in Berengarten's work is the key to a resonant motif. A broad-ranging interview with the American poet Sean Rhys, entitled 'I Must Try This Telling' (2012), starts with discussion of *The Blue Butterfly*. Among his many apt invitations and interventions, Rhys frames this statement and question:

> Your poems are deeply rooted in spiritual and psychological inquiry, in striving after the ineffable. They also inhabit a very physical reality and unfold against an historical backdrop, drawing in at times

to celebrate the mundane occurrences of daily life. How do you negotiate these sometimes discontiguous terrains?

(Berengarten and Rys in RB 2017: 124)

This sparks the following reply:

> The poetic, for me, is closely connected with and engrained in a sense of *the radiance of the commonplace*. This idea is embedded in my poetic philosophy. I've a poem called 'Only the Common Miracle' and in *Under Balkan Light* there's a two-line poem which goes: "Voices in the mirror call / The commonplace is miracle." *I believe strongly that the commonplace is irradiated with wonder, delight, energy, power, beauty* (emphases added) – and that's something that I'm learning more and more these days, now that I'm writing poems […] *rooted in* – Daoism and the *I Ching*. As a learner of *taiji* and *qigong*, I definitely have that sense sometimes, when I'm doing *taiji*, of a kind of radiance – *the radiance of the ordinary*. (*ibid*. 124; emphases added)

Clearly, this response could be variously interpreted. The point I want to address is that here Berengarten is reflecting on ways in which he tends to ground "spiritual and psychological inquiry" by celebrating "the common miracle". This phrase at first seems to embed a contradiction – for how can anything be *miraculous*, if it's no more than *common*? The apparent misfit of these two elements yields to pleasurable paradox as it dawns on us, in all likelihood contrarily to expectation, that commonness and miraculousness needn't be opposed at all, but rather, that the so-called 'ordinary world' around us is itself – and *in* itself – miraculous.

In my readings across Berengarten's writings, I find that his "common miracle" is identical to and co-extensive with the experience *of* the moment *in* the moment, *of* the here-and-now *in* the now-and-here. What is more, he tends to celebrate this by precisely *attending* (attending on, attending to *and* drawing attention to) the apparently most mundane and most banal occurrences of daily life. This way of making poems itself often brings out (discovers, reveals, realises) *intrinsic* poetic qualities among a wide variety of phenomena and occurrences – which, at first glance, may appear entirely disparate and distant from one another, and hardly more than humdrum. But by investment of this kind of attentivity to and in the commonplace, what at first seemed no more than mere *occurrences*, and of little interest or consequence, gets quietly but quickly transformed into multiple *occasions*, invested with beauty and radiance. And what connects and conjoins this diversity is precisely the quality that

Berengarten finds *poetic*: the inherent "radiance of the commonplace" which is he finds engrained in all things.

To return to *Changing*, the phrase "the common miracle" recurs in the cluster devoted to hexagram 55 ('Abounding, Brimming'). This poem's title is 'Ad*her*ing, in*her*ing' (emphases added) which both echoes and magnifies the already-double presence of the sound *here* or *hear* in both words. The poem's subject is the "way" (i.e. the *dao*) in which "light" – which "is constant / in its changing" – sticks "to or in things", "as part of their fabric, stuff, // very grain." The poem concludes:

Whatever else

may go or come
this light changing
on surfaces

is delight, is
glory, the unique
common miracle.   (55/1: 441)

This slender poem's final line expresses the motif that has been present in Berengarten's poetry since its first enunciation in *Black Light* (1983). Yet this recurrence is no mere retrospective, nostalgic or fanciful echo. Through and by means of the poem, apparently plain, ordinary, commonplace light – which always belongs intrinsically, ineluctably and irreducibly to the here-and-now – itself becomes transformative, radiant, miraculous.

ᘒ

Equally revealingly, in another as-yet-unpublished prose-text that has arisen out of *Changing*, Berengarten comments on the term *synchronicity* itself:

I'm tempted to substitute the neologism *synkairistic* for Jung's own neologism *synchronistic*. The Greek word καιρός ['*kairos*'] treats time from the qualitative rather than sequential point of view. In modern Greek this word has survived several thousand years to mean 'weather, season', hence καλοκαίρι ['*kalokairi*'] 'summer', i.e. lit. 'good season, fine weather'. I think we also need a term like *syntopistic*, after Greek τόπος ['*topos*'] 'place', to indicate the 'meaningful coincidence' of places or of two or more occurrences in one place. (RB 2021e, unpaginated, n.p.)

This identical idea also occurs in his latest prose-book, *Balkan Spaces*:

> Varying Jung's term, I suggest that equally appropriate coinages might be *syntopicity*, i.e. 'coincidence of place at and across different times', and, indeed, *synkairicity*, i.e. 'coincidence of moments considered qualitatively rather than merely sequentially (RB 2021a: 23).

It might well be suggested that Berengarten's recent desire to consider time "qualitatively rather than merely sequentially" involves another way of perceiving, experiencing and celebrating *the common miracle*, which is also a subtle aspect of *notness*. What is more, this emphasis is one of the main developments, already latent in previous books, which thoroughly irradiates *Changing*. To be attentive to *kairos* rather than *chronos* is the key.

∽

Thanks to some features and qualities outlined here, among many others, *Changing* stands as a sustained outpouring of captured and contemplated moments of life. These are both ordinary and radiant. they invite both analysis and continuing contemplation. And bearing in mind the title of Ming Dong Gu's essay in this book, 'From the *Book of Changes* to the Book of *Changing*: A Route to World Literature' (89 above), I return, finally, to the elective affinities between Paz and Berengarten. As one of the epigraphs to *Avebury* (1972), Berengarten quotes a sentence from the Mexican poet's book, *The Labyrinth of Solitude*: "For the first time in our history we are contemporaries of all mankind" (Paz 1967: 182). In the light of this comment, it is interesting, across a gulf of more than two thousand years, to consider commonalities between the *I Ching* and *Changing*. Similarly, in his memoir on Paz, Berengarten picks out several further comments by the Mexican poet. First, this sentence: "Today we all speak, if not the same tongue, the same *universal* language." And then, the phrase "the *universal* modern tradition" (Paz 1973: 21 and 34). Berengarten highlights the word *universal* in both quotes, and comments: "I share Octavio's belief that throughout the modern period, all literatures have necessarily and *de facto* become part of one literature, all poetries part of one poetry" (RB 2015a).

The preceding essays in this current volume yield a testament to Berengarten's commitment to this belief: to its subtle *stuff*, its *fabric*, ὕφασμα (*úphasma*), indeed, its entire *spectrum*, φάσμα (*phasma*). For this is woven of perceived analogies, experienced affinities, as-yet-undiscovered potentialities, and an open receptivity to the instresses and inscapes of synchronicity.

References

Auerbach, Erich. 1957 [1946]. *Mimesis: The Representation of Reality in Western Literature*. Trask, Willard (trans.). Princeton, NJ: Princeton University Press.

Berengarten, Richard. 1993. 'A Grove of Trees and a Grove of Stones'. In Burns, Richard and Markovich, Stephen (eds.), *Out of Yugoslavia*: 34-39.

———. 2003. *Book With No Back Cover*. London: David Paul.

———. 2011 [2001] *The Manager*. Bristol: Shearsman Books.

———. 2011 [2004]. *For the Living: Selected Longer Poems, 1965–2000*. Exeter: Shearsman Books.

———. 2011 [2006]. *The Blue Butterfly*. Bristol: Shearsman Books.

———. 2014. *Manual*. Bristol: Shearsman Books.

———. 2015a. 'Octavio Paz in Cambridge, 1970: Reflections and Iterations'. *The Fortnightly Review*. Online at: https://fortnightlyreview.co.uk/2015/07/octavio-paz/

———. 2015b. *Notness: Metaphysical Sonnets*. Bristol: Shearsman Books.

———. 2016. *Changing*. Bristol: Shearsman Books.

———. 2017. *Richard Berengarten: A Portrait in Inter-Views*. Nikolaou, Paschalis and Dillon, John (eds.). Bristol: Shearsman Books.

———. 2018. 'A Synchronistic Experience in Serbia'. *Margutte*. Online at: http://www.margutte.com/?p=30557&lang=en.

———. 2020. 'A Synchronistic Experience in Serbia'. In McMillan, Christian *et al.* (eds.). *Holism: Possibilities and Problems*. London: Routledge and Kegan Paul, 159-169.

———. 2021a. 'A Synchronistic Experience in Serbia'. In *Balkan Spaces*. Bristol: Shearsman Books, 25-37.

———. 2021b. 'Divination, Derivation and Tinkering: Some Notes on the Composition of *Changing*'. n.p.

———. 2021c. 'Change, Chance, Choice, Appropriation: Some notes on John Cage and the *I Ching*'. n.p.

———. 2021d. 'Connectivity, Grounding and Amplification: Some Notes on the Relationship between the *I Ching* and *Changing*'. n.p.

———. 2021e. Concurrence, Convergence, Deepening and Flow: Some Notes on Synchronistic Experience in *I Ching* Divination and in Poetic Composition. n.p.

Berengarten, Richard and Limburg, Joan. 'Managing the Art'. In Berengarten 2017.

Burns, Richard. 1972. *Avebury*. London: Anvil Press with Routledge and Kegan Paul. Reprinted (under the name Berengarten) 2018. Bristol: Shearsman Books.

———. 1983. *Black Light: poems in memory of George Seferis*. Cambridge: Los Poetry Press.

———. 1996. 'With Peter Russell in Venice 1965–1966'. In James Hogg (ed.). *The Road to Parnassus: Homage to Peter Russell on His Seventy-Fifth Birthday*. Salzburg: University of Salzburg, 107-123.

Burns, Richard and Markovich, Stephen (eds.). 1993. *Out of Yugoslavia. North Dakota Quarterly* 61/1.

Eliot, T. S. 1944. *Four Quartets*. London: Faber and Faber.

Gery, John. 2016 [2010]. 'Explicit and Implicit: Ezra Pound's Influence on Richard Berengarten's "Angels"'. In Jope, Derrick and Byford: 144-163.

Johnson, B. S. 1969. *The Unfortunates*. London: Panther Books.

Jope, Norman. Derrick, Paul S. and Byfield, Catherine, (eds.). 2026 [2010] *The Companion to Richard Berengarten*. Bristol: Shearsman Books.

Jung, C. G. 1955. 'Synchronicity: an acausal connecting principle'. In Jung, C. G. and Pauli, Wolfgang. *The Interpretation of Nature and The Psyche*. Hull. R. F. C (trans.). London: Routledge and Kegan Paul, 5-146.

———. 2014 [1960]. 'Synchronicity: An Acausal Connecting Principle'. In *The Structure and Dynamics of the Psyche. Collected Works*, vol. 8. Hull, R. F. C. (trans.). London, Routledge: 427-531.

Keightley, David N. 1978. *Sources of Shang History: the Oracle Bone Inscriptions of Bronze Age China*. Berkeley and Los Angeles, CA: University of California.

———. 2000. *The Ancestral Landscape: Time, Space and Community in Late Shang China* (ca. 1200–1045 B.C.). Berkeley, CA: Institute of East Asian Studies, University of California.

———. 2012. *Working for His Majesty: Research notes on Labor Mobilization in Late Shang China (ca. 1200–1045.B.C)*. Berkeley, CA: Institute of East Asian Studies, University of California.

Palmer, Martin, *et al.* (trans.). 2006 [1996]. *The Book of Chuang Tzu*. London: Penguin Books.

Paz, Octavio. 1967 [1951]. *The Labyrinth of Solitude*: Kemp, Lysander (trans.). London: Allen Lane The Penguin Press.

———. 1973. *Alternating Current*. Lane, Helen R. (trans.). New York, Viking Press.

———. 1986 [1975]. 'On Poets and Others, The Graphics of Charles Tomlinson'. In *On Poets and Others*. Schmidt, Michael (trans. and ed.) New York: Seaver Books.

———. 1989. 'The Other Voice'. 1989. In *The Other Voice: Essays on Modern Poetry*. Lane, Helen (trans.). New York: Harcourt, Brace, Jovanovich.

Pound, Ezra. 1964a. *The Cantos of Ezra Pound*. London: Faber and Faber.

———. 1964b [1931]. 'How to Read'. In *Literary Essays of Ezra Pound*. Eliot, T. S. (ed.). London: Faber and Faber.

Russell, Peter (ed.). 1950. *An Examination of Ezra Pound*. Norfolk, CT: New Directions.

Shaughnessy, Edward L. 2016. 'Preface'. In Berengarten, Richard, *Changing*.

Smith, Richard J. 2012. *The I Ching: A Biography*. Princeton, NJ: Princeton University Press.

THE CONTRIBUTORS

MIKE BARRETT is from Chicago. He has a BA in Economics from the University of Notre Dame, and a PhD in Creative Writing from the University of Illinois-Chicago. As a founding member of the Chicago Poetry Ensemble, he helped establish the Uptown Poetry Slam, the birthplace of slam poetry. Since then he has written ten books of poetry: *Babylons/Other Poems, A is for Acts, Radical Two, The Book of Morpheme, 50 Easy Pieces, Recto Verso (V. 1&2), A Missouri Diptych, Walking with my Doppelgänger,* and *Nutz and the Boltzmann Brainz.* He is recently retired from a long teaching career at Moberly Area Community College. He lives in Missouri with his wife, fiction writer Trudy Lewis. A comprehensive source for his poetry, prose, and visual art can be found online at mikebarrettarchive.com.

BOB DEVINE is a visual artist whose focus is bearing witness to the parallels among world myths, images and symbols. The process of appropriation and the meshing of gathered images from varied eras and cultures are strong elements in his work. His art has been exhibited throughout the Pacific Northwest and is in collections throughout the USA. Exhibitions include: 'ArtQuake' (Portland, Oregon, 1981); 'Heads' (Wentz Gallery, Portland, 1988); 'New Works: From Oak Hill & Main Street' (Jacobs Gallery, Eugene, OR, 1999); and 'Ends and Beginnings' (DIVA, Eugene, 2004). Illustrated works include: Robert Hunter's *Infinity Minus Eleven* (1993) and Hal Hartzell's *The Yew Tree: A Thousand Whispers* (Eugene, 1990). Awards and commissions include the Requiem Poster (Oregon Bach Festival, 1988) and 'The Well: Hexagram 48' (2000). He currently teaches at Lane Community College, Eugene, Oregon.

PAUL SCOTT DERRICK is a Senior Lecturer, retired, in American literature at the University of Valencia. He has published three collections of essays and co-authored various bilingual critical editions of works by Ralph Waldo Emerson, Emily Dickinson, Henry Adams and Sarah Orne Jewett. He is co-editor of *Modernism Revisited: Transgressing Boundaries and Strategies of Renewal in American Poetry* (Rodopi, 2007) and is also one of the co-editors of *The Companion to Richard Berengarten* (Shearsman, 2016) and

Managing The Manager: *Critical Essays on Richard Berengarten's Book-length Poem* (Cambridge Scholars, 2019). With Miguel Teruel, he has translated Berengarten's *Black Light* into Spanish (JPM Ediciones, 2012) and with Viorica Patea, has translated three volumes by Romanian poet Ana Blandiana into English (*My Native Land A4; The Sun of Hereafter & Ebb of the Senses* and *Five Books*: Bloodaxe, 2014/2017/2021). A further volume of Blandiana's poetry, *The Shadow of Words*, is forthcoming from Bloodaxe in 2023. His critical essays, translations and poems have appeared in print and electronic journals in both Europe and the US.

ELEANOR GOODMAN (顾爱玲, Gu Ailing) is the award-winning author of the poetry collection *Nine Dragon Island* (Enclave/Zephyr, 2016). Her translation of *Something Crosses My Mind: Selected Poems of Wang Xiaoni* (Zephyr, 2014) received the 2015 Lucien Stryk Prize and a PEN/Heim Translation Grant, and was shortlisted for the International Griffin Prize. She has also translated the anthology *Iron Moon: An Anthology of Chinese Workers Poetry* (White Pine, 2017), *The Roots of Wisdom: Poems by Zang Di* (Zephyr, 2017), which received the 2020 Patrick D. Hanan Book Prize, and *Days When I Hide My Corpse in a Cardboard Box: Poems of Natalia Chan* (Zephyr, 2018), shortlisted for the 2019 Lucien Stryk Prize. She is a Research Associate at the Harvard University Fairbank Center. Her latest translation is a book of selected poems by Zheng Xiaoqiong (Giramondo, 2022).

MING DONG GU (顾明栋) is a Distinguished Professor of Foreign Studies at Shenzhen University, China, and Professor of Comparative Literature at the University of Texas at Dallas. He is author of *Sinologism: An Alternative to Orientalism and Post-colonialism* (Routledge, 2013), *Chinese Theories of Fiction* (SUNY, 2006) and *Chinese Theories of Reading and Writing* (SUNY, 2005). He is also editor of *Translating China for Western Readers* (SUNY, 2014); *Why Traditional Chinese Philosophy Still Matters* (Routledge, 2018); and the *Routledge Handbook of Modern Chinese Literature* (Routledge, 2019). He has published more than 150 essays and papers in English and Chinese.

TZE-KI HON (韓子奇) is a researcher at the Research Center for History and Culture of Beijing Normal University (Zhuhai campus). He is the Acting Dean of the Faculty of Humanities and Social Sciences, BNU-HKBU United International College, Zhuhai, China. Previously, he taught at City University of Hong Kong, Hanover College, Indiana, and

State University of New York, Geneseo. Specializing in classical studies and intellectual history, topics of his books and the collections of essays he has co-edited include commentaries on the *I Ching*, Neo-Confucianism of the Song-Ming period, the social and intellectual history of late Qing and Republican China, the global order after WWI, and the rise of Confucianism since 1979. Current research includes paradigm shifts in *I Ching* commentaries, the philosophy of divination of Zhu Xi (1130–1200), and the transformation of the *I Ching* into a global classic since WW1.

JEREMY HOOKER is a poet, literary critic and diarist. The most recent of his many volumes of poetry are *Word and Stone* (2019), *Selected Poems 1965–2018* (2020) and *The Release* (2022), all published by Shearsman. The last of these was the quarterly 'Wild Card' choice of the Poetry Book Society. His equally many prose books include: *John Cowper Powys and David Jones: A Comparative Study* (1979); *Poetry of Place* (1982); *Art of Seeing*, (2020); *Welsh Journal* (2001), *Imagining Wales* (2001), *Openings: A European Journal* (2014) and *Ditch Vision* (2017). He received the Cholmondeley Award for Poetry (2014), and his features for BBC Radio 3 include *A Map of David Jones*, first broadcast in 1995. He is an Emeritus Professor of the University of South Wales and a member of the Learned Society of Wales, and in 2021, he was elected to be a Fellow of the Royal Society of Literature.

SOPHIA KATZ (柯書斐, Ke Shufei) is a Lecturer in the Department of East Asian Studies, Tel-Hai College, Israel, and Director of the Tel-Hai Center for the Study of Religions. She specializes in Chinese philosophy and literature. Her interests include: 11th to 17th century Confucian thought; the philosophical poetry of Chinese literati; and comparative philosophy, theology and religion vis-à-vis thinkers from China and other cultures. Her publications include: "The Way of Silent Realization: Ineffability and Rationality in the Philosophical Mysticisms of Śankara and Zhan Ruoshui" (in *Brahman and Dao: Comparative Studies of Indian and Chinese Philosophy and Religion*, 2014), and "Free to Obey: Gao Panlong and Dietrich Bonhoeffer on Selflessness, Fate, and Freedom" (in *Ching Feng: A Journal on Christianity and Chinese Religion and Culture*, vol. 16/1-2, 2017). She is currently researching Chinese influences on the writings of Martin Buber.

LUCAS KLEIN (柯夏智, Ke Xiazhi) is a father, writer, and translator. His scholarship and criticism have appeared in *The Organization of Distance: Poetry, Translation, Chineseness* (Brill, 2018) as well as in numerous journals, such as *Sino-Platonic Papers, Comparative Literature Studies, LARB, Jacket, CLEAR*, and *PMLA*. His translation of *Notes on the Mosquito: Selected Poems of Xi Chuan* (New Directions, 2012) was awarded the Lucien Stryk Prize in 2013. Other translations include Mang Ke, *October Dedications* (Zephyr and Chinese University Press, 2018); contributions to *Li Shangyin* (New York Review Books, 2018); and Duo Duo, *Words as Grain: New and Selected Poems* (Yale University Press, 2021), for which he received a 2019 PEN/Heim Translation Fund grant. He is an associate professor of Chinese at Arizona State University.

HANK LAZER has published thirty-two books of poetry, including *COVID19 SUTRAS* (2020, Lavender Ink), *Slowly Becoming Awake (N32)* (2019, Dos Madres Press), *Poems That Look Just Like Poems* (2019, PURH – one volume in English, one in French), *Evidence of Being Here: Beginning in Havana (N27)*, (2018, Negative Capability Press), *Thinking in Jewish (N20)* (2017, Lavender Ink). Previous books include *Poems Hidden in Plain View* (2016, in English and in French), *Brush Mind: At Hand* (2016). Lazer has performed jazz-poetry improvisations in the US and Cuba with musicians Davey Williams, Omar Pérez, Andrew Raffo Dewar, Holland Hopson, and others. In 2015, Lazer received Alabama's most prestigious literary prize, the Harper Lee Award, for lifetime achievement in literature.

OWEN LOWERY was born on 24 November 1968 and died on 14 May 2021. At the age of 18, he was holder of the British Judo under-21 title, when an accident during a charity tournament left him paralysed from the shoulders down. Confronting his tetraplegic condition with extraordinary courage, he turned to poetry, and in 1998 he obtained a first class honours degree in Creative Writing from Bolton University. He then went on to complete his PhD on the extrospective poetry of Keith Douglas, and he became a prolific and widely published poet in his own right. His work appeared in *Stand, PN Review*, the *Guardian*, on the *BBC* and in the *Albero Project* on the *Margutte* website. Owen was also an accomplished performer of his poetry and appeared regularly at a wide range of major festivals and venues. Northern House and Carcanet have published three of his poetry collections, *Otherwise Unchanged* (2012), *Rego Retold* (2015) and *The Crash Wake Poems* (2021). Owen also had a number of reviews and essays published, including on the work of Richard Berengarten.

RODERICK MAIN works at the University of Essex, UK, where he is Professor in the Department of Psychosocial and Psychoanalytic Studies and Director of the Centre for Myth Studies. He has a BA and MA in Classics from the University of Oxford and a PhD in Religious Studies from Lancaster University. He is author of *The Rupture of Time: Synchronicity and Jung's Critique of Modern Western Culture* (Brunner-Routledge, 2004), *Revelations of Chance: Synchronicity as Spiritual Experience* (SUNY, 2007), and *Breaking the Spell of Disenchantment: Mystery, Meaning, and Metaphysics in the Work of C. G. Jung* (Chiron Publications, 2022). He is also editor of *Jung on Synchronicity and the Paranormal* (Princeton/ Routledge, 1997), and co-editor of *Myth, Literature, and the Unconscious* (Karnac, 2013), *Holism: Possibilities and Problems* (Routledge, 2020), and *Jung, Deleuze, and the Problematic Whole* (Routledge, 2021).

PASCHALIS NIKOLAOU, co-editor of this book, is Associate Professor in Literary Translation at the Ionian University, Greece. He is author of the monograph *The Return of Pytheas: Scenes from British and Greek Poetry in Dialogue* (2017) and of essays published in, among others: *Translation and Creativity: Perspectives on Creative Writing and Translation Studies* (2006); *Translating and Interpreting Conflict* (2007); and *Translating the Literatures of Small European Nations* (2020). He has edited *12 Greek Poems After Cavafy* (2015) and *Encounters in Greek and Irish Literature: Creativity, Translations and Critical Perspectives* (2020), guest edited *Synthesis* 12 ('Recomposed: Anglophone Presences of Classical Literature' (2019), and co-edited *Translating Selves: Experience and Identity Between Languages and Literatures* (2008) and *Richard Berengarten: A Portrait in Inter-Views* (2017). He was a Fulbright Visiting Scholar for 2021 at the Department of Classics, Ohio State University. His study, *Creative Classical Translation*, was published in 2023 by Cambridge University Press.

GEOFFREY REDMOND (雷文德, Lei Wende) MA, MD. With a dual background in biomedical science and literature, Dr. Geoffrey Redmond's current work is Sinological, concentrating on the *I Ching*. He found that the evidence-based nature of philology fit comfortably with his scientific background. Educated at Cornell, the University of Virginia, and Columbia, Redmond's related books include *Teaching the Book of Changes (I Ching)* with Hon Tze-ki (Oxford, 2014); and *The I Ching (Book of Changes): A Critical Translation of the Ancient Text* (Bloomsbury Academic, 2017). This reconstruction depicts an earlier, but not necessarily simpler, time. He is currently working on *Reading the I Ching (Book of Changes): Structure, Imagery, Rhetoric, Philosophy, and Ethics* (also Bloomsbury

Academic). Redmond has lectured on the *I Ching* in Hong Kong, Jinan, Taipei, Kaohsiung, and in Japan and Thailand, as well as at American, Canadian, and European venues.

HEYONG SHEN (申荷永) is Professor of Psychology at CityU (the City University of Macao) and SCNU (South China Normal University). He is a Jungian analyst and member of the International Association of Analytical Psychology (IAAP) and, as a Sandplay Therapist, a member of the International Society of Sandplay Therapy (ISST). He is also Founding President of the Chinese Federation for Analytical Psychology and Sandplay Therapy; and he has organized the International Conference of Analytical Psychology and Chinese Culture (1998–2018). He has been speaker at Eranos Conferences in 1997 and 2007. Heyong is Chief Editor for the Chinese translation of the *Collected Works* of C. G. Jung, as well as chief editor of the *Chinese Journal of Analytical Psychology*.

RICHARD J. SMITH (司馬富, Sima Fu), co-editor of this book, is currently George and Nancy Rupp Professor of Humanities emeritus, a Baker Institute Scholar, and a Research Professor at the Chao Center for Asian Studies, Rice University. He is also an Adjunct Professor at the Center for Asian Studies, University of Texas, Austin, and a member of several professional advisory boards. A specialist in modern Chinese history and traditional Chinese culture, Smith also has strong interests in transnational, global and comparative studies. He has published nine single-authored books, the most recent of which is *The Qing Dynasty and Traditional Chinese Culture* (2015). He has also co-edited or co-authored eight volumes, the most recent of which are *Reexamining the Sinosphere: Cultural Transmissions and Transformations in East Asia* (2020) and *Rethinking the Sinosphere: Poetics, Aesthetics, and Identity Formation* (2020).

RICO SNELLER has taught philosophy and ethics at Leiden University. He is currently a lecturer in philosophy and psychoanalysis at the Mandeville Academy and the Jungian Institute (the Netherlands), and a guest lecturer in philosophy at Al Farabi University in Almaty, Kazakhstan. His PhD thesis was dedicated to the French philosopher Jacques Derrida and his relation to negative theology and Jewish philosophy. Recently, he published *Perspectives on Synchronicity, Inspiration, and the Soul* (Cambridge Scholars, 2020); in this study, Berengarten's poetry is often resorted to in order to clarify the main argument. Sneller has also published an earlier essay on Berengarten's poetry under the title

'Spirituality as Poetry. On Richard Berengarten's Balkan Trilogy' (in *Studies in Spirituality* 29, 2019: 315-331).

TAN CHEE LAY (陈志锐) has lived in Singapore, Taiwan and the UK, and has studied Chinese Literature, English Studies and Business Administration. He completed his doctorate in Oriental Studies (Chinese literature) at St John's College, Cambridge University, specialising in Chinese poetry and exile poets. Chee Lay was awarded the coveted Young Artist Award by the National Arts Council in 2004 and the Singapore Youth Award (Culture and the Arts), the highest accolade for youth, in 2006. A former tutor of the Chinese Language Elective Programme, he is currently an Associate Professor in Chinese in Nanyang Technological University (NTU), Singapore. Chee Lay has published and edited over 20 creative writing and academic books in both Chinese and English languages.

ALAN TRIST is a Cambridge-educated anthropologist, who was publisher and editor with the Hulogosi publishing cooperative in Eugene, Oregon in the 1980s and, in the 1970s and from 1995 to 2014, administrator of the Grateful Dead's song catalogue at Ice Nine Publishing Company in California. His *Paros Poems: An Island Sequence,* co-authored with Alexis Lykiard, appeared in 1967 (Difros, Athens), and *The Water of Life: a Tale of the Grateful Dead* in 1987 (Hulogosi, Eugene, Oregon). He edited *The Grateful Dead Family Album*, authored by Jerilyn Lee Brandelius (Warner Books New York, 1989), and *The Complete Annotated Grateful Dead Lyrics*, annotated and co-edited by David Dodd (Simon and Schuster, New York: 2005). He continues to work with the cultural and arts legacy of the 1960s.

The Trigrams
and Hexagrams
of the *I Ching*

APPENDIX 1

The Primary *I Ching* Trigrams
(*Bagua*)

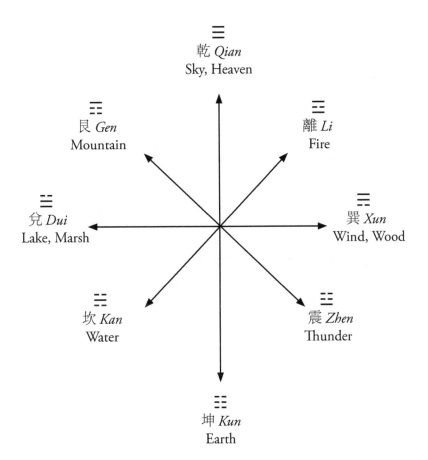

乾 *Qian*
Sky, Heaven

艮 *Gen*
Mountain

離 *Li*
Fire

兌 *Dui*
Lake, Marsh

巽 *Xun*
Wind, Wood

坎 *Kan*
Water

震 *Zhen*
Thunder

坤 *Kun*
Earth

(One possible configuration)

The *I Ching* Hexagrams
and Cluster-Names in *Changing* (1)

	FORM	NAME	NAME IN *CHANGING*
1	䷀	乾 *Qian* (*)	Initiating
2	䷁	坤 *Kun* (*)	Responding, Corresponding
3	䷂	屯 *Zhun*	Beginning
4	䷃	蒙 *Meng*	Bringing up
5	䷄	需 *Xu*	Waiting, Needing
6	䷅	訟 *Song*	Clashing
7	䷆	師 *Shi*	Mustering, Conscripting
8	䷇	比 *Bi*	According, Binding
9	䷈	小畜 *Xiao Xu*	Small Blessing, Possessing
10	䷉	履 *Lü*	Treading
11	䷊	泰 *Tai*	Harmonising, Prospering
12	䷋	否 *Pi*	Stagnating, Decaying
13	䷌	同人 *Tong Ren*	Gathering, Togethering
14	䷍	大有 *Da You*	Huge Having
15	䷎	謙 *Qian*	Humbling
16	䷏	豫 *Yu*	Delighting

(*) Doubled trigrams

The *I Ching* Hexagrams
and Cluster-Names in *Changing* (2)

	FORM	NAME	NAME IN *CHANGING*
17	䷐	随　*Sui*	Following
18	䷑	蠱　*Gu*	Rotting, Remedying
19	䷒	臨　*Lin*	Approaching
20	䷓	觀　*Guan*	Watching
21	䷔	噬嗑 *Shi He*	Biting through
22	䷕	賁　*Bi*	Grace Adorning
23	䷖	剝　*Bo*	Peeling
24	䷗	復　*Fu*	Returning
25	䷘	无妄 *Wu Wang*	Untwisting
26	䷙	大畜 *Da Xu*	Big Blessing, Possessing
27	䷚	頤　*Yi*	Nourishing
28	䷛	大過 *Da Guo*	Overbrimming
29	䷜	坎　*Kan* (*)	Falling (in a pit)
30	䷝	離　*Li* (*)	Clinging
31	䷞	咸　*Xian*	Reciprocating
32	䷟	恒　*Heng*	Enduring

(*) Doubled trigrams

The I Ching Hexagrams
and Cluster-Names in Changing (3)

	Form	Name	Name in Changing
33	䷠	遯 *Dun*	Retreating
34	䷡	大壯 *Da Zhuang*	Powering
35	䷢	晉 *Jin*	Dawning
36	䷣	明夷 *Ming Yi*	Darkening
37	䷤	家人 *Jia Ren*	Dwelling, Householding
38	䷥	睽 *Kui*	Separating
39	䷦	蹇 *Jian*	Struggling, Stumbling
40	䷧	解 *Xie*	Relieving, Releasing
41	䷨	損 *Sun*	Decreasing
42	䷩	益 *Yi*	Increasing
43	䷪	夬 *Guai*	Breaking through
44	䷫	姤 *Gou*	Coupling
45	䷬	萃 *Cui*	Massing
46	䷭	升 *Sheng*	Climbing
47	䷮	困 *Kun*	Exhausting
48	䷯	井 *Jing*	Welling, Replenishing

The *I Ching* Hexagrams
and Cluster-Names in *Changing* (4)

	FORM	NAME	NAME IN *CHANGING*
49	䷰	革 *Ge*	Shedding
50	䷱	鼎 *Ding*	Cooking, Sacrificing
51	䷲	震 *Zhen* (*)	Shaking, Quaking
52	䷳	艮 *Gen* (*)	Stilling
53	䷴	漸 *Jian*	Shifting
54	䷵	歸妹 *Gui Mei*	Wooing, Courting
55	䷶	豐 *Feng*	Abounding, Brimming
56	䷷	旅 *Lü*	Travelling
57	䷸	巽 *Xun* (*)	Blowing, Billowing
58	䷹	兌 *Dui* (*)	Joying, Enjoying
59	䷺	渙 *Huan*	Dispersing
60	䷻	節 *Jie*	Restricting
61	䷼	中孚 *Zhong Fu*	Inner Trusting
62	䷽	小過 *Xiao Guo*	Overstepping
63	䷾	既濟 *Ji Ji*	After crossing over
64	䷿	未濟 *Wei Ji*	Before crossing over

(*) Doubled trigrams

Appendix 3

Transliterating Chinese names, titles and terms: some common alternatives

The transliteration or "romanization" of Chinese sounds has always been a challenge for Westerners. For more than a century the scholarly (and popular) Anglophone convention was to use the so-called Wade-Giles system for rendering Chinese names, terms, and titles, which is why so many people in English-speaking countries know the *Changes* as the *I Ching*. But there are perhaps a dozen other transliterated names by which the classic is known, including *I-ching*, *I Ging*, *Yi King*, *Yih-King*, *Yi Jing* and *Yijing*. The last two of these reflect the Pinyin system of transliteration, invented by the Chinese in the 1950s, adopted by most Western newspapers after 1978, and increasingly used by China specialists since that time.

But there is still no agreement, even among scholars, regarding either the transliteration of the standard Chinese name for the book 易經 or the best translation of the title. By far the most common English rendering is the *Book of Changes*, but the *Classic of Changes* is perhaps a bit closer to the mark. Other Western-language translations of the title include *Das Buch der Wandlungen* (German), *Le Livre des mutations*, *Le Livre des changements*, *Le Classique du changement*, *Yi king* (French), and *El libro de las mutaciones* (Spanish). The earliest versions of the book are known in Chinese as the *Zhou Changes* 周易 (variously transliterated into English as *Chou-i*, *Djohi*, *Zhouyi*, etc.).

In the face of this unavoidable complexity, the editors have accorded their authors a good deal of latitude in the choice not only of transliterations and translations of Chinese names, book titles and terms, but also in their use of "traditional" (繁體, *fanti*) or "simplified" (簡體, *jianti*) characters. As a guide to readers, here follow examples of some of the equivalent Pinyin and Wade-Giles transliterations as they appear in this book. These are tabulated in three categories: Names of people and dynasties; Book titles; and Terms and concepts. Chinese characters are presented in their "traditional" form.

Richard J. Smith

1. Names of people and dynasties

Pinyin	Wade-Giles	Chinese	Name or Description
Fuxi or *Fu Xi*	*Fu-hsi* or *Fu Hsi*	伏羲 *or* 伏犧	Mythical inventor of the *Changes*
Kongzi or *Kongfuzi*	*K'ung-tzu* or *Kung-fu-tzu*	孔子 *or* 孔夫子	Philosopher known in English as Confucius (c. 51–479 BCE)
Laozi	*Lao-tzu*	老子	Daoist philosopher (trad. date 5th century BCE)
Mengzi	*Meng-tzu*	孟子	Philosopher known in English as Mencius (372–289 BCE)
Shang or *Yin*	*Shang* or *Yin*	商 *or* 殷	Dynasty name (c. 1556–1046 BCE)
Zhuangzi	*Chuang-tzu*	莊子	Daoist philosopher (d. 288 BCE)
Zhou	*Chou*	周	Dynasty name (c. 1046–256 BCE)

2. Book titles

Pinyin	Wade-Giles	Chinese	Name or Description
Daodejing	*Tao-te ching*	道德經	The Book *or* Classic of the Way and its Power
Shijing	*Shih-ching*	詩經	The Book *or* Classic of Poetry
Shujing	*Shu-ching*	書經	The Book *or* Classic of History *or* Documents
Yijing	*I Ching* or *I-ching*	易經	The Book *or* Classic of Change(s)
Zhouyi	*Chou-I*	周易	The Zhou *or* Chou Change(s)

3. Terms and concepts

Pinyin	Wade-Giles	Chinese	Name or description
Chan	*Ch'an*	禪	Chan *or* Zen Buddhism
Dao	*Tao*	道	The Way, Nature
dao	*tao*	道	road, path
qi	*ch'i*	氣	energy, life force, *pneuma*, etc.
Taiji	*T'ai-chi*	太極	The Supreme Ultimate
Taiji or *Taiji quan*	*T'ai-chi* or *T'ai-chi ch'üan*	太極 *or* 太極拳	an 'internal' Chinese martial art
wuwei	*wu-wei*	無為	not striving, not overdoing
xin	*hsin*	心	heart, heart-mind

INDEXES

NOTES ON INDEXING

A book that explores correlative thinking, as this one does, necessarily requires correlative indexing. Since the patterning of *Changing* is modelled on the intricate correspondences and entanglements of the *I Ching*'s eight trigrams and sixty-four hexagrams, it is to be expected that multiple interconnections and intervolvements will be in play throughout this book. Combined with the Appendixes (339-349 above), the two indexes below identify some of these links, and thereby, hopefully, enable multiple modes of referencing.

In Index 1, terms, motifs and themes are cross-referenced with the names of trigrams and hexagrams in the *I Ching*, as well as with titles of similarly named poems in *Changing*. This first index is close-grained, detailed and multi-functional. The considerably simpler Index 2 (391-398) presents titles – first, of poem-clusters in *Changing*, and then, of its poem-titles. However, while RB's poem-cluster titles in *Changing* correspond in nearly all respects to the *I Ching*'s hexagram-names, and while text-references for hexagram-names and those of his cluster-titles overlap, the two categories are not absolutely identical. In fact, the latter are rooted in the former, just as *Changing* itself has grown out of the *I Ching*.

The hexagrams listed in Index 1 are limited to those mentioned in this book. Under the abbreviation 'Hex',[1] they are ordered numerically according to the 'received' (standard) sequence, followed by the name in Pinyin transliteration and the title or 'name-tag' in traditional Chinese characters (*fantizi*). These entries may be collocated with the comprehensive list of hexagrams in Appendix 2 (342-345 above), where their names are listed numerically, again according to the 'received' order, and again in traditional characters.

For trigrams, all eight are presented under the abbreviation 'Trig'. These are sequenced alphabetically in Pinyin, also followed by traditional Chinese characters, and are cross-referenced both with their corresponding hexagrams ('doubled trigrams') and with their diagrammatic presentation in Appendix 1 (341 above).

---

[1] Abbreviations used in Index 1 are listed at the beginning of this book. See p. x ('x' as the Roman numeral).

A small number of key Chinese terms appear. While these are listed alphabetically in Pinyin, some of these entries are cross-referenced in Wade-Giles transliteration too, in order to reflect contributors' preferred uses – as explained both in the Editorial Notes and Appendix 3 above (ix and 346, respectively). As for the entries in Index 1 that include Chinese script in addition to transliterations, either traditional or simplified characters may appear – and sometimes both in a single entry. Here too, the appearance of one or other variant (or both) depends on usages preferred by the book's contributors.

Index 2 provides two alphabetical lists of titles. The first (391-392) includes all the poem-clusters in *Changing* that are discussed, referenced or quoted in this book. The second (393-398) includes all the poems similarly mentioned, quoted or explored. Although this second index does not provide a comprehensive list of all 64 clusters and 450 poems in *Changing*, 41 clusters and 168 poems are referenced.

Editors

INDEX 1: GENERAL

< concentration camps; Nazi; Hex 36, 'Darkening'

Auschwitz, 41, 43, 117f, 149, 157, 167 n2; < Adorno; concentration camps; Nazi; Hex 36, 'Darkening'

auspicious, 21f, 93, 96f, 246, 261; < divination; favourable

bagua 八卦, 'eight trigrams', 341; < hex; trig; *cuogua*; *gua*; *guaming*; *zonggua*

balance, -ing, 74, 131ff, 135ff, 139, 142f, 219, 282, 318; /wholeness, 8, 130; between hex(s), 120; between oppositions/polarities, 8, 131, 133, 312; of body, 238, 240; of heaven, 245; self-checking, 158, 302; < binary; equilibrium; harmony; order (A); wholeness; *dao*; *Taiji*; *Taiji tu*; *yinyang*; *zhongdao*

Barrett, Michael, 6, 10f, 14, 243-256

base-line, 61, 108, 127, 133, 200, 204, 211, 218, 254; as metatext, 278; functions of, 237, 300

Baynes, Cary F., 27, 161; < Wilhelm /Baynes; trans. of *IC*

beauty, -iful, 40, 55, 62ff, 66f, 71, 79, 103, 150f, 241f, 281, 298, 300ff, 302, 307, 323; 'Beautiful September Morning' (*CH* 364), 62, 78 n6; 'Changing into Beautiful' (*CH* 163), 235; < delight; grace, glory; radiance; star; << Hex(s) 16; 22; 35; 55

beginning, 12, 109ff, 140, 278; /end, 63, 133, 136, 169f; /middle /end, 12, 316; /motherhood, 120; beginningless, 134, 136, 170; Biblical, 111f, 118; Hex 3, 'Beginning'; < birth; child; family; home; mother

Belsen, 167 n2; < concentration camps; Holocaust; Nazi; Hex 36, 'Darkening'

Benjamin, Walter, 9, 165, 181

Berengarten, Richard (*aka* Burns, *aka* Li Dao 李道) abbr. RB

(A) *miscellaneous*: celebratory, 42; European, 48; hospitable, 42; Jewish identity, 70; lineage, 59; major poet, 49; originality, 16, 112, 208, 271, 309; praise poet, 42, 241; religious, 5f, 38, 44, 53, 71; synchronicity in, 9, 188; 223 n7, 321; world poet, 249; < influences (C)

(B) *writings / projects*: *Albero*, 288 n3, 334; *Avebury*, 41 n1, 45, 307f, 313, 325; *Balkan Spaces*, 325; Balkan Trilogy, 320f; *Black Light*, 48 n2, 324, 332; *Blue Butterfly, The*, 51, 139, 198, 212, 284, 320ff; *Book With No Back Cover*, 13 n8, 131, 157, 176, 316f; 'Common Miracle, The', 79, 241, 322ff; 'Connectivity, Grounding and Amplification', 312; 'Following', 316; 'Grove of Trees and a Grove of Stones, A', 322; *Manager, The*, 37, 39, 45, 51, 57, 61 n6, 247, 313, 315, 317, 332; *Notness: Metaphysical Sonnets*, 223 n7; 224 n9, 282ff, 321ff; *Portrait in Inter-Views, A*, 44, 322f, 335; 'Synchronistic Experience in Serbia, A', 321f; 'Tree', 134, 212, 287, 288 n3; *Under Balkan Light,* 139, 323; < Burns; Li Dao; long poem

bi 比, 'analogy/comparison', 92, 351 n1; < Hex 8 (also *Bi*) 'According, Binding'; analogy; compare; *bixing*; *xiang*; *xing*

Bible, -ical: / *CH*, 167 n2, 172; / *IC*, 26f, 61 n6, 162, 314; /prophetic tradition; 167, /voice of silence, 119; Eden, 170; *Exodus*, 258; *Genesis*, 169f, 172, 174; "in the beginning", 112, 118; *Jeremiah*, 165, 174, 178ff, 182; *John*, 110,

bright, 19, 61f, 98, 208; 'Brightness Diffusing' (*CH* 518), 63, 74, 143; < dawn; glory; heaven; light; radiance; sky; star; sun; Hex 1, 'Initiating'; Trig *Qian*, 'Heaven'

broken, 95, 171 n9, 177, 257, 299; friendship, 171; harmony, 107-127; heart, 174; world, 55; < balance; line; order; revolution

broken/unbroken (solid) line (*yao* 爻), 8, 20, 131, 161, 163, 264, 283; < balance; equilibrium; hex; line; opposite; order (A); polarity; oneness; transformation; wholeness; *yinyang*

Bronze Age, 45, 155, 157, 246

Buber, Martin, 9, 174, 180, 333

Buchenwald, 112f ; < concentration camps; Holocaust; Nazi

Buddhism, -ist, 4, 11, 26, 71, 76, 78 n5; 121, 132, 238, 240, 349; koan / *Zen*, 84, 233, 240, < meditation; Xiao Yao

Buddhist IC, The, < Cleary

Burns, Richard (*aka* Berengarten), x, 4, 70 n2, 188 n2, 307; < Berengarten; Li Dao

Cage, John: / *IC*, 31, 155, 309, 311; aleatory, 312; displacement of self, 82; < chance; random

Cambridge, 15, 42, 47, 145, 156, 159, 160 n4, 242, 270 n1, 284, 307, 317, 321, 337; Pembroke (College), 287; Poetry Festival, 70 n2; poetry orthodoxy, 70 n2

Capra, Fritjof, *The Tao of Physics*, 155

Cardenal, Ernesto, *Cosmic Canticle*, 7, 106-129; broken (harmony, order), 112, 116f, 122, 124; Christian, 109, 111, 123; cosmic song, 110f; *Dao*, 109, 111, 123; dialectics, 110; harmony, 107ff;

liberation theology, 108 n9; Marxism, 7, 112ff; Nicaragua, 7, 108 n9, 113; violence, 108ff, 122ff; Weimar, 112ff; < cosmic; heart; Katz; Merton; praise; revolution; wholeness; *Dao*; *yinyang*; Hex 36, 'Darkening'; Hex 49, 'Shedding'

Casella, Stefano Maria, 134

central/middle path/way (*zhongdao* 中道), 127; < balance; base-line; equilibrium; harmony; *Dao*; *Taiji*; *Taiji tu*; *yinyang*

centre, 130, 220; centripetal/fugal, 321; home as, 213; nervous system, 84; of cosmic energy, 37f; of psyche, 217; well as c. of *IC*, 76, 194ff, 204, 259; 'Himself at the centre' (*CH* 33), 212f; < central path; core

Chan 禪 (pronounced *Zen* in Japanese) < *Zen*

chance (A) *aleatory*: 141; random: 47; aleatory, 312; /analogy/connectivity, 160, 308, 316; / Cage, 312; /divination with *IC*, 58, 83; /inscape/order, 39, 57; as portal to Tao, 291; Jungian version of, 162; leaven of, 288; meaning of, 287; net of, 296; odds of, 149; < acausal; Cage; coincidence; Hopkins; random; synchronicity; *Dao*

chance (B) *opportunity*: 142, "to see patterns/images of heaven", 73; to survive, 95

change, 5, 39, 42, 48, 78f, 111, 117, 126, 209, 225f 252, 255, 259, 262, 274, 282, 284, 303; *Bianhua* / *Zhuanhua*, 209; constants of, 306ff; cyclic, 209; into opposite, 209 n2; laws of, 223; oneself, 304 n24; radical, 107, 119 n13, 139, 209, 223; significance of, 139f; social, 127; spirit of, 270; winds of, 293; < *Book* (*Classic*) *of Change(s)*;

change-line; opposite; polarity; revolution; synchronicity; time; transformation; transience

change-line, 146ff, 150ff, 153, 209 n2, 263, 310; < hex; line

chaos, 149; /disorder, 113, 139; /order, 44; /*ruah* (breath, spirit), 170, 170 n8, 171; /word, 174, 174 n16; "unsealed", 179 n20

child(hood), 139, 142, 212, n4; 213, 268, 286; /language, 83; counting, 212; nourishing, 214; offspring, 94f; playing, 117; raising, 268; upbringing, 21; < birth; education; family; home; mother; Hex 3, 'Beginning'; Hex 4, 'Bringing up'

Chouraqui, André, 174, 182 n24

Christian(ity): in China 27, 333; poets, 44, 46; < Bouvet; Cardenal; Figurist; Jesuit; missionary

Chuang Tzu / Chuang-tzu / Chuang-tse / Zhuangzi 莊子 (*person*), 81, 123, 314, 347; (*book*), 348; < *Dao*; Daoism

Classics: < *Book of Changes*; *Book of Documents*; *Book of Music*; *Book of Rites*; *Book of Songs*; Confucius; '*I*' / *Yi*; *Zhouyi*

Cleary, Thomas, 289 n6, 291, 296 n13, 299, 301 n22; *Buddhist IC, The*, 301 n22; *Taoist IC, The*, 291, 301 n22; trans. of *IC*

cloud(s), 48, 98, 122, 140, 161, 177, 236, 241, 242, 280, 288; -less, 42; -puffs, 54; < rain; water; wind

cluster(s), 295; bundling, 280; imagem, 280; meaning, 10, 77, 314; of names/titles in *CH*, 12, 126, 342-346, 353, 391f, 393; (< gerund, -ing); of poems in *CH*, viii, 8, 9, 11, 12, 38, 58 n4, 98, 101, 107, 114ff, 119, 124, 131, 188,

191ff, 195, 198ff, 204ff, 212 n4, 214, 296, 301, 321, 324; of poetic skills, 319; < field (A); hex; imagem; non-linear; pattern; polysemy; set; suite; symbol; word

coherence, 15, 58ff; cosmic, 250f, 312; holistic, 73, 77, 308; in *IC*, 261, 264, 271, 315; in Paz, 160; in RB / *CH*, 56f, 58 n4, 60ff, 66ff, 73ff, 84, 143, 252, 261; meanings, 223, 261; of solid line, 283; original, primordial, 109, 118; "I cannot make it cohere" / "it coheres all right" (Pound), 39, 53, 57, 58, 66, 159; '(A) coherent language' (*CH* 190); 77, 117, 139, 167 n2, 211, 273f; 'Cohering, Inhering' (*CH* 7), 59, 73f, 135; 'Adhering, inhering' (*CH* 441), 135; < entanglement; harmony; oneness; order (A); pattern; synchronicity; wholeness

coincidence, -ental, 47, 141, 188, 189, 325; *coincidentia oppositorum*, 130, 130 n1; meaningful, 14, 47, 132, 316, 320, 324; < acausal; chance; Jung; Main; meaning(s) (A/B/C); synchronicity

collective unconscious, 141 n2, 190, 199; < archetype; Jung; Main; synchronicity

Communism, -ist, 28, 113

community, -al, 61, 65, 113f, 124, 126, 195, 217, 259, 262, 267, 297; < family, friend(s); kin

compare, -ison; 32; 82; *CH* / *Cosmic Canticle,* 7, 107-129; *CH* / *IC*, 105ff, 244; *CH* / Oliver, 60 n5; *CH* / mosaic, 13, 13 n8, 318; *CH* / *Of Being Numerous*, 6; *CH* / *Paterson*, 273; *CH* / other writings by RB, 317ff, 320ff; hex titles in *CH* /trans. of *IC*, 146; *IC* / computer code, 29; *IC* / well, 261ff;

cosmic, -os, -ology, 37, 40, 44, 161,
203; change, 111; Chinese, 23,
39, 47, 81; creativity, 39; dance,
312; design, 250; energy, 37f;
harmony, 112; in *CH* / *IC*, 3, 8,
11, 30, 38, 47, 71, 81f; 172, 193,
208f, 221ff, 234, 245f, 250, 291,
249ff, 251ff, 263f, 291, 297f,
311f; in Jewish tradition, 166,
169, 171; in Jung, 203 n9, 204;
measure, 250f; order/coherence,
221, 312, 251, 312; < Cardenal, *Cosmic Canticle*; correlative
cosmos-building; microcosm
/macrocosm
creatures, 100, 102, 110, 112, 131,
142, 180, 220, 165; dragon, 98,
211; worms, 177, 235; < animals;
birds; insects
crossing, across, 141, 216, 251, 295f,
cultures, 7, 105; frontiers, 15; the
road, 142; water/river, 21, 142,
147, 293, 295f, 303, 303 n23;
< Hex 63, 'After crossing over';
Hex 64, 'Before crossing over'
Cultural Revolution, 3, 121
cuogua 錯卦, 'counter-changed hex',
119, 119 n13; < hex; trig; *gua*;
zonggua

Dazhuan 大傳, 'Great Treatise, The',
193
Dao / *dao* (also *Tao* / *tao*) 道, 11, 37ff,
82, 111, 193, 231ff, 288ff, 293,
299 n20, 314, 333, 349; /heart,
212; /poetry, 297; /primordial
oneness, 109; chance as portal to,
291 n 9; cosmic, 30; energy of,
39; Great, 222f; *IC* /, 193, 208f,
291 n9; in *CH* / RB, 66, 209,
224, 231f, 303, 324; meanings
of, 71; sincerity of, 123; web/
weave of, 297, 301; *Tao of Phys-*

ics, The (Capra), 155; 'Zen of
the Tao, The' (Trist, DeVine),
13, 286-305; < balance; central
path; Daoism; harmony; Nature;
Way; *Daodejing*; Lao Zi; *Taiji tu*;
yinyang; *zhongdao*; Zhuangzi
Daodejing / *Tao te ching* 道德經, 73,
109, 282, 286, 299 n20, 348;
< Cleary; *Dao*; Daoism; Laozi;
Zhuangzi
Daoism/Taoism, -ist (*Daojia* 道家),
1, 26, 71, 100, 220; 236; 347,
349; /analogical thinking, 38f,
90, 187, /central way, 130; / *IC*,
4, 291, 30 n22, 315; /landscape
painting, 297; /meditation, 238;
/nothingness, 282, 282 n2; /phys-
ics/quantum mechanics, 40, 287
n14; /*qingtan* 'witty discourse',
288 n4; in Cardenal, 123; in Paz,
159; influence on/presence in RB,
6, 8, 11, 37, 71, 73f, 80ff, 84, 99,
130ff, 314, 323; < Cleary; Huang;
Lao Zi; Nature; Way; Zhuangzi;
Dao; *Daodejing*
daoyin 導引, a Chinese form of
physical/mental cultivation, 99;
< *qigong*; *taijiquan*
dāvār דבר (*Hebr* 'word)', 175, 166;
/ *ruah* ('wind, spirit'), 9, 173ff,
181; < Bible; Judaism; Kabbalah;
prophecy; Sneller; speech; spirit;
spirituality; wind; word
dawn, 61, 113, 241, 243; < bright;
glory; light; radiance; sky; sun;
Hex 35, 'Dawning'; << Hex 1,
'Initiating'; Trig *Qian*, 'Heaven'
death, 41ff, 81f, 100ff, 139, 140, 157
172, 243, 265; /heroism, 149;
"breath of", 172, 296; Daoist
attitude to, 99ff; -call, 80; -mak-
ers, 118; defeat of, 123; fear of,
181, 192f; life/, 8, 19, 42, 45,

121, 130ff, 140, 149; inevitability of, 61 n6; mortality, 73, 79, 135; of friends, 71, 79

delight(ful), 79, 115, 137, 157, 177, 241, 301, 317, 323f; "energy is eternal delight" (Blake), 39; heart's, 174, 178; < beauty; glory; miracle; radiance; Hex 16, 'Delighting'; << Hex 22, 'Grace Adorning'; Hex 55, 'Abounding, Brimming'

Delphic Oracle, 12 n6, 319; < divination; Herodotus; oracle; sacrifice; << Hex 50, 'Cooking, Sacrificing'

Derrick, Paul Scott, ix, 5f, 10, 11, 51-68, 69 n1, 148 n1, 241, 241 n2, 243, 331f; 'An unexpected European Voice', 241

Derrida, Jacques, 9, 71, 165f, 169 n7, 336

DeVine, Bob, 13f, 72 n4, 266 n3, 286-305, 331; < Trist

Di 地 ('Earth' as cosmic principle/power), 209; < Earth/earth; Hex 2, 'Responding, Corresponding'; Trig *Kun*, 'Earth; << Heaven/heaven; *Tian*

'Diagram of the Supreme Ultimate' (*Taiji tu* 太極圖), 132; < balance; cosmic; Daoism; harmony; oneness; polarity; *Supreme Ultimate*; Way; *Dao*; *Taiji*

Dick, Philip K., 32, 155

Dickinson, Emily, 54, 331; < well

disorder, 19, 74, 113, 139; < chaos; order (A)

divination, diviner, 92, 96, 181, 267, 277, 297, 313, 315, 333; / *IC*, 1, 3, 8f, 12f, 24f, 28, 47, 72f, 78, 89, 145, 148, 286, 308, 310, 313; 317ff; /prophecy, 53, 181; do-it-yourself, 155; history of, 19-34; *IC*, world's most revered book of, 195; method/procedure,

177, 234, 310, 315; poems in *CH* based on, 131, 156, 311, 314, 316, 320; < consulting; fortune, oracle

divinity, divine, 165, 170, 170 n8, 215; word, 174, 177f; < Bible; God; spirit; *dāvār*; *ruah*

doubled trigram (applying to 'paired' hex[s]: 1/2, 29/30, 51/52, 57/58), 215, 341ff, 353; < hex, trig

dream, 38, 114, 226; /destiny, 226; / soul/psyche, 212, 217; day-, 103; in *CH*, 108, 179, 294; -land, 120; in *Jeremiah*, 180, 182; in Jung, 188, 212, of a spring, 214; -time, 179; synchronicity, 179

Du Fu, 159, 222

Duo Duo, 159, 334

Dylan, Bob, 32, 155

Earth, earth(ly), 6 , 74, 112, 114, 124, 139, 161, 225, 235, 239, 292, 341; /heaven, 5, 30, 37f, 48, 63, 73, 81, 193, 202f, 209, 212, 216, 221, 224, 243, 246, 249ff, 251f, 279; /sky/skies, 179f, 242; as *Di* (cosmic principle/power), 209; mother, 44, 278f; earthiness, 198; 'Earth' (*CH* 14), 74; < *yin*; Hex 2, 'Responding, Corresponding'; Trig *Kun*, 'Earth'; << Heaven /heaven; *Tian*

education, 214, 268; discipline in, 267; Eastern, 225; primary, 213; < child; Hex 4, 'Bringing up'

ego, 197f; /identity, 199; blights poetry, 45; contamination by, 52; diminution of, 81; dissolving, 239, 241; dominant, 197; interference of, 46; < Self/self

Eliot, T. S.: *Four Quartets*, 46; / Pound, 39, 158, 159 n3, 307; influence on RB, 102f, 105; "objective correlative", 102, 104,

191, 319; 'Tradition and the Individual Talent', 16; < Pound

Emerson, Ralph Wardo, 59, 62, 64ff, 66 n8; *Nature*, 55f

energy, -etic: 8, 10, 39, 80, 93, 109, 127, 131, 145f, 223, 242, 282, 288, 323, 349; as violence, 109; cosmic/heavenly/universal, 37f, 46; dark, 250; generative, 46; harmonious, 291; natural, 49; of Tao, 39; original, 65; physical, 46; poetic, 8, 10, 319; primal, 46; sexual, 40, 93; spiritual, 46; < breath; fire; flow; spirit; thunder; water; wave; wind; *pneuma*; *qi, ruah*

entanglement, 1, 14, 134, 136, 254, 287, 287 n2, 290, 297, 353; < cohere; quantum; synchronicity

equilibrium, 19, 44, 74, 131ff, 140; /meaning, 57; broken, 7, 112, 122, 124; cosmic, macro-, 221, 225, 312; dynamic, 39, 57, 59, 64, 112, 122, 125, 135, 137ff, 174, 248, 250, 253, 299 n20; existential, 123; in being, 27, 48; moral, 112; natural, 208, 222; return of, 136; social, 248; < balance; harmony; order (A); polarity; wholeness; *Dao; Taiji tu; yinyang; Zhong dao*; Hex 11, 'Harmonising, Prospering'

eternal, -ity, 200, 251; beauty, 55, 62; constancy, 223; cosmic dance, 312; cycle, round, 41, 225; "energy is eternal delight" (Blake), 39; entangled, 297 n14; forms, 236; light/darkness, 57, 114; now, 47; Tao, 297

etymology (-ical), 54, 169, 180, Chinese, 10, 210, 220, 222; < meaning(s) (C); origin; word

fabric: of poems, 43; of things under light, 79, 324; *úphasma*, 325; 'Fabric of the human orgasm', 172 n12; 119; < stuff

family, 43, 70 n2, 71, 151ff, 213; as *jia*, 213; daughter, 43, 93, 119, 236, 278; father, 152; husband, 20, 91f, 95ff, 152; parent, 94, 222; patriarchal, 92, 152f; relationships, 20; son, 152; roles, 152; upbringing, 214; wife, 12 n9, 114, 247f; < beginning; birth; child; home; mother; Hex 37, 'Dwelling, Householding; Hex 3, 'Beginning'; Hex 4, 'Bringing up'

fantizi 繁體字, traditional characters / 'old script', viii, 209, 346, 353f; examples of, 10, 221f; < simplified characters; *jiantizi*

favorable, 21, 22, 95; < auspicious; divination

fenghuang 鳳凰 (mythical bird), 102; < phoenix

field (A) *conceptual*: 70, 72, 204; algebra, 29; diagrams, 196f; as discipline/specialism, 4, 24f, 309; linguistic, 14; model/pattern of composition, 12, 12 n7, 15f, 15 n9; of action, 291; of hex, 299; of interpretation/meaning, 17, 174; organization, 265; poetics, i, 12 n7, 15, 15 n9; poetry, influence on RB, 16; of synchronicity, 189, 289, 294; of text, 14, of time, 37, 47, 169, 179, 180; of time/space, 95; of vision, 15; sequential, 75, 145, 313; trans-subjective, 284; < cluster; composition; imagem; mosaic; non-narrative; Olson; poetics; polysemic; set; suite; space; spatiality; structure; symbol

field (B) *physical*: 47, 65, 147, 198, 259; battle-, 137; electromagnetic, 250; on fire, 167; soaked, sodden, 280, 295; terraced, 162; 194; 'Fields frost' (*CH* 40), 280; < well-field social system (*jingtian*)

Figurist, 26-27; < Bouvet; Christian; Jesuit; missionary

fire, 102, 121, 167, 188, 215f, 216 n6, 243, 254, 279, 300, 319, 341; air/, 98; /phoenix, 102; inexhaustible, 45f, 122; "*No fire flames once,*" 61, water/, 30, 108, 279; word like, 174, 178; < flame; *qi*; Hex 30, 'Clinging'; Trig *Li*, 'Fire'

Five Agents (*wuxing* 五行), 22

flame, 61ff, 64, 167, 279; in the heart, 254; < fire; *qi*; Hex 30, 'Clinging'; Trig *Li*, 'Fire'

flood, 60, 171 n9, 279, 281, 292, 294; above trees, 279; dark, of chaos, 170f, 179 n20; great flood (*Gilgamesh*), 257; lake, 300; of time, 47, 281; river, 142, 295; 'Floods' (*CH* 230), 295, 296; < flow; lake; *qi*; rain; storm; water; Hex 28, 'Overbrimming'

flow, 5, 28, 37, 48, 60, 66f, 217, 281f; empathetic, 10, 220; energy, 145; grace, 242; *IC* as "solid yet flowing", 37, 49, 76, 200, 260; information, 72; inspiration, 172; over-, 40, 136; river, 257, 295; spatial/temporal, 281; stream, 141; sympathetic, 10, 220; time, 47, 197, 281, 321; water, 201f, 217, 257, 261, 280; < breath; heart/heart-mind; stream; time; *qi*; Hex 57, 'Blowing, Billowing'; << Hex 28, 'Overbrimming'

flower, 60, 91, 245, 332; arranging, 23; campanula, 60; elderflower, 43, 151; gorse, 163; hibiscus, 60; orchids, 60; sun-, 64, 143; tulip, 242; Thomas, "The force that through the green fuse drives the flower", 46

follow(ing), 100, 210; a divination, 131; a hero, 149; /in *IC* / hex(s), 89f, 108, 116, 160, 176, 193, 302; balance of heaven, 245; Chinese worldview, 109; *Dao / Tao*, 66, 314; inspiration, 265; "other voices", 175; the heart, 117, 210f, 217f, 271, 274; the wind, 303; whims, 152; 'Following' (in RB, *Book With No Back Cover*, 13-51), 316; < Hex 17, 'Following'

forest, 104, 239, 245, 287; rain-, 288 n3; < tree; wood

fortune/misfortune, 91, 93, 96f, 147, 151; < auspicious; divination

fractal, 15, 311, 318

friend(s), -ship, 59, 94, 103, 161; affirmation of, 71; /family, 42; /love, 208 n 1; bread of, 171, 176f; Cardenal/Merton, 123, 123 n16; covenant of, 171; death of, 71, 78f, 140; *IC* as, 76, 200, 260, 286 n1, 288; in *CH*, 100, 142, 163; of Jung, 188, 219, 320; RB / Nikolaou, 121; RB / others, 161; RB / Paz, 69, 308f; RB / Yang, 160; 'My Friend Walt Whitman' (Wilson), 65; < community; family; kinship; love

fu 孚, 'sincere, trustworthy', 22; < sincerity; trust

Fu Xi 伏羲 / Fu Hsi 伏犧, 161, 235, 347

gan 感, 'influence', 218, 220ff; < heart; heartfelt influence; influence; *ganying*; *xin*; Hex 31, 'Reciprocating'

ganying 感應, 'mutual influence, sensory stimulus/response, induction', 222; < heart; heartfelt influence; *gan*; *xin*; Hex 31, 'Reciprocating'; << correlative

118, 127, 153, 171 n9, 175, 178, 208-228, 301; in *IC*, 10, 29; in *Jeremiah*, 174, 178; in Oliver, 147; injunctions/path of, 117, 211, 274; of fire, 121; of heaven /earth, 212; open, 127; seed in /from the, 210, 214, 218; solitude of the, 118; stimulation of the, 231, 349; thinking with the, 219; wisdom of the, 208; 'Poetry, Heart and Soul' (Shen), 208-228; < core; mind; heal; heartfelt influence; heartsickness, Shen, *xin* (A); *xin* (B); << *gan*; *ganying*

heartfelt influence, 218, 220ff; < core; heart/heart-mind; heartsickness; sincere; < *gan*; *ganying*; *xin* (A/B); *xinbing*; Hex 31, 'Reciprocating'

heartsickness (*xinbing* 心病), 30; < anxiety; *you*; Hex 29, 'Falling (in a pit)' ; << Shen; *yongxin*; *yu*

Heaven/heaven(ly), 79, 146, 171 n9, 235, 241, 279, 300, 301, 303; /earth, 5, 30, 37f, 48, 63, 73, 169, 193, 202f, 212, 216, 221, 224, 243, 246, 249ff, 252, 279, 341; / Hell, 44; /man/humanity, 30, 246; as *Tian* (cosmic principle/power) 209; balance of, 245; bodies, 111, 252; "endless beginningless", 136, 170; "-filling", 94; in Robert Frost, 54; Way / Tao of, 19, 193, 291 n9; '*Heaven*' (*CH* 4), 133f, 170; 'Heaven-stuff' (*CH* 445), 81, 251; < bright; glory; light; radiance; sky; star; sun; Hex 1, 'Initiating'; Trig *Qian* << Earth/ earth; *Di*

Heidegger, Martin, 6, 51ff, 54ff, 61f, 66, 80; *Science and Reflection*, 52

Herodotus, 12 n6, 319; < Delphic Oracle; oracle; sacrifice

hexagram(s), abbr. Hex/hex(s), viii, 20ff, 353, 391, 393; cosmology, 24, 250, 263f; cluster; 58; Mawangdui sequence, 276; meaning(fulness), 20, 113, 313; name (< *guaming*), 20, 353, 391; received order/sequence, viii, 19f, 353; structure, 20; tables (of all 64), 342-345; titles in *CH*, 12, 126, 342-345; 353; trans. of titles: 126, 299 n18, 352-345; < doubled trig; field (A); geometry; gerund; judgment; Mawangdui; order (B); translations of *IC*; trig; Wilhelm/Baynes; *bagua*; *cuogua*; *gua*; *guaming*; *tuan*; *xici*; *yao*; *yaoci*; *zonggua*

Hex 1, *Qian* 乾, 'Initiating', 8, 133, 169, 215f; < '*Heaven*' (*CH* 4), 133; << Trig (also *Qian*) 'Heaven/ Sky'; bright; dawn; doubled trig; glory; heaven; light; radiance; sky; star; sun; *yang*

Hex 2, *Kun* 坤, 'Responding, Corresponding', 20, 139, 215, 216, 251, 342; < 'Earth' (*CH* 14), 74; << Trig (also *Kun*) 'Earth'; doubled trig; earth; mother; *Di*; *yin*

Hex 3, *Zhun* 屯, 'Beginning', 120, 278, 342; < beginning; birth; child; family; home; pregnancy

Hex 4, *Meng* 蒙, 'Bringing Up', 212ff, 267f, 342; constituent trigs, 212, 219; /dream, 214; /heart, 214; < child; education; family; home

Hex 8, *Bi* 比, 'According, Binding', 29, 342; < affinity; analogy; compare; correlative cosmos-building; correspondence; inspiration; *bi*; *bixing*; *xing*

Hex 9, *Xiao Xu* 小畜, 'Small Blessing, Possessing', 146, 342

Hex 10, *Lü* 履, 'Treading', 20, 21,

290, 215; of *yinyang*, 299 n20; of youth, 214; < analogy; archetype; correspondence; image (B/C); imagem; imagination; metaphor; symbol; *bixing*; *xiang*; *xiang siwei*; *xiangshu*; *xianxiang*

image, imagery (B) *in CH*: 8, 11, 47, 93, 105, 114, 120, 166f, 170, 180 n23, 196, 197, 200ff, 215, 226, 267, 280, 301; /analogical/associational thinking (*bixing*), 91, 93; frequencies/key/recurrent motifs in, 10, 278; Homeric, 143; *IC* "radiating images", 37, 76, 200, 260; of a *hamsah*, 116f; of an egg, 136 of birds, 95, 98, 102, 270; of black light, 48; of fluttering, 174; of *Genesis*, 170; of harmony, 119; of heaven, 73, 171 n9, 216, 300; of light, 300; of lovers, mingling/interbreeding, 119, 166; of moon, 42; of seafaring, 100; of Tao, 301, 303; of water, 281, 300; of well, 54, 194, 262; of well/star, 202f; of wind/waves, 172 n12; of *zhong*, 130; on cover of *CH*, 270; < analogy; archetype; correspondence; image (A/C); imagem; imagination; metaphor; symbol; *bixing*; *xiang*; *xiang siwei*; *xiangshu*; *xianxiang*

image, imagery (C) *miscellaneous*: 54, 267, 278-279; /Fu Hsi, 235; /heart, 210ff, 213, 225, 226; /inspiration, 264; /Jung, 11, 190, 209, 214, 217, 222; archetype, -al, 30, 190, 197, 200, 209, 211f, 214; Chinese, 104; of boat, 217; of Dao/Tao, 222, 286, 301, 303; of healing, 217; of parenting, 222; of poet, 190; of seed, 210; Paz on, 42; Pound on, 104, 105; < analogy; correspondence; image (A/B); imagem; imagination;

metaphor; symbol; *bixing*; *xiang*; *xiang siwei*; *xiangshu*; *xianxiang*

imagem, 6, 41 n1, 76, 278, 280f; < cluster; field (A); image (A/B/C); intuition; metaphor; polysemy, symbol; word; *bixing*; *xiang*; *xiang siwei*; *xiangshu*; *xianxiang*

imagination, 38, 54, 59, 313; poetic, 11, 290, 308; Romantic idea of, 38; scientists on, 31; < correlative cosmos-building; image (A/B/C); inspiration; intuition; *bixing*; *xiang*; *xiang siwei*; *xiangshu*; *xianxiang*

Imagism, 49, 104

immanent, -ence, 174, 200, 237, 279; /transcendence, 168 n4, 190f, 199, 203; < harmony; transcend(ent)

infinity, -ite, 56, 123, 136, 157, 223, 270 n1, 290, 322 < number; space

influence (A) *heartfelt, via heart*: 219ff, mutual/reciprocal/two-way, 132, 139, 218-222; < heart; heartfelt; trust; truth; *gan*; *ganying*; *xin*; Hex 31, 'Reciprocating'; << Hex 61, 'Inner Trusting'

influence (B) *of IC / Chinese culture*: 1, 23ff, 285; in East Asia, 25ff, 28; in the West, 30ff, 306

influence (C) *on RB / CH*: 142, 307f; Chinese, 70 n2, 99, 284; countercultural, 37; dominant, 16; Italian, 70 n2; of *IC* on *CH*, 17, 284, 307, 311; of symbolists, modernists, surrealists, 102: open to, 11; Slavic / Yugoslav, 70 n2; < Blake; Daoism; Eliot; Greece; Hopkins; Jewish; Olson; Paz; Pound; Romantics; Russell; Seferis; Wordsworth; Zen

influence (D) *miscellaneous*: non-
local, 287 n2; of "a cosmic
order", 221; of *qi* on poetry, 10;
of social, political, cultural shifts,
in China, 28; of the *IC* question,
240; of wind, 279ff

inscape, 39, 43, 57, 235; Hopkins;
instress;

insects, 177, 235; butterfly, 242;
scarab beetle, 188; < RB, *Blue
Butterfly, The*

inspiration, -spire, 167, 172, 222,
226, 263, 283, 298, 321; /soul,
336-337; /synchronicity, 336f;
creative, 89f, 105, 172; literary,
23; - comparison (*bixing*), 7, 90ff;
of Chinese culture/tradition, 66,
109, 271; of hex(s), 93ff, 133f;
288; of *IC / Zhouyi*, 25, 31, 70,
89f, 92, 105, 155, 166, 169, 181,
193, 209, 222, 268, 271, 289; of
Jewish prophetic tradition, 166ff;
poetic/in poetry, 51, 89f, 197 n6,
226, 264f, 321; < breath; image
(A/B/C); imagination; influence;
intuition; prophecy; soul; spirit;
spirituality; *bi*; *bixing*; *xiang*; *xiang
siwei*; *xiangshu*; *xianxiang*; *xing*

instress, 64; Hopkins; inscape;

intuition, -ive, -iveness, 4, 6, 55f,
119, 190, 195, 199, 222, 236, 316;
/the heart, 222; as 'image-thinking'
(< *xiang siwei*), 31, 31 n13; of the
poet, 213; < imagem; imagination

Jabès, Edmond, 157, 166, 166 n1

Japan(ese), 28, 140; 303 n23; martial
arts, 282 n2; poets, 159; spread of
IC to, 4, 25, 26, 26 n7

Jesuit, 25, 26, 27, 161, 250; < Bouvet; missionary

Jew(s), Jewish, 37, 78 n5, 165f, 166
n1, 167, 174, 180; /identity in/

influence on RB / *CH*, 9, 37, 45,
70 n2, 71, 166f, 167 n2, 236,
245, 307; *CH* as Jewish/Buddhist,
78 n5; *CH* as Sino-Jewish, 169;
Jewish identity not pinpointable,
166; mysticism, 45; persecution
of, 115, 137f; philosophy, 182;
prophecy, 9, 165-183, 197 n6;
< Benjamin; Bible; concentration
camps; God; Holocaust; Judaism;
Kabbalah; Neher; Sneller; *dāvār*;
ruah; *tikkun*

jia 家, 'home, family', 213; < family;
home; Hex 37, *Jia Ren*, 'Dwelling,
Householding'

jiantizi 簡體字, simplified characters
/ 'new script', viii, 209, 346; 353f;
examples of, 10, 221, 222; < traditional characters; *fantizi*

jingtian 井田, 'well-field' (socio-
economic system), 191

Johnson, B. S., *The Unfortunates*, 315,
317; < book-in-a-box; field (A);
loose-leaf; non-linear

Jope, Norman, 5, 139

joy(ful), enjoy(ing), 8, 94, 96, 110,
125, 131ff, 157, 174, 178, 288,
309, 345; < Hex 58, 'Joying,
Enjoying'

Judaism, Judaic, 9, 166, 167; < God;
Jew, Jewish; Kabbalah; prophecy;
spirituality; *dāvār*; *ruah*; *tikkun*

judgment/statement/decision (*tuan*
彖), 20; < hex

Jung, C. G, 11, 14, 90, 141, 187-228;
/correlative thinking, 9, 188, 189
n4; / *IC*, 9f, 29f, 38, 47f, 130,
161, 196, 197 n6, 209, 211, 214,
222, 225f, 286 n1, 297 n16, 298,
n17, 320f, /love, 41, 110, 118; /
Mountain Lake, 219; / Pauli, 287
n2, 320; /truth, 7, 108, 124; *coincidentia oppositorum*, 130, 130 n1;

influence on RB, 8, 9, 44f, 130ff, 141, 187, 191ff, 200ff, 205, 214f, 226, 307ff, 308, 320ff, 324ff; on justice, 108, 248; on religion, 44f; on the mandala, 203, n9; on therapy/analysis, 10, 217f; on Wilhelm / *IC*, 297 n16; *Interpretation of Nature and the Psyche, The*, 320; *Mysterium Conjunctionis*, 130 n1; *Red Book, The*, 212; < archetype; collective unconscious; dream(s); Jungian; synchronicity; synkairicity; syntopicity; *unus mundus*

Jungian, 1, 10, 16, 29, 161f, 217, 335f; interpretations of *CH*: Main, 9f, 187-207; Shen, 10f, 29, 208-228; < Baynes; Kalff; Wilhelm; << *yongxin* ('Jungian therapy'); *yu* ('healing')

Kabbalah, -istic, 7, 9, 11, 118, 171 n10, 233, 245; < God; Jewish; Judaism; mend; *dāvār*; *ruah*; *tikkun*
kairos, 324, 325; < synkairicity; time
Kalff, Dora (sandplay), 217, 218
Kant, Immanuel, 162
Karcher, Stephen, 289 n6, 290, 293, 296 n13, 297 n16, 299 nn18/19, 301 n22; < trans. of *IC*
Katz, Sophia (Ke Shufei 柯書斐), ix, 7f 12 n5, 107-129, 333; < Cardenal; harmony
Keats, John, negative capability, 6, 11, 233ff
Kierkegaard, 168; < heartsickness; << Hex 29, 'Falling (in a pit)'
kinship: *CH* / *IC*, 72, 80; voices, 175; < family; friend(s)
King Wen sequence/received order, 266; < hex; order (B); *gua*
Klein, Lucas (Ke Xiazhi 柯夏智), ix, 8f, 155-164; 334
Kongfuzi 孔夫子 < Confucius

Ko Un 高銀 (Korean poet), 248
Korea, 28; martial arts, 282 n2; spread of *IC* to, 4, 25, 26, 26 n7
K'ung-fu-tzu < Confucius

lake, 108, 146, 157, 163, 218f, 221, 236, 243, 279f, 300ff; /mountains, 8, 155ff, 158, 218f, 302; Lake District, 157; of language, 83; '*A lake on a mountain*' (*CH* 248), 133, 158, 218f, 301f; 'The lake rises above the trees' (*CH* 224), 160, 279, 281, 294, 302; '*Two lakes, joined*' (*CH* 464), 8, 131ff, 156f, 163, 310f; < marsh; Mountain Lake; Hex 58, 'Joying, Enjoying'; Trig *Dui*, 'Lake, Marsh; << flood; flow; water; Hex 28, 'Overbrimming'
Lao Zi / Laozi / Lao Tzu 老子, 71, 73, 282, 347; < *Dao; Daodejing*; Daoism; Way
Lazer, Hank, ix, 6, 11, 12, 14, 56, 69-85, 334
Legge, James, 27
Leibniz, Gottfried Wilhelm, 27, 27 n8, 16, 250; < binary; opposite; *yinyang*
Levinas, Emmanuel, 9, 182
Lévi-Strauss, Claude, 309
Li Dao 李道, 209; < Berengarten; Burns
light (A) *uncountable*: 278, 282, 286; /beauty, 242; /darkness, 110, 123f, 147; day-, 147; eternal, 57; fund of, 201f, 260; in *CH*, 63f, 66, 74, 79, 82, 108, 119, 122, 125, 133f, 140, 142f, 150f, 240, 242f, 261, 300f, 318, 324; morning, 114; of understanding, 56; rat-, 142; spokes of, 54; striations on water, 177, 235; sun-, 63, 143, 262, 279; twi-, 226; web of,

22; hidden/beyond words, 31, 31 n13; *IC* as generator/distributor of meanings, 313; in Confucian commentary, 244; in hex(s)/line statements, 20f, 95f, 107 133, 151f, 212 n4, 214, 215, 216, 219ff, 268, 291, 299; in the *Ten Wings*, 22; literary/cosmological, 263f; mysterious, 301, 315; of Hex 4, *Meng*, 214; of Hex 29, *Kan*, 215; of Hex 48, *Jing*, 259ff; of *Yi* 易 graph/title, 12, 223, 289 n7, 312; personal, 292; spiritual, 299 n20

meaning(s) (B) *in CH / RB*: 59, 62, 65, 119, 133, 137ff, 158, 169, 197, 200, 279; 298, 301; /order, 57; as *logopoeia*, 311; as non-contiguous connectivity, 14; complexities/layers of, 15, 65; far-reaching, 226; "hidden in words", 77; image of ship, crushed, 171; in bodymind spirituality, 45; in *Book With No Back Cover*, 316; in *scintillae*, 283; in 'Welling' (cluster 48), 191ff, 197, 200, 202; -ful(ness), 14, 117; of *Bianhua / Zhuanhua*, 209, 209 n 2; of chance, 287; polysemic/mult-iple/uncertain, 14, 209, 224, 279, 314f; "wait for meanings to grow", 77, 177, 238, 314f

meaning(s) (C) *miscellaneous*: /accurate seeing, 244; /entangle-ment, 14; /'heart'/'heart' radical, 209f, 214, 217f, 220f, 225; /reflection (Heidegger), 52; as pattern-finding, 13; clusters of, in Chinese words, 10; Confucius on, 244; fields of, 174; in Cardenal, 113; in Emerson, 55, 59, 62; -ful coincidence (in synchronicity), 14, 47, 132, 188ff, 200, 202, 316, 320, 324; -ful life, lives, 113,

283; -less(ness), 45, 114, 116; objective, 189f, 197, 200, 202; of *bo*, 114; of *dāvār*, 173f, 174 n18; of *ganying*, 222; of *geming*, 107; of *I am against*, 182; of *kairos*, 324; of *pu*, 254; of *religio*, 44; of *ruah*, 167ff, 174, 174 n18; of *svemir*, 61; of *Tao*, 71; of think/thank, 80; of *tikkun*, 118; of *wu*, 282 n2; of *zhong*, 130; transcenden-tal, 190; < etymology; field (A); image (A/B/C), Jung, polysemy; symbol; synchronicity; word

measure(ment), 58, 70 n2, 74, 127, 182, 192, 242, 250f; < order (B); random; sequence

meditation, -ative, 6, 47, 51, 82, 99, 111, 143, 219, 239ff, 244, 260, 311; / *IC*, 233f, 240; Buddhist / Zen, 80, 238; Daoist / Taoist, 6, 81, 238ff; images, 235; 'Medita-tion at Majdanek' (*CH* 288), 42; < contemplation; reflection; Hex 33, 'Retreating'; << Hex 52, 'Stilling'

mend, 7, 55, 60, 95, 114ff, 118, 122ff, 185, 245; /change the real, 78, 117, 139, 255, 274; beauty, 62; society, 199, 201; the fallen, 78; the well, 198f, 201, 204, 217; the world, 125, 171 n10; < heal; *tikkun*; Hex 23, 'Peeling'

Merton, Thomas, 123, 123 n16

metaphor, -orical, 22, 246, 291ff, 295f; /metonymy, 236; as yoke, 53; of the well, 12, 202ff, 262; of water, 257; of wind, 278-280; total, 104; 'twisted' (< conceit; *quyu*), 103; < affinity; analogy; conceit; correlative cosmos-building; correspondence; image (A/B/C); imagem; symbol; word; << poetics; *bi*; *bixing*; *xing*; Hex 8, 'According, Binding'

narrative: Biblical, 167 n2, 169; of *IC*'s origins, 161f; RB's rejection of, 307; < Aristotle; Fu Xi; non-narrative; order (B); sequence; structure; time

Nature/nature, 46; /energy, 46, 49, 282; /heart, 147; /mind/imagination, 38, 61; /number, 249; /physics/science, 52, 287; /psyche, 172, 320; as stranger, 54; as *Dao*, 19, 37, 39, 349; at home, 242; ever-changing, 270; form of, 19; Great, 303; in American writers, 54ff; in *IC*, 19ff, 23ff, 46, 217, 226, 268, 279ff; in RB / *CH*, 46, 48, 65, 69, 76, 81, 84, 100, 134, 149, 224, 312; law/order, 149, 208; mastery/power over, 48, 52; Mother, 278; numinous, 241; observation of, 46; of change, 284; of consciousness, 71f; of heaven/earth/reality, 190, 204, 221; of perception, 59; of social memory, 248; of water/stone, 303; patterns of, 161, 177; poet/, 46, 148; power of, 257; prophetic, 173; psyche/, 173, 320; reason/, 303 n23; Taoist, 81, 84; teleonomy in, 302; trust of/unity with, 82, 127; *Nature* (Emerson), 55; < animal; creatures; Way; Whitman; Wordsworth; *Dao*

Nazi, 8, 42, 113, 115, 125, 321; < atrocity; concentration camps; Holocaust; Hex 36, 'Darkening'

Needham, Joseph, 14

negative capability < Keats

Neher, André, *L'Essence du prophétisme*, 9, 166ff, 168 n5, 170, 170 n8, 172 n13, 173f, 174 nn15-18, 181

Nikolaou, Paschalis, i, ix, 3-18, 53, 59, 121, 188 n2, 198, 200 n7, 266 n2, 306-328, 335

non-linear(ity), 11f; in *CH,* 12, 12 n 7, 13; order/reading, 313, 317; vision, 15; < book-in-a-box; cluster; field (A); line; loose-leaf; non-narrative; space; spatial(ity)

non-narrative: in Cardenal, 109f; in *IC*, 12, 13 n7, 75, 145, 267; in RB, *Avebury*, 313; in *CH,* 12f, 13 n7, 15 n9, 17, 253, 265, 315; in *The Manager*, 313; < cluster; field (A); mosaic; narrative; non-linear; set; structure; suite

nothing, 6, 60, 62, 97, 101, 170, 248, 281ff; absolute –, 240, 283; /everything, 45, 122, 134, 240; "deep –", 239; "doing –", 74; figment of, 283; frequency of word, 278, 282; hexagrams "say –," 196, 258; "– else," 78; "– in particular", 43, 151; -ness, 282f; "-saying, 157; "reason knows –," 212; "sheer –", 134; – unfavorable, 21, 91f; RB, 'Nada: hope or nothing', 51; 'Nothing happens, (*CH* 421), 283; < Daoism; notness; *wu*; *wuwei*

notness, 254, 321f, 325; /Dao, 224; /isness, 44, 136, 282f; RB, *Notness: Metaphysical Sonnets*, 223 n 7, 282, 321; < Daoism; nothing; *wu*; *wuwei*

objective correlative, 102, 104, 191, 319; < Eliot

Oliver, Mary, 59, 60 n5, 64f, 147f

Olson, Charles, 46, 155, influence on RB, 16; < field (A); poetics

oneness, 119, 283; musical, 122; original/primordial, 109, 118; < harmony, music; oneness; wholeness; *Taiji*; *Taiji tu*; *unus mundus*; *yinyang*

Ong, Walter, 265; < linear

Oppen, George, *Of Being Numerous*, 6, 74

opposite, -ition, 8, 108, 123, 134, 182, 312; < balance; binary; change; *Taiji*; *Taiji tu*; *yinyang*

oracle, -ular, 3, 201, 293; Delphic, 12 n6, 319; pronouncements, 23, 197, 297; text, 289f; < divination; Herodotus; sacrifice; Hex 50, 'Cooking, Sacrificing'

order (A) *opp. disorder*: 19, 59, 64, 125, 248; /chaos/disorder, 74, 138; /harmony/wholeness, 122ff, 139, 208; /meaning, 57, 58, 202; / Supreme Ultimate, the 137; "appetite for", 59, 74, 135, 250; broken, 7, 112ff, 122ff; Cartesian, 134; "chance left free to act falls into an order," 39, 57 (< Hopkins, *inscape*); cohering, 312; cosmic /macrocosmic/overall, 74, 112, 221, 225, 248, 312; earthly/natural, 112, 208; implicate, 8, 40, 53, 53 n2 (< Bohm); in/of *CH*, 39, 75; in/of *IC*, 73, 75, 199 n20; return of, 136; poet/, 233; social, 248; "There is order in being," 37, 48; < Hex 11, balance; harmony; pattern; wholeness

order (B) *sequence*: 19, 72, 75, 112, 266, 226 n2, 251, 351; fixed, 266; Mawangdui, 276; random, 265, 315ff; < book-in-a box; cluster; loose-leaf, order (A); hex; received; set; sequence; suite; time

Orientalism, 65, 90, 159ff, 332

origin(ary), 169, 180ff, 270, 297, 303, 303 n23, 317; acts of creation, 11; /ends, 136, 170; beauty, 55, 62; chaos, 170; harmony, 118; *IC* as, 11, 23, 208; in *ruah* ('wind/spirit'), 170, 170 n8; in synchronicity, 321; meaning, 22, 44, 75, 225; of *CH* in *IC*, 53, 66,

260, 310, 311, 319; of *IC*, 3, 4, 12, 22, 45, 51, 161, 315; of trigs, 20, 235f; of *IC*'s purpose, 29, 226, 286; of *IC*'s sequence, 266; Supreme Ultimate as, 136; "turning of antennae/towards", 192, 193, 260; < oneness; source(s)

Oulipo poets, 309

Pascal, Blaise, 157, 211f

patience, -ient, 78, 117, 126f, 139, 273; contemplation in *CH*, 6, 51; naturalists, 56; "patience within patience", 77, 177, 238, 314

pattern (A) *in IC*: 75; binary/mathematical, 90, 265; cosmic, 3, 312; in Chinese graphs, 211; of composition, 92; of diffusion, 26

pattern (B) *in CH*: 15f, 48, 74, 84, 92, 132, 279, 314, 316, 353, architectonic, 89, 271; emergent, 292; field, 12 n12, 47; geometrical, 15; in inner/outer worlds, 249; inhering, 250; "Instress, pattern, glory", 64; internal 11ff; of flow, 141; "of heaven and earth", 73; of images/symbols, 8, 15; of *mise-en-page*, 271; of nature, 46; of wind in grass, 47; pattern-finding, 13; synaesthetic, 318; system of, 311; 'Patterns of our own' (*CH* 166), 48, 180

pattern (C) *in RB's other writings*: 16, 46, 53, 58, 306ff, 320f; in *Book With No Back Cover*, 316; in *The Manager*, 315; non-linear, 12 n7; synaesthetic, 318; < cluster; cohere; harmony; mosaic; order (A); space; structure

Pauli, Wolfgang, 287 n2, 320p; < Jung

Paz, Octavio, 32, 42, 155; / China / *IC*, 48, 159f, 309; elective affinities with RB, 325; influence on

/friendship with RB, 5, 9, 10 n4, 16, 38, 41, 41 n1, 43f, 69, 158f, 307ff, 317; on analogy/chance /parallelism, 308f; *Blanco*, 308, 317; *Labyrinth of Solitude, The*, 41, 325; *Monkey Grammarian, The*, 159; *Piedra de sol (Sunstone)*, 160, 308; < *Dao*, Daoism

peripeteia (Greek περιπέτεια) 'diametrical reversal', 209 n2; < Aristotle; opposite; polarity; transformation; *anagnorisis*; *yinyang*

phasma (Greek φάσμα) 'spectrum', 325; < *úphasma*

phoenix, 101f, 102 n8; < *fenghuang*; << fire; flame; sun; Hex 30, 'Clinging'

Pinyin, viii, 187 n1, 346-349, 353f; transliterating; Wade-Giles

Platonism, -ic, 173, 249, 251

pneuma, -tic, 165, 265, 297, 349; response, 168; < breath; spirit, wind; *qi*; *ruah*

poetics, 16, 354; Aristotle, 209 n2, 316; *CH* as *ars poetica*, 205; Chinese, 103, 336; contemporary, 12; cross-cultural, 89; Eastern/Western, 7, 105; field-, 1, 12 n7, 15; of Emerson, 55f; of Olson, 16; of Paz, 43, 160; of Pound, 158ff; of RB, 158, 166, 284; relativistic, 15; universalist/particularist, 16, 43; < affinity; analogy; compare; composition; correlative cosmos building; correspondence; field (A); metaphor; mosaic; pattern; related; *bi*; *bixing*; *xiang*; *xing*; Hex 8, 'According, Binding'; << *gan*; *ganying*; Hex 31, 'Reciprocating'

polarity, 7, 8, 130ff, 166, 246; < balance; binary; change; equilibrium; opposite; transformation; *peripeteia*; *Taiji*; *Taiji tu*; *yinyang*

polysemy, -ic, -ous, 9, 12, 14, 22, 91, 126, 166, 168f, 169 n7, 181, 209, 223, 226, 236, 279, 313ff, 354; in *CH*, 170; pre-theological, 169; < ambiguity; cluster; field (A); imagem; meaning (A/B/C); symbol; word

Pound, Ezra, 66, 105, 159, 307; / Chinese poetry, 39, 49, 102, 104, 159 n3, 306; / Confucius, 39, 91; / Ernest Fenollosa, 39; / Imagism, 104, 233; / Peter Russell, 307; anti-Semitism, 307; Fascism, 159 "I cannot make it cohere" / "it coheres all right" 39, 53, 57, 58, 66, 159; influence on RB, 5f, 12, 16, 102, 158f, 307; *An Examination of Ezra Pound, An*, 307; *Cantos, The*, 12, 16, 39, 53, 57f, 64, 264f, 306, 307; < Eliot; Russell

praise: in *CH*, 202; RB as praise poet, 5, 43; *"without praise or hope"*, 77, 177, 238, 314; < Cardenal

prayer, 147, 165, 240; /poetry, 53, 69 n1; /prediction, 92; /prophecy, 53, 69 n1; *CH* as, 54, 56

pregnancy, -ant, 93, 95ff, 119, 140, 278; < beginning; birth; child; mother; Hex 3, 'Beginning'

prophecy, -et, 93, 173, 178f, 182; / *dāvār* (word, 166, 174ff); /divination, 53, 181; / God, 168 n6, 197 n6; poets/poetry, 53, 69 n1, 178ff, 189, 233; /prayer, 53, 69 n1; /*ruah* (spirit), 166ff, 170; Biblical, 167, 174; Hebrew, 173; in RB, 165-183; in Shelley, 233; Isaiah, 180 n21; Jewish, 9, 165-183; mystery of, 167f; Old Testament, 197 n6; prophetology, 169, 175; Roman (*Vates*), 233; *Essence du prophétisme, l'*, 166;

ren 人, 'human/man/person', 209f

repetition, 318, 321; /memory, 168 n4; as poetic effects; 132, 200, 241; in villanelle, 136; key in poetry; 273; non-identical, 311

return(ing), 80, 136, 259, 321; /Dao /Tao, 82, 111, 212; "before birth", 80, 101; home, 95, 97; to dust, 172; to source, 311; to wholeness, 52, 169; 'The Return' (Pound), 159; < Hex 24, 'Returning'

revelation, 170; Biblical, 27; of God, 170 n8; of relationships, 308; *Revelations of Chance* (Main), 335

revolution(ary), 7, 107ff, 120ff, 125ff; /love, 124; /recklessness, 124; /violence, 109, 122; as break-through, 127; as dynamic harmony, 123ff; as evolution, 122f; as 'shedding the mandate' (< *geming*), 107; cultural, 3, 121; dangers of, 108; in *CH* / RB, 7, 107ff, 120ff, 124ff; inner, 121ff; Marxist, 7; murderous, 125f; ongoing, 107-129; 'Revolution-ary Cadre' (*CH* 392), 107-108; < Cardenal; change; heal; transfor-mation; *tikkun*; Hex 49, 'Shed-ding'; << Hex 23, 'Peeling'

rhyme, 24, 64, 95, 239, 273; half-, 62

Rhys, Sean, 322

rhythm, 46, 151, 332; cosmic/univer-sal, 110f; in/of *CH*, 195, 198ff, 274; in/of poetry, 209 n3, 226; of singing, 209 n3, 226; sprung, 241; < harmony; music

ridgepole, 13, 286ff, 290ff, 293, 293 n10; 294, 302f; < home; house; roof; Hex 37, 'Dwelling, House-holding'; << flood; lake; rain; river; water; Wilhelm/Baynes; *qi*; Hex 28, 'Overbrimming

river, 98, 121, 156, 170, 241, 281, 321; -bank, 142, 224; *CH* as "river of poems", 289, 293f; crossing the, 21, 142, 147, 293, 295f, 303, 303 n23; "Great River called Change", 303; Yellow River Chart, 29; < bridge; crossing; energy; flood; stream; Hex 28. 'Overbrimming'; Hex 63, 'After crossing over'; Hex 64, 'Before crossing over'

Romantic, -ism, 48, 52, 55f, 59, 157, 242, 312; affinities with/ influences on RB, 38f, 46, 62, 66, 308; German, 162; imagination, 38; < Blake, Emerson, Stevens, Wordsworth; << inspiration

roof, 40, 152, 194, 213, 222, 292; < home; house; ridgepole; Hex 37, 'Dwelling, Householding

Rosenzweig, Franz, 174, 180, 182

ruah רוח (*Hebr* 'wind, spirit'), 9, 16, 165-171, 172 n11, 173f, 174 nn15/16; / *dāvār* (*Hebr* 'word'), 173ff, 181; < breath; divine; in-spiration; spirit; spirituality; word; *pneuma*; *qi*; Hex 57, 'Blowing, Billowing'

Rudolf, Anthony, ix, 166 n1

Russell, Peter: influence on RB, 16, 307; *Ephemeron*, 308; *Examina-tion of Ezra Pound, An*, 307; < Pound

Rutt, Richard, 264, 266; < trans. of *Zhouyi*

sacrifice, -ing, -ial, 152; cauldron, 319; human, 246; 'A sacrifice' (*CH* 102), 149f; < Delphic; Herodotus; oracle; Hex 50, 'Cooking, Sacrificing'

science, -tific, 28, 31, 51ff, 91, 109, 165; / *IC*, 23ff, 27 n8, 29, 291

sincere, -erity, 30, 217, 220, 238; *fu*,
22; of Tao, 123; < heart; heartfelt;
trust; truth; Hex 32, 'Enduring';
Hex 61, 'Inner Trusting'

singing, song, 59, 61 n6, 94, 301;
/poetry, 209 n3; 273; bird, 245;
cosmic, 110; crane, 94f; *Song of
Myself* (< Whitman), 64; < *Book
of Songs*, harmony; music: Hex
11, 'Harmonising, Prospering'

sky, skies, 235, 301; /earth/ground,
179, 193, 235; cloudless/un-
clouded, 42, 223; infallible,
196f; reflection in lake/water, 54,
243, 300f; sky-filled, 211; "sky's
forehead", 202ff; Trig *Qian*, 'Sky',
341; way of, 9, 98; 'Bird falling
out of sky' (*CH* 502), 42, 101;
< heaven; Hex 1, 'Initiating'; Trig
Qian, 'Heaven'; << bright; dawn;
glory; heaven; light; radiance; star;
sun

Smith, Richard J. (Sima Fu 司馬富),
i, viii, 1, 4, 19-34, 37, 39, 161,
189n4, 248, 310, 336, 346; *The
I Ching, A Biography*, 19 n1, 246

Sneller, Rico, 8ff, 165-183, 336f;
< Jewish; prophecy; spirit; word

solid line < broken/unbroken line; *yao*

Song 漢 (dynasty), 92, 270 n1; *aka
Sung*, 103, 158; *Song-Ming*, 333

soul, 55f, 71, 172, 212, 293, 296,
336; /heart, 208, 226, 254;
/synchronicity, 335; bodymind,
45; concept of, 71; concerns,
192; darknesses in, 114; divine,
of God, 172; heritage, 254; in *IC*,
31; poetry/, 208; redemption of,
55; soulless West, 155; < psyche;
wisdom

source, 169, 235, 286, 303, 304 n24;
IC as, 19, 23, 29, 70, 70 n3, 83,
89, 90, 182, 208, 222, 289; in

human heart, 226; of *CH* in correlative thinking, 90; of *CH* in *IC*,
53, 56, 105, 187, 205, 262, 271,
286, 311, 319; of nourishment,
246; psychoid archetype as, 197;
ruah as, 170, 170 n8; well as,
194f, 199, 201; < origin; << Hex
48, 'Welling, Replenishing'

space, -tial(ity), 61, 110, 124, 153,
192, 193, 251, 314, 317f; /light,
119; /time/relativity/spacetime, 4,
15, 16, 23, 45, 47, 81, 95, 121,
147, 170, 179, 180, 189f, 192,
226, 238, 241, 252, 264, 270,
281f, 287, 297, 312f; hermeneutic, 237; hidden, 245; infinite,
157; intellectual/emotional/
moral, 32, 317; limitations, 202;
model for *CH*, 12, 15; "tune
space to music," 318; RB, *Balkan
Spaces*; 325; < diagram; field (A);
geometry; infinite; line; mosaic;
non-linear; pattern

spectrum, *úphasma* (Greek ὑφασμα),
325; < *phasma* (φάσμα)

speech, 8, 102, 131, 147, 165; inner,
175, 179f; meaningful, 168;
< word; *dāvār*

spirit/Spirit, 9, 19, 55, 102, 123, 147,
174 n15, 175, 249, 296, 301 n22;
/body, 99, 203; /heart, 178, 208,
226; /poetry, 180, 208; /wind,
167ff, 172; /word, 9, 165ff, 173ff,
181; divine/of God/holy, 165,
168, 168 n5, 169ff; hovering (over
waters), 169ff, 174, 174 n16, 178,
180; in Blake, 40, 49; in *CH* / RB,
170, 172, 205, 254; of China,
225, 297; of creation/life, 101,
178; of *IC*, 226, 303; of *IC* as spirit-guide, 76, 200, 260; of the time,
212; *spiritus*, 165; 'In the spirit of
Walt Whitman (*CH* 58), 66 n7,

453; 'The Spirit of Art According
to the Book of Changes' (Wilhelm
R.), 254; < breath; prophecy;
spiritual(ity); wind; word; *pneuma*;
ruah; Hex 57, 'Blowing, Billowing'
spiritual(ity), 55, 71, 147, 171, 248;
/heart, 208, 226, 254; /body-
mind, 45; energy, 46; in *CH*
/RB, 71, 192f, 200, 322f, 337;
in/of *IC*, 31, 192; meaning, 299
n20; sustenance, 31; wisdom,
168, 200, 208; < breath; divine;
inspiration; spirit
spring (A) *season*: 123; rain, 241;
wind, 103; *Spring and Autumn
Annals*, 208
spring (B) *water*: 160, 208, 214, 214
n5; 257ff; *IC* as wellspring, 159
star, 48, 111, 134, 170, 204, 251;
"consoling, abundant, terrifying",
81; earth as particle of, 270; reflected in well, 202f; -*rooted*, 211;
'Tracks to stars and back' (*CH*
204), 82; < beauty; delight; glory;
heaven; radiance; sky; << Hex 1,
'Initiating'; Trig *Qian*, 'Heaven'
Stevens, Wallace, 6, 66; 'The Idea of
Order at Key West', 59
still(ness), 19, 42, 44, 76, 182, 163,
200, 221, 238, 253, 260, 278,
300; < mountain; Hex 52, 'Stilling'; << meditation; Hex 33,
'Retreating'
stone, 48, 105, 120, 152, 179, 258,
303; Age, 42; heart penetrates,
30; lime- 137, 157; metal/, 30;
way of, 98; "wood, clay, hide,
stone", 48, 177, 180, 235; RB,
'A Grove of Trees and a Grove of
Stones,' 322; *Sunstone* (Paz), 160,
308; 'The stone carver' (*CH* 309),
175 n19; 'Water in a stone jug'
(*CH* 80), 300

storm, 104f, 172 n11, 261, 292;
< cloud; rain; thunder; wind; Hex
51, 'Shaking, Quaking'; Hex 57,
'Blowing, Billowing'
stream, 45, 59, 93, 122, 141, 280;
'From underground streams' (*CH*
387), 171 n9, 198ff, 201, 259;
< flow; river; water; well; *qi*; Hex
48, 'Welling, Replenishing'
structure, -al, 83. 290; archetypal,190; atomic, 29; change as,
111; entanglement, 134; field,
12; geometrical, 15, 263ff; infra-,
246; numerical, 38; of/in *CH*, 4,
11ff, 16, 48, 65, 69, 69 n1, 70,
72, 75, 89f, 108f, 136,146, 187,
193, 213, 249, 263ff, 271, 289,
298, 303, 307, 311ff, 316, 320;
of/in *IC*, 22, 148, 20 n2, 215,
264, 300 n21; of Chinese, 71; of
DNA / *IC*, 251; of metaphor, 53;
symmetrical, 75; teleonomic, 84;
< cohere; equilibrium; field (A);
mosaic; narrative; non-narrative;
order (A); pattern (A/B/C)
stuff: of heaven, 81, 251, 322; of
metaphor, 53; of things under
light, 79, 324; subtle (< *úphasma*),
325; vegetable, 198, 259; < fabric
stylometric, 13, 270ff, 283; < Tan
suan 算, 'predict, calculate', 249;
< mathematical
summer, 54, 65, 104, 147, 157, 324;
'*Summer, svemir*' (*CH* 216), 60f
sun, -light, -rise, -set, -flower, 37, 54,
61, 63, 64, 101f, 143, 171 n9,
241ff, 262, 279; /moon, 193,
223, 225, 301; < bright; dawn;
glory; heaven; radiance; sky; Hex
30, Clinging'; Hex 35, 'Dawning'
Sung (dynasty) < *Song*
supreme, 304 n24; good fortune,
258, 262; power, 193

< Hex 51 (also *Zhen*) 'Shaking, Quaking'; thunder; rain; storm

Trist, Alan, ix, 13f, 72 n4, 226 n3, 286-305, 337; < DeVine

trust, 76, 157, 200, 221f, 260, 288; in nature/Tao, 82; -worthy (*fu*), 22; < heart; heartfelt; mutual influence; sincere; truth; Hex 61, 'Inner Trusting'; *gan*; *ganying*; *xin*; Hex 31, 'Reciprocating'

truth, 41f, 56, 100, 118, 138, 219, 251, 283; /harmony, 108; /justice, 7, 108, 124; 'Ring of Truth' (*CH* 488), 221; < sincere; trust; Hex 61, 'Inner Trusting'

tuan 彖, judgment/statement/decision', 20; < hex

unbroken line < broken/unbroken line; *yao*

unhewn block/uncarved wood (*pu*) 254; < Daoism

unus mundus, 130, 190, 203 n9, 204; < Jung; oneness; synchronicity; wholeness

úphasma (Greek ὑφασμα) 'subtle stuff, fabric', 325; < fabric; stuff; *phasma*

Vietnam, -ese, 28; spread of *IC* to, 4, 25f, 26 n7

villanelle, 51, 69 n1, 136, 171; extra line-reading, 191 n 5

voice(s): ancient Chinese, 82; core /central voice of *IC*, 6, 76; female, 278; in dream (< Shen), 214; "in the mirror", 323; influences on RB, 142; of *CH*, 303; of *CH*, multiple, 8, 141; of collective consciousness, 108; of finest silence, 119; of God, 197 n6; of humanity, 41f; of the past, 143; of the singer, 59; personal/individ-

ual, 81, 108, 197 n6, 272; RB's, 65, 83, 143, 272; supra-personal, 57; timbre, 24; Whitman's, 65; 'An unexpected European Voice' (Derrick), 241; 'Other voices' (*CH* 138), 175, 177, 211; < breath; mouth

Wade-Giles, viii, 145, 187 n1, 346-349, 354; < Pinyin; transliterating

Waley, Arthur, 90

Wang Bi 王弼, 268

Wang Fuzhi 王夫之, 19

Wang Wei 王維, 159

water, 215, 216, 216 n6; /fire, 30, 108, 279; /heart, 211; /lake, 131, 219; /mountain; 163; /stone 303; blue, 114; crossing the, 147; dowsing, 195; dripping, 301f; flexibility, flow, flux of, 141, 217, 258, 281f; fresh, 258f, 261f; in Cardenal, 114; in *CH*, 83, 99, 142, 146, 153, 157, 158, 163, 211, 221, 247, 257ff, 279, 291, 293, 300; in Paz, 160; in Stevens, 59; in well, 195, 198, 203f; irrigate, 279, 280; light/reflection on/in, 54, 177, 235, 300; power of, 257; riding on, 217; rising, 290; under –, 83, 142; underground, 171 n9, 198ff, 258f; -wisdom, 171 n9, 195, 201f, 240, 261; 'Water in a stone jug' (*CH* 80), 300; '*We thirst but drink too little water*' (*CH* 376), 211; < cloud; flood; lake; mist; rain; river; spring; stream; wave; well; *qi*; Hex 29, 'Falling (in a pit'); Trig *Kan*, 'Water'; Hex 48, 'Welling, Replenishing'

wave, 59, 139, 141, 172 n11, 177, 322; < energy; water; wind; *qi*

Way/way, 91, 97, 100, 201, 215, 286, 289; Heavenly, 19, 291 n9; of/in

Index 2A

POEM-CLUSTERS

Since the cluster-titles in *Changing* correspond to the versions of names ascribed by RB to the *I Ching*'s hexagrams, cluster-titles in the first column are followed in the second column, by names of hexagrams in Pinyin. Both cluster-names and Pinyin hexagram-names appear in italics, as they do throughout this book. In the third column, for each of these items, the set of bracketed numbers indicates its reference in *Changing* by means of its position in the *I Ching*'s 'received' (standard) sequence, and its page-range in *Changing*. In the fourth column, non-bracketed numbers refer to pages in this book.

Cluster Title	Hex Name	Reference in *Changing*	Page numbers
Increasing	*Yi*	(42: 335-342)	299, 344
Initiating	*Qian*	(1: 3-10)	133, 169f, 216, 251, 342
Inner Trusting	*Zhong Fu*	(61: 487-494)	94, 221ff, 345
Joying, Enjoying	*Dui*	(58: 463-470)	125, 132ff, 156, 345
Nourishing	*Yi*	(27: 215-222)	147, 343
Overbrimming	*Da Guo*	(28: 223-230)	294, 301ff, 343
Overstepping	*Xiao Guo*	(62: 495-502)	101, 345
Peeling	*Bo*	(23: 183-190)	114f, 119f, 137ff, 343
Reciprocating	*Xian*	(31: 247-254)	218ff, 236, 301ff, 343
Responding, Corresponding	*Kun*	(2: 13-22)	139, 170, 216, 251, 342
Retreating	*Dun*	(33: 263-270)	121, 344
Returning	*Fu*	(24: 191-198)	82, 212, 343
Shaking, Quaking	*Zhen*	(51: 407-414)	172 n11, 345
Shedding	*Ge*	(49: 391-398)	107, 114, 120, 124, 345
Shifting	*Jian*	(53: 423-430)	95, 345
Stagnating, Decaying	*Pi*	(12: 95-102)	148ff, 342
Stilling	*Gen*	(52: 161-168)	162, 239, 345
Struggling, Stumbling	*Jian*	(39: 311-318)	167 n2, 344
Small Blessing, Possessing	*Xiao Xu*	(9: 71-78)	146, 342
Travelling	*Lü*	(56: 447-454)	175 n19, 345
Treading	*Lü*	(10: 79-86)	243f, 299, 299 n18, 300, 342
Untwisting	*Wu Wang*	(25: 199-206)	241, 343
Watching	*Guan*	(20: 159-166)	235, 314, 343
Welling, Replenishing	*Jing*	(48: 383-390)	6, 9f, 12. 54 n3, 76, 126, 171, 190-205, 257-262, 344

Index 2B

Poems

Bracketed numbers indicate: (1) the cluster or hexagram that a poem belongs to according to the 'received' *I Ching* sequence; (2) the poem's place in its cluster; and (3) its page-number in *Changing*. An italicised title indicates that the poem heads its cluster. Non-bracketed numbers refer to pages in this book.